T0329081

Abraham Lincoln
Letters to His Generals
1861–1865

Abraham Lincoln

Letters to His Generals

1861–1865

Edited and with Annotation

by

Brett F. Woods, Ph.D.

Algora Publishing
New York

Library of Congress Cataloging-in-Publication Data —

Lincoln, Abraham, 1809–1865.
   [Correspondence. Selections]
   Abraham Lincoln : letters to his generals, 1861-1865 / edited and with annotation by
Brett F. Woods, Ph.D.
      pages cm
   Includes bibliographical references and index.
      ISBN 978-1-62894-000-8 (soft cover : alk. paper) — ISBN 978-1-62894-001-5 (hard
cover : alk. paper) — ISBN 978-1-62894-002-2 (ebook) 1. Lincoln, Abraham, 1809-1865—
Correspondence. 2. Lincoln, Abraham, 1809–1865—Military leadership. 3. Presidents—
United States—Correspondence. 4. United States—History—Civil War, 1861–1865. I.
Woods, Brett F., editor. II. Title.
      E457.962 2013
      973.7092--dc23
      [B]
                              2013027638

Printed in the United States

TABLE OF CONTENTS

STRATEGIC PERSPECTIVES: THE WAR OF 1862   39

CORRESPONDENCE: 1862   57

STRATEGIC PERSPECTIVES: THE WAR OF 1863

CORRESPONDENCE: 1863

Table of Contents

Table of Contents

EDITOR'S NOTE

> I have just read your dispatch about sore-tongued
> and fatigued horses. Will you pardon me for asking what the
> horses of your army have done since the battle of Antietam
> that fatigues anything?
>
> - Abraham Lincoln to General George B. McClellan,
> October 25, 1862

I have long believed that the most comprehensive portrait of historical figures might be seen in their personal correspondence and journal entries. Abraham Lincoln is certainly no exception, and those letters and telegrams he penned
as commander-in-chief—throughout one of the most critical episodes in American history—are of singular importance. This is particularly true when one re-
views them in their entirety, as opposed to selected excerpts that, if indeed they
have been reprinted at all, have been available only in part, reduced to excerpts,
citations, or references which, in many instances, have been repeatedly cited as
the foundation for a particular interpretation of events, or conclusion of fact.

Accordingly, in this selection of a comparatively few items from the volumi-
nous body of Lincoln correspondence that has been preserved, my intention is
twofold: first, to add to the body of literature exploring leadership and gover-
nance during the American Civil War; and, secondly, and perhaps more impor-
tantly, to provide an additional glimpse into the character and thought processes
of Abraham Lincoln as president and commander-in-chief.

Admittedly, interpreting the thoughts and actions of Abraham Lincoln can
be a challenging exercise for, from a historical perspective; he emerges as an extraordinary individual—one who was clearly many things to many people. But,

too, precisely because of this same complexity, he has become so much a part of America's ongoing search for itself, so deeply entwined in the tapestry of American history, that in many instances succeeding generations have been largely unable to picture him clearly and objectively in his own life and times. To be sure, Lincoln was not a natural strategist. He worked hard to master the subject, just as he had done to become a lawyer. Still, despite being forced to learn the functions of a commander-in-chief on the job, he demonstrates an oftentimes striking understanding of the issues. And, whether the subject might be a general memorandum of military policy, a reflection on the sentencing of a deserter, or pressing the attack on Confederate forces, he writes with remarkable clarity, insight, and concise eloquence.

The primary source material for this compilation is the eight-volume reference *The Collected Works of Abraham Lincoln*, edited by Roy P. Basler, which was published in 1953 under the auspices of the Abraham Lincoln Association. This represented the first major scholarly effort to collect and publish the complete writings of Abraham Lincoln and remains an indispensable research tool. A second principal text is the venerable *American Military History*, edited by Maurice Matloff, which was published in 1969 under the auspices of the Chief of Military History of the United States Army. Similar to the Basler volumes, Matloff's conclusions remain a standard in American Civil War studies and I have freely used the text in order for the reader to be able to place Lincoln's correspondence against the relevant tactical, strategic, and political circumstances.

The format of the correspondence, as drafted by Lincoln, has been preserved whenever possible. My efforts have been directed to refining the presentation, identifying the addressees, many of whom have been lost to history, and, where indicated, providing explanatory notes so as to assist the reader in placing the correspondence in, once again, its particular historical, political, or conceptual context. This methodology, I believe, serves to make the material more palatable and more useful to a general readership, as well as to students of military, diplomatic, or political history. Additionally, it will also permit—or, at a minimum, encourage—readers to arrive at their own conclusions as to the intention of a particular piece of correspondence.

Any errors in selection, fact, transcription, and interpretation remain, of course, my responsibility.

Brett F. Woods, Ph.D.

Santa Fe, New Mexico

CIVIL WAR CHRONOLOGY[1]

January 1861 - The South Secedes: When Abraham Lincoln, a known opponent of slavery, was elected president, the South Carolina legislature perceived a threat. Calling a state convention, the delegates voted to remove the state of South Carolina from the union known as the United States of America. The secession of South Carolina was followed by the secession of six more states—Mississippi, Florida, Alabama, Georgia, Louisiana, and Texas—and the threat of secession by four more—Virginia, Arkansas, Tennessee, and North Carolina. These eleven states eventually formed the Confederate States of America.

February 1861 - The South Creates a Government: At a convention in Montgomery, Alabama, the seven seceding states created the Confederate Constitution, a document similar to the United States Constitution but with greater stress on the autonomy of each state. Jefferson Davis was named provisional president of the Confederacy until elections could be held.

February 1861 - The South Seizes Federal Forts: When President Buchanan—Lincoln's predecessor—refused to surrender Southern federal forts to the seceding states, Southern state troops seized them. At Fort Sumter, South Carolina troops repulsed a supply ship trying to reach federal forces based in the fort. The ship was forced to return to New York, its supplies undelivered.

March 1861 - Lincoln's Inauguration: At Lincoln's inauguration on March 4, the new president said he had no plans to end slavery in those states where it already existed, but he also said he would not accept secession. He hoped to resolve the national crisis without warfare.

April 1861 - Attack on Fort Sumter: When President Lincoln planned to send supplies to Fort Sumter, he alerted the state in advance, in an attempt to avoid hostilities. South Carolina, however, feared a trick; the commander of the fort, Robert Anderson, was asked to surrender immediately. Anderson offered to sur-

---

1 Excerpted from Freeman (Library of Congress) 2013.

render, but only after he had exhausted his supplies. His offer was rejected, and on April 12, the Civil War began with shots fired on the fort. Fort Sumter eventually was surrendered to South Carolina.

April 1861 – Four More States Join the Confederacy: The attack on Fort Sumter prompted four more states to join the Confederacy. With Virginia's secession, Richmond was named the Confederate capitol.

June 1861 – West Virginia is Created: Residents of the western counties of Virginia did not wish to secede along with the rest of the state. This section of Virginia was admitted into the Union as the state of West Virginia on June 20, 1863.

June 1861 – Four Slave States Stay in the Union: Despite their acceptance of slavery, Delaware, Kentucky, Maryland, and Missouri did not join the Confederacy. Although divided in their loyalties, a combination of political maneuvering and Union military pressure kept these states from seceding.

July 1861 – First Battle of Bull Run: Public demand pushed General-in-Chief Winfield Scott to advance on the South before adequately training his untried troops. Scott ordered General Irvin McDowell to advance on Confederate troops stationed at Manassas Junction, Virginia. McDowell attacked on July 21, and was initially successful, but the introduction of Confederate reinforcements resulted in a Southern victory and a chaotic retreat toward Washington by federal troops.

July 1861 – General McDowell Is Replaced: Suddenly aware of the threat of a protracted war and the army's need for organization and training, Lincoln replaced McDowell with General George B. McClellan.

July 1861 – A Blockade of the South: To blockade the coast of the Confederacy effectively, the federal navy had to be improved. By July, the effort at improvement had made a difference and an effective blockade had begun. The South responded by building small, fast ships that could outmaneuver Union vessels. November 8:

November 1861 – Coastal Actions: Captain Samuel F. Dupont's warships silenced Confederate guns in Fort Walker and Fort Beauregard. This victory enabled General Thomas W. Sherman's troops to occupy first Port Royal and then all the famous Sea Islands of South Carolina, where Timothy H. O'Sullivan recorded them making themselves at home.

January 1862 – Abraham Lincoln Takes Action: On January 27, President Lincoln issued a war order authorizing the Union to launch a unified aggressive action against the Confederacy. General McClellan ignored the order.

March 1862 – McClellan Loses Command: On March 8, President Lincoln—impatient with General McClellan's inactivity—issued an order reorganizing the Army of Virginia and relieving McClellan of supreme command. McClellan was given command of the Army of the Potomac, and ordered to attack Richmond. This marked the beginning of the Peninsular Campaign.

April 1862 – The Battle of Shiloh: On April 6, Confederate forces attacked Union forces under General Ulysses S. Grant at Shiloh, Tennessee. By the end of the day, the federal troops were almost defeated. Yet, during the night, reinforcements arrived, and by the next morning the Union commanded the field. When Confederate forces retreated, the exhausted federal forces did not follow. Casualties were heavy—13,000 out of 63,000 Union soldiers died, and 11,000 of 40,000 Confederate troops were killed.

April 1862 - New Orleans: Flag Officer David Farragut led an assault up the Mississippi River. By April 25, he was in command of New Orleans.

April 1862 - The Peninsular Campaign: In April, General McClellan's troops left northern Virginia to begin the Peninsular Campaign. By May 4, they occupied Yorktown, Virginia. At Williamsburg, Confederate forces prevented McClellan from meeting the main part of the Confederate army, and McClellan halted his troops, awaiting reinforcements.

May 1862 - "Stonewall" Jackson Defeats Union Forces: Confederate General Thomas J. "Stonewall" Jackson, commanding forces in the Shenandoah Valley, attacked Union forces in late March, forcing them to retreat across the Potomac. As a result, Union troops were rushed to protect Washington, D.C.

June 1862 - The Battle of Seven Pines (Fair Oaks): On May 31, the Confederate army attacked federal forces at Seven Pines, almost defeating them; last-minute reinforcements saved the Union from a serious defeat. Confederate commander Joseph E. Johnston was severely wounded, and command of the Army of Northern Virginia fell to Robert E. Lee.

July 1862 - The Seven Days' Battles: Between June 26 and July 2, Union and Confederate forces fought a series of battles: Mechanicsville (June 26-27), Gaines's Mill (June 27), Savage's Station (June 29), Frayser's Farm (June 30), and Malvern Hill (July 1). On July 2, the Confederates withdrew to Richmond, ending the Peninsular Campaign.

July 1862 - A New Commander of the Union Army: On July 11, Major-General Henry Halleck was named general-in-chief of the Union army.

August 1862 - Pope's Campaign: Union General John Pope suffered defeated at the Second Battle of Bull Run on August 29-30. General Fitz-John Porter was held responsible for the defeat because he had failed to commit his troops to battle quickly enough; he was forced out of the army by 1863.

September 1862 - Harper's Ferry: Union General McClellan defeated Confederate General Lee at South Mountain and Crampton's Gap in September, but did not move quickly enough to save Harper's Ferry, which fell to Confederate General Jackson on September 15, along with a great number of men and a large body of supplies.

September 1862 - Antietam: On September 17, Confederate forces under General Lee were caught by General McClellan near Sharpsburg, Maryland. This battle proved to be the bloodiest day of the war; 2,108 Union soldiers were killed and 9,549 wounded—2,700 Confederates were killed and 9,029 wounded. The battle had no clear winner, but because General Lee withdrew to Virginia, McClellan was considered the victor. The battle convinced the British and French—who were contemplating official recognition of the Confederacy—to reserve action, and gave Lincoln the opportunity to announce his Preliminary Emancipation Proclamation (September 22), which would free all slaves in areas rebelling against the United States, effective January 1, 1863.

December 1862 - The Battle of Fredericksburg: General McClellan's slow movements, combined with General Lee's escape, and continued raiding by Confederate cavalry, dismayed many in the North. On November 7, Lincoln replaced McClellan with Major-General Ambrose E. Burnside. Burnside's forces were defeated in a series of attacks against entrenched Confederate forces at Fredericksburg, Virginia, and Burnside was replaced with General Joseph Hooker.

January 1863 - Emancipation Proclamation: In an effort to placate the slaveholding border states, Lincoln resisted the demands of radical Republicans for complete abolition. Yet some Union generals, such as General B. F. Butler, declared slaves escaping to their lines "contraband of war," not to be returned to their masters. Other generals decreed that the slaves of men rebelling against the Union were to be considered free. Congress, too, had been moving toward abolition. In 1861, Congress had passed an act stating that all slaves employed against the Union were to be considered free. In 1862, another act stated that all slaves of men who supported the Confederacy were to be considered free. Lincoln, aware of the public's growing support of abolition, issued the Emancipation Proclamation on January 1, 1863, declaring that all slaves in areas still in rebellion were, in the eyes of the federal government, free.

March 1863 - The First Conscription Act: Because of recruiting difficulties, an act was passed making all men between the ages of 20 and 45 liable to be called for military service. Service could be avoided by paying a fee or finding a substitute. The act was seen as unfair to the poor, and riots in working-class sections of New York City broke out in protest. A similar conscription act in the South provoked a similar reaction.

May 1863 - The Battle of Chancellorsville: On April 27, Union General Hooker crossed the Rappahannock River to attack General Lee's forces. Lee split his army, attacking a surprised Union army in three places and almost completely defeating them. Hooker withdrew across the Rappahannock River, giving the South a victory, but it was the Confederates' most costly victory in terms of casualties.

May 1863 - The Vicksburg Campaign: Union General Grant won several victories around Vicksburg, Mississippi, the fortified city considered essential to the Union's plans to regain control of the Mississippi River. On May 22, Grant began a siege of the city. After six weeks, Confederate General John Pemberton surrendered, giving up the city and 30,000 men. The capture of Port Hudson, Louisiana, shortly thereafter placed the entire Mississippi River in Union hands. The Confederacy was split in two.

June–July 1863 - The Gettysburg Campaign: Confederate General Lee decided to take the war to the enemy. On June 13, he defeated Union forces at Winchester, Virginia, and continued north to Pennsylvania. General Hooker, who had been planning to attack Richmond, was instead forced to follow Lee. Hooker, never comfortable with his commander, General Halleck, resigned on June 28, and General George Meade replaced him as commander of the Army of the Potomac. On July 1, a chance encounter between Union and Confederate forces began the Battle of Gettysburg. In the fighting that followed, Meade had greater numbers and better defensive positions. He won the battle, but failed to follow Lee as he retreated back to Virginia. Militarily, the Battle of Gettysburg was the high-water mark of the Confederacy; it is also significant because it ended Confederate hopes of formal recognition by foreign governments. On November 19, President Lincoln dedicated a portion of the Gettysburg battlefield as a national cemetery.

September 1863 - The Battle of Chickamauga: On September 19, Union and Confederate forces met on the Tennessee-Georgia border, near Chickamauga Creek. After the battle, Union forces retreated to Chattanooga, and the Confederacy maintained control of the battlefield.

November 1863 - The Battle of Chattanooga: On November 23-25, Union forces pushed Confederate troops away from Chattanooga. The victory set the stage for General Sherman's Atlanta Campaign.

May 1864 - Grant's Wilderness Campaign: General Grant, promoted to commander of the Union armies, planned to engage Lee's forces in Virginia until they were destroyed. North and South met and fought in an inconclusive three-day battle in the Wilderness. Lee inflicted more casualties on the Union forces than his own army incurred, but unlike Grant, he had no replacements.

May 1864 - The Battle of Spotsylvania: General Grant continued to attack Lee. At Spotsylvania Court House, he fought for five days, vowing to fight all summer if necessary.

June 1864 - The Battle of Cold Harbor: Grant again attacked Confederate forces at Cold Harbor, losing over 7,000 men in twenty minutes. Although Lee suffered fewer casualties, his army never recovered from Grant's continual attacks. This was Lee's last clear victory of the war.

June 1864 - The Siege of Petersburg: Grant hoped to take Petersburg, below Richmond, and then approach the Confederate capital from the South. The attempt failed, resulting in a ten-month siege and the loss of thousands of lives on both sides.

July 1864 - Confederate Troops Approach Washington, D.C.: Confederate General Jubal Early led his forces into Maryland to relieve the pressure on Lee's army. Early got within five miles of Washington, D.C., but on July 13, he was driven back to Virginia.

August 1864 - General William T. Sherman's Atlanta Campaign: Union General Sherman departed Chattanooga, and was soon met by Confederate General Joseph Johnston. Skillful strategy enabled Johnston to hold off Sherman's force—almost twice the size of Johnston's. However, Johnston's tactics caused his superiors to replace him with General John Bell Hood, who was soon defeated. Hood surrendered Atlanta, Georgia, on September 1; Sherman occupied the city the next day. The fall of Atlanta greatly boosted Northern morale.

November 1864 - General William T. Sherman's March to the Sea: General Sherman continued his march through Georgia to the sea. In the course of the march, he cut himself off from his source of supplies, planning for his troops to live off the land. His men cut a path 300 miles in length and 60 miles wide as they passed through Georgia, destroying factories, bridges, railroads, and public buildings.

January 1865 - The Fall of the Confederacy: Transportation problems and successful blockades caused severe shortages of food and supplies in the South. Starving soldiers began to desert Lee's forces, and although President Jefferson

Davis approved the arming of slaves as a means of augmenting the shrinking army, the measure was never put into effect.

February 1865 - Sherman Marches through North and South Carolina: Union General Sherman moved from Georgia through South Carolina, destroying almost everything in his path.

February 1865 - A Chance for Reconciliation Is Lost: Confederate President Jefferson Davis agreed to send delegates to a peace conference with President Lincoln and Secretary of State William Seward, but insisted on Lincoln's recognition of the South's independence as a prerequisite. Lincoln refused, and the conference never occurred.

April 1865 - Fallen Richmond: On March 25, and April 1, General Lee repeatedly attacked General Grant's forces near Petersburg, but was defeated . On April 2, Lee evacuated Richmond, the Confederate capital, and headed west to join with other forces.

April 1865 - Surrender at Appomattox Courthouse: General Lee's troops were soon surrounded, and on April 7, Grant called upon Lee to surrender. On April 9, the two commanders met at Appomattox Courthouse, and agreed on the terms of surrender. Lee's men were sent home on parole - soldiers with their horses, and officers with their side arms. All other equipment was surrendered.

April 1865 - The Assassination of President Lincoln: On April 14, as President Lincoln was watching a performance of "Our American Cousin" at Ford's Theater in Washington, D.C., he was shot by John Wilkes Booth, an actor from Maryland obsessed with avenging the Confederate defeat. Lincoln died the next morning. Booth escaped to Virginia. Eleven days later, cornered in a burning barn, Booth was fatally shot by a Union soldier. Nine other people were involved in the assassination; four were hanged, four imprisoned, and one acquitted.

April–May 1865 - Final Surrenders among Remaining Confederate Troops: Remaining Confederate troops were defeated between the end of April and the end of May. Jefferson Davis was captured in Georgia on May 10.

PROLOGUE: ABRAHAM LINCOLN'S WAR

During the administration of President James Buchanan, 1857–1861, tensions over the issue of extending slavery into the western territories mounted alarmingly and the nation ran its seemingly inexorable course toward disunion. Along with slavery, the shifting social, economic, political, and constitutional problems of the fast-growing country fragmented its citizenry. After open warfare broke out in the Kansas Territory among slaveholders, abolitionists, and opportunists, the battle lines of opinion rapidly hardened. Buchanan quieted Kansas by calling in the Regular Army, but it was too small and too scattered to suppress the struggles that were almost certain to break out in the border states. In 1859 John Brown, who had won notoriety in "Bleeding Kansas," seized the Federal arsenal at Harpers Ferry, Virginia, in a mad attempt to foment a slave uprising within that slaveholding state. Again Federal troops were called on to suppress the new outbreak, and pressures and emotions rose on the eve of the 1860 elections. Republican Abraham Lincoln was elected to succeed Buchanan; although he had failed to win a majority of the popular vote, he received 180 of the 303 electoral votes. The inauguration that was to vest in him the powers of the presidency would take place March 4, 1861. During this lame-duck period, Mr. Buchanan was unable control events and the country continued to lose its cohesion.

Abraham Lincoln's election to the Presidency on November 6, 1860, triggered the long-simmering political crisis. Lincoln's party was opposed to the expansion of slavery into the new western territories. This threatened both the economic and political interests of the South, since the Southern states depended on slavery to maintain their way of life and their power in Congress. South Carolina on December 20 enacted an ordinance declaring that "the union now subsisting between South Carolina and other States, under the name of the 'United States of America,' is hereby dissolved." Within six weeks, six other deep-South states seceded from the Union and seized Federal property inside their borders, including military installations, save Fort Pickens outside Pensacola and Fort Sumter in Charleston Harbor. To the seven states that formed the Confederate States of America on February 18, 1861, at Montgomery, Alabama, the U.S. government's retention of the forts was equivalent to a warlike act. To provide his fledgling government with a military force, on March 6 the new Confederate Executive, Jefferson Davis, called for a 100,000-man volunteer force to serve for twelve months.

The creation of a rival War Department south of the 35th Parallel on February 21 shattered the composition of the Regular Army and disrupted its activities, particularly in Texas, where Maj. Gen. David E. Twiggs surrendered his entire command. With an actual strength of 1,080 officers and 14,926 enlisted men on June 30, 1860, the Regular Army was based on five-year enlistments. Recruited heavily from men of foreign birth, the U.S. Army consisted of 10 regiments of infantry, 4 of artillery, 2 of cavalry, 2 of dragoons, and 1 of mounted riflemen. It was not a unified striking force. The Regular Army was deployed within seven departments, six of them west of the Mississippi. Of 198 line companies, 183 were scattered in 79 isolated posts in the territories. The remaining 15 were in garrisons along the Canadian border and on the Atlantic coast. They were patently unprepared for the mission of forcibly returning the Southern states to the union.

Created by Secretary of War John C. Calhoun and expanded by Secretary of War Davis in 1853, the departments of the U.S. Army had become powerful institutions by the eve of the Civil War. Within each of the trans-Mississippi departments, a senior colonel or general officer by brevet commanded 2,000 officers and men. All the states east of the Mississippi constituted the Department of the East, where Bvt. Maj. Gen. John E. Wool controlled 929 regulars.

A department commander was responsible for mobilizing and training militia and volunteer forces called into Federal service and for coordinating his resources with any expeditionary force commander who operated inside his territory or crossed through his department. A department commander often doubled in command, having responsibility for the administration of his department as well as for conduct of operations in the field. He often had a dual staff arrangement, one for the department and another for the campaign. For strategic guidance and major decisions he looked to the President and General in Chief; for administrative support he channeled his requirements through the Secretary of War to the appropriate bureau chief. In the modern sense he had no corps of staff experts who could assist him in equating his strategic goals with his logistical needs. In many respects the departmental system was a major reason why the Union armies during the Civil War operated like a team of balky horses. A system well suited to the demands of maintaining a small peacetime force could not effectively organize and manage combat forces consisting of hundreds of thousands of soldiers.

The 1,676 numbered paragraphs of the U.S. Army Regulations governed the actions of a department commander. The provisions concerning Army organization and tactics were archaic in most cases despite Davis' efforts in 1857 to update the regulations to reflect the experience of the Mexican War. During the

Civil War the Regulations would be slightly modified to incorporate the military laws passed by two wartime Congresses. In the South, these same regulations would govern the policy and procedures of the Confederate forces.

The roster of the Regular Army was altered considerably by Davis' action in creating the Confederate Army. Of the 1,080 in the active officer corps, 286 resigned or were dismissed and entered the Confederate service. (Conversely, only 26 enlisted men are known to have violated their oaths.) West Point graduates on the active list numbered 824; of these, 184 were among the officers who turned their backs on the United States and offered their swords to the Confederacy. Of the 900 graduates then in civil life, 114 returned to the Union Army and 99 others sought Southern commissions. General in Chief Winfield Scott and Col. George H. Thomas of Virginia were among the few prominent Southerners who fought for the Union. More serious than their numbers, however, was the high caliber of the officers who joined the Confederacy; many were regimental commanders, and three had commanded at the departmental level.[1]

---

1   Matloff 1969, 184-5, 188.

Strategic Perspectives: The War of 1861

Abraham Lincoln was inaugurated—and officially assumed the responsibility of Commander-in-Chief—on March 4, 1861. However, his direct involvement with military strategy would not seemingly begin to manifest itself until July 1861 when, following the fall of Ft. Sumter, he ordered General Scott to suspend the writ of habeas corpus at his discretion along the military line between Washington and Philadelphia. From this point onward, his presence would be felt in every theater of the conflict.

In the South, with military preparations under way, Jefferson Davis dispatched commissioners to Washington a few days after Lincoln's inauguration to treat for the speedy takeover of Forts Sumter and Pickens. Informally reassured that the forts would not be provisioned without proper notice, the envoys returned to Montgomery expecting an uneventful evacuation of Sumter. President Lincoln had to move cautiously, for he knew Sumter's supplies were giving out. As each March day passed, Sumter aggravated the harshness of Lincoln's dilemma. In case of war, the fort had no strategic value. And if Lincoln reinforced it, Davis would have his act of provocation and Lincoln might drive eight more slaveholding states out of the Union. Yet if Sumter was not succored, the North might cool its enthusiasm for the Union concept and become accustomed to having a confederation south of the Mason-Dixon Line. There were no easy choices for the new President.

President Lincoln spent two weeks listening to the conflicting counsel of his constitutional advisers and made up his own mind on March 29 to resupply Fort Sumter with provisions only. No effort would be made to increase its military power. By sea he soon dispatched a token expedition and on April 8 notified South Carolina's governor of his decision. The next move was up to the local Confederate commander, Brig. Gen. Pierre G. T. Beauregard. On the eleventh, Maj. Robert Anderson, Sumter's commander, politely but firmly rejected a formal surrender demand. At 4:30 the next morning Confederate batteries began a 34-hour bombardment. Anderson's ninety-man garrison returned it in earnest, but Sumter's guns were no match for the concentric fire from Confederate artillery. Offered honorable terms on April 14, Anderson surrendered the Federal fort, saluted his U.S. flag with fifty guns, and, with his command, was conveyed to the fleet outside the harbor to be taken to New York City.

From a political perspective, the Confederate barrage of Ft. Sumter removed many difficulties from Lincoln's path in his efforts to preserve the Union. On the fifteenth Lincoln personally penned a proclamation declaring the seven Southern states in insurrection against the laws of the United States. To strangle the Confederacy, on the nineteenth Lincoln declared the entire coast from South Carolina to Texas under naval blockade. To augment the reduced Regular Army, Lincoln asked the governors of the loyal states for 75,000 militiamen to serve for three months, the maximum time permissible under existing laws. With a unanimity that astonished most people, the Northern states responded with 100,000 men. Within the eight slave states still in the Union, the call for militia to suppress the rebellion was angrily and promptly rejected; and the President's decision to coerce the Confederacy moved Virginia, North Carolina, Tennessee, and Arkansas to join it. The border states of Missouri, Kentucky, Maryland, and Delaware were still undecided; and each side moved cautiously to avoid pushing them into the other's camp.

As spring changed into summer the magnitude of the job that the Union had proclaimed for itself—the conquest of an area the size of western Europe, save Scandinavia and Italy, defended by a plucky and proud people and favored by military geography—was imperfectly understood. Although Lincoln later emerged as a diligent student of warfare, he was as yet unversed in the art. His only service in the military had been as a junior officer of volunteers during the Black Hawk war, and he had seen no combat action. His rival, Davis, from the outset knew his military men quite well and thoroughly understood the mechanics of building a fighting force. He had commanded a volunteer regiment in the Mexican War and was experienced at the national policy level due to his service as Secretary of War. Yet, as time passed, Davis would be seen to mismanage his government and its military affairs.

Virginia's secession caused Col. Robert E. Lee, Scott's choice to be the Union's field leader, to resign his commission and offer his services to his state. The Confederates moved their capital to Richmond, Virginia, site of the largest iron works in the South and 100 miles south of the Union capital, Washington. On May 23 Union forces crossed into northern Virginia and occupied Arlington Heights and Alexandria. With Virginia and North Carolina in rebellion, Lincoln extended the naval blockade and called for a large volunteer army backed by an increased regular force.

Correctly anticipating that Congress in its session to open on July 4 would approve his actions, Lincoln, on his own authority, established 40 regiments of U.S. Volunteers (42,034 men) to serve three years or for the duration of the war. He ordered the Regular Army increased by 1 regiment of artillery, 1 of cavalry, and 8 of infantry (actually, 9 regiments were added), or 22,714 men, and the Navy by 18,000 sailors. The new regular infantry regiments were each to have 3 battalions of about 800 men, in contrast to the 1-battalion structure in the existing regular and volunteer regiments. However, because the recruits preferred the larger bonuses, laxer discipline, and easygoing atmosphere of the volunteers, most of the newly constituted regiments were never able to fill their additional battalions to authorized strength. The volunteer units were state units, not Federal or regular units.

The enthusiastic response to Lincoln's various calls forced him to ask the governors to scale down the induction of men. The overtaxed camps could not handle the increasing manpower. In raising the Army, Lincoln used methods that dated back to Washington's day. The combat efficiency and state of training of the new units varied from good to very poor. Some militia regiments were well trained and equipped, others were regiments in name only. The soldiers often elected their own company officers, and the governors commissioned majors and colonels. The President appointed generals. Although many of the newly eager to learn, incompetents were also appointed. Before the end of 1861, however, officers were being required to prove their qualifications before examining boards of regular officers; those found unfit were allowed to resign.

Frequently advised by governors and congressmen, Lincoln selected generals from among leading politicians to give himself a broader base of political support. Some political generals, such as John A. Logan and Francis P. Blair, Jr., distinguished themselves, whereas many others proved military hindrances. Lincoln gave a majority of the commissions in the first forty volunteer units to regulars on active duty, to former West Pointers like George B. McClellan (who had resigned to pursue a business career) or to those who had held volunteer commissions during the Mexican War. On the other hand, Davis never gave higher than a brigade command to a Confederate volunteer officer until he had proved himself in battle.

Both North and South failed to develop a good system to replace individuals in volunteer units. The Confederacy, though hamstrung by its insistence that Texans be commanded by Texans and Georgians by Georgians and by governors' insistent demands for retaining home guards, did devise a regimental system that stood up well until the closing days of the war. Except for Wisconsin, Illinois, and Vermont, the Union armies never had an efficient volunteer replacement system. As battle losses mounted and the ranks of veteran regiments thinned, commanders were forced to send men back to their home states on recruiting duty or face the disbandment of their regiments. Northern governors with patronage in mind preferred to raise new regiments, allowing battle-tested ones to decline to company proportions.

The enlisted Regular Army was kept intact for the duration of the war. Many critics believed that the Union should have used regulars to cadre the volunteer units. But this practice was initially impossible during the summer of 1861 for at least two reasons. Lincoln did not foresee a long war, and the majority of regulars were needed on the frontier until trained men could replace them. In addition, Lincoln's critics overlooked the breakdown in morale that would have accompanied the breakup of old line regiments, many of which had histories and honors dating back to the War of 1812. An officer holding a regular commission in 1861 had to resign to accept a commission in the volunteers unless the War Department specifically released him. Most regulars were loath to resign, uncertain that they would be recalled to active duty after the war. Thus, during 1861 and part of 1862, promotion in the Regular Army was slow. All regulars could accept commissions in the volunteers by 1862, and in many cases the year they had spent in small unit command seasoning had its reward in advancing them to higher commands. Ulysses S. Grant and William T. Sherman, both U.S. Military Academy graduates returning from civilian life, asked specifically for volunteer regimental commands at first and soon advanced rapidly to general officer posts.[1]

The Opposition

As North and South lined up for battle, the preponderance of productive capacity, manpower, and agricultural potential clearly lay on the side of the North. Its crops were worth more annually than those of the South, which had concentrated on growing cotton, tobacco, and rice. Between February and May 1861 the Confederate authorities missed the opportunity to ship baled cotton to England and draw bills against it for the purchase of arms. In sea power, railroads, material wealth, and industrial capacity to produce iron and munitions, the North was vastly superior to the South. This disparity became even more pronounced as the ever-tightening blockade gradually cut off the Confederacy from foreign imports. The North had more mules and horses, a logistical advantage of great importance since supplies had to be carried to the troops from rail and riverheads.

The difference in manpower was also critical. According to the census of 1860, the population of the United States numbered 31,443,321. About 23 million of them were in the twenty-two Northern states and 9 million in the eleven states that later seceded. Of the latter total, 3.5 million were slaves. The size of the opposing armies would reflect this disparity. At one time or another about 2.1 million men would serve in the Northern armies, while 800,000–900,000 men would serve the South. Peak strength of the two forces would be about 1 million and 600,000, respectively.

Yet not all the advantages lay with the North. The South possessed good interior lines of communications; and its 3,550-mile coastline, embracing 189 harbors and navigable river mouths, was difficult to blockade effectively. Possessors of a rich military tradition in wars against the British, Spanish, Mexicans, and Indians, the Southerners initially managed to form redoubtable cavalry units more easily than the North and used them with considerable skill against the invading infantry. As the war moved along, the armies on both sides demonstrated high degrees of military skill and bravery. Man for man they became almost evenly matched, and their battles were among the bloodiest in modern history. Jefferson Davis hoped that the sympathy or even the intervention of European powers might more than compensate for the Confederacy's lack of material resources. This hope, largely illusory from the start, became less and less likely of realiza-

---

1 Matloff 1969, 188-191.

tion with the emancipation of the slaves, with every Union victory, and with the increasing effectiveness of the blockade.

Militarily, the South's greatest advantage over the North was simply the fact that if not attacked it could win by doing nothing. To restore the Union the Federal forces would have to conquer the Confederacy. Thus the arena of action lay below the strategic line of the Potomac and Ohio Rivers. Here, geography divided the theater of war into three interrelated theaters of operations. The Eastern Theater lay between the Atlantic Ocean and the Appalachian Mountains; the Western Theater embraced the area from the Appalachians to the Mississippi; and the Trans-Mississippi Theater ran westward to the Pacific Ocean.

In the east, the triangular shape of northern Virginia made it a difficult target to attack and provided it some advantage. The northern apex of the state aimed like an arrow at the Federal capital. The Potomac River and the lower Chesapeake Bay formed the right leg of the triangle; its left bounded on the Blue Ridge and the adjacent Shenandoah Valley. The base of the triangle followed the basin of the James and Appomattox Rivers, whereon stood Richmond, halfway between the bay and the valley. For three-and-a-half years Federal commanders would be defeated on the legs and in the center of this triangle as they tried to take Richmond and defeat the Army of Northern Virginia. Operating on these interior lines, General Lee would strike any Union force attempting to invade and follow up with lightning invasions of the North to keep it off balance. In the three neighboring counties of Virginia within this triangle, more than half a million men would clash in mortal combat over the course of four years. More soldiers—Union and Confederate—would die in these three counties than in the Revolutionary War, the War of 1812, the War with Mexico, and all the Indian Wars combined.

The hammer for swinging against the anvil of Union forces in Virginia came from the line of the Ohio River as Union forces moved along the invasion routes of the Green, Cumberland, Tennessee, and Mississippi Rivers. To breach the lower reaches of the Appalachians, the Federals needed the railroad centers at Nashville, Chattanooga, and Atlanta; with them they could strike north through the Carolinas toward the line of the James. But in the spring of 1861, the anvil and hammer concept had not yet occurred to the military leaders in Washington. Only the General in Chief, Scott, had a concrete strategic proposal for waging total war. He recommended that Lincoln take the time to train an army of 85,000 men and that he enforce the naval blockade of the Confederacy. Then the Army was to advance down the Mississippi to divide and conquer the South. The press ridiculed the strategy, calling it the Anaconda Plan, analogous to an anaconda snake's slowly squeezing its prey to death. But few leaders examined the South in terms of its military geography or concentrated on a strategy to prevail over it. Instead, most thought in terms of political boundaries and a short war; or, perhaps even just one major battle, which would end with the capture of Richmond.[1]

---

1 Matloff 1969, 192-195.

First Bull Run (First Manassas)

In the early summer of 1861 the partly trained ninety-day militia, the almost untrained volunteers, and one newly organized battalion of regulars—a total force of 50,000 Federals commanded by Brig. Gen. Irvin McDowell—defended the nation's capital. Thirty miles to the southwest, covering the rail and road hub at Manassas, Virginia, General Beauregard posted 20,000 Confederates, to be joined by 2,000 more within a few days. To the left, on their defensive line along the Potomac, the Confederates stationed another 11,000 men under Brig. Gen. Joseph E. Johnston in the Shenandoah Valley town of Winchester. Opposing Johnston around Martinsburg, with the mission of keeping the Confederates in place, was Maj. Gen. Robert Patterson with 18,000 Federals. On the extreme right of the Confederate northern Virginia defense line was Col. John B. Magruder's force, which had recently repulsed Maj. Gen. Benjamin F. Butler's Union troops at Big Bethel, Virginia, on 10 June and forced them back into their sanctuary at Fort Monroe.

Big Bethel, the first large-scale engagement of the Civil War, demonstrated that neither opponent was as yet well trained. The Confederates had started preparations earlier to protect northern Virginia and therefore might have had a slight edge on their opponents. General McDowell, only recently a major of regulars, had less than three months to weld his three types of units (militia, volunteer, and regular) into a single fighting force. He attempted to do too much himself, and there were few competent staff officers in the vicinity to help him. McDowell's largest tactical unit was a regiment until just before he marched out of Alexandria. Two to four brigades, plus a battery of regular artillery—the best arm against raw infantry—formed a division. In all, thirteen brigades were organized into five divisions. McDowell parceled out his forty-nine guns among his brigade commanders, who in turn attached them to their regiments. His total force for the advance was 35,732 men, but of these, one division of 5,752 men dropped off to guard roads to the rear.

McDowell's advance against Beauregard on four parallel routes was hastened by Northern opinion, expressed in editorials and Congressional speeches, which demanded immediate action. Scott warned Lincoln against undertaking the "On to Richmond" campaign until McDowell's troops had become disciplined units. But Lincoln, eager to use the ninety-day militia before they departed, demanded an advance, fully aware that the Confederates were also unseasoned and cherishing the belief that one defeat would force the South to quit. Scott, influenced by false intelligence that Beauregard would move immediately on Washington, acceded. McDowell's battle plan and preparations accelerated accordingly. The plan, accepted in late June, called for Butler and Patterson to prevent the Confederates facing them from reinforcing Beauregard while McDowell advanced against Manassas to outflank the Southern position. Scott called it a good plan on paper but knew Johnston was capable of frustrating it if given the chance. McDowell's success against the Confederate center depended upon a rapid thirty mile march, if 35,000 Federals were to keep 22,000 Confederates from being reinforced.

On July 16, 1861, the largest army ever assembled on the North American continent up to that time advanced slowly on both sides of the Warrenton pike toward Bull Run. McDowell's marching orders were good, but the effect was ruined by one unwise caution to the brigade commanders: "It will not be pardonable in any commander...to come upon a battery or breastwork without a knowledge of its position." The caution recalled to McDowell's subordinates the currently sensationalized bugbear of the press of the Federal forces' being fooled by "masked batteries." (The term originated at Sumter, where a certain battery was constructed, masked by a house that was demolished just before the guns opened fire.) Accordingly, 35,000 men moved with extreme caution just five miles on the seventeenth. The next day the Federals occupied Centreville, four miles east of Stone Bridge, which carried the Warrenton pike over Bull Run creek.

Beauregard's advance guards made no effort to delay the Federals but fell back across the battle line, now extending three miles along the west bank of Bull Run, which meandered from Stone Bridge southeast until it joined the Occoquan stream. The country was fairly rough, cut by streams and thickly wooded. It presented formidable obstacles to attacking raw troops, but a fair shelter for equally raw troops on the defensive. On the eighteenth, while McDowell's main body waited at Centreville for the trains to close up, the leading division demonstrated against Beauregard's right around Mitchell's Ford. The Federal infantry retired after a sharp musketry fight, and a 45-minute artillery duel ensued. It was the first exchange of four standard types of artillery ammunition for all muzzle loading guns, whether rifled or smoothbore. Solid shot, shell, spherical case or shrapnel, and canister from eight Federal guns firing 415 rounds were answered by seven Confederate pieces returning 310 rounds. Steadily withdrawing its guns, the oldest and best-drilled unit of the South, the Washington Light Artillery of New Orleans, broke off the fight against well-trained U.S. regular artillery. Both sides had used rifled artillery, which greatly increased the accuracy and gave a range more than double that of the smoothbores. Yet throughout the war rifled guns never supplanted the new, easily loaded Napoleons. In the fight, defective Confederate ammunition fired from three new 3-inch iron rifles would not fly point foremost but tumbled and lost range against McDowell's gunners. That the error went undetected for days reveals the haste in which Davis had procured his ordnance.

Sure that his green troops could not flank the Confederate right, McDowell tarried two more fateful days before he attacked in force. Engineers reconnoitered for an undefended ford north of Stone Bridge. Finding no vedettes at the ford near Sudley Springs, McDowell decided to envelop the Confederate left on July 21 and destroy the Manassas Gap Railroad to keep Johnston from reinforcing the outnumbered Beauregard. The idea was excellent, but the timing was slow.

While McDowell frittered away four-and-a-half days before he was ready to envelop in force, new tools of warfare swung the advantages of mobility, surprise, and mass at critical points toward Beauregard. On July 17 spies in Washington told of McDowell's departure from Alexandria. By electric telegraph Beauregard in turn alerted Richmond. Davis, also telegraphing, ordered commanders around Richmond, at Aquia Creek, and at Winchester to concentrate their available strength at Manassas. Johnston lost no time in deceiving Patterson by using Col. J. E. B. Stuart's cavalry as a screen and adroitly maneuvering his infantry away from the valley. Johnston selected the best overland routes for his artillery and cavalry marches and arranged for railroad officials to move his four infantry brigades. Brig. Gen. Thomas Jackson's lead brigade, accompanied by Johnston himself, covered fifty-seven miles in twenty five hours by road and rail to reach Beauregard on the twentieth.

At daylight on the twenty-first McDowell unmasked the first phase of his attack plan. Three brigades of Brig. Gen. Daniel Tyler's division appeared before Stone Bridge; and a huge, 30-lb. Parrott rifle dragged into place by ten horses commenced a slow fire directed by six cannoneers of the 2d U.S. Artillery. Five brigades in two divisions directly under McDowell's command meanwhile marched on an eight-mile circuitous route toward the undefended ford at Sudley Springs. McDowell's goal was the Confederate left rear and a chance to cut the railroad. The movement was not unobserved, however. At 9:00 a.m. a signal flag wigwag from the Henry house announced the point of the enveloping columns at Sudley's crossing, and the intelligence was immediately relayed to Beauregard and Johnston, three miles away on the Confederate right.

The first weight of the Federal attack fell against eleven Confederate companies and two guns. For an hour McDowell's regiments, firing one by one and moving forward cautiously in piecemeal fashion, tried to overrun Beauregard's left flank. The timid tactics gave Beauregard time to redeploy ten regiments across a three-mile front to form a second defensive line across the north face of the hill behind the Henry house. At 10:30 a.m., as the summer sun grew hotter, a portentous dust cloud ten miles northwest of Manassas heralded the arrival of Kirby Smith's brigade, the tail of Johnston's reinforcements from the Shenandoah Valley.

For two hours the roar of the battle swelled in volume. Federal musketry crashes and the thunder from the heavier pieces indicated that McDowell was now committing whole brigades supported by four batteries of artillery. North of the Warrenton turnpike, the Confederate infantry began to lose its brigade cohesion and fall back in disorder. As Beauregard and Johnston rode to the sound of battle, 10,000 Federals were punishing 7,000 Confederates in the vicinity of the Henry and Robinson houses. Johnston, though senior in command, turned the battle over to Beauregard and galloped off toward Manassas to direct the arrival of reinforcements. Brig. Gen. Barnard E. Bee's brigade was pushed back from its advanced position toward the flat-crested hill behind the Henry house, where Jackson's newly arrived brigade had formed. In rallying his routed troops, Bee shouted: "Look at Jackson's Brigade; it stands like a stone wall! Rally behind the Virginians!"[1] Screened by a wooded area, three brigades regrouped behind

---

1 Out of these words came a nickname that Jackson would carry to his grave, and after his death in 1863 the Confederate War Department officially designated his unit the Stonewall Brigade.

Jackson's lines; and the rally became a great equalizer as McDowell's strength dissipated to 9,000 men with no immediate infantry reserves in sight.

The cloud of dust moved closer to Manassas Junction, but McDowell ignored it and allowed a lull to settle over his front for almost two hours. At 2:00 p.m., having deployed two batteries of regular artillery directly to his front around the Henry house with insufficient infantry protection, McDowell renewed the battle. By midafternoon the dust had blended sweaty uniforms into a common hue, and more and more cases of mistaken identity were confusing both sides in the smoke of the battle. Then, as part of the confusion, came a fateful episode. To the right front of McDowell's exposed artillery, a line of advancing blue clad infantry, the 33d Regiment, Virginia Volunteers, suddenly appeared through the smoke. The Federal artillery commander ordered canister, but the chief artillery officer on McDowell's staff overruled the order, claiming that the oncoming blue uniforms belonged to friendly infantry arriving in support. The Virginians advanced to within seventy yards of the Federal guns, leveled their muskets, and let loose. The shock of their volley cut the artillery to shreds; and for the remainder of the day nine Federal guns stood silent, unserved, and helpless between the armies.

About 4:00 p.m., Beauregard, with two additional fresh brigades, advanced his entire line. Shorn of their artillery, the faltering Federal lines soon lost cohesion and began to pull back along the routes they knew; there was more and more confusion as they retired. East of Bull Run, Federal artillery, using Napoleon smoothbores in this initial pullback from the field, proved to the unsuspecting Confederate cavalry, using classic saber-charging tactics, that a determined line of artillerymen could reduce cavalry to dead and sprawling infantry in minutes.

As in so many battles of the Civil War yet to come, there was no organized pursuit in strength to cut the enemy to ribbons while he fled from the immediate area of the battlefield. At Bull Run, the Federal withdrawal turned into a panic-stricken flight about 6:30 p.m., when Cub Run Bridge, about a mile west of Centreville, was blocked by overturned wagons. President Davis, just arrived from Richmond, had two daylight hours to arrive at a decision for pursuit. In council with Johnston and Beauregard, Davis instructed the whole Confederate right to advance against the Centreville road, but apparently his orders were never delivered or Beauregard neglected to follow them. Davis thus lost a splendid opportunity for seeing in person whether the unused infantry and artillery on the right of his line could have made a concerted effort to destroy McDowell's fleeing forces. Logistically, Federal booty taken over the next two days by the Confederates would have sustained them for days in an advance against Washington.

Strategically, Bull Run was important to the Confederates only because the center of their Virginia defenses had held. Tactically, the action highlights many of the problems and deficiencies that were typical of the first year of the war. Bull Run was a clash between large, ill-trained bodies of recruits who were slow in joining battle. The rumor of masked batteries frightened commanders; plans called for maneuvering the enemy out of position, but attacks were frontal; security principles were disregarded; tactical intelligence was nil; and reconnaissance was poorly executed. Soldiers were overloaded for battle. Neither commander was able to employ his whole force effectively. Of McDowell's 35,000 men, only 18,000 crossed Bull Run and casualties among these, including the missing, numbered about 2,708. Beauregard, with 32,000 men, ordered only 18,000 into action and lost 1,982.

Both commanders rode along the front, often interfering in small unit actions. McDowell led his enveloping column instead of directing all his forces from the rear. Wisely, Johnston left the battlefield and went to the rear to hasten his Shenandoah Valley reserves. Regiments were committed piecemeal. Infantry failed to protect exposed artillery. Artillery was parceled out under infantry command; only on the retreat was the Union senior artillery officer on the scene allowed to manage his guns. He saved twenty-one guns of the forty-nine that McDowell had. Beauregard's orders were oral, vague, and confusing. Some were delivered, others were never followed.[1]

The Second Uprising in 1861

The Southern victory near Manassas had an immediate and long-term effect on the efforts of both the Northern and the Southern states. First, it compelled Northern leaders to face up to the nature and scope of the struggle and to begin the task of putting the Union on a full war footing. Second, it made them more willing to heed the advice of professional soldiers directing military operations along a vast continental land front from Point Lookout, Maryland, to Fort Craig in central New Mexico. Third, Confederate leaders, after their feeling of invincibility quickly wore off, called for 400,000 volunteers, sought critical military items in Europe, and turned to planning operations that might swing the remaining slaveholding states and territories into the Confederacy. Finally, the most potent immediate influence of Bull Run was upon the European powers, which eyed the Confederacy as a belligerent with much potential for political intervention and as a source of revenue. Unless the U.S. Navy could make it unprofitable for private merchant ships to deliver arms to Southern ports and depart with agricultural goods, speculative capital would flow increasingly into the contraband trade.

Strategically, in 1861 the Navy made the most important contribution toward an ultimate Union victory. At considerable expense and in haste to make the blockade effective, the Navy by the end of the year had assembled 200 ships of every description, armed them after a fashion, and placed them on station. With new congressional acts regarding piracy, revenue, confiscation, and enforcement in hand, commanders of this motley fleet intercepted more and more swift blockade runners steaming out of Nassau, Bermuda, and Havana on their three-day run to Wilmington, North Carolina; Charleston, South Carolina; or Savannah, Georgia. In two round trips a blockade runner, even if lost on its third voyage, still produced a considerable profit to its owner. By the end of 1861 such profit was no longer easy, because the Navy had many new fast ships specially fitted for blockade duty in service.

---

1 Matloff 1969, 196-201.

After 1861 the naval character of the war changed. There was no Civil War on the high seas except for the exciting exploits of three or four Confederate cruisers that raided commercial shipping. As the war progressed, both opponents perfected the nature and construction of ships and naval ordnance for a war that would be fought in coastal waters or inside defensible harbors. The three main weapons, the rifled naval gun, the armored ram, and the torpedo mine, were developed and used in novel ways. To offset the defensive use of these weapons by the South, the U.S. Navy beginning in August 1861 landed more and more Army expeditionary forces and gradually gained footholds in the vicinity of Mobile, Savannah, Charleston, and Wilmington. By the end of the war, joint Navy–Army expeditions would convert the sea blockade into a military occupation and would seal off all major ports in the South. Even more important were the river fleets of the U.S. Navy on the Ohio, Missouri, and Mississippi Rivers. These fleets, operating closely with the local Army commanders, provided essential elements in the evolving Union strategy of splitting the Confederacy along the natural invasion routes of the river valleys.

The defeat at Bull Run was followed by "a second uprising" in the North that greatly surpassed the effort after Sumter's surrender. President Lincoln and Congress set to with a will to raise and train the large Federal armies that would be required to defeat the South, to select competent Army field commanders, and to reorganize and strengthen the War Department. On July 22, 1861, Lincoln called for a 500,000-man force of three-year volunteers and during the rest of July quickly disbanded the ninety-day militia. The more experienced men entered the newly authorized volunteer force. Meanwhile, the volunteer quota and the increase of regulars, mobilized after Sumter, had so far progressed that camps and garrisons, established at strategic points along the 1,950-mile boundary with the border states and territories, were bustling with activity. As July ended, Congress authorized the volunteers to serve for the duration of the war and perfected their regimental organization. Four regiments were grouped into a brigade, and three brigades formed a division. The infantry corps structure would be fixed when the President directed. In effect, the Lincoln administration was building a Federal force, as opposed to one based on joint state-Federal control and support. State governors, given a quota according to a state's population, raised 1,000-man volunteer regiments, bought locally whatever the units needed, shipped them to federal training centers, and presented all bills to the U.S. government. Accordingly, Congress floated a national loan of $250 million.

Pending the transformation of volunteer forces, both opponents necessarily suspended major military operations in the east for the remainder of 1861. President Lincoln conferred frequently with General Scott and his military advisers about steps already taken to strengthen Union forces along the continental front. Regular Army units were consolidating their position at Fort Craig and Fort Union to protect the upper Rio Grande valley against any Confederate columns coming from Texas. To protect communication lines to the Pacific and the southwest and to guard Federal supplies at Fort Leavenworth, Kansas, and St. Louis, Missouri, Union troops were deployed in eastern Kansas and across central Missouri.

In terms of territorial gain and long-term strategic value, the Western Theater of Operations was more active in 1861 than was the Eastern. Both Union and Confederacy coveted Kentucky and Missouri. The confluence of the Tennessee, Cumberland, and Ohio Rivers lay within Kentucky; while the vast Mississippi–Missouri River network flowed through Missouri. Whoever controlled these two states and these rivers had a great strategic advantage. At the onset of hostilities, Kentucky adopted a policy of neutrality. The loss of Kentucky, in Lincoln's judgment, would be "nearly the same as to lose the whole game," so he carefully respected Kentucky's decision in May to remain neutral. But a Confederate force occupied the strategically important town of Columbus, Kentucky, overlooking the Mississippi River, on fears that Brig. Gen. Ulysses S. Grant, poised across the Ohio River at Cairo, Illinois, would do so first. The rebel move into Kentucky violated that state's neutrality stance, and Kentucky's legislature responded by requesting that Union forces remove the Confederate invaders. On September 6 Grant launched a joint Army–Navy operation into Kentucky and occupied the towns of Paducah and Southland at the mouth of the Tennessee and Cumberland Rivers. This move prevented further Confederate advances in Kentucky and positioned Grant's forces for campaigns in 1862.

In Missouri, pro-Southern and Unionist sympathizers fought a violent campaign for control. A 6,000-man Federal force under Brig. Gen. Nathaniel Lyon defeated Southern militia to occupy the state capital at Jefferson City. A Confederate army of nearly 13,000 moved from Arkansas to destroy the smaller Union force. At Wilson's Creek, Lyon launched a preemptive strike against the rebel camp in the early morning of 10 August, dividing his numerically inferior troops and assaulting from the north and south. The Southern army quickly recovered and regrouped. Outgunned, the Union force fought off three Confederate counterattacks against Bloody Hill before it was able to break contact and withdraw. Based on the number of troops engaged, Wilson's Creek was the most costly Civil War battle in 1861, with the Confederates losing 1,222 killed and wounded. Union casualties were 1,317, including Lyon, the first general officer to be killed in the conflict. The victory at Wilson's Creek buoyed Confederate morale. But Union forces under Charles C. Frémont and later Henry W. Halleck occupied central Missouri and contained rebel forces in the southwestern corner of the state for the remainder of 1861.

A battle with equally long-term consequences was fought for western Virginia. Forty counties elected to secede from Virginia and asked for Federal troops to assist them in repelling any punitive expeditions emerging from the Shenandoah Valley. Between May and early July 1861, Ohio volunteers, under the command of Maj. Gen. George B. McClellan, occupied the Grafton area of western Virginia, hoping to protect the railroad that linked the Ohio Valley with Baltimore. In a series of clashes at Philippi, Beverly, and along the Cheat River, McClellan's forces checked the invading Confederates, paving the way for West Virginia's entrance into the Union. Even the arrival of Jefferson Davis' principal military adviser and Commander of the Confederate forces in Virginia, not yet the Commander of the Army of Northern Virginia, General Robert E. Lee, failed to reverse Union gains. Lee attempted to coordinate several overly ambitious offensives in the Tygart and Kanawha River valleys; but poor roads, dispirited troops, miserable weather, and shortages of supply led to a series of failures. He returned to Richmond after this failure of his first major campaign by the end of October 1861. His reputation as a military commander suffered, while that of his principal foe, General McClellan, soared; some saw McClellan as the "hope of the North."

Although the border strife intensified in the west, Scott attended to the more important front facing Virginia. The nation's capital was imperiled, the Potomac was directly under Confederate guns, and Maryland and Delaware were being used as recruiting areas for the Southern cause. On July 22, Lincoln, following Scott's advice, summoned McClellan, who was thirty-five years old at the time, to Washington, and assigned him command, under Scott, of all the troops in the Washington area. McClellan's reputation was unrivaled, and the public had acclaimed him for his victories in western Virginia. On August 21 McClellan named his force the Army of the Potomac and commenced molding it, with considerable skill, into a formidable machine.

McClellan organized the Army of the Potomac into eleven 10,000-man divisions, each with three brigades of infantry, a cavalry regiment, and four six-gun batteries. In general the other Union armies adopted this structure, and the Confederates deviated from the model only in their cavalry organization. In the Army of Northern Virginia, for example, General Lee treated his cavalry as a tactical arm, grouped first as a division and later as a cavalry corps. Union cavalry consisted of little more than mounted infantry, carrying out a multitude of duties, such as serving as pickets, wagon train escorts, and couriers for the division commander. McClellan planned, once Lincoln activated the corps, to withdraw one-half of the artillery pieces from each infantry division and center them at corps level as a reserve to be deployed under army command. He insisted that the .58-caliber single-shot, muzzle loading Springfield rifle be the standard weapon of the infantry, and most of the Army of the Potomac possessed it when corps were organized on March 8, 1862.

McClellan completely transformed the military atmosphere around Washington before the end of 1861. He was an able administrator, but his critics doubted his abilities as a top field commander. And from the day McClellan activated the Army of the Potomac, he was politically active in trying to oust Winfield Scott. Finally, on November 1, the aged and harassed General in Chief, taking advantage of a new law, retired from the Army. That same day, acting on assurances that McClellan could handle two tasks concurrently, Lincoln made McClellan the General in Chief and retained him in command of the Army of the Potomac. By the ninth, basing his action on Scott's earlier groundwork, McClellan carved out five new departments in the west, all commanded by Regular Army officers. In addition, he continued the work of the new Department of New England, where General Butler was already forming volunteer regiments for scheduled amphibious operations off the Carolina coast and in the Gulf of Mexico.

For the Union cause in Kentucky, the new General in Chief's move came none too soon. After Kentucky declared for the Union on September 20, both sides rapidly concentrated forces in western Kentucky. Maj. Gen. Albert S. Johnston, recently appointed to command Confederate forces in the west, fortified Bowling Green and extended his defensive line to Columbus. Union troops immediately occupied Louisville and planned advances down the railroad to Nashville, Tennessee, and eastward into the Appalachians. By November 15, the commanders of the Departments of the Ohio and the Missouri, dividing their operational boundaries in Kentucky along the Cumberland River, were exchanging strategic plans with McClellan in anticipation of a grand offensive in the spring of 1862.

The outpouring of troops and their preparations for battle disrupted the leisurely pace of the War Department. In haste to supply, equip, and deploy the second quota of volunteers, a score or more of states competed not only against one another but also against the Federal government. Profiteers demanded exorbitant prices for scarce items, which frequently turned out to be worthless. Unbridled graft and extravagance were reflected in the bills that the states presented to the War Department for payment. After Bull Run a concerted, widespread movement emerged for the dismissal of Secretary of War Simon Cameron, who had failed to manage his office efficiently. Cameron selected Edwin M. Stanton, former Attorney General in President Buchanan's Cabinet, as his special counsel to handle all legal arguments justifying the War Department's purchasing policies. Knowing that the cabinet post had considerable potential, Stanton worked hard to restore the War Department's prestige. Behind the scenes Stanton aided his fellow Democrat, McClellan, in outfitting the Army of the Potomac. As the summer faded, Stanton, having once scoffed at Lincoln early in the war, ingratiated himself with the President and his key Cabinet members by urging his pro-Union views. In January 1862 Lincoln replaced Cameron with Stanton, who immediately set out to make his cabinet position the most powerful in Lincoln's administration.

Self-confident, arrogant, abrupt, and contemptuous of incompetent military leaders, Stanton was also fiercely energetic, incorruptible, and efficient. Respecting few men and fearing none, he did his best to eliminate favoritism and see to it that war contracts were honestly negotiated and faithfully filled. Few men liked Stanton, but almost all high officials respected him. Stanton insisted that the Army receive whatever it needed, and the best available, so no campaign by any Union army would ever fail for want of supplies.

From the day that Stanton took office, the structure of the War Department was centralized to handle the growing volume of business. Each bureau chief reported directly to Stanton, but the responsibility became so heavy that he delegated procurement and distribution matters to three assistant secretaries. Because the Quartermaster General's Department transported men and materiel, operated the depot system, constructed camps, and handled the largest number of contracts, it soon became the most important agency of the General Staff. Hardworking, efficient, and loyal, Montgomery C. Meigs as Quartermaster General was an organizing genius and one of the few career officers to whom Stanton would listen. To complete his department, Stanton added three major bureaus during the war: the Judge Advocate General's Office in 1862; the Signal Department in 1863; and the Provost Marshal General's Bureau in 1863 to administer the draft (enrollment) act. In the same year the Corps of Topographical Engineers merged with the Corps of Engineers.

Stanton faced mobilization problems and home front crises of unprecedented magnitude. Loyal states were bringing half a million men under arms. Grain, wool, leather, lumber, metals, and fuel were being turned into food, clothing, vehicles, and guns, and thousands of draft animals were being purchased and shipped from every part of the North. A well-managed Federal authority was needed to assume the states' obligations, to train volunteer units in the use of their tools of war, and then to deploy them along a vast continental front. By exploiting the railroad, steamship, and telegraph, the War Department provided field commanders a novel type of mobility in their operations. Stanton's major task was to control all aspects of this outpouring of the nation's resources. If war contracts were tainted, the Union soldiers might despair. Moral as well as financial bankruptcy could easily wreck Union hopes of victory. In addition, Stanton had the job of suppressing subversion, of timing the delicate matter of enrolling African Americans in the Army, and of cooperating with a radical-dominated Congress, a strong-willed Cabinet, and a conservative-minded Army. With a lawyer's training, Stanton, like Lincoln, knew little about military affairs, and there was little time for him to learn. Anticipating that President Lincoln would soon call for War Department plans for the spring 1862 offensives, Stanton researched every document he could find on Army administration, consulted his bureau chiefs about readiness, and prepared himself to work with the General in Chief on strategic matters.

When he took office, Stanton found that the War Department had a rival in the form of the Joint Congressional Committee on the Conduct of the War. The committee originated in an investigation of a badly executed reconnaissance at Ball's Bluff on the Potomac on October 21, 1861, in which volunteer officer and popular former Senator Col. Edward D. Baker, was killed. By subsequently searching out graft and inefficiency, the committee did valuable service, but it also vexed the President, Stanton, and most of the generals during the war. Composed of extreme antislavery men without military knowledge and experience, the committee probed the battles, tried to force all its views regarding statecraft and strategy on the President, and put forward its own candidates for high command. Suspicious of proslavery men and men of moderate views, it considered that the only generals fit for office were those who had been abolitionists before 1861.

As the year ended both North and South were earnestly preparing for a hard war. Both opponents were raising and training huge armies totaling nearly a million men. Fort Sumter and bloody Bull Run were over, and each side was gathering its resources for the even bloodier struggles to come.[1]

---

1 Matloff 1969, 202-208.

CORRESPONDENCE: 1861

Order Authorizing General Scott to Suspend the Writ of Habeas Corpus, July 2, 1861.[1]

To the Commanding General, Army of the United States:

You are engaged in suppressing an insurrection against the laws of the United States. If at any point on or in the vicinity of any military line which is now or which shall be used between the city of New York and the city of Washington you find resistance which renders it necessary to suspend the writ of habeas corpus for the public safety, you personally, or through the officer in command at the point where resistance occurs, are authorized to suspend that writ.

Given under my hand and the seal of the United States at the city of Washington, this second day of July, 1861, and of the independence of the United States the eighty-fifth.

A. Lincoln.

---

1 None of the powers assumed by the President after the fall of Fort Sumter was so vigorously denounced as his order to General Scott to suspend the writ of habeas corpus at his discretion along the military line between Washington and Philadelphia. In pursuance of this order, one John Merryman, a citizen of Maryland, was arrested upon suspicion of treasonable conduct. His application to the Supreme Court for a writ of *habeas corpus* gave occasion to Chief Justice Taney to record a vigorous dissent from the doctrine that in a crisis the President might suspend the privilege of the writ. The President not only disregarded the protest, but extended the order to suspend the writ along the line from Washington to New York. In this course he was sustained by the Attorney General, whose opinion may be regarded as a reply to the Chief Justice. (Johnson 1912, 474)

Memoranda of Military Policy Suggested By the Bull Run Defeat, July 23, 1861.[1]

1. 1Let the plan for making the blockade effective be pushed forward with all possible dispatch.

2. Let the volunteer forces at Fort Monroe and vicinity under General Butler be constantly drilled, disciplined, and instructed without more for the present.

3. Let Baltimore be held as now, with a gentle but firm and certain hand.

4. Let the force now under Patterson or Banks be strengthened and made secure in its position.

5. Let the forces in Western Virginia act till further orders according to instructions or orders from General McClellan.

6. [Let] General Frémont push forward his organization and operations in the West as rapidly as possible, giving rather special attention to Missouri.

7. Let the forces late before Manassas, except the three-months men, be reorganized as rapidly as possible in their camps here and about Arlington.

8. Let the three-months forces who decline to enter the longer service be discharged as rapidly as circumstances will permit.

9. Let the new volunteer forces be brought forward as fast as possible, and especially into the camps on the two sides of the river here.

When the foregoing shall be substantially attended to:

1. Let Manassas Junction (or some point on one or other of the railroads near it) and Strasburg be seized, and permanently held, with an open line from Washington to Manassas, and an open line from Harper's Ferry to Strasburg the military men to find the way of doing these.

2. This done, a joint movement from Cairo on Memphis; and from Cincinnati on East Tennessee.

---

1 For the new program a new commander was needed. Not that Bull Run commander Irving McDowell had served so badly; it was rather that this unfortunate commander bore the imprimatur of defeat, and that conditions of army morale and popular feeling demanded a change. The name of George B. McClellan was in favor because of a minor but skillfully advertised campaign in western Virginia (June and July, 1861). In an address to his troops he had dramatically acclaimed the achievements of his men; this address, whose publication was not neglected, was dated only five days before McDowell's defeat. More than this, McClellan had real qualities. Training at West Point had been followed by regular army duty, Mexican War service, military surveys, observation in the Crimean War (perfectly reported and published by the United States government), and executive experience with the Illinois Central Railroad. (Randall 1957, 244)

Telegram to General Frémont, Washington, August 15, 1861.[1]

To Major General Frémont:

Been answering your messages since day before yesterday. Do you receive the answers? The War Department has notified all the governors you designate to forward all available force. So telegraphed you. Have you received these messages? Answer immediately.

A. Lincoln.

To General Frémont, Washington, September 2, 1861.[2]

My Dear Sir—Two points in your proclamation of August 30 give me some anxiety.

First. Should you shoot a man, according to the proclamation, the Confederates would very certainly shoot our best men in their hands in retaliation; and so, man for man, indefinitely. It is, therefore, my order that you allow no man to be shot under the proclamation without first having my approbation or consent.

Second. I think there is great danger that the closing paragraph, in relation to the confiscation of property and the liberating slaves of traitorous owners, will alarm our Southern Union friends and turn them against us; perhaps ruin our rather fair prospect for Kentucky. Allow me, therefore, to ask that you will, as of your own motion, modify that paragraph so as to conform to the first and fourth sections of the act of Congress entitled "An act to confiscate property used for insurrectionary purposes," approved August 6, 1861, and a copy of which act I herewith send you.

This letter is written in a spirit of caution, and not of censure. I send it by special messenger, in order that it may certainly and speedily reach you. Yours very truly,

A. Lincoln.

---

1   On the 25th of July, Major General John C. Frémont reached St. Louis, in command of the Western Department. His advent was hailed with great enthusiasm. The newspapers, predicted for him achievements extravagant and impossible as those which the New York journals had foretold for McClellan. In those sanguine days, the whole country made "Young Napoleons" to order. With characteristic energy, Frémont plunged into the business of his new department, where chaos reigned, and he had no spell to evoke order, save the boundless patriotism and earnestness of the people. His headquarters were established on Chouteau Avenue. He was overrun with visitors—every captain, or corporal, or civilian, seeking to prosecute his business with the General in person. He was therefore compelled to shut himself up, and, by the sweeping refusal to admit petitioners to him, a few were excluded whose business was important. (Richardson 1971, 185)

2   Although there were some minor skirmishes in small hamlets and crossroads in Missouri where Confederate guerrillas struck, no single engagement actually amounted to much. However, together, these skirmishes stood for effective harassment. Frémont's answer to these hit-and-run raids came on August 30 in a proclamation that invoked martial law, confiscated the property of all Missourians in arms against the national government, and emancipated their slaves. Antislavery radicals rejoiced, but Lincoln instantly recognized the dangers. Frémont's edict would outrage border-state loyalists and convince a great many Northern Democrats that they had been tricked into supporting a war for the wrong purpose. Herein, Lincoln tactfully offers his counsel to Frémont. (Angle and Miers 1960, 151)

To General Frémont, Washington, September 11, 1861.[1]

Major General John C. Frémont:

Sir—Yours of the 8th, in answer to mine of the 2d instant, is just received. Assuming that you, upon the ground, could better judge of the necessities of your position than I could at this distance, on seeing your proclamation of August 30 I perceived no general objection to it. The particular clause, however, in relation to the confiscation of property and the liberation of slaves appeared to me to be objectionable in its nonconformity to the act of Congress passed the 6th of last August upon the same subjects; and hence I wrote you, expressing my wish that that clause should be modified accordingly. Your answer, just received, express-es the preference on your part that I should make an open order for the modifica-tion, which I very cheerfully do. It is therefore ordered that the said clause of said proclamation be so modified, held, and construed as to conform to, and not to transcend, the provisions on the same subject contained in the act of Congress entitled "An act to confiscate property used for insurrectionary purposes," ap-proved August 6, 1861, and that said act be published at length with this order. Your obedient servant,

A. Lincoln.

To General Scott, Washington, September 16, 1861.[2]

General Scott:

Dear Sir—Since conversing with you I have concluded to request you to frame an order for recruiting North Carolinians at Fort Hatteras. I suggest it to be so framed as for us to accept a smaller force—even a company—if we cannot get a regiment or more. What is necessary to now say about officers you will judge. Governor Seward says he has a nephew (Clarence A. Seward, I believe) who would be willing to go and play colonel and assist in raising the force. Still it is to be considered whether the North Carolinians will not prefer officers of their own. I should expect they would. Yours very truly,

A. Lincoln.

---

1 In response to Lincoln's September 2 note, Freemont remains steadfast in his position, advis-ing Lincoln, "Looking at affairs from this point of view, I am satisfied that strong and vigor-ous measures have now become necessary to the success of our Arms; and hoping that my views may have the honor to meet your approval." Lincoln now replies, ordering a modifica-tion of the proclamation. (Logan 1886, 367)

2 From the very beginning, both Northern military leaders and Lincoln realized the danger that North Carolinians in the Union army faced if captured by Southern soldiers. As a result, a conscious effort was made to protect these men from capture and punishment as traitors to the Confederacy. A serious—albeit unsuccessful in some instances—effort was made by Union leaders in the state to protect Unionists from capture and punishment as traitors by Confederate authorities. (Collins 1998, 53) Governor (William Henry) Seward had been elected in 1830 to the New York State Senate and became governor of the state in 1838 and again in 1840. In Albany he gained a reputation as a reformer and as an advocate of internal improvements as well as a rabid opponent of slavery. A leading Republican, Seward was appointed Secretary of State in President Abraham Lincoln's cabinet and won accolades for his handling of diplomacy during the Civil War. He remained Secretary of State during President Andrew Johnson's administration. (Ritter 1998, 346)

To General Frémont, Washington, September 12, 1861.[1]

Major General Frémont:

Governor Morton telegraphs as follows: "Colonel Lane, just arrived by special train, represents Owensborough, forty miles above Evansville, in possession of secessionists. Green River is navigable. Owensborough must be seized. We want a gunboat sent up from Paducah for that purpose." Send up the gunboat if, in your discretion, you think it right. Perhaps you had better order those in charge of the Ohio River to guard it vigilantly at all points.

A. Lincoln.

To General Thomas W. Sherman, Washington, October 18, 1861.[2]

General Thomas Sherman, Annapolis, Md.:

Your dispatch [sic] of yesterday received and shown to General McClellan. I have promised him not to direct his army here without his consent. I do not think I shall come to Annapolis.

A. Lincoln.

To Brigadier General S.R. Curtis, With Inclosures [sic], Washington, October 24, 1861.[3]

Brigadier General S.R. Curtis:

Dear Sir—On receipt of this, with the accompanying inclosures, you will take safe, certain, and suitable measures to have the inclosure addressed to Major General Frémont delivered to him with all reasonable dispatch, subject to these conditions only: that if, when General Frémont shall be reached by the messen-

---

1 Fremont telegraphed Lincoln the same day, "I have immediately ordered Captain [Andrew H.] Foote with gunboat to...Owensborough, and will take measures to guard the Ohio." (Lincoln v.4, 1953, 533)

2 The War Department appointed Brigadier General Thomas West Sherman to lead some of the earliest amphibian operations on the Atlantic coast. However, from the start, the expeditions encountered exasperating delays. Sherman eventually sailed south from Hampton Roads on October 29. The flagship *Wabash*, out in front, led the parade like a drum major. Eight naval ships in two columns followed. Then came the transports in three columns, each headed by an ocean liner—the *Vanderbilt*, the *Baltic* and the *Atlantic*. Two naval craft guarded each flank of the transport group, and two served as whippers-in in the rear. Off Cape Hatteras the symmetry of the formation was shattered by a hurricane. The *Union*, loaded with horses, and the *Osceola*, an army supply vessel, were wrecked on the North Carolina coast and seventy-three members of their crews were taken as prisoners to Raleigh. The supply vessel *Peerless*, loaded with cattle, broke up in the trough of the waves. Other vessels suffered similar fates. Sherman, however, preserved and was credited with leading the Union occupation of the Confederate garrisons of Fort Walker and Fort Beauregard. (West 1957, 83 and 87)

3 Union general John C. Frémont—considered a folk hero due to the tales of his western exploration and adventures—was an ardent abolitionist who, in 1861, issued an emancipation order in Missouri, which was rescinded by Lincoln. Frémont was subsequently relieved of his military command by the president. (Swint 2006, 196) General David Hunter, West Point graduate and veteran of the Seminole and Mexican Wars was a staunch opponent of slavery and perhaps closer to Lincoln than any other general. (Drumond 1961, 372) Samuel Ryan Curtis commanded Union forces in Missouri and Arkansas. (Winters 1998, 139)

ger—yourself or any one sent by you—he shall then have, in personal command, fought and won a battle, or shall then be actually in a battle, or shall then be in the immediate presence of the enemy in expectation of a battle, it is not to be delivered, but held for further orders. After, and not till after, the delivery to General Frémont, let the inclosure addressed to General Hunter be delivered to him.

Your obedient servant,

A. Lincoln.

(General Orders No. 18.) Headquarters of the Army, Washington, October 24, 1861

Major General Frémont, of the United States Army, the present commander of the Western Department of the same, will, on the receipt of this order, call Major General Hunter, of the United States Volunteers, to relieve him temporarily in that command, when he (Major General Frémont) will report to general headquarters by letter for further orders.

Winfield Scott. By command: E. D. Townsend, Assistant Adjutant General.

To [David Hunter] the Commander of the Department of the West. Washington, October 24, 1861.[1]

Sir—The command of the Department of the West having devolved upon you, I propose to offer you a few suggestions. Knowing how hazardous it is to bind down a distant commander in the field to specific lines and operations, as so much always depends on a knowledge of localities and passing events, it is intended, therefore, to leave a considerable margin for the exercise of your judgment and discretion.

The main rebel army (Price's) west of the Mississippi is believed to have passed Dade County in full retreat upon northwestern Arkansas, leaving Missouri almost freed from the enemy, excepting in the southeast of the State. Assuming this basis of fact, it seems desirable, as you are not likely to overtake Price, and are in danger of making too long a line from your own base of supplies and reinforcements, that you should give up the pursuit, halt your main army, divide it into two corps of observation, one occupying Sedalia and the other Rolla, the present termini of railroads; then recruit the condition of both corps by re-establishing and improving their discipline and instructions, perfecting their clothing and equipment, and providing less uncomfortable quarters. Of course, both railroads must be guarded and kept open, judiciously employing just so much force as is necessary for this. From these two points, Sedalia and Rolla, and especially in judicious cooperation with Lane on the Kansas border, it would be so easy to concentrate and repel any army of the enemy returning on Missouri from the southwest, that it is not probable any such attempt will be made before or during the approaching cold weather. Before spring the people of Missouri

---

1 Although Lincoln always modestly disclaimed any military ability, this letter to that General Hunter on the occasion of his taking command, was seemingly justified in its military views by the subsequent course of events in that Department throughout the war. (Lincoln 1865. 75)

will probably be in no favorable mood to renew for next year the troubles which have so much afflicted and impoverished them during this. If you adopt this line of policy, and if, as I anticipate, you will see no enemy in great force approaching, you will have a surplus of force which you can withdraw from these points and direct to others as may be needed, the railroads furnishing ready means of reinforcing these main points if occasion requires. Doubtless local uprisings will for a time continue to occur, but these can be met by detachments and local forces of our own, and will ere long tire out of themselves.

While, as stated in the beginning of the letter, a large discretion must be and is left with yourself, I feel sure that an indefinite pursuit of Price or an attempt by this long and circuitous route to reach Memphis will be exhaustive beyond endurance, and will end in the loss of the whole force engaged in it.

Your obedient servant,

A. Lincoln.

Order Retiring General Scott and Appointing General McClellan His Successor (General Orders, No. 94)[1]

Executive Mansion, Washington.
November 1, 1861

On the 1st day of November, A.D. 1861, upon his own application to the President of the United States, Brevet Lieutenant General Winfield Scott is ordered to be placed, and hereby is placed, upon the list of retired officers of the Army of the United States, without reduction in his current pay, subsistence, or allowances. The American people will hear with sadness and deep emotion that General Scott has withdrawn from the active control of the army, while the president and a unanimous cabinet express their own and the nation's sympathy in his personal affliction and their profound sense of the important public services rendered by him to his country during his long and brilliant career, among which will ever be gratefully distinguished his faithful devotion to the constitution, the union, and the flag when assailed by parricidal rebellion.

A. Lincoln.

The President is pleased to direct that Major General George B. McClellan assume the command of the Army of the United States. The headquarters of the army will be established in the city of Washington. All communications intended for the commanding general will hereafter be addressed direct to the adju-

---

1 In retirement, Scott traveled to France, wrote his memoirs (published in 1864), and, in full dress uniform, age 78, paid his final respects to the assassinated Lincoln as the body lay in state in New York City in April of 1865. Scott died on May 29, 1866, at West Point. (Binning 1999, 376) Bartlett suggests that the melancholy summer of 1861 turned into an even more melancholy autumn. George B. McClellan, the dandy little general who had taken over the army on the retirement of the ancient Winfield Scott, preened his moustaches, posed like Napoleon and trained his army. McClellan did everything but fight. He had the Napoleonic ego and the Napoleonic stance without the Napoleonic talent for winning battles. (Bartlett 1961, 245)

tant-general. The duplicate returns, orders, and other papers heretofore sent to the Assistant Adjutant General, Headquarters of the Army, will be discontinued.

By Order of the Secretary of War: L. Thomas, Adjutant General.

Order Authorizing General Halleck to Suspend the Writ of Habeas Corpus, December 2, 1861.[1]

Major General H. W. Halleck, Commanding in the Department of Missouri:

General—As an insurrection exists in the United States, and is in arms in the State of Missouri, you are hereby authorized and empowered to suspend the writ of habeas corpus within the limits of the military division under your command, and to exercise martial law as you find it necessary in your discretion to secure the public safety and the authority of the United States.

In witness whereof I have hereunto set my hand and caused the seal of the United States to be affixed at Washington, this second day of December, A.D. 1861.

A. Lincoln.

Letter of Reprimand to General Hunter, Executive Mansion, Washington, December 31, 1861.[2]

Dear Sir:

Yours of the 23d is received, and I am constrained to say it is difficult to answer so ugly a letter in good temper. I am, as you intimate, losing much of the great confidence I placed in you, not from any act or omission of yours touching the public service, up to the time you were sent to Leavenworth, but from the flood of grumbling dispatches and letters I have seen from you since. I knew you were being ordered to Leavenworth at the time it was done; and I aver that with as tender a regard for your honor and your sensibilities as I had for my own, it

---

1 Halleck had never previously mentioned the writ of habeas corpus and neither had Lincoln in any correspondence leading up to the order of December 2 which suggests that the administration recognized no particular distinction between imposing martial law and suspending the writ of habeas corpus. Nevertheless, Halleck and his subordinates urged vigorous action against the disloyal populace in Missouri while attempting at the same time to restrain overzealous commanders from encumbering the makeshift federal prisons with people arrested for trivial offenses. In order to restrict the application of martial law, Halleck declared it in force only in St. Louis and around all railroads in the state. He reiterated the point in a general order on March 13, 1862, saying that "Martial law has never been legally declared in Missouri except in the city of St. Louis and on and in the immediate vicinity of the railroads and telegraph lines." Actually, Halleck had not mentioned telegraph lines in his original order back in December, and he was thereby perhaps unconsciously expanding the suspension. (Neely 1991, 38)

2 On December 23, 1861 Hunter had written Lincoln to complain, "I am very deeply mortified, humiliated, insulted and disgraced. You did me the honor to select me as a Major General and I am confident you intended I should have a Major Generals command. Yet strange as it may appear I am sent here into banishment with not three thousand effective men under my command, while one of the Brigadiers, General [Don Carlos] Buell, is in command of near one hundred thousand men in Kentucky. The only sin I have committed is my carrying out your views in relation to the retrograde movement from Springfield." Although, as previously indicated, David Hunter was a close personal friend, on this occasion, Lincoln found it necessary to issue a reprimand to his friend in response to Hunter's complaints about the size of his command. (Holzer 1993, 251)

never occurred to me that you were being "humiliated, insulted, and disgraced"; nor have I, up to this day, heard an intimation that you have been wronged, coming from anyone but yourself. No one has blamed you for the retrograde movement from Springfield, nor for the information you gave General Cameron; and this you could readily understand, if it were not for your unwarranted assumption that the ordering you to Leavenworth must necessarily have been done as a punishment for some fault. I thought then, and think yet, the position assigned to you is as responsible, and as honorable, as that assigned to Buell—I know that General McClellan expected more important results from it. My impression is that at the time you were assigned to the new Western Department, it had not been determined to replace General Sherman in Kentucky; but of this I am not certain, because the idea that a command in Kentucky was very desirable, and one in the farther West undesirable, had never occurred to me. You constantly speak of being placed in command of only 3000. Now, tell me, is this not mere impatience? Have you not known all the while that you are to command four or five times that many. I have been, and am sincerely your friend; and if, as such, I dare to make a suggestion, I would say you are adopting the best possible way to ruin yourself. "Act well your part, there all the honor lies." He who does something at the head of one regiment, will eclipse him who does nothing at the head of a hundred.

Your friend, as ever,

A. Lincoln.

Telegram to General Halleck, Washington, December 31, 1861.[1,2]

General H. W. Halleck, St. Louis, Missouri.

General McClellan is sick. Are General Buell and yourself in concert? When he moves on Bowling Green, what hinders it being reinforced from Columbus? A simultaneous movement by you on Columbus might prevent it.

A. Lincoln.

---

1 A similar dispatch was sent to Buell on the same date.

2 Between McClellan and Buell only formal communications passed in the latter part of December 1861, while McClellan was too sick to do much planning. On December 29, Buell brought up the subject of operations on the rivers, "It is my conviction that all the force that can possibly be collected should be brought to bear on that front of which Columbus and Bowling Green may be said to be the flanks. The center, that is, the Cumberland and Tennessee where the railroad crosses them, is now the most vulnerable point. I regard it as the most important strategical [sic] point in the whole field of operations." That this center, rightly judged "the most important strategical point," should lie on the sector line dividing the two great departments in the central West was a most serious fault of organization, rendered the more serious by the incapacity through sickness of McClellan, the commanding general, through whose active supervision lay the only prospect of proper coordination. (Conger 1931, 134) Accordingly, with McClelland ill, Lincoln correctly sensed that all was not right and that something must be done about it. He drafted the December 31 telegram.

STRATEGIC PERSPECTIVES: THE WAR OF 1862

In 1862, the armed forces of the United States undertook the first massive campaigns to defeat the Southern Confederacy. Better organization, training, and leadership would be displayed on both sides as the combat became more intense. Young American citizen soldiers would find that war was not a romantic adventure and their leaders would learn that every victory had its price.

As the winter of 1861–62 wore on, McClellan exaggerated his difficulties and the enemy's strength, and discounted the Confederacy's problems. He drilled and trained the Army of the Potomac while western forces under his general command accomplished little. Lincoln and the Union waited impatiently for a conclusive engagement. But neither the Union nor the Confederate Army showed much inclination to move, each being intent on perfecting itself before striking a heavy blow.

The President was particularly eager to support Unionist sentiment in east Tennessee by moving forces in that direction. Above all he wanted a concerted movement to crush the rebellion quickly. In an effort to push matters Lincoln issued General War Order No. 1 on January 27, 1862. This order, besides superfluously telling the armies to obey existing orders, directed that a general movement of land and sea forces against the Confederacy be launched on February 22, 1862. Lincoln's issuance of an order for an offensive several weeks in advance, without considering what the weather and the roads might be like, has been scoffed at frequently. But apparently he issued it only to get McClellan to agree to move. Even before Lincoln sent the directive his intentions were overtaken by events in the western theater.[1]

The Twin Rivers Campaign: Students of the Civil War often concentrate their study upon the cockpit of the war in the east—Virginia. The ri-

---

1 Matloff 1969, 209.

val capitals lay only a hundred miles apart and the country between them was fought over for Pour years. But it was the Union armies west of the Appalachians that struck the death knell of the Confederacy.

These Union forces in late 1861 were organized into two separate commands. Brig. Gen. Don Carlos Buell commanded some 45,000 men from a headquarters at Louisville, Kentucky, while Maj. Gen. Henry W. Halleck with headquarters at St. Louis, Missouri, had 91,000 under his command. These troops were generally raw, undisciplined western volunteers. Logistical matters and training facilities were undeveloped and as Halleck once wrote in disgust to his superior in Washington, "affairs here are in complete chaos."

Affairs were no better among Confederate authorities farther south. Facing Buell and Halleck were 43,000 scattered and ill-equipped Confederate troops under General Albert Sidney Johnston. Charged with defending a line which stretched for more than 500 miles from western Virginia to the border of Kansas, Johnston's forces mostly lay east of the Mississippi River. They occupied a system of forts and camps from Cumberland Gap in western Virginia through Bowling Green, Kentucky, to Columbus, Kentucky, on the Mississippi. Rivers and railroads provided Johnston with most of his interior lines of communications since most of the roads were virtually impassable in winter. To protect a lateral railroad where it crossed two rivers in Tennessee and yet respect Kentucky's neutrality, the Confederates had built Fort Henry on the Tennessee River and Fort Donelson on the Cumberland River just south of the boundary between the two states. On the other hand, hampering the Confederate build-up were Southern governors whose states' rights doctrine led them to believe that defense of their respective states had higher priority than pushing forward the needed men and munitions to a Confederate commander, Johnston, at the front.

At the beginning of 1862, Halleck and Buell were supposed to be co-operating with each other but had yet to do so effectively. On his own, Buell moved in mid-January to give token response to Lincoln's desire to help the Unionists in east Tennessee. One of his subordinates succeeded in breaching theConfederate defense line in eastern Kentucky in a local action near Mill Springs, but Buell failed to exploit the victory.

In Halleck's department, Brig. Gen. Ulysses S. Grant, at the time an inconspicuous district commander at Cairo, Illinois, had meanwhile proposed a river expedition up the Tennessee to take Fort Henry. After some hesitancy and in spite of the absence of assurance of support from Buell, Halleck approved a plan for a joint Army–Navy expedition. On January 30, 1862, he directed 15,000 men under Grant, supported by armored gunboats and river craft of the U.S. Navy under Flag Officer Andrew H. Foote, to "take and hold Fort Henry." The actions of subordinate commanders were at last prodding the Union war machine to move.[1]

Capture of Forts Henry and Donelson: Grant landed his troops below Fort Henry and together with Foote's naval force moved against the Confederate position on February 6. At the Federals' approach the Confederate com-

---

1 Matloff 1969, 209-211.

mander sent most of his men to Fort Donelson. Muddy roads delayed the Union Army's advance, but Foote's seven gunboats plunged ahead and in a short fire fight induced the defenders of Fort Henry to surrender. Indeed, the Confederates had lowered their colors before Grant's infantry could reach the action. The Tennessee River now lay open to Foote's gunboats all the way to northern Alabama.

General Grant was no rhetorician. Sparing with words, he never bombarded his troops with Napoleonic manifestos as McClellan did. After the capture of Fort Henry he simply telegraphed the somewhat surprised Halleck: "I shall take and destroy Fort Donelson on the 8th and return to Fort Henry." But inclement weather delayed the Federal movement until February 12. Then river craft carried some of the troops by water around to Fort Donelson. The rest of the troops moved overland under sunny skies and unseasonably mild temperatures. The spring-like weather caused the youthful soldiers to litter the roadside with overcoats, blankets, and tents.

But winter once more descended upon Grant's forces (soon to swell to nearly 27,000 men) as they invested Fort Donelson. Johnston, sure that the fall of this fort would jeopardize his entrenched camp at Bowling Green, hurried three generals and 12,000 reinforcements to Fort Donelson and then retired toward Nashville with 14,000 men. Even without reinforcements, Fort Donelson was a strong position. The main earthwork stood 100 feet above the river and with its outlying system of rifle pits embraced an area of 100 acres. The whole Confederate position occupied less than a square mile. Grant and Foote first attempted to reduce it by naval bombardment, which had succeeded at Fort Henry. But this time the Confederate defenders handled the gunboats so roughly that they withdrew. Grant then prepared for a long siege, although the bitter cold weather and lack of assault training among his troops caused him to have some reservations.

The Confederates, sensing they were caught in a trap, essayed a sortie on February 15, and swept one of Grant's divisions off the field. But divided Confederate command, not lack of determination or valor on the part of the fighting men, led to ultimate defeat of the attack. The three Confederate commanders could not agree upon the next move, and at a critical moment, Grant ordered counterattacks all along the line. By the end of the day Union troops had captured a portion of the Confederate outer works. Now surrounded by Union forces that outnumbered them almost two to one, the Confederate leaders decided they were in a hopeless situation. In a scene resembling opéra bouffe, Brig. Gen. John B. Floyd, who had been Buchanan's Secretary of War and feared execution as a traitor, passed the command to Brig. Gen. Gideon Pillow. Pillow passed the command immediately to Brig. Gen. Simon B. Buckner, who asked Grant, an old friend, for terms. Soon afterward Grant sent his famous message: "No terms except unconditional and immediate surrender can be accepted. I propose to move immediately upon your works."

Some Confederates escaped with Floyd and Pillow, and Col. Nathan Bedford Forrest led his cavalry through frozen backwaters to safety. But the bulk of the garrison "from 12,000 to 15,000 prisoners . . . also 20,000 stand of arms, 48 pieces of artillery, 17 heavy guns, from 2,000 to 4,000 horses, and large quantities of commissary stores" fell into Federal hands.

Poor leadership, violation of the principle of unity of command, and too strict adherence to position defense had cost the South the key to the gateway of the Confederacy in the west. The loss of the two forts dealt the Confederacy a blow from which it never fully recovered. Johnston had to abandon Kentucky and most of middle and west Tennessee. The vital industrial and transportation center of Nashville soon fell to Buell's advancing army. Foreign governments took special notice of the defeats. For the North the victories were its first good news of the war. They set the strategic pattern for further advance into the Confederacy. In Grant the people had a new hero and he was quickly dubbed "Unconditional Surrender" Grant.[1]

Confederate Counterattack at Shiloh:

As department commander, Halleck naturally received much credit for these victories. President Lincoln decided to unify command of all the western armies, and on March 11 Halleck received the command. Halleck, nicknamed "Old Brains," was well known as a master of the theory and literature of war. Lincoln's decision gave him jurisdiction over four armies—Buell's Army of the Ohio, Grant's Army of the Tennessee, Maj. Gen. Samuel Curtis' Army of the Southwest in Missouri and Arkansas, and Maj. Gen. John Pope's Army of the Mississippi. While Pope, in co-operation with Foote's naval forces, successfully attacked New Madrid and Island No. 10 on the Mississippi River, Halleck decided to concentrate Grant's and Buell's armies and move against Johnston at Corinth in northern Mississippi. Grant and Buell were to meet at Shiloh (Pittsburgh Landing) near Savannah on the Tennessee River. Well aware of the Federal movements, Johnston decided to attack Grant before Buell could join him. The Confederate army, 40,000 strong, marched out of Corinth on the afternoon of April 3. Muddy roads and faulty staff co-ordination made a shambles of Confederate march discipline. Mixed up commands, artillery and wagons bogged down in the mud, and green troops who insisted upon shooting their rifles at every passing rabbit threatened to abort the whole expedition. Not until late in the afternoon of April 5 did Johnston's army complete the 22-mile march to its attack point. Then the Confederate leader postponed his attack until the next morning and the delay proved costly.

Grant's forces were encamped in a rather loose battle line and apparently anticipated no attack. The position at Shiloh itself was not good, for the army was pocketed by the river at its back and a creek on each flank. Because the army was on an offensive mission, it had not entrenched. Grant has often been criticized for this omission, but entrenchment was not common at that stage of the war. The fact that the principle of security was disregarded is inescapable. Very little patrolling had been carried out, and the Federals were unaware that a Confederate army of 40,000 men was spending the night of April 5 just two miles away. The victories at Forts Henry and Donelson had apparently produced over-confidence in Grant's army, which like Johnston's, was only partly trained. Even Grant reflected this feeling, for he had established his headquarters at Savannah, nine miles downstream.

---

1 Matloff 1969, 211-212.

Johnston's men burst out of the woods early on April 6, so early that Union soldiers turned out into their company streets from their tents to fight. Some fled to the safety of the landing, but most of the regiments fought stubbornly and yielded ground slowly. One particular knot of Federals rallied along an old sunken road, named the Hornet's Nest by Confederates because of the stinging shot and shell they had to face there. Although this obstacle disrupted Johnston's timetable of attack, by afternoon the Confederates had attained local success elsewhere all along the line. At the same time the melee of battle badly disorganized the attackers. Johnston's attack formation had been awkward from the beginning. He had formed his three corps into one column with each corps deployed with divisions in line so that each corps stretched across the whole battlefront, one behind the other. Such a formation could be effectively controlled neither by army nor corps commanders.

Then, almost at the moment of victory, Johnston himself was mortally wounded while leading a local assault. General Beauregard, Johnston's successor, suspended the attack for the day and attempted to straighten out and reorganize his command. As the day ended, Grant's sixth division, which had lost its way while marching to the battlefield, reached Shiloh along with advance elements of Buell's army.

The next morning Grant counterattacked to regain the lost ground and the Confederates withdrew to Corinth. There was no pursuit. Shiloh was the bloodiest battle fought in North America up to that time. Of 63,000 Federals, 13,000 were casualties. The Confederates lost 11,000. Fortunate indeed for the Federals had been Lincoln's decision to unify the command under Halleck, for this act had guaranteed Buell's presence and prevented Johnston from defeating the Union armies separately. Grant came in for much denunciation for being surprised, but President Lincoln loyally sustained him. "I can't spare this man; he fights."

Halleck was a master of military maxims, but he had failed to concentrate all his forces immediately for a final defeat of Beauregard. As it was, Pope and Foote took Island No. 10 in April, opening the Mississippi as far as Memphis. Halleck, taking personal command of Grant's and Buell's forces, then ponderously advanced toward Corinth. Remembering Shiloh, he proceeded cautiously, and it was May 30 before he reached his objective. Beauregard had already evacuated the town. Meanwhile Capt. David G. Farragut with a naval force and Maj. Gen. Benjamin F. Butler's land units cracked the gulf coast fortifications of the Mississippi and captured New Orleans. By mid-1862, only strongholds at Vicksburg and Port Hudson on the Mississippi blocked complete Federal control of that vital river.[1]

Perryville to Stones River: Despite these early setbacks the Confederate armies in the west were still full of fight. As Federal forces advanced deeper into the Confederacy it became increasingly difficult for them to protect the long lines of river, rail, and road supply and communications. Guerrilla and cavalry operations by colorful Confederate "wizards of the saddle" like John Hunt Morgan, Joseph Wheeler, and Nathan Bedford Forrest followed Forrest's adage of

---

1 Matloff 1969, 212-215.

"Get 'em sheered, and then keep the sheer on 'em." Such tactics completely disrupted the timetable of Federal offensives.

By summer and fall rejuvenated Confederate forces under General Braxton Bragg, Lt. Gen. Edmund Kirby Smith, and Maj. Gen. Earl Van Dorn were ready to seize the initiative. Never again was the South so close to victory, nor did it ever again hold the initiative in every theater of the war.

Over-all Confederate strategy called for a three-pronged advance from the Mississippi River all the way to Virginia. Twin columns under Bragg and Smith were to bear the brunt of the western offensive by advancing from Chattanooga into east Tennessee, then northward into Kentucky. They were to be supported by Van Dorn, who would move north from Mississippi with the intention of driving Grant's forces out of west Tennessee. The western columns of the Confederacy were then to unite somewhere in Kentucky.

At the same time, these movements were to be coordinated with the planned invasion of Maryland, east of the Appalachians, by General Robert E. Lee's Army of Northern Virginia. Much depended upon speed, good coordination of effort and communications, and attempts to woo Kentucky and Maryland into the arms of the Confederacy. Victory could stimulate peace advocates and the Copperheads in the North to bring peace. Furthermore there was always the possibility that a successful invasion might induce Great Britain and France to recognize the Confederacy and to intervene forcibly to break the blockade This last hope was a feeble one. Emperor Napoleon III was primarily interested in advancing his Mexican schemes; he considered both recognition and intervention but would not move without British support. Britain, which pursued the policy of recognizing de facto governments, would undoubtedly have recognized the Confederacy eventually had it won the war. But the British Government only briefly flirted with the idea of recognition and throughout the war adhered to a policy of neutrality and respect for the Union blockade.

At first things went well for the Confederates in the west. Bragg caught Buell off guard and without fighting a battle forced Federal evacuation of northern Alabama and central Tennessee. But when Bragg entered Kentucky he became engaged in "government making" in an effort to set up a state regime which would bind Kentucky to the Confederacy. Also, the Confederate invasion was not achieving the expected results since few Kentuckians joined Bragg's forces and an attempt at conscription in east Tennessee failed completely.

Buell finally caught up with Bragg's advance at Perryville, Kentucky, on October 7. Finding the Confederates in some strength, Buell began concentrating his own scattered units. The next morning fighting began around Perryville over possession of drinking water. Brig. Gen. Philip H. Sheridan's division forced the Confederates away from one creek and dug in. The battle as a whole turned out to be a rather confused affair as Buell sought to concentrate units arriving from several different directions upon the battlefield itself. Early in the afternoon, Maj. Gen. Alexander M. McCook's Union corps arrived and began forming a line of battle. At that moment Maj. Gen. Leonidas Polk's Confederate corps attacked and drove McCook back about a mile, but Sheridan's troops held their ground. Finally a Union counterattack pushed the Confederates out of the town of Perryville. Buell himself remained at headquarters, only two and a half miles from the field, completely unaware of the extent of the engagement until it was nearly over. The rolling terrain had caused an "acoustic shadow," whereby the sounds of the conflict were completely inaudible to the Federal commander. While the battle ended in a tactical stalemate, Bragg suffered such severe casualties that he was forced to retreat. Coupled with Van Dorn's failure to bypass Federal defenses at Corinth, Mississippi, and carry out his part of the strategic plan, this setback forced the Confederates to abandon any idea of bringing Kentucky into the Confederacy.

By Christmas Bragg was back in middle Tennessee, battered but still anxious to recoup his losses by recapturing Nashville. Buell had been dilatory in pursuing Bragg after Perryville and had been replaced in command of the Army of the Ohio (now restyled the Army of the Cumberland) by Maj. Gen. William S. Rosecrans. In spite of urgent and even threatening letters from the War Department, the new commander would not move against Bragg until he had collected abundant supplies at Nashville. Then he would be independent of the railroad line from Nashville to Louisville, a line of communications continually cut by Confederate cavalry.

On December 26 Rosecrans finally marched south from Nashville. Poorly screened by Union cavalry, his three columns in turn knew little about Confederate concentrations near Murfreesboro, thirty miles southeast of the Tennessee capital. Here Bragg had taken a strong position astride Stones River on the direct route to Chattanooga and proposed to fight it out. Rosecrans moved into line opposite Bragg on the evening of December 30. Both army commanders proceeded to develop identical battle plans—each designed to envelop the opponent's right flank. Bragg's objective was to drive Rosecrans off his communications line with Nashville and pin him against the river. Rosecrans' plan had the same objective in reverse, that of pinning the Confederates against the stream. Victory would probably belong to the commander who struck first and hard.

Insufficient Federal security and Rosecrans' failure to insure that the pivotal units in his attack plan were also properly posted to thwart Confederate counterattacks resulted in Confederate seizure of the initiative as the battle of Stones River opened on December 31. At dawn, Maj. Gen. William J. Hardee's corps with large cavalry support began the drive on the Federal right. Undeceived by their opponent's device of extra campfires to feign a longer battle line, Confederate attacking columns simply pushed farther around the Union flank and promptly rolled the defenders back. Applying the principles of mass and surprise to achieve rapid success, Bragg's battle plan forced Rosecrans to modify his own. The Union leader pulled back his left flank division, which had jumped off to attack Maj. Gen. John C. Breckinridge's Confederate units north of Stones River. While Sheridan's division, as at Perryville, provided stubborn resistance to General Polk's corps in the center, Hardee's units continued their drive, which by noon saw the Union battle line bent back against the Nashville pike. Meanwhile the Confederate cavalry had wrought havoc among Rosecrans' rear area elements. As was typical of many Civil War battles the attacking columns of Polk and Hardee became badly intermingled. Their men began to tire, and by afternoon repeated Confederate assaults against the constricted Union line along the Nashville pike had bogged down.

That night Rosecrans held a council of war. Some of the subordinate commanders wanted to retreat. Rosecrans and two of his corps commanders, Maj. Gen. Thomas L. Crittenden and Maj. Gen. George H. Thomas, vetoed the scheme. Brigades were then returned to their proper divisions, stragglers rounded up, and various other adjustments made in the Federal position. New Year's Day, 1863, dawned quiet and little action occurred that day.

The sunrise of January 2 revealed Rosecrans still in position. Bragg directed Breckinridge to attack the Union left wing, once more thrown across Stones River on the north. But massed Union artillery shattered the assaults and counterattacking Federals drove Breckinridge's men back to their line of departure. The armies remained stationary on January 3 but Bragg finally withdrew from the battlefield that evening, permitting victory to slip from his grasp. Tactically a draw, Stones River so badly mangled the Army of the Cumberland that it would be immobilized for six months. Yet, more than most other battles of the war, Stones River was a conflict between the wills of the opposing army leaders. Rosecrans, supported by Thomas and others, would not admit himself beaten and in the end won a victory of sorts.

The great Confederate counteroffensives of 1862 had failed in the west, yet Chattanooga, the key to east Tennessee and Georgia, remained in Southern hands. Farther west Federal forces had penetrated only slightly into northern Mississippi. The war was simply on dead center in the west at the end of the year.[1]

The Army of the Potomac Moves South:
As the year 1862 began in the eastern theater, plans prepared in Washington were aimed at the capture of Richmond rather than destruction of the army commanded by Joseph E. Johnston, now a full general. Precise methods for reaching the Confederate capital differed. President Lincoln favored an overland advance which would always keep an army between the Confederates and Washington. McClellan agreed at first, then changed his views in favor of a waterborne move by the Army of the Potomac to Urbana on the Rappahannock. From there he could drive to Richmond before Johnston could retire from the Manassas area to intercept him. The Washington fortifications, an elaborate system of earthen forts and battery emplacements then in advanced stages of construction, would adequately protect the capital while the field army was away. Johnston, however, rendered this plan obsolete; he withdrew from Manassas to Fredericksburg, halfway between the two capitals and astride McClellan's prospective route of advance. Early in March McClellan moved his army out to the deserted Confederate camps around Manassas to give his troops some field experience. While he was in the field President Lincoln relieved him as General in Chief, doubtless on the ground that he could not command one army in the field and at the same time supervise the operations of all the armies of the United States. Lincoln did not appoint a successor. For a time he and Stanton took over personal direction of the Army, with

---

1 Matloff 1969, 215-219.

the advice of a newly constituted Army board consisting of the elderly Maj. Gen. Ethan A. Hitchcock and the chiefs of the War Department bureaus.

When events overtook the Urbana scheme, McClellan began to advocate a seaborne move to Fort Monroe, Virginia (at the tip of the peninsula formed by the York and James Rivers), to be followed by an overland advance up the peninsula. If the troops moved fast, he maintained, they could cover the seventy-five miles to Richmond before Johnston could concentrate his forces to stop them. This plan had promise, for it utilized Federal control of the seas and a useful base of operations at Fort Monroe and there were fewer rivers to cross than by the overland route. Successful neutralization of the Merrimac by the Monitor on March 9 had eliminated any naval threat to supply and communications lines, but the absence of good roads and the difficult terrain of the peninsula offered drawbacks to the plan. Lincoln approved it, providing McClellan would leave behind the number of men that his corps commanders considered adequate to insure the safety of Washington. McClellan gave the President his assurances, but failed to take Lincoln into his confidence by pointing out that he considered the Federal troops in the Shenandoah Valley to be covering Washington. In listing the forces he had left behind, he counted some men twice and included several units in Pennsylvania not under his command.

Embarkation began in mid-March, and by April 4 advance elements had moved out of Fort Monroe against Yorktown. The day before, however, the commander of the Washington defenses reported that he had insufficient forces to protect the city. In addition, Stonewall Jackson had become active in the Shenandoah Valley. Lincoln thereupon told Stanton to detain one of the two corps which were awaiting embarkation at Alexandria. Stanton held back McDowell's corps, numbering 30,000 men, seriously affecting McClellan's plans.[1]

Jackson's Valley Campaign: While a small Confederate garrison at Yorktown made ready to delay McClellan, Johnston hurried his army to the peninsula. In Richmond Confederate authorities had determined on a spectacularly bold diversion. Robert E. Lee, who had rapidly moved to the rank of general, had assumed the position of military adviser to Jefferson Davis on March 13. Charged with the conduct of operations of the Confederate armies under Davis' direction, Lee saw that any threat to Washington would cause progressive weakening of McClellan's advance against Richmond. He therefore ordered Jackson to begin a rapid campaign in the Shenandoah Valley close to the northern capital. The equivalent of three Federal divisions was sent to the valley to destroy Jackson. Lincoln and Stanton, using the telegraph and what military knowledge they had acquired, devised plans to bottle Jackson up and destroy him. But Federal forces in the valley were not under a locally unified command. They moved too slowly; one force did not obey orders strictly; and directives from Washington often neglected to take time, distance, or logistics into account. Also, in Stonewall Jackson, the Union troops were contending against one of the most outstanding field

---

1 Matloff 1969, 219-220.

commanders America has ever produced.[1] By mobility and maneuver, achieved by rapid marches, surprise, deception, and hard fighting, Jackson neutralized and defeated in detail Federal forces three times larger than his own. In a classic campaign between March 23 and June 9, 1862, he fought six battles: Kernstown, McDowell, Front Royal, Winchester, Cross Keys, and Port Republic. All but Kernstown were victories. His presence alone in the Shenandoah immobilized McDowell's corps by keeping these reinforcements from joining McClellan before Richmond.[2]

The Peninsular Campaign: Fair Oaks:

When McClellan reached the peninsula in early April he found a force of ten to fifteen thousand Confederates under Maj. Gen. John B. Magruder barring his path to Richmond. Magruder, a student of drama and master of deception, so dazzled him that McClellan, instead of brushing the Confederates aside, spent a month in a siege of Yorktown. But Johnston, who wanted to fight the decisive action closer to Richmond, decided to withdraw slowly up the peninsula. At Williamsburg, on May 5, McClellan's advance elements made contact with the Confederate rear guard under Maj. Gen. James Longstreet, who successfully delayed the Federal advance. McClellan then pursued in leisurely fashion. By May 25, two corps of the Army of the Potomac had turned southwest toward Richmond and crossed the sluggish Chickahominy River. The remaining three corps were on the north side of the stream with the expectation of making contact with McDowell, who would come down from Fredericksburg. Men of the two corps south of the river could see the spires of the Confederate capital, but Johnston's army was in front of them.

Drenching rains on May 30 raised the Chickahominy to flood stage and seriously divided McClellan's army. Johnston decided to grasp this chance to defeat the Federals in detail. He struck on May 31 near Fair Oaks. His plans called for his whole force to concentrate against the isolated corps south of the river, but his staff and subordinate commanders were not up to the task of executing them. Assaulting columns became confused, and attacks were delivered piecemeal. The Federals, after some initial reverses, held their ground and bloodily repulsed the Confederates.

When Johnston suffered a severe wound at Fair Oaks, President Davis replaced him with General Lee. Lee for his part had no intention of defending Richmond passively. The city's fortifications would enable him to protect Richmond with a relatively small force while he used the main body of his army offensively in an attempt to cut off and destroy the Army of the Potomac. He ordered Jackson back from the Shenandoah Valley with all possible speed.[3]

---

1 Jackson's philosophy of war was, "Always mystify, mislead, and surprise the enemy, if possible; and when you strike and overcome him, never give up the pursuit as long as your men have strength to follow; for an army routed, if hotly pursued, becomes panic-stricken and can then be destroyed by half their number. (Matloff 1969, 221)

2 Matloff 1969, 220-221.

3 Matloff 1969, 221-223.

The Seven Days' Battles: McClellan had planned to utilize his superior artillery to break through the Richmond defenses, but Lee struck the Federal Army before it could resume the advance. Lee's dispositions for the Battle of Mechanicsville on June 26 present a good illustration of the principles of mass and economy of force. On the north side of the Chickahominy, he concentrated 65,000 men to oppose Brig. Gen. Fitz-John Porter's V Corps of 30,000. Only 25,000 were left before Richmond to contain the remainder of the Union Army. When Lee attacked, the timing and co-ordination were off; Jackson of all people was slow and the V Corps defended stoutly during the day. McClellan thereupon withdrew the V Corps southeast to a stronger position at Gaines' Mill. Porter's men constructed light barricades and made ready. Lee massed 57,000 men and assaulted 34,000 Federals on June 27. The fighting was severe but numbers told, and the Federal line broke. Darkness fell before Lee could exploit his advantage, and McClellan took the opportunity to regroup Porter's men with the main army south of the Chickahominy.

At this point McClellan yielded the initiative to Lee. With his line of communications cut to White House, his supply base on the York River, and with the James River open to the U.S. Navy, the Union commander decided to shift his base to Harrison's Landing on the south side of the peninsula. His rear areas had been particularly shaky since Confederate cavalry under Brig. Gen. J. E. B. Stuart had ridden completely around the Federal Army in a daring raid in early June. The intricate retreat to the James, which involved 90,000 men, the artillery train, 3,100 wagons, and 2,500 head of cattle, began on the night of June 27 and was accomplished by using two roads. Lee tried to hinder the movement but was held off by Federal rear guards at Savage Station on June 29 and at Frayser's Farm (Glendale) on the last day of the month.

By the first day of July McClellan had concentrated the Army of the Potomac on a commanding plateau at Malvern Hill, northwest of Harrison's Landing. The location was strong, with clear fields of fire to the front and the flanks secured by streams. Massed artillery could sweep all approaches, and gunboats on the river were ready to provide fire support. The Confederates would have to attack by passing through broken and wooded terrain, traversing swampy ground, and ascending the hill. At first Lee felt McClellan's position was too strong to assault. Then, at 3:00 p.m. on July 1, when a shifting of Federal troops deceived him into thinking there was a general withdrawal, he changed his mind and attacked. Again staff work and control were poor. The assaults, which were all frontal, were delivered piecemeal by only part of the army against Union artillery, massed hub to hub, and supporting infantry. The Confederate formations were shattered because Lee failed to carry out the principle of mass. On the following day, the Army of the Potomac fell back to Harrison's Landing and dug in. After reconnoitering McClellan's position, Lee ordered his exhausted men back to the Richmond lines for rest and reorganization.

The Peninsular Campaign cost the Federal Army some 15,849 men killed, wounded, and missing. The Confederates, who had done most of the attacking, lost 20,614. Improvement in the training and discipline of the two armies since the disorganized fight at Bull Run was notable. Also significant was the fact that higher commanders had not yet thoroughly mastered their jobs. Except in Mc-Clellan's defensive action at Malvern Hill, which was largely conducted by his corps commanders, neither side had been able to bring an entire army into coordinated action.[1]

Second Manassas:

Failure of the Union forces to take Richmond quickly forced President Lincoln to abandon the idea of exercising command over the Union armies in person. On July 11, 1862, he selected as new General in Chief Henry W. Halleck, who had won acclaim for the victories in the west. The President did not at once appoint a successor in the west, which was to suffer from divided command for a time. Lincoln wanted Halleck to direct the various Federal armies in close concert to take advantage of the North's superior strength. If all Federal armies coordinated their efforts, Lincoln reasoned, they could strike where the Confederacy was weak or force it to strengthen one army at the expense of another, and eventually they could wear the Confederacy down, destroy the various armies, and win the war.

Halleck turned out to be a disappointment. He never attempted to exercise field command or assume responsibility for strategic direction of the armies. But, acting more as military adviser to the President, he performed a valuable function by serving as a channel of communication between the Chief Executive and the field commanders. He adeptly translated the President's ideas into terms the generals could comprehend, and expressed the soldier's views in language that Mr. Lincoln could understand.

Shortly before Halleck's appointment, Lincoln also decided to consolidate the various Union forces in the Shenandoah Valley and other parts of western Virginia some 45,000 men under the victor at Island No.10, Maj. Gen. John Pope. Pope immediately disenchanted his new command by pointing out that in the west the Federal armies were used to seeing the backs of their enemies. Pope's so-called Army of Virginia was ordered to divert pressure from McClellan on the peninsula. But Jackson had left the valley and Federal forces were scattered. On August 3, Halleck ordered McClellan to withdraw by water from the peninsula to Aquia Creek on the Potomac and to effect a speedy junction at Fredericksburg with Pope. Meanwhile Pope began posting the Army of Virginia along the Orange and Alexandria Railroad to the west of Fredericksburg.

Lee knew that his Army of Northern Virginia was in a dangerous position between Pope and McClellan, especially if the two were to unite. On July 13, he sent Jackson, with forces eventually totaling 24,000 men, to watch Pope. After an initial sparring action at Cedar Mountain on August 9, Jackson and Pope stood watching each other for nearly a week. Lee, knowing that McClellan was leaving Harrison's Landing, had departed Richmond with the remainder of the Army of Northern Virginia and joined Jackson at Gordonsville. The combined Confederate forces outnumbered Pope's, and Lee resolved to outflank and cut off the Army of Virginia before the whole of McClellan's force could be brought to bear.

---

1 Matloff 1969, 223-224.

A succession of captured orders enabled both Lee and Pope to learn the intentions of the other. Pope ascertained Lee's plan to trap him against the Rappahannock and withdrew to the north bank astride the railroad. Lee, learning that two corps from the Army of the Potomac would join Pope within days, acted quickly and boldly. He sent Jackson off on a wide turning movement through Thoroughfare Gap in the Bull Run Mountains around the northern flank of Pope's army and subsequently followed the same route with the divisions commanded by General Longstreet.

Pope took note of Jackson's move, but first assumed that it was pointed toward the Shenandoah Valley. Then Jackson, covering nearly sixty miles in two days, came in behind Pope at Manassas on August 26, destroyed his supply base there, and slipped away unmolested. Pope marched and countermarched his forces for two days trying to find the elusive Confederates. At the same time the Union commander failed to take Lee's other forces into account. As a result he walked into Lee's trap on the site of the old battlefield of Manassas, or Bull Run. Pope attacked Jackson, posted behind an abandoned railroad embankment, but again the attack consisted of a series of piecemeal frontal assaults which were repulsed with heavy casualties. By then Porter's V Corps from the Army of the Potomac had reached the field and was ordered to attack Jackson's right (south) flank. By this time also, Longstreet's column had burst through Thoroughfare Gap, and deploying on Jackson's right, it blocked Porter's move.

Next day, August 30, Pope renewed his attacks against Jackson, whom he thought to be retreating. Seizing the opportunity to catch the Federal columns in an exposed position, Lee sent Longstreet slashing along the Warrenton turnpike to catch Pope's flank in the air. The Federal army soon retired from the field and Pope led it back to Washington, fighting an enveloping Confederate force at Chantilly on the way.

Lee, by great daring and rapid movement, and by virtue of having the Confederate forces unified under his command, had successfully defeated one formidable Union army in the presence of another even larger one. Halleck, as General in Chief, had not taken the field to co-ordinate Pope and McClellan, and Pope lost the campaign despite the advantage of interior lines.

President Lincoln, desiring to use McClellan's admitted talents for training and reorganizing the battered eastern armies, had become convinced that bitter personal feelings between McClellan and Pope prevented them from working effectively in the same theater. On September 5, Halleck, upon the President's order, dissolved the Army of Virginia and assigned its units to the Army of the Potomac. He sent Pope to a command in Minnesota. The Union authorities expected that McClellan would be able to devote several months to training and reorganization, but Lee dashed these hopes.[1]

Lee Invades Maryland:

Lee Invades Maryland: Up to this point the Confederates in the east had been following defensive strategy, though tactically they frequently assumed the offensive. But Davis and Lee, for a complicated set of political and military reasons, determined to take the offensive and invade the North in co-ordination

---

[1] Matloff 1969, 224-227.

with Bragg's drive into Kentucky. Militarily, in the east, an invasion of Maryland would give Lee a chance to defeat or destroy the Army of the Potomac, uncovering such cities as Washington, Baltimore, and Philadelphia, and to cut Federal communications with the states to the west.

The Army of Northern Virginia, organized into 2 infantry commands (Longstreet's consisting of 5 divisions, and Jackson's of 4 divisions) plus Stuart's 3 brigades of cavalry, and the reserve artillery, numbered 55,000 effectives. Lee did not rest after Manassas but crossed the Potomac and encamped near Frederick, Maryland, from which he sent Jackson to capture an isolated Federal garrison at Harpers Ferry. The remainder of Lee's army then crossed South Mountain and headed for Hagerstown, about twenty-five miles northwest of Frederick, with Stuart's cavalry screening the right flank. In the meantime McClellan's rejuvenated Army of the Potomac, 90,000 men organized into 6 corps, marched northwest from Washington and reached Frederick on September 12.

At this time McClellan had a stroke of luck. Lee, in assigning missions to his command, had detached Maj. Gen. D. H. Hill's division from Jackson and attached it to Longstreet and had sent copies of his orders, which prescribed routes, objectives, and times of arrival, to Jackson, Longstreet, and Hill. But Jackson was not sure that Hill had received the order. He therefore made an additional copy of Lee's order and sent it to Hill. One of Hill's orders, wrapped around some cigars, was somehow left behind in an abandoned camp where it was picked up on September Is by Union soldiers and rushed to McClellan. This windfall gave the Federal commander an unmatched opportunity to defeat Lee's scattered forces in detail if he pushed fast through the gaps. McClellan vacillated for sixteen hours. Lee, informed of the lost order, sent all available forces to hold the gaps, so that it was nightfall on the 14th before McClellan fought his way across South Mountain.

Lee retreated to Sharpsburg on Antietam Creek where he turned to fight. Pinned between Antietam Creek and the Potomac with no room for maneuver, and still outnumbered since Jackson's force had yet to return to the main body after capturing Harpers Ferry, Lee relied on the advantage of interior lines and the boldness and the fighting ability of his men.

McClellan delayed his attack until September 17, when he launched an uncoordinated series of assaults which drove back the Confederates in places but failed to break their line. Heavy fighting swelled across ripe fields and up through rocky glens that became known to history as the West Wood, the Cornfield, the East Wood, Bloody Lane, and Burnside's Bridge. One Southerner remembered the attacking Union columns: "With flags flying and the long unfaltering lines rising and falling as they crossed the rolling fields, it looked as though nothing could stop them." But when the massed fire of field guns and small arms struck such human waves, a Union survivor recalled, it "was like a scythe running through our line."

McClellan, like too many leaders during the Civil War, could not bring himself to commit his reserve (the V Corps under Porter) at the strategic moment. Although adored by his men, as one of the veterans wrote after the war, he "never realized the metal that was in his grand Army of the Potomac." Jackson's last division arrived in time to head off the final assaults by Maj. Gen. Ambrose Burnside's corps, and at the end of the day Lee still held most of his line. Casualties were heavy. Of 70,000 Federal troops nearly 13,000 were killed, wounded, or missing, and the 40,000 or more Confederates engaged lost almost as many. Although Lee audaciously awaited new attacks on September 18, McClellan left him unmolested, and that night the Army of Northern Virginia withdrew across the Potomac.[1]

Lincoln's Emancipation Proclamation: Antietam was tactically a draw, but the fact that Lee was forced to call off the invasion made it a strategic victory and gave President Lincoln an opportunity to strike at the Confederacy psychologically and economically by issuing the Emancipation Proclamation on September 22, 1862. Lincoln, while opposed to slavery and its extension to the western territories, was not an abolitionist. He had stated publicly that the war was being fought over union or secession, with the slavery question only incidental, and had earlier overruled several generals who were premature emancipators. But anticipating the total psychological warfare techniques of the twentieth century, he had for some time desired to free the slaves of the Confederate states in order to weaken their economies and to appeal to antislavery opinion in Europe. He had awaited the opportune moment that a Union victory would give him and decided that Antietam was suitable. Acting on his authority as Commander in Chief he issued the Proclamation which stated that all slaves in states or districts in rebellion against the United States on January 1, 1863, would be thenceforward and forever free. The Proclamation set no slaves free on the day it took effect. Negroes in the four slave states still in the Union were not touched, nor were the slaves in those Confederate areas that had been subjugated by Union bayonets. It had no immediate effect behind the Confederate lines, except to cause a good deal of excitement. But thereafter, as Union forces penetrated the South, the newly freed people deserted the farms and plantations and flocked to the colors.

Negroes had served in the Revolution, the War of 1812, and other early wars, but they had been barred from the Regular Army and, under the Militia Act of 1792, from the state militia. The Civil War marks their official debut in American military forces. Recruiting of Negroes began under the local auspices of Maj. Gen. David Hunter in the Department of the South as early as April 1862. There was a certain appeal to the idea that Negroes might assure their freedom by joining in the battle for it even if they served for lower pay in segregated units under white officers. On July 17, 1862, Congress authorized recruitment of Negroes while passing the antislavery Second Confiscation Act. The Emancipation Proclamation put the matter in a new light, and on May 22, 1863, the War Department established a Bureau of Colored Troops, another innovation of the Civil War since it was an example of Federal volunteer formations without official ties to specific states (others being the various U.S. sharpshooter regiments and the invalid Veteran Reserve Corps). By the end of the war 100,000 Negroes were

---

1 Matloff 1969, 227-229.

enrolled as U.S. Volunteers. Many other Negroes served in state units, elsewhere in the armed forces, and as laborers for the Union Army.[1]

Fiasco at Fredericksburg: After Antietam both armies returned to

face each other in Virginia, Lee situated near Culpeper and McClellan at Warren-ton. But McClellan's slowness, his failure to accomplish more at Antietam, and perhaps his rather arrogant habit of offering gratuitous political advice to his superiors, coupled with the intense anti-McClellan views of the joint Congressional Committee on the Conduct of the War, convinced Lincoln that he could retain him in command no longer. On November 7 Lincoln replaced him with Burnside, who had won distinction in operations that gained control of ports on the North Carolina coast and who had led the IX Corps at Antietam. Burnside accepted the post with reluctance.

Burnside decided to march rapidly to Fredericksburg and then advance along the railroad line to Richmond before Lee could intercept him. Such a move by the army now 120,000 strong would cut Lee off from his main base. Burnside's advance elements reached the north bank of the Rappahannock on November 17, well ahead of Lee. But a series of minor failures delayed the completion of ponton bridges, and Lee moved his army to high ground on the south side of the river before the Federal forces could cross. Lee's situation resembled McClellan's position at Malvern Hill which had proved the folly of frontal assaults against combined artillery and infantry strongpoints. But Burnside thought the sheer weight of numbers could smash through the Confederates.

To achieve greater ease of tactical control, Burnside had created three head-quarters higher than corps: the Right, Center, and Left Grand Divisions under Maj. Gens. Edwin V. Sumner, Joseph Hooker, and William B. Franklin, respec-tively, with two corps plus cavalry assigned to each grand division. Burnside originally planned to make the main thrust by Center and Left Grand Divisions against Jackson's positions on a long, low-wooded ridge southeast of the town. The Right Grand Division would cross three ponton bridges at Fredericksburg and attack Marye's Heights, a steep eminence about one mile from the river where Longstreet's men were posted. On the morning of December 15, he weak-ened the attack on the left, feeling that under cover of 147 heavy siege and field guns on the heights on the Union side of the river much could be achieved by a better-balanced attack along the whole line.

Burnside's engineers had begun laying the bridges as early as December 11. But harassment from Confederate sharpshooters complicated the operation, and it was not until the next day that all the assault units were over the river. After an artillery duel on the morning of the 13th, fog lifted to reveal dense Union columns moving forward to the attack. Part of the Left Grand Division, finding a weak-ness in Jackson's line, drove in to seize the ridge, but as Burnside had weakened this part of the assault the Federals were not able to hold against Confederate counterattacks. On the right, the troops had to cross a mile of open ground to reach Marye's Heights, traverse a drainage canal, and face a fusillade of fire from the infamous sunken road and stone wall behind which Longstreet had placed

---

1 Matloff 1969, 229-230.

four ranks of riflemen. In a series of assaults the Union soldiers pushed to the stone wall but no farther. As a demonstration of valor the effort was exemplary; as a demonstration of tactical skill it was tragic. Lee, observing the shattered attackers, commented: "It is well that war is so terrible, we should grow too fond of it."

The Army of the Potomac lost 12,000 men at Fredericksburg while the Army of Northern Virginia suffered only 5,300 casualties. Burnside planned to renew the attack on the following day and Jackson, whose enthusiasm in battle sometimes approached the point of frenzy, suggested that the Confederates strip off their clothes for better identification and strike the Army of the Potomac in a night attack. But Lee knew of Burnside's plans from a captured order and vetoed the scheme. When the Federal corps commanders talked Burnside out of renewing the attack, both armies settled into winter quarters facing each other across the Rappahannock. Fredericksburg, a disastrous defeat, was otherwise noteworthy for the U.S. Army in that the telegraph first saw extensive battlefield use, linking headquarters with forward batteries during the action, a forerunner of twentieth century battlefield communications.[1]

West of the Mississippi: If the major fighting of the Civil War occurred in the "older" populated sections of the United States, the youthful area of the American frontier across the Mississippi saw its share of action also. Missouri and Kansas, and indeed the distant New Mexico Territory (all areas involved in the root causes for the conflict), were touched by the Civil War.

The Southwest was a particularly rich plum, for as one Confederate commander observed: "The vast mineral resources of Arizona, in addition to its affording an outlet to the Pacific, makes its acquisition a matter of some importance to our Govt." Also it was assumed that Indians and the Mormons in Utah would readily accept allegiance to almost any government other than that in Washington.

It was with these motives in mind that early in 1862 Confederate forces moved up the Rio Grande valley and proceeded to establish that part of New Mexico Territory north of the 34th parallel as the Confederate territory of Arizona. Under Brig. Gen. Henry H. Sibley, inventor of a famous tent bearing his name, the Confederates successfully swept all the way to Santa Fe, capital of New Mexico, bypassing several Union garrisons on the way. But Sibley was dangerously overextended, and Federal troops, reinforced by Colorado volunteers, surprised the advancing Confederates in Apache Canyon on March 26 and 28, as they sought to capture the largest Union garrison in the territory at Fort Union.

One of the bypassed Federal columns under Col. Edward R. S. Canby from Fort Craig meanwhile joined the Fort Union troops against the Confederates. Unable to capture the Union posts, unable to resupply his forces, and learning of yet a third Federal column converging on him from California, Sibley began a determined retreat down the Rio Grande valley. By May he was back in Texas and the Confederate invasion of New Mexico was ended. The fighting, on a small scale by eastern standards, provided valuable training for Federal troops

---

1 Matloff 1969, 230-232.

involved later in Indian wars in this area. Indeed, while the Confederate dream of a new territory and an outlet to the Pacific was shattered by 1862, Indian leaders in the mountain territories saw an opportunity to reconquer lost land while the white men were otherwise preoccupied. In 1863 and 1864 both Federal and Confederate troops in the southwest were kept busy fighting hostile tribes.

In Missouri and Arkansas, fighting had erupted on a large scale by the early spring of 1862. Federal authorities had retained a precarious hold over Missouri when Maj. Gen. Samuel R. Curtis with 11,000 men chased disorganized Confederates back into Arkansas. But under General Van Dorn and Maj. Gen. Sterling Price, the Confederates regrouped and embarked upon a counteroffensive which only ended at Pea Ridge on March 7 and 8. Here Van Dorn executed a double envelopment as half his army stole behind Pea Ridge, marched around three-fourths of Curtis' force, and struck Curtis' left rear near Elkhorn Tavern while the other half attacked his right rear. But in so doing the Confederates uncovered their own line of communications and Curtis' troops turned around and fought off the attacks from the rear. After initial success, Van Dorn and Price were unable to continue the contest and withdrew. For three more years guerrilla warfare would ravage Missouri but the Union grip on the state was secure.

The year 1862, which began with impressive Union victories in the west, ended in bitter frustration in the east. Ten full-scale and costly battles had been fought, but no decisive victory had yet been scored by the forces of the Union. The Federals had broken the great Confederate counteroffensives in the fall only to see their hopes fade with the advent of winter. Apparently the Union war machine had lost its earlier momentum.[1]

---

1 Matloff 1969, 232-235.

CORRESPONDENCE: 1862

To General H. W. Halleck, Executive Mansion, January 1, 1862.[1]

Dear General Halleck:

General McClellan is not dangerously ill, as I hope, but would better not be disturbed with business. I am very anxious that, in case of General Buell's moving toward Nashville, the enemy shall not be greatly reinforced, and I think there is danger he will be from Columbus. It seems to me that a real or feigned attack upon Columbus from up the river at the same time would either prevent this or compensate for it by throwing Columbus into our hands. I wrote General Buell a letter similar to this, meaning that he and you shall communicate and act in concert, unless it be your judgment and his that there is no necessity for it. You and he will understand much better than I how to do it. Please do not lose time in this matter.

Yours very truly,

A. Lincoln.

---

1 In response to Lincoln's December 31 notes to Buell and Hallack, on January 1, 1862 the generals responded. Buell: "There is no arrangement between General Halleck, and myself. I have been informed by General McClellan that he would make suitable disposition for concerted action. There is nothing to prevent Bowling Green being re-enforced from Columbus if a military force is not brought to bear on the latter place." Halleck: "I have never received a word from General Buell. I am not ready to co-operate with him. Hope to do so in few weeks. Have written fully on this subject to Major General McClellan. Too much haste will ruin everything." (Conger 1931, 134) So, in response to Lincoln's suggestion that they act together, here they say that they can't. Or won't, or the other one isn't doing his part. Lincoln must have wondered if there was any general in the West who could act decisively when action was needed.

Telegram to General D. C. Buell, Washington City, January 1, 1862.[1]

Brigadier General Buell, Louisville:
General McClellan should not yet be disturbed with business. I think you better get in concert with General Halleck at once. I write you tonight. I also telegraph and write Halleck.
A. Lincoln.

Telegram to General D. C. Buell, Washington, January 4, 1862.[2]

General Buell:
Have arms gone forward for East Tennessee? Please tell me the progress and condition of the movement in that direction. Answer.
A. Lincoln.

To General D. C. Buell, Executive Mansion, Washington, January 6, 1862.[3]

Brigadier General Buell:
My Dear Sir—Your dispatch of yesterday has been received, and it disappoints and distresses me. I have shown it to General McClellan, who says he will write you today. I am not competent to criticize your views, and therefore what I offer is in justification of myself. Of the two, I would rather have a point on the railroad south of Cumberland Gap than Nashville. First, because it cuts a great artery of the enemy's communication, which Nashville does not; and secondly, because it is in the midst of loyal people who would rally around it, while Nashville is not. Again, I cannot see why the movement on East Tennessee would not be a diversion in your favor rather than a disadvantage, assuming that a movement toward Nashville is the main object. But my distress is that our friends in East Tennessee are being hanged and driven to despair, and even now, I fear, are thinking of taking rebel arms for the sake of personal protection. In this we lose the most valuable stake we have in the South. My dispatch, to which yours is an answer, was sent with the knowledge of Senator Johnson and Representative Maynard of East Tennessee, and they will be upon me to know the answer, which I cannot safely show them. They would despair, possibly resign to go and

---

1 There seems to be little room to misinterpret Lincoln's impatience when he states, "I think you better get in concert with General Halleck at once."

2 Buell answered Lincoln's telegram on January 5: "Arms can only go forward for East Tennessee under the protection of the troops. My organization of the troops has had in view two columns with reference to that movement.... But it was necessary also to have regard to contingencies which...might require a modification.... I will confess...I have been bound to it more by...sympathy for the people of Eastern Tennessee, and the anxiety with which yourself and the General in Chief have desired it, than by my opinion of its wisdom...." (Lincoln v.5, 1953, 90)

3 Lincoln's disappointment with Buell is evident in this note.

save their families somehow, or die with them. I do not intend this to be an order in any sense, but merely, as intimated before, to show you the grounds of my anxiety.

Yours very truly,
A. Lincoln.

Telegram to General Buell, Washington, January 7, 1862[1]

Brigadier General D.C. Buell, Louisville:

Please name as early a day as you safely can on or before which you can be ready to move southward in concert with Major General Halleck. Delay is ruining us, and it is indispensable for me to have something definite. I send a like dispatch to Major General Halleck.

A. Lincoln.

Lincoln Indorsement [sic] of a Letter from General Halleck, January 10, 1862[2]

Headquarters Department of the Missouri St. Louis, January 6, 1862.

To His Excellency The President: In reply to your Excellency's letter of the 1st instant, I have to state that on receiving your telegram I immediately communicated with General Buell and have since sent him all the information I could obtain of the enemy's movements about Columbus and Camp Beauregard. No considerable force has been sent from those places to Bowling Green. They have about 22,000 men at Columbus, and the place is strongly fortified. I have at Cairo, Port Holt, and Paducah only about 15,000, which, after leaving guards at these places, would give me but little over 10,000 men with which to assist General Buell. It would be madness to attempt anything serious with such a force, and I cannot at the present time withdraw any from Missouri without risking the loss of this State. The troops recently raised in other States of this department have, without my knowledge, been sent to Kentucky and Kansas.

I am satisfied that the authorities at Washington do not appreciate the difficulties with which we have to contend here. The operations of Lane, Jennison, and others have so enraged the people of Missouri that it is estimated that there is a majority of 80,000 against the government. We are virtually in an enemy's country. Price and others have a considerable army in the southwest, against which I am operating with all my available force.

This city and most of the middle and northern counties are insurrectionary,—burning bridges, destroying telegraph lines, etc.,—and can be kept down only by the presence of troops. A large portion of the foreign troops organized by General Frémont are unreliable; indeed, many of them are already mutinous. They have been tampered with by politicians, and made to

---

1 Regardless of his motives for not moving into East Tennessee, Buell caused trouble for himself by acknowledging his disinterest with the campaign. What the general failed to anticipate was that Tennessee senators Andrew Johnson and Horace Maynard would see his letter, which helped fuel the pressure on Lincoln to get commanders to fight rather than manage the war. More than that, it placed Buell in a bad position with regard to his political views of the war and his understanding of civil-military relationships. (Engle 2001, 35)

2 Once again, Lincoln's disappointment in the conduct of Generals Buell and Halleck is clear.

believe that if they get up a mutiny and demand Frémont's return the government will be forced to restore him to duty here. It is believed that some high officers are in the plot I have already been obliged to disarm several of these organizations, and I am daily expecting more serious outbreaks. Another grave difficulty is the want of proper general officers to command the troops and enforce order and discipline, and especially to protect public property from robbery and plunder. Some of the brigadier-generals assigned to this department are entirely ignorant of their duties and unfit for any command. I assure you, Mr. President, it is very difficult to accomplish much with such means. I am in the condition of a carpenter who is required to build a bridge with a dull axe, a broken saw, and rotten timber. It is true that I have some very good green timber, which will answer the purpose as soon as I can get it into shape and season it a little.

I know nothing of General Buell's intended operations, never having received any information in regard to the general plan of campaign. If it be intended that his column shall move on Bowling Green while another moves from Cairo or Paducah on Columbus or Camp Beauregard, it will be a repetition of the same strategic error which produced the disaster of Bull Run. To operate on exterior lines against an enemy occupying a central position will fail, as it always has failed, in ninety-nine cases out of a hundred. It is condemned by every military authority I have ever read.

General Buell's army and the forces at Paducah occupy precisely the same position in relation to each other and to the enemy as did the armies of McDowell and Patterson before the battle of Bull Run.

Very respectfully, your obedient servant,

H. W. Halleck, Major General

[Indorsement] The within is a copy of a letter just received from General Halleck. It is exceedingly discouraging. As everywhere else, nothing can be done.

A. Lincoln.

To General D. C. Buell, Executive Mansion, Washington, January 13, 1862[1]

Brigadier General Buell:

My Dear Sir— Your dispatch of yesterday is received, in which you say, "I received your letter and General McClellan's, and will at once devote my efforts to your views and his." In the midst of my many cares I have not seen, nor asked to see, General McClellan's letter to you. For my own views, I have not offered and do not now offer them as orders; and while I am glad to have them respectfully considered, I would blame you to follow them contrary to your own clear judg-

---

1 Day and night that winter, and especially in December and January, the President, so we learn from his secretary, was deep in the study of strategical works, maps, and other documents relating to the leadership of armies, their provisioning, their march. Predisposed to draw comparisons and at the same time a realist and a calculator he combining his memories of the little campaign against the Indians with the experiences of the last year, he could achieve a clear pictorial understanding of the extant military situation, and, his eyes on the map, could elaborate plans for encircling the enemy. He taught himself the fundamentals of war-making, as he had taught himself all that he had learned; and even if we do not know the precise course of his studies, the results, at any rate, show the extent of his acquirements. Against this backdrop, he now seemingly begins to take a new tone with his generals, no longer exhibiting toward them the demeanor of a perplexed layman as he writes to Buell in this letter. (Ludwig 1930, 315)

ment, unless I should put them in the form of orders. As to General McClellan's views, you understand your duty in regard to them better than I do.

With this preliminary I state my general idea of this war to be, that we have the greater numbers and the enemy has the greater facility of concentrating forces upon points of collision; that we must fail unless we can find some way of making our advantage an overmatch for his; and that this can only be done by menacing him with superior forces at different points at the same time, so that we can safely attack one or both if he makes no change; and if he weakens one to strengthen the other, forbear to attack the strengthened one, but seize and hold the weakened one, gaining so much.

To illustrate: Suppose last summer, when Winchester ran away to reinforce Manassas, we had forborne to attack Manassas, but had seized and held Winchester. I mention this to illustrate and not to criticise. I did not lose confidence in McDowell, and I think less harshly of Patterson than some others seem to.... Applying the principle to your case, my idea is that Halleck shall menace Columbus and "down river" generally, while you menace Bowling Green and East Tennessee. If the enemy shall concentrate at Bowling Green, do not retire from his front, yet do not fight him there either, but seize Columbus and East Tennessee, one or both, left exposed by the concentration at Bowling Green. It is a matter of no small anxiety to me, and which I am sure you will not overlook, that the East Tennessee line is so long and over so bad a road.

Yours very truly,

A. Lincoln.

[Indorsement] Having today written General Buell a letter, it occurs to me to send General Halleck a copy of it.

A. Lincoln.

To General H. W. Halleck. Executive Mansion, Washington, January 15, 1862[1]

Major General Halleck:

My Dear Sir—The Germans are true and patriotic and so far as they have got cross in Missouri it is upon mistake and misunderstanding. Without a knowledge of its contents, Governor Koerner, of Illinois, will hand you this letter. He is an educated and talented German gentleman, as true a man as lives. With his assistance you can set everything right with the Germans.... My clear judgment is that, with reference to the German element in your command, you should have Governor Koerner with you; and if agreeable to you and him, I will make him a brigadier-general, so that he can afford to give his time. He does not wish to command in the field, though he has more military knowledge than some who do. If he goes into the place, he will simply be an efficient, zealous, and unselfish assistant to you. I say all this upon intimate personal acquaintance with Governor Koerner.

Yours very truly,

A. Lincoln.

---

1 Gustav Koerner, a brilliant German-American, was an Illinois politician and an early friend of Abraham and his wife, Mary Todd Lincoln. (Nevins 1992, 495)

President's General War Order Number 1, Executive Mansion, Washington, January 27, 1862[1]

Ordered, That the 22d day of February, 1862, be the day for a general movement of the land and the naval forces of the United States against the insurgent forces.

That especially the army at and about Fortress Monroe, the Army of the Potomac, the Army of Western Virginia, the army near Munfordville, Kentucky, the army and flotilla at Cairo, and a naval force in the Gulf of Mexico, be ready for a movement on that day.

That all other forces, both land and naval, with their respective commanders, obey existing orders for the time, and be ready to obey additional orders when duly given.

That the heads of departments, and especially the Secretaries of War and of the Navy, with all their subordinates, and the General-in-chief, with all other commanders and subordinates of land and naval forces, will severally be held to their strict and full responsibilities for the prompt execution of this order.

A. Lincoln.

President's Special War Order Number 1, Executive Mansion, Washington, January 31, 1862[2]

Ordered, That all the disposable force of the Army of the Potomac, after providing safely for the defence of Washington, be formed into an expedition for the immediate object of seizing and occupying a point upon the railroad southwest-

---

1 On January 26, 1862, Lincoln, told a naval officer that he believed he must "take these army matters into his own hands." One day later the generals were astonished and the public heartened to read the President's "General War Order Number One," which decreed a general movement on February 22 of all land and naval forces of the United States against the insurgents. On January 31 came his "Special War Order Number One," ordering an advance by the Army of the Potomac directly on Richmond by way of Manassas, this advance to begin by February 22. The orders were not carried out literally. McClellan submitted a long letter explaining why they could not be, and Lincoln consented to waive them. Washington's Birthday passed quietly by without an advance, and it was not until late in March that McClellan shifted his army to Fortress Monroe, whence it was to move on Richmond via the York Peninsula. Nevertheless, the orders had been worth making. They roused the North from its cynical lethargy until the news of Henry and Donelson could fire its spirit; and they gave McClellan a healthy jolt. In December McClellan had hastily penciled his replies to Lincoln's careful inquiries about the coming campaign. In his elaborate communication of February 3 the young Napoleon betrayed a new awareness that Lincoln was, after all, his commander in chief. "From that time," wrote John Hay, "[the President] influenced actively the operations of the campaign. He stopped going to McClellan's and sent for the general to come to him. Everything grew busy and animated after that order." And Stanton remarked after the war that if Lincoln had not issued those orders, "the Armies would have remained in front of Washington to this present." (Bruce 1956, 170)

2 The object of this order was to engage the rebel army in front of Washington by a flank attack, and by its defeat relieve the capital, put Richmond at risk, and break the main strength of the rebellion by destroying the principal army arrayed in its support. Instead of obeying it, General McClellan remonstrated against its execution, and urged the adoption of a different plan of attack, which was to move upon Richmond by way of the Chesapeake Bay, the Rappahannock River, and a land march across the country from Urbana, leaving the rebel forces in position at Manassas to be held in check, if they should attempt a forward movement, only by the troops in the fortifications around Washington. (Henry 1864, 224)

ward of what is known as Manassas Junction, all details to be in the discretion of the commander-in-chief, and the expedition to move before or on the 22d day of February next.

A. Lincoln.

To General G. B. McClellan, Executive Mansion, Washington, February 3, 1862[1]

Major General McClellan:

Dear Sir—You and I have distinct and different plans for a movement of the Army of the Potomac—yours to be down the Chesapeake, up the Rappahannock to Urbana, and across land to the terminus of the railroad on the York River; mine to move directly to a point on the railroad southwest of Manassas. If you will give me satisfactory answers to the following questions, I shall gladly yield my plan to yours.

First. Does not your plan involve a greatly larger expenditure of time and money than mine?

Second. Wherein is a victory more certain by your plan than mine?

Third. Wherein is a victory more valuable by your plan than mine?

Fourth. In fact, would it not be less valuable in this, that it would break no great line of the enemy's communications, while mine would?

Fifth. In case of disaster, would not a retreat be more difficult by your plan than mine?

Yours truly,

A. Lincoln.

To Generals D. Hunter and J. H. Lane, Executive Mansion, Washington, February 4, 1862[2]

Major General Hunter and Brigadier General Lane, Leavenworth, Kansas:

1 McClellan protested Lincoln's plans and asked permission to submit in writing his objections to the overland route, and his reasons for preferring to advance by way of the Chesapeake. These arguments had doubtless already been considered in the course of his recent discussions with the President, yet Mr. Lincoln gave the desired consent. He even furnished McClellan with a basis for his memorandum. But despite McClelland's resistance, Lincoln's confidence in the merits of his own plan remained unshaken. For political, no less than for military reasons, an immediate attack upon the enemy before Washington, by a column which should protect the Union Capital while advancing upon Richmond, appeared wiser to him than a flank movement that, uncovering Washington for a shorter march to the Confederate Capital, would still consume, in transportation down the Chesapeake, much more time and money. Experts, reviewing McClellan's plan since the war, along purely strategical lines, have differed widely in their opinions of its soundness. The President's plan, on the other hand, as more nearly meeting the requirements of the situation, had the approval, at the time, of some able soldiers, and of well-nigh all the civilians whom he consulted. Mr. Stanton, the new Secretary of War, was especially earnest in its support; and he urged Lincoln to insist upon having his way. (Rothschild 1906, 356-7)

2 General David Hunter had received communications from the War Department in January, 1862, announcing that a Southern expedition, consisting of eight or ten thousand Kansas troops and four thousand Indians, had been decided upon, and implying the existence of a definite, mutual understanding that Kansas Senator J. H. Lane should have the chief command. These communications took Hunter by surprise, and, while suspecting political intervention in Washington, in his perplexity he wrote General Halleck, who had succeeded General Frémont in command of the Western Department for clarification. (Spring 309,

My wish has been and is to avail the government of the services of both General Hunter and General Lane, and, so far as possible, to personally oblige both. General Hunter is the senior officer, and must command when they serve together; though in so far as he can consistently with the public service and his own honor oblige General Lane, he will also oblige me. If they cannot come to an amicable understanding, General Lane must report to General Hunter for duty, according to the rules, or decline the service.

A. Lincoln.

To General H. W. Halleck, Executive Mansion, Washington, February 16, 1862[1]

Major General Halleck, St. Louis, Missouri:

You have Fort Donelson safe, unless Grant shall be overwhelmed from outside; to prevent which latter will, I think, require all the vigilance, energy, and skill of yourself and Buell, acting in full co-operation. Columbus will not get at Grant, but the force from Bowling Green will. They hold the railroad from Bowling Green to within a few miles of Fort Donelson, with the bridge at Clarksville undisturbed. It is unsafe to rely that they will not dare to expose Nashville to Buell. A small part of their force can retire slowly toward Nashville, breaking up the railroad as they go, and keep Buell out of that city twenty days. Meanwhile Nashville will be abundantly defended by forces from all South and perhaps from hers at Manassas. Could not a cavalry force from General Thomas on the upper Cumberland dash across, almost unresisted, and cut the railroad at or near Knoxville, Tennessee? In the midst of a bombardment at Fort Donelson, why could not a gunboat run up and destroy the bridge at Clarksville? Our success or failure at Fort Donelson is vastly important, and I beg you to put your soul in the effort. I send a copy of this to Buell.

A. Lincoln.

Executive Order No. 2, In Relation to State Prisoners, War Department, Washington City, February 27, 1862[2]

It is ordered:

First. That a special commission of two persons, one of military rank and the other in civil life, be appointed to examine the cases of the state prisoners re-

---

1885) Bowed down, as these generals knew President Lincoln to be, under the load of anxieties and responsibilities of a disrupted nation's troubles, it does seem as if they might have settled their squabbles by themselves, and there seems to be a flavor of pathetic sadness in the fatherly firmness with which he settles the dispute. (Illinois Infantry 132, 1892)

1 Motion mattered to Abraham Lincoln and to win at Donelson (of which he was unaware at the time he wrote the letter) was of critical importance to the president. Lincoln's letter, with its grasp of essentials, makes it clear that he perceived Grant as a pivotal figure—as a fighter eager for a fight. Aware of this perception, Halleck wanted Grant pushed aside; once a victor, Grant became a rival. (McFeely 1981, 104)

2 Arrests continued to be made under authority of the State Department, not without complaint, certainly, from large numbers of the people, but with the general acquiescence of the whole community, and beyond all question greatly to the advantage of the government and the country. Still, to clarify the issue, Lincoln issued this order, which transferred control of the whole matter to the War Department. (Raymond 1865, 379)

maining in the military custody of the United States, and to determine whether in view of the public Safety and the existing rebellion they should be discharged, or remain in military custody, or be remitted to the civil tribunals for trial.

Second. That Major General John A. Dix, commanding in Baltimore, and the HON. Edwards Pierrepont, of New York, be, and they are hereby, appointed commissioners for the purpose above mentioned; and they are authorized to examine, hear, and determine the cases aforesaid ex parte and in a summary manner, at such times and places as in their discretion they may appoint, and make full report to the War Department.

By order of the President.

President's General War Order No. 2, Executive Mansion, Washington, March 8, 1862[1]

Ordered: 1. That the Major General commanding the Army of the Potomac proceed forthwith to organize that part of the said army destined to enter upon active operations (including the reserve, but excluding the troops to be left in the fortifications about Washington) into four army corps, to be commanded according to seniority of rank, as follows: First Corps to consist of four divisions, and to be commanded by Major General I. McDowell. Second Corps to consist of three divisions, and to be commanded by Brigadier General E. V. Sumner. Third Corps to consist of three divisions, and to be commanded by Brigadier General S. P. Heintzelman. Fourth Corps to consist of three divisions, and to be commanded by Brigadier General E. D. Keyes.

2. That the divisions now commanded by the officers above assigned to the commands of army corps shall be embraced in and form part of their respective corps.

3. The forces left for the defense of Washington will be placed in command of Brigadier General James S. Wadsworth, who shall also be military governor of the District of Columbia.

---

1 Prior to the Civil War, the United States Army never used the corps organization because it never fielded a force large enough to make creation of corps advantageous. In discussing the organization of field armies, the army regulations of 1855 and 1861 did not mention corps, citing "divisions as the basis of the organization and administration of armies in the field." As an authority on the organization of European armies, however, McClellan was well aware of the advantages of organizing the large army that he was creating in 1861 into corps, and it was his intention to do so as soon as "service in the field had indicated what general officers were best fitted to exercise those most important commands." But, in early 1862, when McClellan had taken no action regarding the organization of army corps, he was preempted by Lincoln, who, in this General War Order Number 2, directed "that the Major General commanding the Army of the Potomac proceed forthwith to organize that part of the said army destined to enter upon active operations ... into four army corps." Although McClellan objected to Lincoln's order as being "issued without consulting me and against my judgment," he nevertheless carried it out on 13 March with the issuance of Army of the Potomac General Orders Number 151, dividing his field army into four army corps. In organizing these initial corps, McClellan followed Napoleon's model to create a combined arms organization of three infantry divisions, supported by up to twelve batteries of artillery and one or more regiments of cavalry. (Armstrong 2008, 32)

4. That this order be executed with such promptness and dispatch as not to delay the commencement of the operations already directed to be underwritten by the Army of the Potomac.

5. A fifth army corps, to be commanded by Major general N. P. Banks, will be formed from his own and General Shields's (late General Lander's) divisions.

A. Lincoln.

President's General War Order No. 3, Executive Mansion, Washington, March 8, 1862[1]

Ordered: That no change of the base of operations of the Army of the Potomac shall be made without leaving in and about Washington such a force as in the opinion of the general-in-chief and the commanders of all the army corps shall leave said city entirely secure.

That no more than two army corps (about 50,000 troops) of said Army of the Potomac shall be moved en route for a new base of operations until the navigation of the Potomac from Washington to the Chesapeake Bay shall be freed from enemy's batteries and other obstructions, or until the President shall hereafter give express permission.

That any movements as aforesaid en route for a new base of operations which may be ordered by the general-in-chief, and which may be intended to move upon the Chesapeake Bay, shall begin to move upon the bay as early as the 18th day of March instant, and the general-in-chief shall be responsible that it so move as early as that day.

Ordered, That the army and navy co-operate in an immediate effort to capture the enemy's batteries upon the Potomac between Washington and the Chesapeake Bay.

A. Lincoln.

President's Special War Order No. 3, Executive Mansion, Washington, March 11, 1862[2]

Major General McClellan having personally taken the field at the head of the Army of the Potomac, until otherwise ordered he is relieved from the command

---

1   The following day, on March 9, information was received by General McClellan, at Washington, that the enemy had abandoned his position in front of that city. He at once, crossed the Potomac, and on the same night issued orders for an immediate advance of the whole army towards Manassas; but not with any intention, as he later explained, of pursuing the rebels, and taking advantage of their retreat, but to, among other things, give the troops "some experience of the march and bivouac preparatory to the campaign," and to afford them also a "good intermediate step between the quiet and comparative comfort of the camps around Washington and the vigor of active operations." These objects, in General McClellan's opinion, were sufficiently accomplished by what the Prince de Joinville, of his staff, styled a "promenade" of the army to Manassas. (Raymond 1865, 268-9)

2   Although the Army of the Potomac and McClellan were finally in the field for the first time, McClellan's departure from Washington offered Lincoln an opportunity to take direct control of the conduct of the war, which he did with this March 11 order. Surprisingly, McClellan seemed to accept his relief as general-in-chief amicably. In a March 12 note to Lincoln, McClellan reminded him that at some time past he (McClellan) had stated "that no feeling of self-interest or ambition should ever prevent me from devoting myself to the service." Now, "under the present circumstances," he continued, "I shall work just as cheer-

of the other military departments, he retaining command of the Department of the Potomac.

Ordered further, That the departments now under the respective commands of Generals Halleck and Hunter, together with so much of that under General Buell as lies west of a north and south line indefinitely drawn through Knoxville, Tenn., be consolidated and designated the Department of the Mississippi, and that until otherwise ordered Major General Halleck have command of said department.

Ordered also, That the country west of the Department of the Potomac and east of the Department of the Mississippi be a military department, to be called the Mountain Department, and that the same be commanded by Major General Frémont.

That all the commanders of departments, after the receipt of this order by them, respectively report severally and directly to the Secretary of War, and that prompt, full, and frequent reports will be expected of all and each of them.

A. Lincoln.

To General G. B. McClellan, Executive Mansion, Washington, March 31, 1862[1]

Major General McClellan:

My Dear Sir—This morning I felt constrained to order Blenker's division to Frémont, and I write this to assure you I did so with great pain, understanding that you would wish it otherwise. If you could know the full pressure of the case, I am confident that you would justify it, even beyond a mere acknowledgment that the commander-in-chief may order what he pleases.

Yours very truly,
A. Lincoln.

To General G. B. McClellan, Washington, April 6, 1862[2]

General G. B. McClellan:

---

fully as before, and that no consideration of self will in any manner interfere with the discharge of my public duties." (Armstrong 2008, 20)

1 It can be seen from the tone of these orders, that the President—as arguably most of official Washington—was confounded by the unaccountable delay of the Army of the Potomac to move against the enemy at Manassas, and that this feeling became one of chagrin and mortification when the rebels were allowed to withdraw from that position without molestation, and without suspicion until their design had been carried into complete and successful execution. He was impatiently anxious, therefore, that no more time should be lost in delays. General McClellan, before embarking for the Peninsula, had communicated his intention of reaching, without loss of time, the field of what he believed would be a decisive battle, somewhere between West Point and Richmond. On March 31, the President, in yielding to the demands of General Frémont, and from a belief that this officer needed a much larger force than he then had at his command in the Mountain Department, ordered General Blenker's division, of the Army of the Potomac, to join him, a decision which he announced to General McClellan in this letter. (Brockett 1865, 354)

2 McClelland had a profound contempt for the opinion of the Washington authorities, and in his answer piled up the difficulties with which he had to contend, and complained of the inadequacy of his force. To his wife, with whom he shared his inmost thoughts, he wrote: "The President very coolly telegraphed me yesterday that he thought I had better break

Yours of 11 A.M. today received. Secretary of War informs me that the forwarding of transportation, ammunition, and Woodbury's brigade, under your orders, is not, and will not be, interfered with. You now have over one hundred thousand troops with you, independent of General Wool's command. I think you better break the enemy's line from Yorktown to Warwick River at once. This will probably use time as advantageously as you can.

A. Lincoln, President.

To General G. B. McClellan, Washington, April 9, 1862[1]

Major General McClellan:

My Dear Sir—Your dispatches, complaining that you are not properly sustained, while they do not offend me, do pain me very much.

Blenker's division was withdrawn from you before you left here, and you knew the pressure under which I did it, and, as I thought, acquiesced in it certainly not without reluctance.

After you left I ascertained that less than 20,000 unorganized men, without a single field battery, were all you designed to be left for the defense of Washington and Manassas Junction, and part of this even to go to General Hooker's old position; General Banks's corps, once designed for Manassas Junction, was divided and tied up on the line of Winchester and Strasburg, and could not leave it without again exposing the upper Potomac and the Baltimore and Ohio Railroad. This presented (or would present when McDowell and Sumner should be gone) a great temptation to the enemy to turn back from the Rappahannock and sack Washington. My explicit order that Washington should, by the judgment of all the Commanders of corps, be left entirely secure, had been neglected. It was precisely this that drove me to detain McDowell.

---

the enemy's lines at once! I was much tempted to reply that he had better come and do it himself." (Rhodes 1896, 465)

1 Rhodes' additional comments on the April 9 letter place the document in perspective: Lincoln wrote McClellan the noble, pathetic, and sensible letter which is often reproduced or quoted from, and which contains, as a direction for the future, the remark, and "It is indispensable to you that you strike a blow." The young general failed to take the course which every consideration prompted, from two defects in the working of his mind. He was irresolute; he habitually overestimated the force of the enemy. For a conceited man and unsuccessful general, McClellan wrote and talked too much, and he had at this time various opinions as to the strength of the enemy he must encounter; but on April 7 he was sure that General Joseph E. Johnston had arrived in Yorktown with strong reinforcements, and that he should have the whole force of the enemy on his hands, which was probably not less than 100,000. It is quite true that as soon as McClellan began his advance towards Yorktown, reinforcements commenced to arrive for Magruder, so that by April 11 he had an aggregate of 31,500, but by this time the Union army reached the number of 100,000 men present for duty. Up to this date, therefore, there was no time when McClellan had not three men to one of the Confederates. April 17 Joseph E. Johnston took command in person at Yorktown of an army, which had then reached the number of 53,000. McClellan had missed the golden opportunity for an assault, and perhaps from this time on nothing could have been better than a continuance of the scientific siege operations which he began soon after his arrival before Yorktown. (Rhodes 1896, 465-6) So, it seems, the inexperienced lawyer summed up in three lines the situation which the professional soldier was constitutionally incapable of realizing. "By delay the enemy will relatively gain on you…that is he will gain faster by fortifications and reinforcements than you will by reinforcements alone." (Ballard 1952, 112)

I do not forget that I was satisfied with your arrangement to leave Banks at Manassas Junction; but when that arrangement was broken up and nothing substituted for it, of course I was not satisfied. I was constrained to substitute something for it myself.

And now allow me to ask, do you really think I should permit the line from Richmond via Manassas Junction to this city to be entirely open, except what resistance could be presented by less than 20,000 unorganized troops? This is a question which the country will not allow me to evade.

There is a curious mystery about the number of the troops now with you. When I telegraphed you on the 6th, saying you had over 100,000 with you, I had just obtained from the Secretary of War a statement, taken as he said from your own returns, making 108,000 then with you and en route to you. You now say you will have but 85,000 when all enroute to you shall have reached you. How can this discrepancy of 23,000 be accounted for?

As to General Wool's command, I understand it is doing for you precisely what a like number of your own would have to do if that command was away. I suppose the whole force which has gone forward to you is with you by this time; and if so, I think it is the precise time for you to strike a blow. By delay the enemy will relatively gain upon you—that is, he will gain faster by fortifications and reinforcements than you can by reinforcements alone.

And once more let me tell you it is indispensable to you that you strike a blow. I am powerless to help this. You will do me the justice to remember I always insisted that going down the bay in search of a field, instead of fighting at or near Manassas, was only shifting and not surmounting a difficulty; that we would find the same enemy and the same or equal entrenchments at either place. The country will not fail to note—is noting now—that the present hesitation to move upon an entrenched enemy is but the story of Manassas repeated.

I beg to assure you that I have never written you or spoken to you in greater kindness of feeling than now, nor with a fuller purpose to sustain you, so far as in my most anxious judgment I consistently can; but you must act.

Yours very truly,
A. Lincoln.

To General H. W. Halleck, Executive Mansion, Washington, April 9, 1862[1]

Major General Halleck, Saint Louis, Mo.:

If the rigor of the confinement of Magoffin (Governor of Kentucky) at Alton is endangering his life, or materially impairing his health, I wish it mitigated as far as it can be consistently with his safe detention.

A. Lincoln.

---

1 Ebenezer Magoffin, brother of the pro-Southern governor of Kentucky, Beriah Magoffin, was a prominent prisoner. Ebenezer had settled in Boone County, Missouri, in the mid-1850s and supported the Confederate cause. He had been captured and paroled before the battle of Lexington. Now, in violation of the condition of his parole, he faced trial by a military commission in St. Louis. Lincoln's letter aside, on February 20, 1862, the commission sentenced Magoffin to death. Beriah Magoffin, with the help of the Kentucky moderate John J. Crittenden, sought Lincoln's intervention. On March 25, 1862, Lincoln would suspend the death sentence pending a review of the case. However, on July 24, 1862 Ebenezer Magoffin escaped from the Alton military prison. (Gerteis 2012, 125)

Telegram to General G. B. McClellan, Washington, April 21, 1862[1]

Major General McClellan:

Your dispatch of the 19th was received that day. Fredericksburg is evacuated and the bridges destroyed by the enemy, and a small part of McDowell's command occupies this side of the Rappahannock, opposite the town. He purposes moving his whole force to that point.

A. Lincoln.

Telegram to General G. B. McClellan, Washington, April 29, 1862[2]

Major General McClellan:

Would it derange or embarrass your operations if I were to appoint Captain Charles Griffin a brigadier-general of volunteers? Please answer.

A. Lincoln.

Telegram to General McClellan, Executive Mansion, Washington, May 1, 1862[3]

Major General McClellan:

1 It would not be until May 2 that Federal troops began a period of occupation of Fredericksburg proper. These troops, as part of the recently organized Department of the Rappahannock under the overall command of Major General Irvin McDowell, would continue to cause tension among Fredericksburg's residents. McDowell called Fredericksburg "a position of Manifest importance to us and to the enemy, whatever course the war may take. His troops would serve as strategic reinforcements for Federal operations in Virginia. Fredericksburg became a central communications network, a major supply base and route of transportation to quickly aid the Army of the Potomac under Major General George McClellan attempting to capture the Confederate capital at Richmond to the southeast or assist Federal forces under Major General Nathaniel P. Banks to the northwest in the Shenandoah Valley fighting Confederate forces under Major General Thomas J. "Stonewall" Jackson. Federal forces remained in Fredericksburg until August 31 in the aftermath of the defeat of Major General John Pope's Army of Virginia by General Robert E. Lee and the Confederate Anny of Northern Virginia at the Battle of Second Bull Run, also known as Second Manassas. (Bryant 2010, 9)

2 Charles Griffith was serving as a West Point instructor until early 1861, when, during the early years of the war, he organized a new artillery unit with the academy's enlisted men. The battery distinguished itself in the first major battle of the Civil War at Bull Run and later during the Peninsular Campaign. He transferred to the infantry in 1862 to become (following Lincoln's desire) a brigadier general of volunteers and to subsequently lead his brigade at the second battle of Bull Run and at Antietam. Griffin's irascibility frequently led to conflict with his superiors, but his leadership abilities brought steady promotion. He commanded a division in the battles at Fredericksburg, Chancellorsville, and Gettysburg, and in the Virginia Campaign (1864–65). He became a major general in command of the Fifth Corps in April 1865 and was one of the Union generals who received Robert E. Lee's surrender at Appomattox. (Baggett 2012)

3 Once again, Lincoln's frustration with McClelland seems evident; however, his feelings were well-founded. As Holland (answering Lincoln's question) suggests, there was indeed something to be done; but the Confederates did it. After the absolute waste of a month's time, opportunities, and resources of strength and material, the rebels quietly evacuated their position, and retired up the Peninsula. It was the old story of great preparations to fight, and no fighting or weakening of the enemy. General McClellan thought the success brilliant, if we judge by his dispatches, but it was the costly victory of an engineer. He telegraphed

Your call for Parrott guns from Washington alarms me, chiefly because it argues indefinite procrastination. Is anything to be done?

A. Lincoln.

Telegram to General H. W. Halleck, War Department, May 1, 1862[1]

Major General Halleck, Pittsburgh Landing, Tennessee:

I am pressed by the Missouri members of Congress to give General Schofield independent command in Missouri. They insist that for want of this their local troubles gradually grow worse. I have forborne, so far, for fear of interfering with and embarrassing your operations. Please answer telling me whether anything, and what, I can do for them without injuriously interfering with you.

A. Lincoln.

To General G. B. McClellan, Fort Monroe, Virginia, May 9, 1862[2]

Major General McClellan:

My Dear Sir—I have just assisted the Secretary of War in framing part of a dispatch to you relating to army corps, which dispatch, of course, will have reached you long before this will. I wish to say a few words to you privately on this subject. I ordered the army corps organization not only on the unanimous opinion of the twelve generals whom you had selected and assigned as generals of divisions, but also on the unanimous opinion of every military man I could get an opinion from, and every modern military book, yourself only excepted. Of

---

to Stanton, on the fourth, that he held the entire line of the enemy's works; that he had thrown all his cavalry and horse artillery, supported by infantry, in pursuit; that no time should be lost, and that he should "push the enemy to the wall." The enemy retired to his second line of works at Williamsburgh without pushing, and took his position behind the wall. Here was fought the battle of Williamsburgh, which McClellan designated in his final report as "one of the most brilliant engagements of the war." He bestows the highest praise upon General Hancock, though Hooker had fought with equal gallantry, and encountered greater losses. All did their duty; and when, between four and five o'clock in the afternoon, General McClellan arrived at the scene, although the battle had commenced early in the morning. On the next morning, there was no enemy; and, owing to the bad roads, the lack of food, and the exhaustion of the troops, McClellan determined there could be no immediate pursuit. (Holland 1866, 368)

1 Able notes that the scenario of Schofield ultimately being given an independent command in Missouri was much to be regretted as indicative of a surrender to politicians and an abandonment of the idea, so fundamentally conducive to military success, that all parts must contribute to the good of the whole. (Abel 1992, 106)

2 After battle of Williamsburg, McClelland had written Lincoln indicating his wish to return to the organization by divisions, or else to be authorized "to relieve from duty with this army, commanders of corps or divisions who find themselves incompetent." This was a fresh manifestation of his hostility to Generals Sumner, Heintzelman, and Keyes, shown when the President had overruled him in March by organizing the army into corps, and giving the command of them to those generals who were entitled to it by rank. A few days later, despite McClelland's protestations, Lincoln authorized the formation of two *additional* provisional army corps, to be commanded by Generals Porter and Franklin. They were numbered the 5th and 6th. The order announcing this was promulgated by General McClellan May 18. (Gorham 1899, 394-6)

---

course, I did not on my own judgment pretend to understand the subject. I now think it indispensable for you to know how your struggle against it is received in quarters which we cannot entirely disregard. It is looked upon as merely an effort to pamper one or two pets, and to persecute and degrade their supposed rivals. I have had no word from Sumner, Heintzleman, or Keyes the command-ers of these corps are, of course, the three highest officers with you; but I am constantly told that you have no consultation or communication with them; that you consult and communicate with nobody but General Fitz John Porter, and perhaps General Franklin. I do not say these complaints are true or just; but at all events, it is proper you should know of their existence. Do the commanders of corps disobey your orders in anything?

When you relieved General Hamilton of his command the other day, you thereby lost the confidence of at least one of your best friends in the Senate. And here let me say, not as applicable to you personally, that Senators and Represen-tatives speak of me in their places without question, and that officers of the army must cease addressing insulting letters to them for taking no greater liberty with them.

But to return. Are you strong enough—are you strong enough even with my help—to set your foot upon the necks of Sumner, Heintzelman, and Keyes all at once? This is a practical and very serious question to you?

The success of your army and the cause of the country are the same, and, of course, I only desire the good of the cause.

Yours truly,

A. Lincoln.

Telegram to General G. B. McClellan, Washington City, May 15, 1862[1]

Major General McClellan, Cumberland, Virginia:

Your long dispatch of yesterday is just received. I will answer more fully soon. Will say now that all your dispatches to the Secretary of War have been promptly shown to me. Have done and shall do all I could and can to sustain you. Hoped that the opening of James River and putting Wool and Burnside in communication, with an open road to Richmond, or to you, had effected some-thing in that direction. I am still unwilling to take all our force off the direct line between Richmond and here.

A. Lincoln.

---

1 It should be noted that, while McClellan had active enemies working against him, at this time he had some cabinet support. He had been intimate with Seward, and now Seward came to his help. The Secretary of State visited McClellan at Cumberland Landing and heard his story. From this place Seward wrote Lincoln on May 14, "The battle will be fought, probably, this side of Richmond. We think that you should order whole or major part of General McDowell's, with Shields, up the York River as soon as possible....We find General McClellan confident of success. He moves to White House tomorrow morning." This pow-erful interposition had some effect. At that moment Stanton and Seward were in opposi-tion. On May 15, McClellan wired Stanton that he was detained by having to make roads. "News from front indicate enemy in large force. Raining today. No time will be lost in bring-ing about a decisive battle." (Eckenrode and Conrad 1941, 57)

Proclamation Revoking General Hunter's Order of Military Emancipation, May 19, 1862[1]

By The President of the United States of America:

A Proclamation: Whereas there appears in the public prints what purports to be a proclamation of Major general Hunter, in the words and figures following, to wit:

(General Orders No. 11) Headquarters Department of the South, Hilton Head, Port Royal, S. C., May 9, 1862.

The three States of Georgia, Florida, and South Carolina, comprising the military department of the South, having deliberately declared themselves no longer under the protection of the United States of America, and having taken up arms against the said United States, it became a military necessity to declare martial law. This was accordingly done on the 25th day of April, 1862. Slavery and martial law in a free country are altogether incompatible. The persons in these three States: Georgia Florida, and South Carolina—heretofore held as slaves are therefore declared forever free.

"By command of Major General D. Hunter: "(Official.) Ed. W. Smith, "Acting Assistant Adjutant General."

And whereas the same is producing some excitement and misunderstanding: therefore,

I, Abraham Lincoln, President of the United States, proclaim and declare that the Government of the United States, had no knowledge, information, or belief of an intention on the part of General Hunter to issue such a proclamation; nor has it yet any authentic information that the document is genuine. And further, that neither General Hunter nor any other commander or person has been authorized by the Government of the United States to make a proclamation declaring the slaves of any State free; and that the supposed proclamation now in question, whether genuine or false, is altogether void so far as respects such a declaration.

I further make known that whether it be competent for me, as commander-in-chief of the army and navy, to declare the slaves of any State or States free, and whether, at any time, in any case, it shall have become a necessity indispensable to the maintenance of the government to exercise such supposed power, are questions which under my responsibility I reserve to myself, and which I cannot feel justified in leaving to the decision of commanders in the field.

These are totally different questions from those of police regulations in armies and camps.

---

1 Revoking Hunter's emancipation proclamation in May 1862 caused less criticism than the controversy over Frémont, and the language in his order made clear, as Lincoln had stated to others, that no commanding general shall do such a thing without first consulting him. Still, Lincoln was too astute not to sense that the center of opinion was shifting. As he privately told Chase and publicly told Hunter, he too was moving. He was warning both sides that emancipation might be near. But how fast Lincoln moved, what he did about freedom, was tied to the state of the Union and its power. For political and military purposes, Lincoln needed to settle on a policy that addressed a problem of logistics and dealt with morale by reinvigorating the war effort against an institution so basically antithetical to freedom. (Green 2004, 154-5)

On the sixth day of March last, by special message, I recommended to Congress the adoption of a joint resolution, to be substantially as follows:

Resolved, That the United States ought to co-operate with any State which may adopt gradual abolishment of slavery, giving to such State pecuniary aid, to be used by such State, in its discretion, to compensate for the inconvenience, public and private, produced by such change of system.

The resolution in the language above quoted was adopted by large majorities in both branches of Congress, and now stands an authentic, definite, and solemn proposal of the nation to the States and people most immediately interested in the subject-matter. To the people of those States I now earnestly appeal. I do not argue—I beseech you to make arguments for yourselves. You cannot, if you would, be blind to the signs of the times. I beg of you a calm and enlarged consideration of them, ranging, if it may be, far above personal and partisan politics. This proposal makes common cause for a common object, casting no reproaches upon any. It acts not the Pharisee. The change it contemplates would come gently as the dews of heaven, not rending or wrecking anything. Will you not embrace it? So much good has not been done, by one effort, in all past time, as in the providence of God it is now your high privilege to do. May the vast future not have to lament that you have neglected it.

In witness whereof, I have hereunto set my hand and caused the seal of the United States to be affixed.

Done at the city of Washington, this nineteenth day of May, in the year of our Lord one thousand eight hundred and sixty-two, and of the independence of the United States the eighty-sixth.

A. Lincoln.

Telegram to General G. E. McClellan, Washington, May 21, 1862[1]

Major General McClellan:

I have just been waited on by a large committee who present a petition signed by twenty-three senators and eighty-four representatives asking me to restore General Hamilton to his division. I wish to do this, and yet I do not wish to be understood as rebuking you. Please answer at once.

A. Lincoln.

Telegram to General G. B. McClellan, Washington City, May 22, 1862[2]

Major General McClellan:

---

1 McClellan's replied the following day: "The discipline of the army will not permit the restoration of General Hamilton to his Division.... Genl Hamilton is not fit to command a Division.... The cause of his removal...was ample to justify me in the course pursued. You cannot do anything better calculated to injure my army and diminish the probabilities of success...than to restore Gen Hamilton...." (Lincoln v.5, 1953, 227)

2 As additional background to what came to be known as the Peninsula Campaign, when McClellan reached the Virginia peninsula in early April he found a force of ten to fifteen

Your long dispatch of yesterday just received. You will have just such control of General McDowell and his forces as you therein indicate. McDowell can reach you by land sooner than he could get aboard of boats, if the boats were ready at Fredericksburg, unless his march shall be resisted, in which case the force resisting him will certainly not be confronting you at Richmond. By land he can reach you in five days after starting, whereas by water he would not reach you in two weeks, judging by past experience. Franklin's single division did not reach you in ten days after I ordered it.

A. Lincoln, President, United States.

Telegram to General McClellan, Washington, May 24, 1862[1]

Major General G. B. McClellan:

---

thousand Confederates under Maj. Gen. John B. Magruder barring his path to Richmond. Magruder, a student of drama and master of deception, so dazzled McClellan that instead of brushing the Confederates aside he spent a month in a siege of Yorktown. But Johnston, who wanted to fight the decisive action closer to Richmond, decided to withdraw slowly up the peninsula. At Williamsburg, on May 5, McClellan's advance elements made contact with the Confederate rear guard under Maj. Gen. James Longstreet, who successfully delayed the Federal advance. McClellan again pursued in leisurely fashion, always believing that he was outnumbered and about to be attacked in overwhelming force by Johnston. By May 25 two corps of the Army of the Potomac had turned southwest toward Richmond and crossed the sluggish Chickahominy River. The remaining three corps were on the north side of the stream with the expectation of making contact with McDowell, who would come down from Fredericksburg. Men of the two corps south of the river could see the spires of the Confederate capital, but Johnston's army was in front of them. Drenching rains on May 30 raised the Chickahominy to flood stage and seriously divided McClellan's army. Johnston decided to grasp this chance to defeat the Federals in detail. He struck on May 31 near Fair Oaks. His plans called for his whole force to concentrate against the isolated corps south of the river, but his staff and subordinate commanders were not up to the task of executing them. Assaulting columns became confused, and attacks were delivered piecemeal. The Federals, after some initial reverses, held their ground and bloodily repulsed the Confederates. When Johnston suffered a severe wound at Fair Oaks, President Davis replaced him with General Lee. Lee for his part had no intention of defending Richmond passively. The city's fortifications would enable him to protect Richmond with a relatively small force while he used the main body of his army offensively in an attempt to cut off and destroy the Army of the Potomac. He ordered Jackson back from the Shenandoah Valley with all possible speed. (Stewart, 2005, 227-8) From the perspective of the President, and as the late May and early June 1862 correspondence reflects, Lincoln could scarcely be more engaged, "Commander in chief Lincoln was acting up to his title. He was designing both strategy and tactics. His plan for capturing Jackson was specific in nature; order to Frémont to march to a specific point was tactical. He also gave McDowell strategic and tactical instructions." (Williams 2000, 98)

1 For the next several days—indeed until the end of the month—Lincoln repeatedly attempted to coordinate the actions of his generals. His overall plan directed Banks to reform on or near the Potomac while Frémont moved towards Jackson's rear at Harrisonburg. McDowell would meanwhile advance west from Fredericksburg in case Stonewall moved east across the Blue Ridge. Either Frémont or McDowell alone supposedly had enough strength to defeat Jackson; if the two Union forces combined, the Valley could be cleared and Jackson eliminated. The plan looked very good on paper and could well have succeeded, except for the unpredictability of one man—Stonewall Jackson himself. In his own eyes, Lincoln knew he was taking a risk by sending so many troops after Jackson. He was genuinely afraid that Jackson might escape from the Valley and descend on Washington, whose ragtag garrison might not have held back a determined enemy force. For that reason Lincoln ordered McDowell to send one of his brigades to Manassas and another to Washington; in

In consequence of General Banks's critical position, I have been compelled to suspend General McDowell's movements to join you. The enemy are making a desperate push upon Harper's Ferry, and we are trying to throw General Frémont's force and part of General McDowell's in their rear.

A. Lincoln, President.

Telegram to General McClellan, Washington, May 24, 1862[1]

Major General George B. McClellan:

I left General McDowell's camp at dark last evening. Shields's command is there, but it is so worn that he cannot move before Monday morning, the 26th. We have so thinned our line to get troops for other places that it was broken yesterday at Front Royal, with a probable loss to us of one regiment infantry, two Companies cavalry, putting General Banks in some peril.

The enemy's forces under General Anderson now opposing General McDowell's advance have as their line of supply and retreat the road to Richmond.

If, in conjunction with McDowell's movement against Anderson, you could send a force from your right to cut off the enemy's supplies from Richmond, preserve the railroad bridges across the two forks of the Pamunkey, and intercept the enemy's retreat, you will prevent the army now opposed to you from receiving an accession of numbers of nearly 15,000 men; and if you succeed in saving the bridges you will secure a line of railroad for supplies in addition to the one you now have. Can you not do this almost as well as not while you are building the Chickahominy bridges? McDowell and Shields both say they can, and positively will, move Monday morning. I wish you to move cautiously and safely.

You will have command of McDowell, after he joins you, precisely as you indicated in your long dispatch to us of the 21st.

A. Lincoln.

Telegram to General Rufus Saxton, War Department, May 24, 1862, 2 P.M.[2]

General Saxton:

---

addition, Stanton issued a call for militia from neighboring states. What concerned Lincoln most was McClellan's isolated position in far-off eastern Virginia. McClellan had been impossibly slow in mounting his campaign, and Lincoln's patience was now running thin. On 25 May, Lincoln warned McClellan, "I think the time is near when you must either attack Richmond or give up the job and come to the defense of Washington." (Martin 1994, 131)

1 No reply to this telegram has been located.
2 Born 19 October 1824 at Greenfield, Massachusetts, Rufus Saxton attended nearby Deerfield Academy and worked on the family farm until, at age 20, he received appointment to West Point from which he graduated in 1849. He was appointed Second Lieutenant, Artillery, and he served in that Branch against the Seminole Indians in Florida, on the Northern Pacific Railroad, in garrison on several posts, on the Coastal Survey in the East, as an Instructor of Artillery Tactics at West Point and on other Eastern duty. During this period, he patented a self-registering thermostat for deep-sea soundings. When the Civil War broke out in 1861, he was in command of an artillery detachment at the St. Louis Arsenal, but after assisting General Nathaniel Lyon in dispersing the disloyal Missouri State Guard at Camp Jackson, he became Lyon's Chief Quartermaster. He then joined General George B. McClellan's staff in West Virginia and later accompanied the Port Royal Expedition as Quartermaster. He

Geary reports Jackson with 20,000 moving from Ashby's Gap by the Little River turnpike, through Aldie, toward Centreville. This he says is reliable. He is also informed of large forces south of him. We know a force of some 15,000 broke up Saturday night from in front of Fredericksburg and went we know not where. Please inform us, if possible, what has become of the force which pursued Banks yesterday; also any other information you have.

A. Lincoln.

Telegram to General J. C. Frémont, War Department, May 24, 1862, 4 P.M. [1]

Major General Frémont, Franklin:

You are authorized to purchase the 400 horses, or take them wherever or however you can get them. The exposed condition of General Banks makes his immediate relief a point of paramount importance. You are therefore directed by the President to move against Jackson at Harrisonburg and operate against the enemy in such way as to relieve Banks. This movement must be made immediately. You will acknowledge the receipt of this order, and specify the hour it is received by you.

A. Lincoln.

Telegram to General J. C. Frémont, War Department, May 24, 1862, 7:15 P.M. [2]

Major General Frémont, Franklin, Virginia:

Many thanks for the promptness with which you have answered that you will execute the order. Much—perhaps all—depends upon the celerity with which you can execute it. Put the utmost speed into it. Do not lose a minute.

A. Lincoln.

was appointed Brigadier General of U.S. Volunteers as of April 15, 1862 and commanded the defenses of Harpers Ferry in May and June. During the balance of the war he commanded at various points in the South under a multiplicity of formal titles. However, his principal occupation was the enlistment and organization of Negroes, principally ex-slaves, into the Federal Army. At the end of the war, he passed naturally into the newly created Freedman's Bureau, acting as its Assistant Commissioner for the States of South Carolina, Georgia and Florida until January 1866, when he was mustered out of the volunteer service. He was awarded the Medal of Honor on April 25, 1893 for service as a Brigadier General, United States Volunteers, at Harpers Ferry, Virginia, where he displayed "Distinguished gallantry and good conduct in the defense." He was breveted Major General of Volunteers and Brigadier General in the Regular Army, but returned to his pre-war grade of Major to the Quartermaster Department, where he served faithfully and competently in various districts and departments across the country for 22 years. He became a Lieutenant Colonel in 1872 and Colonel and Assistant Quartermaster General in 1882. During his last five years of service, he commanded the Quartermaster Depot, Jeffersonville, Kentucky. (Patterson 2012)

1 Gallagher suggests that Lincoln's May 24 instructions to Generals Frémont and McDowell should not be construed as evidence of panic on Lincoln's part growing out of fear for the safety of Washington, but as yet another effort to get McClellan to apply offensive pressure against the rebel force defending Richmond. They also demonstrate that Lincoln hoped to inaugurate some manner of offensive against Jackson from the outset, as opposed to simply assuming more defensive measures directed to saving Washington. (Gallagher 2003, 10)

2 Fremont replied: "Your telegram received at five (5) o'clock this afternoon will move as ordered & operate against the enemy in such way as to afford prompt relief to Genl Banks." (Lincoln v.5, 1953, 231)

Telegram to General I. McDowell, War Department, May 24, 1862[1]

Major General McDowell, Fredricksburg:

General Frémont has been ordered by telegraph to move from Franklin on Harrisonburg to relieve General Banks, and capture or destroy Jackson's and Ewell's forces. You are instructed, laying aside for the present the movement on Richmond, to put 20,000 men in motion at once for the Shenandoah, moving on the line or in advance of the line of the Manassas Gap railroad. Your object will be to capture the forces of Jackson and Ewell, either in co-operation with General Frémont, or, in case want of supplies or of transportation, interferes with his movements, it is believed that the force which you move will be sufficient to accomplish this object alone. The information thus far received here makes it probable that if the enemy operate actively against General Banks, you will not be able to count upon much assistance from him, but may even have to release him. Reports received this moment are that Banks is fighting with Ewell eight miles from Winchester.

A. Lincoln.

Telegram to General McDowell, War Department, Washington City, May 24, 1862[2]

Major General I. McDowell:

I am highly gratified by your alacrity in obeying my order. The change was as painful to me as it can possibly be to you or to any one. Everything now depends upon the celerity and vigor of your movement.

A. Lincoln.

Telegram to General John W. Geary, War Department, May 25, 1862, 1:45 P.M.[3]

General Geary, White Plains:

1 In reply to Lincoln's telegram of 5 P.M., McDowell telegraphed Stanton: "The President's order has been received and is in process of execution. This is a crushing blow to us." (Ibid, 233)

2 McDowell's replied at 9:30 P.M.: "I obeyed your orders immediately...perhaps as a subordinate there I ought to stop; but...I beg to say that co-operation between General Fremont and myself to cut Jackson and Ewell there is not to be counted upon, even if it is not a practical impossibility. Next, that I am entirely beyond helping distance of General Banks; no celerity or vigor will avail so far as he is concerned.... It will take a week or ten days for the force to get to the valley by the route which will give it food and forage, and by that time the enemy will have retired. I shall gain nothing for you there, and shall lose much for you here.... I have ordered General Shields to commence the movement by to-morrow morning. A second division will follow in the afternoon. Did I understand you aright, that you wished that I personally should accompany this expedition? I hope to see Governor Chase to-night and express myself more fully to him." (Ibid)

3 Much changed on May 24 after Jackson's attack at Front Royal. The Virginian's sudden appearance and victory in the lower Valley shocked Washington. For the first time since the Federals had begun active operations in the Valley more than two months earlier, Jackson represented a significant threat rather than a nuisance. Lincoln and Stanton, distant from the field of events, had little idea of what was happening. "We are left in extraordinary state of uncertainty as to the real state of affairs," Stanton wrote on May 24. From Lincoln's perspective, things must have looked serious indeed when General Geary, commander of

Please give us your best present impression as to the number of the enemy's forces north of Strasburg and Front Royal. Are the forces still moving north through the gap at Front Royal and between you and there?

A. Lincoln.

Telegram to General G. B. McClellan, Washington, May 25, 1862, 2 P.M.[1]

Major General McClellan:

The enemy is moving north in sufficient force to drive General Banks before him—precisely in what force we cannot tell. He is also threatening Leesburg and Geary, on the Manassas Gap railroad, from both north and south—precisely what force we cannot tell. I think the movement is a general and concerted one, such as would not be if he was acting upon the purpose of a very desperate defense of Richmond. I think the time is near when you must either attack Richmond or give up the job and come to the defense of Washington. Let me hear from you instantly.

A. Lincoln, President.

Telegram to General R. Saxton, War Department, May 25, 1862.[2]

General Saxton, Harper's Ferry:

If Banks reaches Martinsburg, is he any the better for it? Will not the enemy cut him from thence to Harper's Ferry? Have you sent anything to meet him and assist him at Martinsburg? This is an inquiry, not an order.

A. Lincoln.

2,200 railroad guards in an independent brigade on the Manassas Gap Railroad east of Front Royal, telegraphed (erroneously) on May 24 that Jackson was already east of the Blue Ridge and moving through Aldie Gap in the Bull Run Mountains toward Centreville with 20,000 men. As one of Washington's chief informants during the next few days, Geary badly misled his superiors and contributed immeasurably to the chaos. (Gallagher 2003, 63)

1 When McClelland received Lincoln's first telegram of May 25, he was writing a letter to his wife. After reading the telegram, he wrote her that the President was "terribly scared" and wanted him to come back and save Washington. "Heaven help a country governed by such counsels," he exclaimed. At ten o'clock that night he got Lincoln's second telegram, and he added to his letter to Mrs. McClellan that they were in a panic at the capital. He was glad they were frightened: "A scare will do them good, and may bring them to their senses." The next day he found out they were not as scared as he had thought. Lincoln had learned that Banks was safely over the Potomac with his army, and the President dispatched McClellan that things looked better. McClellan was vastly relieved. He had feared he would be ordered back to Washington, and being in Washington was the worst fate he could think of. (Williams 2000, 100)

2 Saxton replied: "General Banks cannot reach Harper's Ferry from Martinsburg. He had two lines of retreat: one to Harper's Ferry, one to Martinsburg. He took the latter.... It is 19 miles from Winchester to Martinsburg, and 23 miles from here to Martinsburg, and 11 or 12 from Williamsport. His only chance is to go there. We could do nothing to assist him, as we could not ascertain line of retreat until it was too late. The whole force here does not amount to over 2,500 men, and 1,000 of these did not get ready to march before 12 o'clock to-day. I am looking anxiously for artillery." (Lincoln v.5, 1953, 237)

Telegram to General R. Saxton, War Department, May 25, 1862, 6:30 P.M.[1]

General Saxton, Harper's Ferry:

One good six-gun battery, complete in its men and appointments, is now on its way to you from Baltimore. Eleven other guns, of different sorts, are on their way to you from here. Hope they will all reach you before morning. As you have but 2500 men at Harper's Ferry, where are the rest which were in that vicinity and which we have sent forward? Have any of them been cut off?

A. Lincoln.

Telegram to General R. Saxton, War Department, May 25, 1862.[2]

General Saxton, Harper's Ferry:

I fear you have mistaken me. I did not mean to question the correctness of your conduct; on the contrary! I approve what you have done. As the 2500 reported by you seemed small to me, I feared some had got to Banks and been cut off with him. Please tell me the exact number you now have in hand.

A. Lincoln.

Telegram to General G. B. McClellan [Cipher] War Department, Washington City, May 25, 1862, 8:30 P.M.[3]

1 Jackson's forces attacked Harpers Ferry on May 30, but Saxton mounted a successful defense and, in 1893, he would be awarded the Congressional Medal of Honor for his actions that day. Three months later, Harpers Ferry was again of critical strategic importance. Robert E. Lee was commencing his first invasion of the North and wanted to secure his supply lines from the Shenandoah Valley and cover a possible line of retreat behind the Blue Ridge. In a risky move, he divided his army, sending part of it with Jackson to take the town, which the general did on September 15, 1862, defeating the approximately 14,000 Union troops garrisoned there under Colonel Dixon Miles. Jackson, however, was then forced to race to Maryland for the Battle of Antietam on September 17, which ended with Lee's retreat back into Virginia. A week later, Union troops were back in control of Harpers Ferry. (Noyalas 2011) Saxton's reply was received at 10:10 P.M.: "All the troops which were in this vicinity...are here. None of the troops which have arrived since I came here have been cut off.... The First Regiment District Volunteers...arrived at Winchester just as...Banks commenced retreating. Three companies only got out of the cars. The train returned with the regiment, with the above-mentioned line of retreat, until it was too late...." (Lincoln v.5, 1953, 238)

2 Saxton replied the following day: "I have had as careful an estimate made of the force here as is possible at present. It amounts to 6,700 men. Many more are on the way. A portion of the artillery has arrived, including one light battery...." (Ibid)

3 Lincoln's endorsement appears on the back of the document: "Draft of Tel. Despatch to Gen. McClellan, May 25, 1862." General Banks had telegraphed from Martinsburg at 2:40 P.M.: "The rebels attacked us this morning at daybreak in great force. Their number was estimated at 15000, consisting of Ewells & Jackson's divisions the fire of pickets began with light, was followed by the artillery until the lines were fully under fire on both sides. The left wing stood firmly, holding its ground well & right did the same for a time when two regiments broke the lines under the fire of the enemy. The right wing fell back & was ordered to withdraw & the troops pressed through the town in considerable confusion. They were quickly reformed on the other side, & continued their march in good order to Martinsburg where they arrived at 2.40 P.M. a distance of twenty-two miles. Our trains are in advance & will cross the river in safety. Our entire force engaged was less than 4000 consisting of

Major General McClellan:

Your dispatch received. General Banks was at Strasburg, with about 6,000 men, Shields having been taken from him to swell a give up the column for McDowell to aid you at Richmond, and the rest of his force scattered at various places. On the 23d a rebel force of 7000 to 10,000 fell upon one regiment and two companies guarding the bridge at Front Royal, destroying it entirely; crossed the Shenandoah, and on the 24th (yesterday) pushed to get north of Banks, on the road to Winchester. Banks ran a race with them, beating them into Winchester yesterday evening. This morning a battle ensued between the two forces, in which Banks was beaten back into full retreat toward Martinsburg, and probably is broken up into a total rout. Geary, on the Manassas Gap railroad, just now reports that Jackson is now near Front Royal, With 10,000, following up and supporting, as I understand, the forces now pursuing Banks, also that another force of 10,000 is near Orleans, following on in the same direction. Stripped here, as we are here, it will be all we can do to prevent them crossing the Potomac at Harper's Ferry or above. We have about 20,000 of McDowell's force moving back to the vicinity of Front Royal, and General Frémont, who was at Franklin, is moving to Harrisonburg; both these movements intended to get in the enemy's rear.

One more of McDowell's brigades is ordered through here to Harper's Ferry; the rest of his force remains for the present at Fredericksburg. We are sending such regiments and dribs from here and Baltimore as we can spare to Harper's Ferry, supplying their places in some sort by calling in militia from the adjacent States. We also have eighteen cannon on the road to Harper's Ferry, of which arm there is not a single one yet at that point. This is now our situation.

If McDowell's force was now beyond our reach, we should be utterly helpless. Apprehension of something like this, and no unwillingness to sustain you, has always been my reason for withholding McDowell's force from you. Please understand this, and do the best you can with the force you have.

A. Lincoln.

Telegram to General G. B. McClellan, Washington, May 26, 1862, 12:40 P.M.[1]

Major General McClellan:

We have General Banks's official report. He has saved his army and baggage, and has made a safe retreat to the river, and is probably safe at Williamsport. He reports the attacking force at 15,000.

A. Lincoln, President.

[George H.] Gordon's & [Dudley] Donnelly's brigades, with two reg'ts of cavalry under Gen. [John P.] Hatch. & two batteries artillery. Our loss is considerable as was that of the enemy, but cannot now be stated. We were reinforced by 10th Maine which did good service, & a regt. of cavalry." (Ibid, 237)

1 No "official report" from Banks has been located.

Telegram to General I. McDowell, War Department, May 26, 1862, 1 P.M.[1]

Major General McDowell, Falmouth, Virginia:

Despatches from Geary just received have been sent you. Should not the remainder of your forces, except sufficient to hold the point at Fredericksburg, move this way—to Manassas Junction or Alexandria? As commander of this department, should you not be here? I ask these questions.

A. Lincoln.

Telegram to General McClellan. Washington, May 26, 1862.[2]

Major General George B. McClellan:

Can you not cut the Alula Creek railroad? Also, what impression have you as to intrenched works for you to contend with in front of Richmond? Can you get near enough to throw shells into the city?

A. Lincoln, President.

Telegram to General J. C. Frémont, May 27, 1862, 9:58 P.M.3

Major General Frémont:

I see that you are at Moorefield. You were expressly ordered to march to Harrisonburg. What does this mean?

A. Lincoln.

---

1 General Geary telegraphed Stanton from White Plains at 12:10 P.M. that Stonewall Jackson was advancing with a large force through Middleburg, and again from Broad Run at 12:30 which confirmed the information. McDowell replied that he thought the available forces sufficient and added, "I have not thought my presence needed elsewhere as much as here, but since there is a sufficient doubt to cause you to ask the question I will immediately leave here to go to Washington and will arrive early to-morrow morning, but will not move my headquarters till I have seen you...." (Ibid, 240)

2 McClellan's replied: "Have cut the Virginia Central Rail Road in three places between Hanover C.H. and the Chickahominy. Will try to cut the other. I do not think Richmond entrenchments formidable, but am not certain. Hope very soon to be within shelling distance. Have Rail road in operation from White House to Chickahominy. Hope to have Chickahominy bridge repaired tonight. Nothing of interest today." (Ibid)

3 Fremont replied May 28: "My troops were not in condition to execute your order...otherwise than has been done. They have marched day & night to do it. The men had had so little to eat that many were weak for want of food & so reported by the Chief Surgeon Having for main object as stated in your telegram, the relief of Genl Banks the line of march followed was a necessity. In executing any order rec'd I take it for granted that I am to exercise discretion concerning it's literal execution according to circumstances if I am to understand that literal obedience to orders is required please say so. I have no desire to exercise any power which you do not think belongs of necessity to my position in the field." (Ibid, 244)

Telegram to General G. B. McClellan, Washington, May 28, 1862.1

Major General McClellan:
What of F.J. Porter's expedition? Please answer.
A. Lincoln.

Telegram to General I. McDowell, Washington, May 28, 1862.²

General McDowell, Manassas Junction:
General McClellan at 6.30 P.M. yesterday telegraphed that Fitz-John Porter's division had fought and driven 13,000 of the enemy, under General Branch, from Hanover Court-House, and was driving them from a stand they had made on the railroad at the time the messenger left. Two hours later he telegraphed that Stoneman had captured an engine and six cars on the Virginia Central, which he at once sent to communicate with Porter. Nothing further from McClellan.

If Porter effects a lodgment on both railroads near Hanover Court-House, consider whether your forces in front of Fredericksburg should not push through and join him.
A. Lincoln.

Telegram to General I. McDowell, Washington, May 28, 1862, 4 P.M.³

General McDowell, Manassas Junction:

---

1 Apparently, this message was not received at McClellan's headquarters until after McClellan had telegraphed a report of General Fitz-John Porter's action of the previous day. McClellan's report dated May 28 stated: "Porter's action of yesterday was truly a glorious victory. Too much credit cannot be given to his magnificent division and its accomplished leader. The route of rebels was complete...not a defeat, but a complete rout. Prisoners are constantly coming in; two companies have this moment arrived, with excellent arms. There is no doubt that the enemy are concentrating everything on Richmond. I will do my best to cut off Jackson, but am doubtful whether I can. It is the policy and duty of the Government to send me by water all the well-drilled troops available. I am confident that Washington is in no danger. Engines and cars in large numbers have been sent up to bring down Jackson's command. I may not be able to cut them off, but will try. We have cut all but the Fredericksburg and Richmond Railroad. The real issue is in the battle about to be fought in front of Richmond. All our available troops should be collected here...not raw regiments, but the well-drilled troops. It cannot be ignored that a desperate battle is before us. If any regiments of good troops remain unemployed it will be an irreparable fault committed." (Ibid, 244)

2 McDowell's replied: "I beg leave to report, in reply to your telegram of this morning directing me to consider whether my force in front of Fredericksburg should not push through and join the army under General McClellan, that I do not think, in the present state of affairs, it would be well to attempt to push through a part of that force, or to leave Fredericksburg otherwise than strongly held which could not be done as the troops are now posted. I trust in a few days to be able to effect the object you have in view, and which no one desires more than I do." (Ibid, 245)

3 This in response to a note from McDowell to Stanton that stated: "General Geary reports this a.m. that his scouts find nothing of the enemy this side of the Blue Ridge. Nothing else of importance." (Ibid, 246)

You say General Geary's scouts report that they find no enemy this side of the Blue Ridge. Neither do I. Have they been to the Blue Ridge looking for them. A. Lincoln.

Telegram to General I. McDowell, Washington, May 28, 1862, 5:40 P.M.[1]

General McDowell, Manassas Junction:

I think the evidence now preponderates that Ewell and Jackson are still about Winchester. Assuming this, it is for you a question of legs. Put in all the speed you can. I have told Frémont as much, and directed him to drive at them as fast as possible. By the way, I suppose you know Frémont has got up to Moorefield, instead of going into Harrisonburg.

A. Lincoln.

Telegram to General G. B. McClellan, Washington May 28, 1862, 8:40 P.M.[2]

Major General McClellan:

I am very glad of General F. J. Porter's victory. Still, if it was a total rout of the enemy, I am puzzled to know why the Richmond and Fredericksburg railroad was not seized again, as you say you have all the railroads but the Richmond and Fredericksburg. I am puzzled to see how, lacking that, you can have any, except the scrap from Richmond to West Point. The scrap of the Virginia Central from Richmond to Hanover Junction, without more, is simply nothing. That the whole of the enemy is concentrating on Richmond, I think cannot be certainly known to you or me. Saxton, at Harper's Ferry informs us that large forces, supposed to be Jackson's and Ewell's, forced his advance from Charlestown today. General King telegraphs us from Fredericksburg that contrabands give certain information that 15,000 left Hanover Junction Monday morning to reinforce Jackson. I am painfully impressed with the importance of the struggle before you, and shall aid you all I can consistently with my view of due regard to all points.

A. Lincoln.

---

1 McDowell replied: "I beg to assure you that I am doing everything which legs and steam are capable of to hurry forward matters in this quarter. I shall be deficient in wagons when I get out of the way of the railroad for transporting supplies, but shall push on nevertheless." (Ibid, 246)

2 The movement here referred to was against rebel forces at Hanover Court House, which threatened McDowell, and was in a position to re-enforce Jackson. The expedition was under command of General Fitz-John Porter, and proved a success. General McClellan on the 28th announced it to the Government as a "complete rout" of the rebels, and as entitling Porter to the highest honors. In the same dispatch he said he would do his best to cut off Jackson from returning to Richmond, but doubted if he could. The great battle was about to be fought before Richmond, and he adds: "It is the policy and the duty of the Government to send me by water all the well-drilled troops available. All unavailable troops should be collected here." Porter, he said, had cut all the railroads but the one from Richmond to Fredericksburg, which was the one concerning which the President had evinced the most anxiety. Another expedition was sent to the South Anna River and Ashland, which destroyed some bridges without opposition. This was announced to the government by McClellan as another "complete victory" achieved by the heroism of Porter and accompanied by the statement that the enemy were even in greater force than he had supposed. (Raymond 1865, 283)

Telegram to General Marcy, Washington, May 29, 1862, 10 A.M.[1]

General R. B. Marcy, McClellan's Headquarters:

Yours just received. I think it cannot be certainly known whether the force which fought General Porter is the same which recently confronted McDowell. Another item of evidence bearing on it is that General Branch commanded against Porter, while it was General Anderson who was in front of McDowell. He and McDowell were in correspondence about prisoners.

A. Lincoln.

Telegram to General G. B. McClellan, War Department, Washington City, May 29, 1862, 10:30 A.M.[2]

Major General McClellan:

I think we shall be able within three days to tell you certainly whether any considerable force of the enemy—Jackson or anyone else—is moving on to Harper's Ferry or vicinity. Take this expected development into your calculations.

A. Lincoln.

Telegram to General N. P. Banks, Washington, May 29, 1862.[3]

Major General Banks, Williamsport, Maryland:

General McDowell's advance should, and probably will, be at or near Front Royal at twelve (noon) tomorrow. General Frémont will be at or near Strasburg as soon. Please watch the enemy closely, and follow and harass and detain him if he attempts to retire. I mean this for General Saxton's force as well as that immediately with you.

A. Lincoln.

Telegram to General Frémont, Washington, May 29, 1862, 12 M.[4]

Major General Frémont, Moorefield, Virginia:

---

1 Marcy replied: "In answer to your dispatch of this morning I have the honor to state that several rebel officers, taken prisoners on the 27th, say they confidently expected to have been re-enforced on that day by Anderson's command. General Porter reports that South Anna railroad bridge was fired this morning, and a large amount of Confederate property destroyed at Ashland. General Porter's command is now on its march back to this place, having executed his instructions." (Lincoln v.5, 1953, 248)

2 No response located.

3 Banks replied: "My command is much disabled, but we will do what we can to carry out your views." (Lincoln v.5, 1953, 247)

4 On May 28, Stanton telegraphed Lincoln's direction that Fremont should halt at Moorefield and await orders unless the enemy should be in the general direction of Romney, in which case Fremont should move upon him. Fremont telegraphed to Stanton the following day that Lincoln's order, "Will be obeyed as promptly as possible, and I am now engaged in drawing forward my force. My reconnoitering parties out last night 22 miles, to Wardensville, report Jackson's force 4 miles below Winchester; rear guard at Strasburg; head-quarters, Winchester. Reconnaissance returned to Romney at 11 last night from 15

General McDowell's advance, if not checked by the enemy, should, and probably will, be at Front Royal by twelve (noon) tomorrow. His force, when up, will be about 20,000. Please have your force at Strasburg, or, if the route you are moving on does not lead to that point, as near Strasburg as the enemy may be by the same time. Your dispatch No.30 received and satisfactory.

A. Lincoln.

Telegram to General I. McDowell, Washington, May 29, 1862.[1]

Major General McDowell, Manassas Junction:

General Frémont's force should, and probably will, be at or near Strasburg by twelve (noon) tomorrow. Try to have your force, or the advance of it, at Front Royal as soon.

A. Lincoln.

Telegram to General Marcy, Washington, May 29, 1862, 1:20 P.M.[2]

General R. B. Marcy:

Your dispatch as to the South Anna and Ashland being seized by our forces this morning is received. Understanding these points to be on the Richmond and Fredericksburg railroad, I heartily congratulate the country, and thank General McClellan and his army for their seizure.

A. Lincoln.

Telegram to General I. McDowell, Washington, May 30, 1862, 10 A.M.[3]

Major General McDowell, Manassas Junction:

---

miles out. Report Jackson, [Edward] Johnson, and Ewell at Chester, and rebel cavalry sent from Winchester toward Harper's Ferry and Martinsburg." (Ibid)

1 McDowell responded to Stanton: "Shields reported an accident on the railroad at Thoroughfare Gap which he feared could not be repaired under twenty-four hours.... I sent him the President's telegram and he reports he will make such arrangements that will enable him to be in Front Royal before 12 o'clock m. to-morrow, with his other two brigades within 4 miles of the town by the same hour. Since then the locomotive and force sent from here have repaired the break in the road...." (Ibid)

2 No response located.

3 McDowell replied: "I am pushing forward everything to the utmost as I telegraphed the Secy of War last night. Major General Shields did not think he could make Front Royal before tonight. I sent him your telegraph and asked what could be done by extraordinary exertions, towards accomplishing your wishes that the advance of my force should be at Front Royal by twelve oclock noon today I informed him of the position of affairs and how necessary it was to forward He fully appreciated the course and said he would...be at Front Royal by noon and two other Brigades within five miles of Front Royal by the same time. It will require driving to accomplish this and the day is hot. I am urging Genl Ord forward with all the physical power of the Rail Road & of the moral power of a strong representation of the urgency of the cause he may be beyond Rectorstown tonight. Genl Shields has ten thousand nine hundred...men & Genl Ord nine thousand about 20000 between them Bayards cavalry brigade will amount to about two thousand 2000 Gearys will amount to about fifteen hundred (1500) All this will give me about twenty one thousand 21000 men for offensive

I somewhat apprehend that Frémont's force, in its present condition, may not be quite strong enough in case it comes in collision with the enemy. For this additional reason I wish you to push forward your column as rapidly as possible. Tell me what number your force reaching Front Royal will amount to.

A. Lincoln.

Telegram to General N. P. Banks, Washington, May 30, 1862, 10:15 A.M.[1]

Major General Banks, Williamsport, Maryland, via Harper's Ferry:

If the enemy in force is in or about Martinsburg, Charlestown, and Winchester, Or any or all of them, he may come in collision with Frémont, in which case I am anxious that your force, with you and at Harper's Ferry, should so operate as to assist Frémont if possible; the same if the enemy should engage McDowell. This was the meaning of my dispatch yesterday.

A. Lincoln.

Telegram to General I. McDowell, Washington, May 30, 1862, 12:40 P.M.[2]

Major General McDowell, Rectortown:

Your dispatch of today received and is satisfactory. Frémont has nominally 22,000, really about 17,000. Blenker's division is part of it. I have a dispatch from Frémont this morning, not telling me where he is; but he says:

"Scouts and men from Winchester represent Jackson's force variously at 30,000 to 60,000. With him Generals Ewell and Longstreet."

The high figures erroneous, of course. Do you know where Longstreet is? Corinth is evacuated and occupied by us.

A. Lincoln.

Telegram to General Frémont, Washington, May 30, 1862, 2:30 P.M.[3]

Major General Frémont, Moorefield, Virginia:

---

purposes...the others being required to guard Bridges and Rail road in the rear.... May I ask the force which...Fremont will have with him at Strasburg...." (Lincoln v.5, 1953, 251)

1 Banks replied: "Your communication received. Have sent part of our force to Antietam Ford, near Shepherdstown. Will do all we can to harass the enemy's rear. No indication of enemy this side of Martinsburg, and we believe no considerable force there." (Ibid, 249)

2 No response located.

3 Fremont's dispatch of May 29, read, in part: "My command is not yet in marching order. It has been necessary to halt to-day to bring up parts of regiments and to receive stragglers, hundreds of whom from Blenker's division strewed the roads. You can conceive the condition of the command from the fact that the medical director this morning protested against its farther advance without allowing one day's rest.... I could not venture to proceed with it in disorder, and cannot with safety undertake to be at the point you mention earlier than by 5 o'clock on Saturday afternoon. At that hour I will be at or near it, according to position of the enemy.... Will be on the road early to-morrow...and couriers will be provided to bring on your answer, which please send to-night, and let me know if General McDowell's force can be so controlled as to make this combination." (Lincoln v.5, 1953, 250)

Yours, saying you will reach Strasburg or vicinity at 5 P.M. Saturday, has been received and sent to General McDowell, and he directed to act in view of it. You must be up to the time you promised, if possible.

Corinth was evacuated last night, and is occupied by our troops today; the enemy gone south to Okolotia, on the railroad to Mobile.

A. Lincoln.

Telegram to General I. McDowell, War Department Washington City, May 30, 1862, 9:30 P.M.[1]

Major General McDowell, Rectortown, Virginia:

I send you a dispatch just received from Saxton at Harper's Ferry: "The rebels are in line of battle in front of our lines. They have nine pieces of artillery, and in position, and cavalry. I shelled the woods in which they were, and they in return threw a large number of shells into the lines and tents from which I moved last night to take up a stronger position. I expect a great deal from the battery on the mountain, having three 9 inch Dahlgren bearing directly on the enemy's approaches. The enemy appeared this morning and then retired, with the intention of drawing us on. I shall act on the defensive, as my position is a strong one. In a skirmish which took place this afternoon I lost one horse. The enemy lost two men killed and seven wounded. R. Saxon, Brigadier General."

It seems the game is before you. Have sent a copy to General Frémont.

A. Lincoln.

Telegram to General G. B. McClellan, Washington, May 31, 1862, 10:20 P.M.[2]

Major General McClellan:

A circle whose circumference shall pass through Harper's Ferry, Front Royal, and Strasburg, and whose center shall be a little northeast of Winchester, almost certainly has within it this morning the forces of Jackson, Ewell, and Edward Johnson. Quite certainly they were within it two days ago. Some part of their forces attacked Harper's Ferry at dark last evening, and are still in sight this morning. Shields, with McDowell's advance, retook Front Royal at 11 A.M. yesterday, with a dozen of our own prisoners taken there a week ago, 150 of the enemy, two locomotives, and eleven cars, some other property and stores, and saved the bridge.

General Frémont, from the direction of Moorefield, promises to be at or near Strasburg at 5 P.M. today. General Banks at Williamsport, with his old force and his new force at Harper's Ferry, is directed to co-operate. Shields at Front Royal reports a rumor of still an additional force of the enemy, supposed to be Anderson's, having entered the valley of Virginia. This last may or may not be true. Corinth is certainly in the hands of General Halleck.

A. Lincoln.

---

1 No response located.
2 No response located.

Telegram to General G. B. McClellan, Washington City, June 1, 1862, 9:30 A.M.[1]

Major General McClellan:

You are probably engaged with the enemy. I suppose he made the attack. Stand well on your guard, hold all your ground, or yield any only inch by inch and in good order. This morning we merge General Wool's department into yours, giving you command of the whole, and sending General Dix to Port Monroe and General Wool to Fort McHenry. We also send General Sigel to report to you for duty.

A. Lincoln.

Telegram to General G. B. McClellan, Washington, June 3, 1862.[2]

Major General McClellan:

With these continuous rains I am very anxious about the Chickahominy so close in your rear and crossing your line of communication. Please look to it.

A. Lincoln, President.

Telegram to General I. McDowell, Washington, June 3, 1862, 6:15 P.M.[3]

Major General McDowell, Front Royal, Virginia:

Anxious to know whether Shields can head or flank Jackson. Please tell about where Shields and Jackson, respectively, are at the time this reaches you.

A. Lincoln.

Telegram to General H. W. Halleck, Washington, June 4, 1862.[4]

Major General Halleck, Corinth:

---

1 No response located.

2 McClellan replied: "Your dispatch of Five PM just received. As the Chickahominy has been almost the only obstacle in my way for several days your Excellency may rest assured that it has not been over-looked Every effort has been made and will continue to be to perfect the communication across it Nothing of importance except that it is again raining." (Lincoln v.5, 1953, 258)

3 The following day, McDowell replied that he could only infer the position of "Stonewall" Jackson's army, "...as I have nothing on that point from either Genl Fremont or Genl Shields Since Fremont has been in Woodstock Jackson has had time to be south of Mt Jackson with macadamized turnpike. Shields is at Luray---his advance at the Shenandoah on the road to New Market with an indifferent road which the constant rains are making bad and with the Shenandoah impassable and rising." (Ibid)

4 Halleck had telegraphed Stanton on June 4 that General John Pope was thirty miles south of Corinth and "...already reports 10,000 prisoners and deserters...and 15,000 stand of arms captured." Pope later denied ever having made such a report, but Halleck maintained that he had telegraphed "the exact language of General Pope. If it was erroneous, the responsibility is his, not mine." On June 5 Halleck telegraphed that "dispatch from Grand Junction says it was reported there that Memphis was evacuated on Saturday I have nothing to confirm the report & can hear nothing of the flotilla in the Mississippi River." (Ibid, 259)

Your dispatch of today to Secretary of War received. Thanks for the good news it brings. Have you anything from Memphis or other parts of the Mississippi River? Please answer.

A. Lincoln.

To General G. B. McClellan [Cipher] War Department, Washington, June 7, 1862.[1]

Major General McClellan:

Your dispatch about Chattanooga and Dalton was duly received and sent to General Halleck. I have just received the following answer from him: We have Fort Pillow, Randolph, and Memphis.

A. Lincoln.

Telegram to General H. W. Halleck, Washington, June 8, 1862.[2]

Major General Halleck, Corinth, Mississippi:

We are changing one of the departmental lines, so as to give you all of Kentucky and Tennessee. In your movement upon Chattanooga I think it probable that you include some combination of the force near Cumberland Gap under General Morgan. Do you?

A. Lincoln.

Telegram to General N. P. Banks., Washington, June 9, 1862.[3]

Major General Banks, Winchester:

We are arranging a general plan for the valley of the Shenandoah, and in accordance with this you will move your main force to the Shenandoah at or opposite Front Royal as soon as possible.

A. Lincoln.

Telegram to General J. C. Frémont, Washington, June 9, 1862.[4]

Major General Frémont:

Halt at Harrisonburg, pursuing Jackson no farther. Get your force well in hand and stand on the defensive, guarding against a movement of the enemy ei-

---

1 Halleck's telegram of June 7 reported: "Preparations for Chattanooga made five days ago & troops moved in that direction." (Ibid, 263)

2 *General Orders No. 62*, June 8, 1862, extended the Department of the Mississippi to include the whole of Tennessee and Kentucky. No reply from Halleck to Lincoln's question has been located, but Brigadier General George W. Morgan was at Bowman, Tennessee, on June 13. (Ibid, 264)

3 Banks replied: "Your orders shall be faithfully executed...." (Ibid, 264)

4 This in response to Fremont's June 7 note to Stanton that reported the arrival of his army at Harrisonburg "...at 2 o'clock yesterday afternoon, driving out the enemy's rear guard.... The condition of the force is extremely bad, for want of supplies...." (Ibid)

ther back toward Strasburg or toward Franklin, and await further orders, which will soon be sent you.

A. Lincoln.

To General J. C. Frémont, Washington, June 12, 1862.[1]

Major General Frémont:

Accounts, which we do not credit, represent that Jackson is largely reinforced and turning upon you. Get your forces well in hand and keep us well and frequently advised; and if you find yourself really pressed by a superior force of the enemy, fall back cautiously toward or to Winchester, and we will have in due time Banks in position to sustain you. Do not fall back upon Harrisonburg unless upon tolerably clear necessity. We understand Jackson is on the other side of the Shenandoah from you, and hence cannot in any event press you into any necessity of a precipitate withdrawal.

A. Lincoln.

P.S. Yours, preferring Mount Jackson to Harrisonburg, is just received. On this point use your discretion, remembering that our object is to give such protection as you can to western Virginia. Many thanks to yourself, officers, and men for the gallant battle of last Sunday. A. L.

To General J. C. Frémont, Washington, June 13. 1862.[2]

Major General Frémont:

We cannot afford to keep your force and Banks's and McDowell's engaged in keeping Jackson south of Strasburg and Front Royal. You fought Jackson alone and worsted him. He can have no substantial reinforcements so long as a battle is pending at Richmond. Surely you and Banks in supporting distance are capable

---

1 Fremont had telegraphed from Harrisonburg, Virginia, June 11, "Will you allow me to halt at Mount Jackson instead of Harrisonburg, which is not a line of defense, and exposes me to be cut off.... My troops are very much distressed for want of supplies...." Generals McDowell and [Franz] Sigel reported to Stanton June 12, that "Jackson has been re-enforced to the number of 30,000 or 35,000 men." Stanton telegraphed Sigel on June 12 that "It cannot be possible that Jackson has any such re-enforcement as 30,000 or 35,000.... The President directs that your forces and Banks' shall not fall back from Front Royal and their present positions until further developments." (Ibid, 268)

2 Fremont replied from Mount Jackson on June 12: "Upon intelligence of Genl Shields defeat and withdrawal towards Richmond I retired upon this place which is a defensible and good position. The Regiments composing my command have been rendered very weak by illness casualties and deaths. I request that orders be given to recruit them to full strength immediately. Their condition necessitates that they have some days rest and good and sufficient food. The demand made upon them in the pursuit of Jackson has exhausted them for the present and they should be supported by fresh troops. At any hour they may be attacked by the Enemy now reported strong [sic] reinforced and I ask that Genl Sigel be telegraphed to report to me with his force without delay. I respectfully suggest to the President that it may prove disastrous to separate the small corps now operating in this region...consolidated they could act offensively and efficiently against the enemy. I also suggest that Gen Shields may be attacked on his march Eastward unless supported. My strength should be sufficient to enable me to occupy the Monteray passes & aid Gen [J. D.] Cox and Col [George] Crook against whom I think the Enemy is likely to concentrate a superior force. I have asked for Sigel.... If possible Banks also should come. A disaster now would have consequences difficult to remedy." (Ibid, 269-70)

---

of keeping him from returning to Winchester. But if Sigel be sent forward to you, and McDowell (as he must) be put to other work, Jackson will break through at Front Royal again. He is already on the right side of the Shenandoah to do it, and on the wrong side of it to attack you. The orders already sent you and Banks place you and him in the proper positions for the work assigned you. Jackson cannot move his whole force on either of you before the other can learn of it and go to his assistance. He cannot divide his force, sending part against each of you, because he will be too weak for either. Please do as I directed in the order of the 8th and my dispatch of yesterday, the 12th, and neither you nor Banks will be overwhelmed by Jackson. By proper scout lookouts, and beacons of smoke by day and fires by night you can always have timely notice of the enemy's approach. I know not as to you, but by some this has been too much neglected.

    A. Lincoln.

To General J. C. Frémont, War Department, Washington City, June 15, 1862.[1]

Major General Frémont:

Your letter of the 12th by Colonel Zagonyi is just received. In answer to the principal part of it, I repeat the substance of an order of the 8th and one or two telegraphic dispatches sent you since.

We have no definite power of sending reinforcements; so that we are compelled rather to consider the proper disposal of the forces we have than of those we could wish to have. We may be able to send you some dribs by degrees, but I do not believe we can do more. As you alone beat Jackson last Sunday, I argue that you are stronger than he is today, unless he has been reinforced; and that he cannot have been materially reinforced, because such reinforcement could only have come from Richmond, and he is much more likely to go to Richmond than Richmond is to come to him. Neither is very likely. I think Jackson's game—his assigned work—now is to magnify the accounts of his numbers and reports of his movements, and thus by constant alarms keep three or four times as many of our troops away from Richmond as his own force amounts to. Thus he helps his friends at Richmond three or four times as much as if he were there. Our game

---

1 As Jackson's successful Shenandoah Valley campaign moved to a close in early June 1862, Lincoln nonetheless emerged in a favorable light. Far from panicking when Jackson advanced toward the Potomac River during the last week of May, Lincoln used the rebel threat in an effort to force McClellan to attack the Confederate army protecting Richmond. Lincoln manifested a sound grasp of Union and Confederate strategy, an understanding of his generals' personalities, and a resolute determination to prod—almost to will— his commanders to act in such a way as to forge victories outside Richmond and in the Shenandoah Valley. From the Confederate perspective, Jackson began the campaign with a reputation based largely on his role at the battle of First Manassas. Although generally admired and blessed with one of the best sobriquets ("Stonewall") in American military history, he did not rank alongside more famous Confederate generals such as the Johnstons and Beauregard. It was Valley campaign that catapulted him into national prominence. In stark contrast to Jackson, the principal Federal generals in the Valley campaign have been criticized, or even ridiculed, by innumerable historians and other writers. Banks, Frémont, Shields, Milroy, and McDowell appear as clumsy foils to the brilliant Stonewall, bumbling their way—some historians have detected no martial genius in any of these men—through a comedy of errors and frustrating Lincoln in the process. (Gallagher 2003, 3, xviii-xix)

is not to allow this. Accordingly, by the order of the 8th, I directed you to halt at Harrisonburg, rest your force, and get it well in hand, the objects being to guard against Jackson's returning by the same route to the upper Potomac over which you have just driven him out, and at the same time give some protection against a raid into West Virginia.

Already I have given you discretion to occupy Mount Jackson instead, if, on full consideration, you think best. I do not believe Jackson will attack you, but certainly he cannot attack you by surprise; and if he comes upon you in superior force, you have but to notify us, fall back cautiously, and Banks will join you in due time. But while we know not whether Jackson will move at all, or by what route, we cannot safely put you and Banks both on the Strasburg line, and leave no force on the Front Royal line—the very line upon which he prosecuted his late raid. The true policy is to place one of you on one line and the other on the other in such positions that you can unite once you actually find Jackson moving upon it. And this is precisely what we are doing. This protects that part of our frontier, so to speak, and liberates McDowell to go to the assistance of McClellan. I have arranged this, and am very unwilling to have it deranged. While you have only asked for Sigel, I have spoken only of Banks, and this because Sigel's force is now the principal part of Bank's force.

About transferring General Schenck's commands, the purchase of supplies, and the promotion and appointment of officers, mentioned in your letter, I will consult with the Secretary of War tomorrow.

Yours truly,

A. Lincoln.

To General J. C. Frémont, Washington, June 16, 1862.[1]

Major General Frémont, Mount Jackson, Virginia:

Your dispatch of yesterday, reminding me of a supposed understanding that I would furnish you a corps of 35,000 men, and asking of me the "fulfilment of this understanding," is received. I am ready to come to a fair settlement of accounts with you on the fulfilment of understandings.

---

1 As background to this letter, it is well to remember that a new department had been created for Frémont, in the hope that he would early occupy Knoxville, or at least effectively break the railway communication between that city and Lynchburg. After two months, however, he was still remote from the intended scene of his main operations. When Jackson was putting Banks to flight in the latter part of May, Frémont was at Franklin, in West Virginia, midway between Beverly and Harrisonburg, with lagging trains forty miles in his rear, at Moorefield. He was ordered on the 24th to "move against Jackson at Harrisonburg," in support of Banks, and was told that the movement "must be made immediately." The distance from his position directly across the mountain to Harrisonburg was comparatively short, and the road, though not of the best, was passable. Frémont, nevertheless, countermarched to Moorefield, and crossed from that place into the Shenandoah Valley well down toward Winchester, spoiling the President's carefully laid plan to corner Jackson. Frémont arrived just too late, though the enemy did not escape without some trouble. Fighting with Frémont on the 8th of June, and the next day with a brigade of Shields (of McDowell's corps) at Port Republic, Jackson freed himself from his opponents and retired from the valley without serious loss. The President was disappointed and chagrined. (Barrett 1904, 69-70)

Early in March last, when I assigned you to the command of the Mountain Department, I did tell you I would give you all the force I could, and that I hoped to make it reach 35,000. You at the same time told me that within a reasonable time you would seize the railroad at or east of Knoxville, Tenn., if you could. There was then in the department a force supposed to be 25,000, the exact number as well known to you as to me. After looking about two or three days, you called and distinctly told me that if I would add the Blenker division to the force already in the department, you would undertake the job. The Blenker division contained 10,000, and at the expense of great dissatisfaction to General McClellan I took it from his army and gave it to you. My promise was literally fulfilled. I have given you all I could, and I have given you very nearly, if not quite, 35,000.

Now for yours. On the 23d of May, largely over two months afterward, you were at Franklin, Va., not within 300 miles of Knoxville, nor within 80 miles of any part of the railroad east of it, and not moving forward, but telegraphing here that you could not move for lack of everything. Now, do not misunderstand me. I do not say you have not done all you could. I presume you met unexpected difficulties; and I beg you to believe that as surely as you have done your best, so have I. I have not the power now to fill up your Corps to 35,000. I am not demanding of you to do the work of 35,000. I am only asking of you to stand cautiously on the defensive, get your force in order, and give such protection as you can to the valley of the Shenandoah and to western Virginia.

Have you received the orders, and will you act upon them?

A. Lincoln.

To General C. Schurz, Washington, June 16, 1862.[1]

Brigadier General Schurz, Mount Jackson, Virginia:

Your long letter is received. The information you give is valuable. You say it is fortunate that Frémont did not intercept Jackson; that Jackson had the superior force, and would have overwhelmed him. If this is so, how happened it that Frémont fairly fought and routed him on the 8th? Or is the account that he did fight and rout him false and fabricated? Both General Frémont and you speak of Jackson having beaten Shields. By our accounts he did not beat Shields. He had no engagement with Shields. He did meet and drive back with disaster about 2000 of Shields's advance till they were met by an additional brigade of Shields's,

---

1 A superior politician and abolitionist, Carl Schurz was educated at the universities in Cologne and Bonn. He served the German Revolution as a junior officer and, upon the defeat of the revolution, he fled, first to Switzerland and then to France. Expelled from France, he lived briefly in England and then migrated to the United States in 1852. At the start of the war he was minister to Spain, but resigned in 1862 to urge immediate emancipation of the slaves. Lincoln demurred, but made Schurz a brigadier general of volunteers, a political move designed to enhance German-American support for the war. Schurz led a division with some ability in the Second Bull Run Campaign. Made a major general in March of 1863, his division performed poorly as part of XI Corps at Chancellorsville that spring. At Gettysburg he briefly commanded the corps, but neither it, nor his division performed with brilliance, though he did manage to hold the line on Cemetery Hill on 2 July. Later that year Schurz went West with his division, where it again did poorly at Chattanooga. Relieved, he spent the next year in administrative posts and stumping the country for Lincoln's reelection. (Nofi 1995, 158-9)

when Jackson himself turned and retreated. Shields himself and more than half his force were not nearer than twenty miles to any of it.

A. Lincoln.

Telegram to General H. W. Halleck, Washington, June 18, 1862.[1]

Major General Halleck, Corinth, Mississippi:

It would be of both interest and value to us here to know how the expedition toward East Tennessee is progressing, if in your judgment you can give us the information with safety.

A. Lincoln.

Telegram to General G. B. McClellan, War Department, Washington, June 18, 1862.2

Major General McClellan:

Yours of today, making it probable that Jackson has been reinforced by about 10,000 from Richmond, is corroborated by a dispatch from General King at Fredericksburg, saying a Frenchman, just arrived from Richmond by way of Gordonsville, met 10,000 to 15,000 passing through the latter place to join Jackson.

If this is true, it is as good as a reinforcement to you of an equal force. I could better dispose of things if I could know about what day you can attack Richmond, and would be glad to be informed, if you think you can inform me with safety.

A. Lincoln.

Telegram to General G. B. McClellan, Washington, June 19, 1862.[3]

Major General McClellan:

Yours of last night just received, and for which I thank you.

If large reinforcements are going from Richmond to Jackson, it proves one of two things: either they are very strong at Richmond, or do not mean to defend the place desperately.

On reflection, I do not see how reinforcements from Richmond to Jackson could be in Gordonsville, as reported by the Frenchman and your deserters. Have not all been sent to deceive?

A. Lincoln.

---

1 Halleck replied on June 21, "Genl Buell's column is at Tuscumbia As soon [as] the bridge at that place is rebuilt he will move east more rapidly. The enemy has evacuated Cumberland Gap. Must very soon leave all East Tennessee. Out troops have reached Memphis & the Railroad connection will be complete in a few days." (Lincoln v.5, 1953, 276)

2 McClellan telegraphed Stanton at 10:30 A. M., June 18, that several deserters had stated that troops including "a considerable portion of Longstreets Division" had left Richmond to reinforce Jackson. (Ibid.)

3 McClellan's reply argued that "If ten 10 or fifteen 15 thousand men have left Richmond to reinforce Jackson it illustrates their strength and confidence. After tomorrow, we shall fight the rebel Army as soon as Providence will permit. We shall await only a favorable condition of the earth and sky and the completion of some necessary preliminaries." (Ibid, 277)'

Telegram to General G. B. McClellan, War Department, Washington, June 20, 1862.[1]

Major General McClellan:

In regard to the contemplated execution of Captains Spriggs and Triplett the government has no information whatever, but will inquire and advise you.

A. Lincoln.

Telegram to General G. B. McClellan, Washington City, June 20, 1862.[2]

Major General McClellan:

We have this morning sent you a dispatch of General Sigel corroborative of the proposition that Jackson is being reinforced from Richmond. This may be reality, and yet may only be contrivance for deception, and to determine which is perplexing. If we knew it was not true, we could send you some more force; but as the case stands we do not think we safely can. Still, we will watch the signs and do so if possible.

In regard to a contemplated execution of Captains Spriggs and Triplett the government has no information whatever, but will inquire and advise you.

A. Lincoln.

Telegram to General G. B. McClellan, Washington, June 21, 1862, 6 P.M.[3]

Major General George B. McClellan:

---

1   Captains John Spriggs, and Marshall Triplett, Virginia Partisan Rangers, were captured by Union forces and branded as outlaws, not soldiers. They were sentenced to be hung as common criminals. Confederate authorities were outraged when word of this reached them, and they were ready to retaliate with the execution of two captured Union officers. After the intervention of Lee, Lincoln, Stanton and host of other influential Union and Confederate officials both sides eventually agreed that the prisoners in question would be treated as prisoners of war. (Sutherland 2009, 96-96)

2   At this juncture, Lincoln was not particularly satisfied with this new command arrangement in the Shenandoah. He knew that lack of good central control over the three commands there—Frémont, Banks and McDowell—had helped Jackson escape his trap of late May. Less than two weeks after he organized the new command setup he again altered command arrangements by joining McDowell's, Banks' and Frémont's commands into the Army of Virginia under command of a newcomer, Maj. Gen. John Pope, who had had some success on the Mississippi. Pope's assigned objective was to coordinate the defense of the Shenandoah with an offensive towards Richmond. As Lincoln rearranged his armies in the Valley, Lee decided to take advantage of the suspension of activity. Jackson would not be hurled against the Yankee defenders of Winchester. Instead, he was called to Richmond on 16 June, to help drive off McClellan. On 17 June, Jackson and his battle-hardened veterans began leaving the Valley to join Lee's army before Richmond. Their arrival meant much more than their mere numbers. (Martin 1994, 192)

3   McClellan's reply reported further on the "great... difficulties" confronting him and his "inferiority in numbers," and concluded by suggesting that "I would be glad to have permission to lay before your Excellency by letter or telegram my views as to the present state of Military affairs throughout the whole country. In the mean time I would be pleased to learn the disposition as to numbers and position of the troops not under my command in Virginia and elsewhere." (Lincoln v.5, 1953, 279-280)

Your dispatch of yesterday (2 P. M.) was received this morning. If it would not divert too much of your time and attention from the army under your immediate command, I would be glad to have your views as to the present state of military affairs throughout the whole country, as you say you would be glad to give them. I would rather it should be by letter than by telegraph, because of the better chance of secrecy. As to the numbers and positions of the troops not under your command in Virginia and elsewhere, even if I could do it with accuracy, which I cannot, I would rather not transmit either by telegraph or by letter, because of the chances of its reaching the enemy. I would be very glad to talk with you, but you cannot leave your camp, and I cannot well leave here.

A. Lincoln, President.

Telegram to General N. P. Banks, War Department, June 22, 1862.[1]

Major General Banks, Middletown:
I am very glad you are looking well to the west for a movement of the enemy in that direction. You know my anxiety on that point.

All was quiet at General McClellan's headquarters at two o'clock today.

A. Lincoln.

To General G. B. McClellan, Washington, June 26, 1862.[2]

Major General McClellan:
Your three dispatches of yesterday in relation to the affair, ending with the statement that you completely succeeded in making your point, are very gratifying.

The later one of 6:15 P.M., suggesting the probability of your being overwhelmed by two hundred thousand, and talking of where the responsibility will belong, pains me very much. I give you all I can, and act on the presumption that you will do the best you can with what you have, while you continue, ungenerously I think, to assume that I could give you more if I would. I have omitted, and shall omit, no opportunity to send you reinforcements whenever I possibly can.

A. Lincoln.

P. S. General Pope thinks if you fall back it would be much better towards York River than towards the James. As Pope now has charge of the capital, please confer with him through the telegraph.

---

1 Banks and Frémont were at Middleton, in the Shenandoah Valley. Neither Corps was well supplied and Frémont's was in especially bad condition in every respect. (Pope 1998, 128)

2 On this same date McClellan was officially notified of the consolidation of the forces of McDowell, Banks, and Fremont, constituting the Army of Virginia, which was to be under the command of Major-General John Pope, called east for that purpose after the occupation of Corinth. The assurance was given that this army would promptly co-operate with that under McClellan, moving southward by land. (Barrett 1904, 61)

Order Constituting the Army of Virginia, Executive Mansion, Washington, June 26, 1862.[1]

Ordered:

1st. The forces under Major Generals Frémont, Banks, and McDowell, including the troops now under Brigadier General Sturgis at Washington, shall be consolidated and form one army, to be called the Army of Virginia.

2d. The command of the Army of Virginia is specially assigned to Major General John Pope, as commanding general. The troops of the Mountain Department, heretofore under command of General Frémont, shall constitute the First Army Corps, under the command of General Frémont; the troops of the Shenandoah Department, now under General Banks, shall constitute the Second Army Corps, and be commanded by him; the troops under the command of General McDowell, except those within the fortifications and city of Washington, shall form the Third Army Corps, and be under his command.

3d. The Army of Virginia shall operate in such manner as, while protecting western Virginia and the national capital from danger or insult, it shall in the speediest manner attack and overcome the rebel forces under Jackson and Ewell, threaten the enemy in the direction of Charlottesville, and render the most effective aid to relieve General McClellan and capture Richmond.

4th. When the Army of the Potomac and the Army of Virginia shall be in position to communicate and directly co-operate at or before Richmond, the chief command, while so operating together, shall be governed, as in like cases, by the Rules and Articles of War.

A. Lincoln.

Telegram to General A. E. Burnside, Washington, June 28, 1862.[2]

General Burnside:

I think you had better go, with any reinforcements you can spare, to General McClellan.

A. Lincoln.

---

1 Lincoln created the Army of Virginia under Major General John Pope, drawn from the forces of McDowell, Frémont, Banks, and those guarding the capital. Lincoln ordered them to protect Washington and western Virginia from Confederate depredations, particularly those of Jackson and Ewell (who, unknown to Lincoln, had already rejoined Lee's army). They would also provide another prong of a Union attack against Richmond; however, Lee's offensive, and McClellan's retreat to the James River, thwarted this strategy. (Stoker 210, 159)

2 On June 25 McClellan had ordered Burnside at New Bern, North Carolina, to "advance on Goldsborough [North Carolina] with all your available forces at the earliest practicable moment...destroying all the railroad communications in the direction of Richmond in your power...." Stanton telegraphed Burnside at 6 P.M. on June 28, "Since the dispatches of the President and myself to you of to-day we have seen a copy of one sent to you by...McClellan on the 25th, of which we were not aware. Our directions were not designed to interfere... but only to authorize...any aid in your power." (Lincoln v.5, 1953, 288)

Telegram to General G. B. McClellan, War Department, Washington City, June 28, 1862.[1]

Major General McClellan:

Save your army, at all events. Will send reinforcements as fast as we can. Of course they cannot reach you today, tomorrow, or next day. I have not said you were ungenerous for saying you needed reinforcements. I thought you were ungenerous in assuming that I did not send them as fast as I could. I feel any misfortune to you and your army quite as keenly as you feel it yourself. If you have had a drawn battle, or a repulse, it is the price we pay for the enemy not being in Washington. We protected Washington, and the enemy concentrated on you. Had we stripped Washington, he would have been upon us before the troops could have gotten to you. Less than a week ago you notified us that reinforcements were leaving Richmond to come in front of us. It is the nature of the case, and neither you nor the government is to blame. Please tell at once the present condition and aspect of things.

A. Lincoln.

Telegram to General J. A. Dix, War Department, Washington, June 28, 1862. [2]

General Dix:

Communication with McClellan by White House is cut off. Strain every nerve to open communication with him by James River, or any other way you can. Report to me.

A. Lincoln.

Telegram to General J. A. Dix, War Department, Washington City, June 30, 1862.[3]

Major General Dix, Fort Monroe:

---

1 In this note, Lincoln offers a few conciliatory words to McClelland who had been shaken by defeat in the battle of Gaines's Mill, the second of the Seven Days engagement. Lee had saved Richmond and, from Gaines's Mill on the north to Harrison's Landing on the south, the whole country-side was covered with freshly made graves and still unburied dead, with abandoned munitions of war. For weeks the agents of the Confederacy gathered in the spoils. (Beymer 2003, 129)

2 All telegraphic communication with McClellan had ceased shortly before noon on Saturday, June 28, at the time of the Confederate seizure of White House, McClellan's base of operations. (Andrews 1955, 689) It should be noted that "White House" was, in fact, the 4,000-acre plantation in New Kent County, Virginia, which William Henry Fitzhugh "Rooney" Lee, the general's second son, inherited from his grandfather G. W. P. Custis. (Allan 1996, 21)

3 Dix telegraphed Stanton at 11 A.M., "Will you please say to President Lincoln that the report from Williamsburg is just in. The enemy had not been at White House at 8 o'clock last evening. Our pickets extend to New Kent Court-House, 6 miles this side." At 2 P.M. he replied to Lincoln's dispatch, "We have no doubt that McClellan intended to abandon the White House. Our only line of communication with him by telegraph from that point would be along the railroad, which the enemy will hardly give up. "The communication of... Goldsborough, telegraphed to Gideon Welles, will have advised you that the general relies on the James River for all his communications hereafter. The commodore was with me an hour ago. I suggested we should extend our wires from Williamsburg to the mouth of the

---

Is it not probable that the enemy has abandoned the line between White House and McClellan's rear? He could have but little object to maintain it, and nothing to subsist upon. Would not Stoneman better move up and see about it? I think a telegraphic communication can at once be opened to White House from Williamsburg. The wires must be up still.

A. Lincoln.

Telegram to General H. W. Halleck, Washington, June 30, 1862.[1]

Major General Halleck, Corinth, Mississippi:

Would be very glad of 25,000 infantry; no artillery or cavalry; but please do not send a man if it endangers any place you deem important to hold, or if it forces you to give up or weaken or delay the expedition against Chattanooga. To take and hold the railroad at or east of Cleveland, in East Tennessee, I think fully as important as the taking and holding of Richmond.

A. Lincoln.

Telegram to General McClellan, Washington, July 1, 1862, 3:30 P.M.[2]

Major General George B. McClellan:

It is impossible to reinforce you for your present emergency. If we had a million of men, we could not get them to you in time. We have not the men to send. If you are not strong enough to face the enemy, you must find a place of security, and wait, rest, and repair. Maintain your ground if you can, but save the army at all events, even if you fall back to Fort Monroe. We still have strength enough in the country, and will bring it out.

A. Lincoln.

To General G. B. McClellan, War Department, Washington, July 2, 1862.[3]

Major General McClellan:

Chickahominy and there communicate by the James River by steamers or carry them on the left bank of the river to Turkey Island Point.... The general has all the materials of the working party with him.... We have no material here. I will make a reconnaissance in the vicinity of the White House, to ascertain whether the enemy are there." (Lincoln v.5, 1953, 294-295)

1 Halleck was able to convince Lincoln that sending so many men would indeed endanger Buell's campaign, but the president was so pressured by events in Virginia that he repeated his request on July 2 and 4th, receiving the same general reply from Halleck. (Hess 2000, 15)

2 This in response to McClellan's June 30 telegram to Stanton that stated, "Another day of desperate fighting. We are hard pressed by superior numbers.... You must send me very large reinforcements by way of Fort Monroe and they must come very promptly.... My Army has... done all that men could do, if none of us escape we shall at least have done honor to the country. I shall do my best to save the Army...." (Lincoln v.5, 1953, 298)

3 When this letter was written, there can be no doubt of Lincoln's intention to support McClellan in an early resumption of his campaign. From every available source, meanwhile, from Hunter at Hilton Head, Burnside at New Berne, Halleck at Corinth, and certain commands around Washington, detachments were ordered to the Peninsula. Most of these, it should be said, for one reason or another, never reached McClellan. (Rothschild 1906, 394)

Your dispatch of Tuesday morning induces me to hope your army is having some rest. In this hope allow me to reason with you a moment. When you ask for 50,000 men to be promptly sent you, you surely labor under some gross mistake of fact. Recently you sent papers showing your disposal of forces made last spring for the defense of Washington, and advising a return to that plan. I find it included in and about Washington 75,000 men.

Now, please be assured I have not men enough to fill that very plan by 15,000. All of Frémont's in the valley, all of Banks's, all of McDowell's not with you, and all in Washington, taken together, do not exceed, if they reach, 60,000. With Wool and Dix added to those mentioned, I have not, outside of your army, 75,000 men east of the mountains. Thus the idea of sending you 50,000, or any other considerable force, promptly, is simply absurd.

If, in your frequent mention of responsibility, you have the impression that I blame you for not doing more than you can, please be relieved of such impression. I only beg that in like manner you will not ask impossibilities of me. If you think you are not strong enough to take Richmond just now, I do not ask you to try just now. Save the army, material and personal, and I will strengthen it for the offensive again as fast as I can. The governors of eighteen States offer me a new levy of 300,000, which I accept.

A. Lincoln.

To General H. W. Halleck, Washington, D.C. July 2, 1862.[1]

Major General Halleck, Corinth, Mississippi:

Your several dispatches of yesterday to Secretary of War and myself received. I did say, and now repeat, I would be exceedingly glad for some reinforcements from you. Still do not send a man if in your judgment it will endanger any point you deem important to hold, or will force you to give up or weaken or delay the Chattanooga expedition.

Please tell me could you not make me a flying visit for consultation without endangering the Service in your department.

A. Lincoln.

To General G. B. McClellan, War Department Washington, July 3, 1862[2]

Major General George B. McClellan:

---

1 Halleck replied: "The Enemy attacked us at Booneville yesterday in considerable force.... Particulars not yet received.... According to reports...[Braxton] Bragg is preparing to attack us.... Under these circumstances I do not think I could safely be absent from my Army, although being somewhat broken in health and wearied...a trip to Washington would be exceedingly desirable." (Lincoln v.5, 1953, 301)

2 McClellan's dispatch of 5:30 P.M., July 2, sent from Berkeley, Harrison's Bar, via Fort Monroe, read in part: "I have succeeded in getting this army to this place on the banks of the James.... I have lost but one gun.... An hour and a half ago the rear of the wagon train was within a mile of camp, and only one wagon abandoned. As usual, we had a severe battle yesterday and beat the enemy badly, the men fighting even better than before. We fell back to this position during the night and morning. Officers and men thoroughly worn-out by fighting

Yours of 5:30 yesterday is just received. I am satisfied that yourself, officers, and men have done the best you could. All accounts say better fighting was never done. Ten thousand thanks for it.

On the 28th we sent General Burnside an order to send all the force he could spare to you. We then learned that you had requested him to go to Goldsborough; upon which we said to him our order was intended for your benefit, and we did not wish to be in conflict with your views.

We hope you will have help from him soon. Today we have ordered General Hunter to send you all he can spare. At last advices General Halleck thinks he cannot send reinforcements without endangering all he has gained.

A. Lincoln, President.

To General G. B. McClellan, War Department, Washington City, July 4, 1862.[1]

Major General McClellan:

I understand your position as stated in your letter and by General Marcy. To reinforce you so as to enable you to resume the offensive within a month, or even six weeks, is impossible. In addition to that arrived and now arriving from the Potomac (about 10,000 men, I suppose), and about 10,000 I hope you will have from Burnside very soon, and about 5000 from Hunter a little later, I do not see how I can send you another man within a month. Under these circumstances the defensive for the present must be your only care. Save the army first, where you are, if you can; secondly, by removal, if you must. You, on the ground, must be the judge as to which you will attempt, and of the means for effecting it. I but give it as my opinion that with the aid of the gunboats and the reinforcements mentioned above you can hold your present position—provided, and so long as, you can keep the James River open below you. If you are not tolerably confident you can keep the James River open, you had better remove as soon as possible. I do not remember that you have expressed any apprehension as to the danger of having your communication cut on the river below you, yet I do not suppose it can have escaped your attention.

---

every day and working every night for a week. They are in good spirits, and after a little rest will fight better than ever. If not attacked during this day I will have the men ready to repulse the enemy to-morrow.... Our losses have been very heavy, for we have fought every day since last Tuesday. I have not yielded an inch of ground unnecessarily, but have retired to prevent the superior force of the enemy from cutting me off and to take a different base of operations. I thank you for the re-enforcements. Every 1,000 men you send at once will help me much." At Lincoln's direction Stanton ordered Hunter at Hilton Head, South Carolina, to forward "all the infantry force that can be spared.... It is believed that you can forward 10,000...." (Ibid, 303)

1   On July 3, McClellan had one again pleaded for one hundred thousand men—"more rather than less"— in order to enable him to "accomplish the great task of capturing Richmond, and putting an end to the rebellion." McClellan said he hoped the enemy was as completely worn out as his own army, though he feared a new attack, from which, however, he trusted the bad condition of the roads might protect him. On the 4th, he repeated his call for heavy reinforcements, but said he held a very strong position, from which, with the aid of the gunboats, he could only be driven by overwhelming numbers. (Raymond and Carpenter 1865, 295) On the same day he received this patient response from a patient, but increasingly "McClellan weary" Lincoln

Yours very truly,

A. Lincoln.

P.S. If at any time you feel able to take the offensive, you are not restrained from doing so. A.L.

Telegram to General H. W. Halleck, War Department, July 4, 1862.[1]

Major General Halleck, Corinth, Mississippi:

You do not know how much you would oblige us if, without abandoning any of your positions or plans, you could promptly send us even 10,000 infantry. Can you not? Some part of the Corinth army is certainly fighting McClellan in front of Richmond. Prisoners are in our hands from the late Corinth army.

A. Lincoln.

Telegram to General G. B. McClellan, Washington, July 5, 1862. 9 A.M.[2]

Major General George B. McClellan:

A thousand thanks for the relief your two dispatches of 12 and 1 P.M. yesterday gave me. Be assured the heroism and skill of yourself and officers and men is, and forever will be, appreciated.

If you can hold your present position, we shall have the enemy yet.

A. Lincoln.

---

1 Halleck replied on July 5: "For the last week there has been great uneasiness among Union men in Tennessee on account of the secret organizations of insurgents to co-operate in any attack of the enemy on our lines. Every commanding officer from Nashville to Memphis has asked for re-enforcements.... I submitted the question of sending troops to Richmond to the principal officers of my command. They are unanimous in opinion that if this army is seriously diminished the Chattanooga expedition must be revoked or the hope of holding Southwest Tennessee abandoned. I must earnestly protest against surrendering what has cost us so much... and which in a military point of view is worth more than Richmond...." (Lincoln v.5, 1953, 305)

2 This note is in response to a lengthy McClellan letter detailing the engagement at Harrison's Landing that McClellan began with, "The enemy attacked the left of our lines, and a fierce battle ensued, lasting until night. They were repulsed with great slaughter." (McClellan 1864, 595) Burton, however, suggests a more modest perspective, noting that, on July 2, the Army of the Potomac marched to Harrison's Landing in a driving rain. Lee followed the next day, having been alerted by Jeb Stuart that McClellan had left Evelington Heights, a bluff commanding Harrison's Landing, unoccupied. But McClellan, perhaps reminded by Stuart's shelling him with a single gun, moved troops to the heights before Lee could arrive. The Seven Days' Battles were over, and with them not only McClellan's and the Union's best chance to take Richmond for more than two years, but also the best chance to restore the Union to a status quo that resembled 1860. From this moment on, the end of the war would likely mean revolutionary change in the political and social fabric of the nation. In the meantime, Confederate spirits soared. Despite a series of tactical defeats,. Lee had won a strategic victory, and he would maintain the initiative until September 17 along Antietam Creek near Sharpsburg, Maryland, where McClellan finally forced him to retreat. (Burton 2012)

To General H. W. Halleck, War Department, Washington City, July 6, 1862.[1]

Major General Halleck, Corinth, Mississippi:

This introduces Governor William Sprague, of Rhode Island. He is now Governor for the third time, and senator-elect of the United States.

I know the object of his visit to you. He has my cheerful consent to go, but not my direction. He wishes to get you and part of your force, one or both, to come here. You already know I should be exceedingly glad of this if, in your judgment, it could be without endangering positions and operations in the southwest; and I now repeat what I have more than once said by telegraph: "Do not come or send a man if, in your judgment, it will endanger any point you deem important to hold, or endangers or delays the Chattanooga expedition."

Still, please give my friend, Governor Sprague, a full and fair hearing.

Yours very truly,

A. Lincoln.

Order Making Halleck General-In-Chief, Executive Mansion, Washington, July 11, 1862.2

Ordered: That Major General Henry W. Halleck be assigned to command the whole land forces of the United States, as general-in-chief, and that he repair to this capital so soon as he can with safety to the positions and operations within the department now under his charge.

A. Lincoln.

Telegram to General H. W. Halleck. War Department, July 11, 1862.[3]

Major General Halleck, Corinth:

1 William Sprague (1830– 1915) had been elected governor of Rhode Island as a Democrat in 1859 and again in 1861. (Cooling 2007, 37) Kate Chase, daughter of Salmon Chase, Lincoln's treasury secretary, would wed William Sprague in October, 1863. (Guelzo 1999, 387)

2 Lincoln felt overwhelmed by his dual duties as general in chief and chief executive, and he began to search for someone to fill the top military post. There was no question that Buell was unsuitable, both for political reasons and for his lack of military success. Governor Johnson had no faith in the general's ability to "redeem east Tennessee." Halleck seemed the most likely choice. He was an effective administrator although a terrible field commander and Grant's successes had been made possible, in part, by his management of the western department. On July 11, Lincoln issued this order making Halleck general in chief. Other westerners, including Pope and Maj. Gen. Franz Sigel, had already been transferred to the East. (Hess 2000, 15)

3 Early July 1862 began a period of difficulty for Lincoln when two of the Confederacy's ablest and boldest cavalry leaders rode forth on raids deep behind Union lines to wreak havoc and capture supply depots all over central Kentucky and Tennessee. On July 4 John Hunt Morgan left Knoxville with eight hundred troopers, Kentucky rebels to a man. They headed north into their native state where during the next twenty-four days they rode a thousand miles, destroyed several supply depots, captured and paroled twelve hundred prisoners at various Union posts, and returned home with the loss of fewer than ninety men. Meanwhile Nathan Bedford Forrest rode out of Chattanooga on July 6 at the head of a thousand men.

Governor Johnson, at Nashville, is in great trouble and anxiety about a raid into Kentucky. The governor is a true and valuable man—indispensable to us in Tennessee. Will you please get in communication with him, and have a full conference with him before you leave for here? I have telegraphed him on the subject.

A. Lincoln.

To General G. B. McClellan, Executive Mansion, Washington, July 13, 1862.[1]

Major General McClellan:

I am told that over 160,000 men have gone into your army on the Peninsula. When I was with you the other day we made out 86,500 remaining, leaving 73,500 to be accounted for. I believe 23,500 will cover all the killed, wounded, and missing in all your battles and skirmishes, leaving 50,000 who have left otherwise. No more than 5000 of these have died, leaving 45,000 of your army still alive and not with it. I believe half or two-thirds of them are fit for duty today. Have you any more perfect knowledge of this than I have? If I am right, and you had these men with you, you could go into Richmond in the next three days. How can they be got to you, and how can they be prevented from getting away in such numbers for the future?

A. Lincoln.

Bluffing the Union garrison of equal size at Murfreesboro into surrendering, Forrest tore up the railroad, captured a million dollars' worth of supplies, and then burned three bridges on the line south of Nashville that Buell depended on for supplies. When Union crews finally repaired the damage, Morgan's merry men struck again, capturing a train and pushing the flaming boxcars into an 800-foot tunnel north of Nashville, causing the timbers to burn and the tunnel to collapse. All of this was embarrassing enough and convinced Union commanders that to cope with enemy cavalry raids they must develop effective cavalry of their own—something that was a long time in coming. But the damage to the Union cause was more than psychological. The Richmond Enquirer may have exaggerated when it claimed that "Forrest in Tennessee and Morgan in Kentucky have done much to retrieve the disasters that lost us parts of both those States." But it did not exaggerate much. "Our cavalry is paving the way for me in Middle Tennessee and Kentucky," wrote General Braxton Bragg in late July. (McPherson 2004, 75)

1 Responding to reports of ever-shrinking army personnel numbers, Lincoln realized he could not hope to learn the true facts from McClellan's inconsistent messages. Nor was he disposed, in view of the partisan feelings that had been aroused, to rely on the reports of others. Consequently, there appeared to be no alternative for him but to judge of the situation at Harrison's Landing with his own eyes. So, on the 8th of July, Lincoln paid McClellan a visit. The President stayed less than twenty-four hours, but he spent the time to advantage. A hasty inspection of the army, and conferences with principal officers, sufficiently revealed the condition of affairs. McClellan's 50,000 men had unaccountably become 86,500. But what troubled Lincoln more than this discrepancy between the commander's understated figures and his actual strength was the large number of soldiers, a host in itself, still missing from the ranks. "Sending men to that army," he once said, "is like shoveling fleas across a barn-yard...not half of them get there." Shortly after this visit to Harrison's Landing, Lincoln, with official returns before him, summed up his conclusions on the subject in this July 13 dispatch to McClellan. (Rothschild 1906, 395)

Telegram to General H. W. Halleck, War Department, July 13, 1862.[1]

Major General Halleck, Corinth, Mississippi:

They are having a stampede in Kentucky. Please look to it.

A. Lincoln.

Telegram to General J. T. Boyle, Washington, July 13, 1862.[2]

General J. T. Boyle, Louisville, Kentucky:

Your several dispatches received. You should call on General Halleck. Telegraph him at once. I have telegraphed him that you are in trouble.

A. Lincoln.

Telegram to General J. T. Boyle, War Department, July 13, 1862.[3]

General J. T. Boyle, Louisville, Kentucky:

We cannot venture to order troops from General Buell. We know not what condition he is in. He may be attacked himself. You must call on General Halleck, who commands, and whose business it is to understand and care for the whole field. If you cannot telegraph to him, send a messenger to him. A dispatch has this moment come from Halleck at Tuscombia, Alabama.

A. Lincoln.

Telegram to General H. W. Halleck, War Department, July 14, 1862.[4]

Major General Halleck, Corinth, Mississippi:

I am very anxious—almost impatient—to have you here. Have due regard to what you leave behind. When can you reach here?

A. Lincoln.

---

1 On July 14, Halleck ordered Buell to "Do all in your power to put down the Morgan raid even if the Chattanooga expedition should be delayed." (Lincoln v.5, 1953, 322)

2 From Louisville, Boyle had telegraphed both Halleck and Stanton on July 12 that Confederate General John H. Morgan was reported raiding in the vicinity of Danville, Harrodsburg, and Glasgow, Kentucky, with a cavalry force too large to be driven back with infantry alone. (Ibid., 321)

3 Boyle's dispatches to Stanton on July 13 reported Morgan's force at 2,800 to 3,000, and that requests for reinforcements from Buell remained unanswered. (Ibid.)

4 Halleck replied on July 15, "General Grant has just arrived from Memphis. I am in communication with General Buell and Governor Johnson in Tennessee. Hope to finally arrange disposition of troops and re-enforcements for General Curtis by to-morrow and to leave Thursday morning, the 17th." (Ibid, 323)

Telegram to General G. B. McClellan, War Department, Washington City, July 14, 1862.[1]

Major General McClellan:

General Burnside's force is at Newport News, ready to move, on short notice, one way or the other, when ordered.

A. Lincoln.

Telegram to General G. B. McClellan, War Department, Washington City, July 21, 1862.[2]

Major General McClellan:

This is Monday. I hope to be able to tell you on Thursday what is to be done with Burnside.

A. Lincoln.

Telegram to General S. R. Curtis, Washington, D.C. August 12, 1862.[3]

Major General Curtis, St. Louis, Missouri:

Would the completion of the railroad some distance farther in the direction of Springfield, Mo., be of any military advantage to you? Please answer.

A. Lincoln.

Telegram to General Burnside or General Parke, Washington, August 21, 1862. [4]

To General Burnside or General Parke:

What news about arrival of troops?

A. Lincoln.

Telegram to General G. B. McClellan, Washington City, August 27, 1862, 4 P.M.[5]

Major General McClellan, Alexandria, Virginia:

---

1 McClellan replied on July 14: "Nothing new of interest.... Everything going on very well. I am very anxious to have my old regiments filled up rather than have new ones formed. What of Burnside?" (Ibid, 323)

2 McClellan had telegraphed on July 20: "....If I am to have Burnsides troops I would be glad to avail myself of at least a portion of them to occupy a point on south bank of James River...." Burnside's troops were not to be assigned to McClellan, but to Major General John Pope. Since Burnside ranked Pope, his troops were placed under Major General Jesse L. Reno and assigned to Pope's command on August 1, 1862, with orders to take position near Fredericksburg. (Ibid, 334)

3 No reply has been located.

4 Major General John G. Parke (Burnside's chief of staff) replied: "Telegram received. Two brigades of Porter's corps arrived, with [Erastus B.] Tyler's heavy artillery, of over forty pieces. A large number of steamers in sight below Aquia. Will telegraph what troops are on board as soon as I learn. Over 6,000 troops were landed yesterday and I hope double that will be landed to-day. All that I can't land here at once I will send to Alexandria." (Lincoln v.5, 1953, 385)

5 No reply has been located.

What news from the front?
A. Lincoln.

Telegram to General A. E. Burnside, August 28, 1862, 2:40 P. M.[1]

Major General Burnside, Falmouth, Virginia:
Any news from General Pope?
A. Lincoln.

Telegram to General A. E. Burnside, Washington, August 29, 1862, 2:30 P.M.[2]

Major General Burnside, Falmouth, Virginia:
Any further news? Does Colonel Devon mean that sound of firing was heard in direction of Warrenton, as stated, or in direction of Warrenton Junction?
A. Lincoln.

Telegram to General G. B. McClellan, Washington, August 29, 1862, 2:30 P.M.[3]

Major General McClellan:
What news from direction of Manassas Junction? What generally?
A. Lincoln.

---

1 Burnside replied the same day: "All quiet in our front" and relayed a dispatch sent from the advance telegraph station by Captain James B. McIntyrthat stated : "I heard from Colonel [Thomas C.] Devin at 1.30 P.M. All quiet here. A cavalry force on the Culpeper road, 12 miles from Barnett's Ford; a force of all arms at Stevensburg, 16 miles from the ford. This, he says, is from information gained, but he has seen no enemy, except a small scout on the south side of the river. He reports General Pope, with the main body of his army, at Warrenton Junction. He has sent to Rappahannock Station and will report to me. When the scout returns I will telegraph you. Everything is perfectly quiet in this neighborhood." (Lincoln v.5, 1953, 397)

2 Burnside had forwarded a dispatch from Colonel Thomas C. Devin (then at Barnett's Ford) to Halleck and McClellan that indicated, "heavy firing this morning, apparently in the direction of Brensville and being at this hour toward Warrenton." At 5:15 P.M. he then forwarded to Halleck a dispatch from General Porter (then at Bristol) that provided more detail: "Sigel had severe fight last night; took many prisoners. Banks is at Warrenton Junction; McDowell near Gainesville; Heintzelman and Reno at Centreville.... A large body of enemy reported opposite...." (Ibid, 398-399)

3 McClellan replied: "The last news I recd from the direction of Manassas was from stragglers to the effect that the enemy were evacuating Centreville & retirring towards Thorofare Gap this by no means reliable. I am clear that one of two courses should be adopted. First to concentrate all our available forces to open communication with Pope. Second to leave Pope to get out of his scrape & at once use all our means to make the capital perfectly safe. No middle course will now answer. Tell me what you wish me to do & I will do all in my power to accomplish it. I wish to know what my orders & authority are. I ask for nothing but will obey whatever orders you give. I only ask a prompt decision that I may at once give the necessary orders. It will not do to delay longer." (Ibid, 399)

Telegram to General Banks, August 30, 1862, 8:35 P.M.[1]

Major General Banks, Manassas Junction, Virginia:
Please tell me what news.
A. Lincoln.

Telegram to General J. T. Boyle, War Department, August 31, 1862.[2]

General Boyle, Louisville, Kentucky:
What force, and what the numbers of it, which General Nelson had in the engagement near Richmond yesterday?
A. Lincoln.

Order to General H. W. Halleck, Washington, September 3, 1862.[3]

Ordered, That the general-in-chief, Major General Halleck, immediately commence, and proceed with all possible dispatch; to organize an army, for active operations, from all the material within and coming within his control, independent of the forces he may deem necessary for the defense of Washington when such active army shall take the field.
By order of the President:
A. Lincoln.

Telegram to General H. G. Wright, War Department, Washington, September 7, 1862.[4]

General Wright, Cincinnati, Ohio:

---

1 Banks replied: "It is represented to me that the engagement yesterday evening was very severe but successful for our arms. Another engagement occurred this afternoon but I have not yet learned the result." (Ibid, 400)

2 General Horatio Wright had earlier telegraphed Halleck: "Nelson has been badly beaten, I fear, in an encounter with the enemy near Richmond, Ky.; his force being, as he says, hopelessly broken and scattered. He is in Lexington, Ky., wounded, and I leave for that place in a couple of hours to see what can be done. He gives me no particulars. My orders were to make the Kentucky River the line of defense, and his orders in pursuance seem to have been disregarded. At any rate his force has been routed." To Lincoln's telegram Boyle answered: "I am not accurately informed of the force Gen Nelson had in the Engagement but believe that he had seven or eight thousand men all of them new lev[i]es except eighteenth Ky. His force may have been greater. The enemy's force estimated at fifteen to twenty thousand Morgan has moved from Glasgow in direction of Lebanon. Col Bruce, at Bowling Greene says Buckner, with force of Forest, Stearns & Co is moving from Tomkinsville toward Columbia & Lebanon. We need drilled troops & drilled artillery." (Ibid, 402)

3 At this juncture, Halleck's functions had seemingly been reduced to mere routine work. Lincoln had, in fact, assumed direct responsibility for all military affairs and had even personally written this September 3 order for the reorganization of an army for the field. (Carman and Pierro 2008, 64)

4 In fact, Braxton Bragg, with his Army of Tennessee, had initiated an invasion of Kentucky on 28 August. He reached Glasgow, Kentucky, on 13 September, and marched north to capture Munfordville on 17 September, the day of the battle of Antietam. Instead of pushing on to unite with Smith, Bragg spread his army out in the center of the state from Bardstown to Harrodsburg in order to better gather up supplies and recruits. At the end of the month

---

Do you know to any certainty where General Bragg is? May he not be in Virginia?

A. Lincoln.

Telegram to General J. T. Boyle, War Department, Washington, September 7, 1862.[1]

General Boyle, Louisville, Kentucky:

Where is General Bragg? What do you know on the subject?

A. Lincoln.

Telegram to General J. E. Wool, War Department, Washington, September 7, 1862.[2]

Major General Wool, Baltimore:

What about Harper's Ferry? Do you know anything about it? How certain is your information about Bragg being in the valley of the Shenandoah?

A. Lincoln.

Telegram to General D. C. Buell, War Department, Washington, September 8, 1862, 7:20 P.M.[3]

General Buell:

---

he conferred with Smith, who had been forced to pull back from Covington because of the strong defenses encountered there. One of the invasion's major objectives was fulfilled on 4 October when Bragg set up Richard Hawes as provisional Confederate governor of the state. (Cannan 1994, 56)

1 Boyle initially replied: "I do not know...but believe he is in Tennessee threatening Genl Buell... ."A second telegram received at. confirmed the first and conjectured that Bragg would cross the Cumberland River above Nashville, and "as Buell crosses at that place he will move into Ky at Burkesville or Tompkinsville." A third telegram added, "Intelligent persons who left Nashville on Sixth Inst say that nothing is known of Bragg's army in Tennessee. There is some conjecture that Bragg may have joined the forces near Washington. My view of their plans is likely all wrong." (Lincoln v.5, 1953, 409)

2 Wool had telegraphed Halleck: "Colonel [George R.] Dennis, at Gettysburg, communicates the following...from undoubted authority: 'Brig. Gen. B. [T.] Johnson, with 5,000 infantry, came into Frederick about 12 m. yesterday.... Jackson followed with 25,000 at 2.30 p.m.... Johnson's brigade encamped a mile north of the city.... He said he would be there only one day; then for Pennsylvania or Baltimore. General Bragg was advancing up the Shenandoah Valley for Pennsylvania, with 40,000 troops....'" Wood replied to Lincoln: "Your dispatch rec'd Genl Hill is menacing Harper's Ferry but with what force is not stated I think Harpers Ferry will be defended. Bragg is reported to be advancing through Valley of Shenandoah with forty thousand.... More than thirty thousand...were reported in & near Frederick yesterday with three.... Batteries & more coming. Number of Cavalry not started [sic] & not included in above Estimate Rebels proclaimed that [sic] were going Either to Philadelphia or Baltimore All my information is second hand...." (Ibid.)

3 Buell replied: "Bragg is certainly this side of the Cumberland Mountains with his whole force, except what is in Kentucky under [E. Kirby] Smith. His movements will probably depend on mine. I expect that for the want of supplies I can neither follow him nor remain here. Think I must withdraw from Tennessee. I shall not abandon Tennessee while it is possible to hold on. Cut off effectually from supplies, it is impossible for me to operate in force where I am; but I shall endeavor to hold Nashville, and at the same time drive Smith out of Kentucky and hold my communications." (Ibid.)

What degree of certainty have you that Bragg, with his command, is not now in the valley of the Shenandoah, Virginia?

A. Lincoln.

Telegram to General G. B. McClellan, War Department, Washington City, September 10, 1862, 10:15 A.M.[1]

Major General McClellan, Rockville, Maryland:

How does it look now?

A. Lincoln.

Telegram to General C. B. McClellan, Executive Mansion, September 11, 1862, 6 P.M.[2]

Major General McClellan:

This is explanatory. If Porter, Heintzelman, and Sigel were sent you, it would sweep everything from the other side of the river, because the new troops have been distributed among them, as I understand. Porter reports himself 21,000 strong, which can only be by the addition of new troops. He is ordered tonight to join you as quickly as possible. I am for sending you all that can be spared, and I hope others can follow Porter very soon,

A. Lincoln.

---

1 McClellan responded: "In reply to your dispatch of the morning I have the honor to state that Genl Pleasanton at Barnesville reports that a movement of the Enemy last night is said to have been made across the Potomac from this side to the other Side. We shall know the truth of this rumor soon. Pleasanton is watching all the fords as high as Conrad's ferry & has pickets out to the mouth of the Monocacy He has sent out this morning to occupy Sugar Loaf Mountain from which a large extent of country can be seen in all directions. Genl Burnside had his scouts out last night to Ridgeville & within 3 miles of New Market. No Enemy seen with the exception of a few pickets. They were told that Stuart's Cavalry 5000 in number occupied New Market & that the main Rebel force under Jackson was still at Frederick. Burnside has sent a strong reconnaissance today to the mountain pass at Ridgeville I propose if the information I have rec'd proves reliable regarding the natural strength of this position to occupy it with a sufficient force to resist an advance of the Enemy in that direction. I have scouts & spies pushed forward in every direction shall soon be in possession of reliable & definite information The statements I get regarding the Enemy's forces that have crossed to this side range from 80 to 150,000. I am perfectly certain that none of the Enemy's troops have crossed the Potomac within the last 24 hours below the mouth of the Monocacy. I was informed last night by Genl Pleasanton that his information rendered it probable that Jackson's forces had advanced to New Market with Stuart's Cavalry at Urbana. In view of this I ordered the army forward this morning to the line along the high ridge from Ridgeville through Damascus[,] Clarksburg &c but the information subsequently obtained from Genl Burnside's Scouts that the mass of the Enemy was still at Frederick induced me to suspend the movement of the right wing until I could verify the truth of the reports by means of Burnside's reconnaissance in force today. My extreme left advances to Poolesville this morning. The work of reorganization & re-fitting is progressing very satisfactorily with the new heads of staff Dept's. Dispatch this instant rec'd from Genl Pleasanton dated Barnesville 10.30 a.m. says 'My Scouts occupy the ferry at the mouth of the Monocacy They found no Enemy except a few pickets on the other side of the Monocacy at Licksville. About 3 miles from that Stream it was reported there was a force of 6,000 men.'" (Ibid, 412)

2 Earlier, McClellan had telegraphed Halleck for "...all the troops you can spare from Washington, particularly Porter's, Heintzelman's, Sigel's, and all the other old troops." (Ibid, 415)

Telegram to General G. B. McClellan, Washington City, September 12, 1862.[1]

Major General McClellan, Clarksburg, Maryland:
How does it look now?
A. Lincoln.

Telegram to General J. T. Boyle, Washington, September 12, 1862.[2]

Major General Boyle, Louisville, Kentucky:
Your dispatch of last evening received. Where is the enemy which you dread in Louisville? How near to you? What is General Gilbert's opinion? With all possible respect for you, I must think General Wright's military opinion is the better. He is as much responsible for Louisville as for Cincinnati. General Halleck telegraphed him on this very subject yesterday, and I telegraph him now; but for us here to control him there on the ground would be a babel of confusion which would be utterly ruinous. Where do you understand Buell to be, and what is he doing?
A. Lincoln.

Telegram to General H. G. Wright, Military Telegraph, Washington, September 12, 1862.

Major General Wright, Cincinnati, Ohio:
I am being appealed to from Louisville against your withdrawing troops from that place. While I cannot pretend to judge of the propriety of what you are do-

---

1 No reply has been located.
2 General Boyle had telegraphed on September 11: "Genl Wrights withdrawing the troops from this place and sending to Cincinnati is creating a panic and will ruin the State." Major General Charles C. Gilbert telegraphed Lincoln on September 12: "The Enemy must destroy Buells army...before attempting the capture of Cincinnati. If we secure Buells line of communication with this place an attack on Cincinnati in force is an impossibility unless by the way of the Kanawha and Western Va...." Boyle replied to Lincoln's telegram: "I expect no Enemy here unless when [Kirby] Smith and he unites they may move on Louisville. Genl Gilberts opinion may be inferred from dispatch he sent you. I believe he concurs with me. I have no idea there is any considerable force of the Enemy near Cincinnati. Bragg is reported already in the State with large force on the lines I indicated some days ago. I do not believe it. There is some force but it is not large Bragg may enter soon Buell is at Nashville. Part of his Army are at Bowling Green. [Alexander M.] McCooks Division which was no this side the Cumberland, now is reported to have recrossed to the Nashville side. I have heard nothing from Buell. My information is from Col Bruce at Bowling Green. I concur with you that Genl Wrights military opinion is better than I ever thought mine to be but I can know facts as well as the ablest military man. There are many reports Deserters from Buckner report him with ten thousand 10000 men near Tompkinsville. Bragg reported at Burkesville and Columbia advancing into the centre of the State. I do not believe any of the reports of an early attack at any point. They can and I hope will be driven out before they attack." (Ibid, 416-417)

ing, you would much oblige me by furnishing me a rational answer to make to the governor and others at Louisville. [1, 2]

A. Lincoln.

Telegram to General G. B. McClellan, Washington City, September 12, 1862, 5:45 P.M. [3]

Major General McClellan:

Governor Curtin telegraphs me: "I have advices that Jackson is crossing the Potomac at Williamsport, and probably the whole rebel army will be down from Maryland."

Receiving nothing from Harper's Ferry or Martinsburg today, and positive information from Wheeling that the line is cut, corroborates the idea that the enemy is crossing the Potomac. Please do not let him get off without being hurt.

A. Lincoln.

---

1   Horatio Gouverneur Wright graduated from the U.S. Military Academy ranked second in the class of 1841. He had served in the Army Corps of Engineers and later taught French and engineering at West Point. When the Civil War broke out, he assisted in the construction of the fortifications in Washington and served as engineer at the first battle of Bull Run. Wright received a promotion to brigadier general and participated in the operations along the Carolina, Georgia, and Florida coastlines, where he gained little combat experience. After participating in the Union defeat at the battle of Secessionville in June of 1862, Wright left the department and assumed command of the Department of the Ohio the following September. He began his tenure there with Confederate Maj. Gen. Braxton Bragg's Confederate army threatening Louisville and Cincinnati. Although Wright displayed solid organizational skills, he saw no combat in Kentucky. Furthermore, the campaign tarnished Wright's reputation when the congressional commission investigating the campaign blamed him for the capture of a Union garrison at Munfordville. (Patchan 2007, 30)

2   In addition to General Boyle's earlier commentary, Lincoln had received communications from Governor Robinson and numerous other influential Kentuckians. Wright replied on September 13, 10 P.M., "Your dispatch of yesterday by some mistake was not laid before me. I see it now for the first time. I have no intention of abandoning Louisville or of leaving it without adequate protection. Two regiments only were withdrawn, and that at a time when Cincinnati was seriously threatened, leaving at Louisville about thirty regiments and more than thirty guns.... Louisville has not been threatened at all, while Kirby Smith's forces did approach to within 8 miles of Cincinnati. He is now retreating from before the force hastily collected." (Lincoln v.5, 1953, 419)

3   By good fortune, McClellan, on the 13th, received the full text of General Lee's order for the investment and capture of Harper's Ferry. The order directed Jackson, with three divisions, to move via Williamsport and Martinsburg, on Harper's Ferry; McLaws, with two divisions, to Maryland Heights; Walker, with one division, was to re-cross the Potomac below Harper's Ferry and occupy Loudoun Heights; Longstreet, with two divisions, all the reserve, supply, and baggage trains, was ordered to Boonsboro; Hill's division was to form the rear guard; the cavalry, after detaching a sufficient force to accompany each of the moving columns, was to bring up the stragglers in the rear. Five divisions of the Confederate Army were thus separated from the separated the artillery and trains from the whole Army of the Potomac. Never was a more brilliant opportunity presented to a commander. Another opportunity had presented itself for ending the Rebellion. Unfortunately the telegraph brought news of divided councils at the capital. The President a few days before had relinquished control, but he had not yet learned the importance of signifying his wishes through a General in Chief. So, while the President was telegraphing, "Please do not let him (the enemy) get off without being hurt," General Halleck was urging more caution. (Upton 1917, 378)

Telegram to General H. G. Wright, War Department, Washington, September 14, 1862.[1]

General Wright, Cincinnati, Ohio:

Thanks for your dispatch. Can you not pursue the retreating enemy, and relieve Cumberland Gap?

A. Lincoln.

Telegram to General G. B. McClellan, War Department, Washington, September 15, 1862, 2:45 P.M.[2]

Major General McClellan:

Your dispatch of today received. God bless you, and all with you. Destroy the rebel army if possible.

A. Lincoln.

Telegram to General Ketchum, Executive Mansion, Washington, September 20, 1862.[3]

General Ketchum, Springfield, Illinois:

How many regiments are there in Illinois, ready for service but for want of arms? How many arms have you there ready for distribution?

A. Lincoln.

To General Halleck, McClellan's Headquarters, October 3, 1862.[4]

Major General Halleck:

General Stuart, of the rebel army, has sent in a few of our prisoners under a flag of truce, and evidently seeking to commit us to their right to parole prisoners in that way. My inclination is to send the prisoners back with a definite notice

---

1 No reply has been located.

2 This in response to news that McClellan had moved forward, and on the 14th, to the great alarm of the Confederate commanders, had captured the line of South Mountain, but not without a loss of more than 2,000 men. (Upton 1917, 378)

3 Inspector General William S. Ketchum, who had been sent to Illinois to expedite the forwarding of new troops, replied: "Six regiments under orders; nine armed, but want pay; ten mustered, but not filled or paid; eighteen organizing. Governor insists on ordering regiments off, but not ordered until paid, and delayed for want of money. Not been able to see Governor for several days, but have had eight regiments ordered within last three days. Arms for distribution 16,429, but no accouterments." (Lincoln v.5, 1953, 431)

4 Concerning the Union troops paroled by Confederate General James E. B. Stuart, Halleck at first replied that he thought there was "nothing against" proposal, but, later in the day, he added: "When I telegraphed you this morning I had only heard the cartel read by the Secretary of War. I have since examined the original document and withdraw my opinion. I am disposed to think the parole is made by the cartel to include all military duty." On October 4, he concluded, "After full consultation with the Secretary of War and Colonel Holt it is concluded that the parole under the cartel does not prohibit doing service against the Indians." But Attorney General Bates on October 18 gave his opinion that "The terms of the contract are...explicit...beyond a doubt.... It is the plainly declared purpose of the Cartel to prevent the use of prisoners paroled...in the discharge of any of the duties of a soldier...." (Ibid, 449)

---

that we will recognize no paroles given to our prisoners by the rebels as extending beyond a prohibition against fighting them, though I wish your opinion upon it, based both upon the general law and our cartel. I wish to avoid violations of the law and bad faith. Answer as quickly as possible, as the thing, if done at all, should be done at once.

A. Lincoln, President

Telegram to General U. S. Grant, Washington, October 8, 1862.[1]

Major General Grant:

I congratulate you and all concerned in your recent battles and victories. How does it all sum up? I especially regret the death of General Hackleman, and am very anxious to know the condition of General Oglesby, who is an intimate personal friend.

A. Lincoln.

Telegram to General J. T. Boyle, War Department, October 11, 1862, 4 P.M.[2]

General Boyle, Louisville, Kentucky:

Please send any news you have from General Buell today.

A. Lincoln.

Telegram to General J. T. Boyle, War Department, October 12, 1862, 4:10 P.M.[3]

General Boyle, Louisville, Kentucky:

---

1 This message was sent upon receiving the intelligence from Grant announcing the Union victories at Corinth and on the Hatchie. (Headley 1869, 180) These successes relieved West Tennessee from all immediate danger and, although a brief campaign, it displayed Grant's military judgment, the clearness of his perceptions, and made the way clear for his campaign against Vicksburg. (Remlap 1885, 66)

2 At this point in time, Lincoln and his advisers had long been dissatisfied with Buell's performance and, despite his being (at least partially) credited with saving Kentucky, Buell was targeted by many people who believed he had not done enough to punish the Confederates. One correspondent talked with his soldiers at the end of the campaign and found them to be utterly disgusted. "No words were too harsh to apply to Buell," he wrote. "None differed from the general opinion about him. Major Generals and privates talked alike." Some believed that this dissatisfaction in the ranks threatened the men's combat effectiveness. Treasury Secretary Salmon P. Chase became convinced that Buell's "heart is not in the war" because of his opposition to the emancipation policy. For whatever reason, Buell's halting movements infuriated the Northern public. An Indianapolis editor scored him, writing: "His career is a blank, without one vigorous action, one wise measure, one bold movement, or one patriotic impulse. The country has had just one year too much of him." (Hess 2000, 117)

3 Boyle replied: "Your dispatches received. Have no reliable information since 10th instant. Battle was fought on Wednesday by two divisions of McCook's corps, and most of rebel force, under [William J.] Hardee and [Leonidas] Polk, [Braxton] Bragg commanding the whole. We lost Generals [James S.] Jackson and [William R.] Terrill, Colonel [George] Webster, Lieutenant-Colonel [George P.] Jouett, Major [William P.] Campbell.... Our loss estimated at 1,500 to 2,000 killed and wounded. The enemy's loss as great, and believed to be greater.... My understanding is that Buell is pressing the enemy. Heavy fighting reported

We are anxious to hear from General Buell's army. We have heard nothing since day before yesterday. Have you anything?

A. Lincoln.

Telegram to General Curtis, Washington, October 12, 1862.[1]

Major General Curtis, Saint Louis, Missouri:

Would the completion of the railroad some distance further in the direction of Springfield, Mo., be of any military advantage to you? Please answer.

A. Lincoln.

To General G. B. McClellan, Executive Mansion, Washington, October 13, 1862.[2]

Major General McClellan:

My Dear Sir—You remember my speaking to you of what I called your over-cautiousness. Are you not over-cautious when you assume that you cannot do what the enemy is constantly doing? Should you not claim to be at least his equal in prowess, and act upon the claim?

As I understand, you telegraphed General Halleck that you cannot subsist your army at Winchester unless the railroad from Harper's Ferry to that point be put in working order. But the enemy does now subsist his army at Winchester, at a distance nearly twice as great from railroad transportation as you would have to do, without the railroad last named. He now wagons from Culpepper Court-House, which is just about twice as far as you would have to do from Harper's Ferry. He is certainly not more than half as well provided with wagons as you are. I certainly should be pleased for you to have the advantage of the railroad from Harper's Ferry to Winchester; but it wastes the remainder of autumn to give it to you, and, in fact, ignores the question of time, which cannot and must not be ignored.

Again, one of the standard maxims of war, as you know, is "to operate upon the enemy's communications as much as possible, without exposing your own." You seem to act as if this applies against you, but cannot apply in your favor. Change positions with the enemy, and think you not he would break your communication with Richmond within the next twenty-four hours? You dread his going into Pennsylvania. But if he does so in full force, he gives up his communications to you absolutely, and you have nothing to do but to follow and ruin him; if he does so with less than full force, fall upon and beat what is left behind all the easier.

---

at Harrodsburg. Expect to receive news by courier to night. Will send it to you." (Lincoln v.5, 1953, 458-459)

1 No reply has been located.

2 In this letter, Lincoln showed not only his impatience with McClellan but also his own growing self-confidence about how to conduct military operations. He did not order McClellan to follow any particular recommendations as to the line of march, but he expected McClellan to act forcefully. When McClellan continued to find excuses rather than push on against Lee's army after Antietam, Lincoln would soon sack him. (Miller 2012, 29)

Exclusive of the water line, you are now nearer to Richmond than the enemy is, by the route that you can and he must take. Why can you not reach there before him, unless you admit that he is more than your equal on a march? His route is the arc of a circle, while yours is the chord. The roads are as good on yours as on his.

You know I desired, but did not order, you to cross the Potomac below instead of above the Shenandoah and Blue Ridge. My idea was, that this would at once menace the enemy's communications, which I would seize if he would permit. If he should move northward, I would follow him closely, holding his communications. If he should prevent our seizing his communications, and move toward Richmond, I would press closely to him, fight him if a favorable opportunity should present, and at least try to beat him to Richmond on the inside track. I say "try;" if we never try, we shall never succeed. If he makes a stand at Winchester, moving neither north or south, I would fight him there, on the idea that if we cannot beat him when he bears the wastage of coming to us, we never can when we bear the wastage of going to him. This proposition is a simple truth, and is too important to be lost sight of for a moment. In coming to us he tenders us an advantage which we should not waive. We should not so operate as to merely drive him away. As we must beat him somewhere or fail finally, we can do it, if at all, easier near to us than far away. If we cannot beat the enemy where he now is, we never can, he again being within the entrenchments of Richmond.

[And, indeed, the enemy was let back into Richmond and it took another two years and thousands of dead for McClelland cowardice—if that was all that it was. I still suspect, and I think the evidence is overwhelming that he was, either secretly a supporter of the South, or, what is more likely, a politician readying for a different campaign: that of the Presidency of the United States.]

Recurring to the idea of going to Richmond on the inside track, the facility of supplying from the side away from the enemy is remarkable, as it were, by the different spokes of a wheel extending from the hub toward the rim, and this whether you move directly by the chord or on the inside arc, hugging the Blue Ridge more closely. The chord line, as you see, carries you by Aldie, Hay Market, and Fredericksburg; and you see how turnpikes, railroads, and finally the Potomac, by Aquia Creek, meet you at all points from WASHINGTON; the same, only the lines lengthened a little, if you press closer to the Blue Ridge part of the way.

The gaps through the Blue Ridge I understand to be about the following distances from Harper's Ferry, to wit: Vestal's, 5 miles; Gregory's, 13; Snicker's, 18; Ashby's, 28; Manassas, 38; Chester, 45; and Thornton's, 53. I should think it preferable to take the route nearest the enemy, disabling him to make an important move without your knowledge, and compelling him to keep his forces together for dread of you. The gaps would enable you to attack if you should wish. For a great part of the way you would be practically between the enemy and both Washington and Richmond, enabling us to spare you the greatest number of troops from here. When at length running for Richmond ahead of him enables him to move this way, if he does so, turn and attack him in rear. But I think he should be engaged long before such a point is reached. It is all easy if our troops march as well as the enemy, and it is unmanly to say they cannot do it. This letter is in no sense an order.

Yours truly,

A. Lincoln.

To General U. S. Grant, Executive Mansion, Washington, October 21, 1862.[1]

Major General U. S. Grant:

The bearer of this, Thomas R. Smith, a citizen of Tennessee, goes to that State seeking to have such of the people thereof as desire to avoid the unsatisfactory prospect before them, and to have peace again upon the old terms, under the Constitution of the United States, to manifest such desire by elections of members to the Congress of the United States particularly, and perhaps a Legislature, State officers, and a United States senator friendly to their object.

I shall be glad for you and each of you to aid him, and all others acting for this object, as much as possible. In all available ways give the people a show to express their wishes at these elections.

Follow law, and forms of law, as far as convenient, but at all events get the expression of the largest number of the people possible. All see how such action will connect with and affect the proclamation of September 22. Of course the men elected should be gentlemen of character, willing to swear support to the Constitution as of old, and known to be above reasonable suspicion of duplicity.

Yours very respectfully,

A. Lincoln.

Telegram to General Jameson, Executive Mansion, Washington, October 21, 1862.[2]

General Jameson, Upper Stillwater, Me.:

How is your health now? Do you or not wish Lieut. R. P. Crawford to be restored to his office?

A. Lincoln.

Telegram to General G. B. McClellan, War Department, Washington City, October 25, 1862.[3]

Major General McClellan:

---

1 To prevent any practical result from Lincoln's message to Grant, General Bragg moved his forces to within striking distance of Nashville. (Headley 1869, 181)

2 A prosperous businessman and commander of a state militia regiment at the start of the Civil War, he was elected colonel of the 2nd Maine. His promotion as brigadier general ranked from September 1861. At the Battle of Seven Pines on May 31, 1862, his horse was killed and fell on Jameson's leg. The horse was lifted off him, and he was helped away from the field. Soon afterward, he contracted a fever, took a leave of absence, and returned to Maine. According to his attending physician, he died in his residence on November 6, 1862, at Oldtown, Maine, of typhoid fever. (Welsh 1996, 183)

3 In response to this, not-so-gentle chiding, McClellan replied that they had been engaged in making reconnaissances, scouting, and picketing. Lincoln answered McClellan on the following day, October 26, 1862. (Raymond 1864, 283)

I have just read your dispatch about sore-tongued and fatigued horses. Will you pardon me for asking what the horses of your army have done since the battle of Antietam that fatigues anything?

A. Lincoln.

Telegram to General G. B. McClellan, Executive Mansion, Washington, October 26, 1862, 11:30 A.M.[1]

Major General McClellan:

Yours, in reply to mine about horses, received. Of course, you know the facts better than I; still two considerations remain: Stuart's cavalry out marched ours, having certainly done more marked service on the Peninsula and everywhere since. Secondly, will not a movement of our army be a relief to the cavalry, compelling the enemy to concentrate instead of foraging in squads everywhere? But I am so rejoiced to learn from your dispatch to General Halleck that you begin crossing the river this morning.

A. Lincoln.

To General Dix [Private and Confidential] Executive Mansion, Washington, October 26, 1862.[2]

Major General Dix, Fort Monroe, Virginia:

Your dispatch to Mr. Stanton, of which the enclosed is a copy, has been handed me by him. It would be dangerous for me now to begin construing and making specific applications of the proclamation.

---

1 McClellan replied later that evening: "I have the honor to acknowledge the receipt of your telegram of this morning. You will pardon me for most respectfully differing with you in regard to the expression in your dispatch 'Stuart's cavalry has done more marked service on the Peninsula and everywhere since.' I cannot resist the strength of my own conviction that some one has conveyed to your mind an erroneous impression in regard to the service of our cavalry, for I know you would not intentionally do injustice to the excellent officers and men of which it is composed.... With the exception of the two raids by Stuart, I am unconscious of a single instance where the rebel cavalry has exhibited any superiority over ours. The fact that Stuart out marched Pleasonton in his last raid is easily accounted for. It is said that he received a relay of fresh horses when he crossed the river at McCoy's Ferry. From that point he had extra lead horses to take the places of those that gave out on the road, besides which he stole some 1,000 horses in Pennsylvania, which contributed toward giving him another relay. Notwithstanding all this, he dropped a great many broken-down horses along the road. Pleasonton made his entire trip without a change of horses. After this statement of facts has been placed before you, I feel confident you will concur with me that our cavalry is equally as efficient as that of the rebels." (Lincoln v.5, 1953, 477)

2 Dix's October 23 telegram to Stanton read: "Will a congress District being in an Insurgent State and represented on the 1st. of January next in the congress of the United States by a member chosen at an election wherein a majority of the qualified Voters of the District shall have participated be considered not in rebellion & exempt from the penalty announced in the Presidents Proclamation of the 22nd. of September?" Dix replied to Lincoln's letter on October 28: "I have just received your private and confidential letter of the 26th inst. My despatch to the Secretary of War was dictated by an earnest desire, not without hope, to induce the people of the Congress District, of which Norfolk is a part, to return to their allegiance and send a loyal member to the House ...I am about to call on them, through their Military Governor, to take the oath of allegiance, and I wish to give them the assurance, if I can, that, by complying with the conditions of your Proclamation of the 22nd of Sept. they will avoid the penalties of disloyalty...." (Ibid.)

It is obvious to all that I therein intended to give time and opportunity. Also, it is seen I left myself at liberty to exempt parts of States. Without saying more, I shall be very glad if any Congressional district will, in good faith, do as your dispatch contemplates.

Could you give me the facts which prompted you to telegraph?

Yours very truly,

A. Lincoln.

Telegram to General G. B. McClellan, Executive Mansion, Washington, October 27, 1862, 12:10 P.M.

Major General McClellan:

Yours of yesterday received. Most certainly I intend no injustice to any, and if I have done any I deeply regret it. To be told, after more than five weeks' total inaction of the army, and during which period we have sent to the army every fresh horse we possibly could, amounting in the whole to 7918, that the cavalry horses were too much fatigued to move, presents a very cheerless, almost hopeless, prospect for the future, and it may have forced something of impatience in my dispatch. If not recruited and rested then, when could they ever be? I suppose the river is rising, and I am glad to believe you are crossing.

A. Lincoln.

Telegram to General G. B. McClellan, Executive Mansion, Washington, October 27, 1862, 3:25 P.M.[1]

Major General McClellan:

Your dispatch of 3 P.M. today, in regard to filling up old regiments with drafted men, is received, and the request therein shall be complied with as far as practicable.

And now I ask a distinct answer to the question, Is it your purpose not to go into action again until the men now being drafted in the States are incorporated into the old regiments?

A. Lincoln.

Order Relieving General G. B. McClellan, Executive Mansion Washington, November 5, 1862.[2]

By direction of the President, it is ordered that Major General McClellan be relieved from the command of the Army of the Potomac, and that Major Gen-

---

1 Lincoln drafted this note in response to a McClellan telegram that detailed the extent to which the line of the Potomac should be guarded after he left it, so as to cover Maryland and Pennsylvania from further invasions. McClellan thought strong garrisons should be left at certain points, complained that his forces were inadequate, and made some suggestion concerning the position of the rebel army under Bragg, which led General Halleck in reply to remind him that Bragg was four hundred miles away, while Lee was but twenty. McClellan opined that it was necessary to "fill up the old regiments of his command before taking them again into action." (Raymond 1864, 284)

2 In reply to Lincoln's second October 27 telegram, McClellan, explained that the language of the dispatch, which was prepared by one of his aids, had incorrectly expressed his meaning, and that he should not postpone the advance until the regiments were filled by drafted

eral Burnside take the command of that army. Also that Major General Hunter take command of the corps in said army which is now commanded by General Burnside. That Major General Fitz. John Porter be relieved from command of the corps he now commands in said army, and that Major General Hooker take command of said corps.

The general-in-chief is authorized, in [his] discretion, to issue an order substantially as the above forthwith, or so soon as he may deem proper.

A. Lincoln.

Telegram to General J. Pope, Executive Mansion, Washington, November 10, 1862.[1]

Major General Pope, St. Paul, Minnesota:

Your dispatch giving the names of 300 Indians condemned to death is received. Please forward as soon as possible the full and complete record of their convictions; and if the record does not fully indicate the more guilty and influential of the culprits, please have a careful statement made on these points and forwarded to me. Send all by mail.

A. Lincoln.

Telegram to General Blair, Executive Mansion, Washington, November 17, 1862.[2]

Hon. F. P. Blair:

Your brother says you are solicitous to be ordered to join General McLernand [sic, McClernand]. I suppose you are ordered to Helena; this means that you are to form part of McLernand's expedition as it moves down the river; and General McLernand is so informed. I will see General Halleck as to whether the additional force you mention can go with you.

A. Lincoln.

---

men. The army was gradually crossed over, and, on the 5th of November, McClellan announced that it was all on the Virginia side. This was just a month after the order to cross had been given—the enemy meantime having taken possession of all the strong points, and falling back, at his leisure, towards his base of operations. These unaccountable delays in the movement of the army created the most intense dissatisfaction in the public mind, and completely exhausted the patience of the Lincoln and his senior staff. On November 5 this order was issued relieving General McClellan from the command of the Army of the Potomac, and directing General Burnside to take his place, thus closing a most remarkable chapter in the history of the war. (Raymond 1864, 284)

1 The Santee Sioux had entered into treaty agreements with the U.S. government. In 1862, the Santees rose up in revolt over the failure of the government to honor certain treaty agreements, resulting in Santee people dying of starvation. What began as a small conflict turned into widespread warfare, and after a few days, nearly five hundred settlers were killed, with atrocities carried out by both the Santees and the settlers during the short war. As large numbers of troops poured into the state, the Santees surrendered. Over three hundred Santee men, almost all the Santee warriors who had surrendered, were sentenced to die for their part in the war. Lincoln ultimately commuted the sentence of all but thirty-nine men, who were executed in a mass hanging, the largest mass execution ever held in the United States. (Birchfield 1997, 894)

2 Francis Preston Blair Jr. was the son of the Republican party founder Francis P. Blair. He was an ardent Unionist who played a central role in keeping Missouri in the Union in 1861. (Pope 1998, 261)

Telegram to General J. A. Dix, Washington, November 18, 1861.[1]

Major General Dix, Fort Monroe:

Please give me your best opinion as to the number of the enemy now at Richmond and also at Petersburg.

A. Lincoln.

To General N. P. Banks, Executive Mansion, Washington, November 22, 1862.[2]

My Dear General Banks:

Early last week you left me in high hope with your assurance that you would be off with your expedition at the end of that week, or early in this. It is now the end of this, and I have just been overwhelmed and confounded with the sight of a requisition made by you which, I am assured, cannot be filled and got off within an hour short of two months. I enclose you a copy of the requisition, in some hope that it is not genuine—that you have never seen it. My dear General, this expanding and piling up of impedimenta has been, so far, almost our ruin, and will be our final ruin if it is not abandoned. If you had the articles of this requisition upon the wharf, with the necessary animals to make them of any use, and forage for the animals, you could not get vessels together in two weeks to carry the whole, to say nothing of your twenty thousand men; and, having the vessels, you could not put the cargoes aboard in two weeks more. And, after all, where you are going you have no use for them. When you parted with me you had no such ideas in your mind. I know you had not, or you could not have expected to be off so soon as you said. You must get back to something like the plan you had then, or your expedition is a failure before you start. You must be off before Congress meets. You would be better off anywhere, and especially where you are going, for not having a thousand wagons doing nothing but hauling forage to feed the animals that draw them, and taking at least two thousand men to care for the wagons and animals, who otherwise might be two thousand good soldiers. Now, dear General, do not think this is an ill-natured letter; it is the very reverse. The simple publication of this requisition would ruin you.

Very truly your friend,

A. Lincoln.

---

1 Dix replied: "My only reliable information...comes from a man who has not been here for four weeks. It was then 11,000 on and near the Blackwater...at Petersburg, 700; at Richmond, 7,000; between the James and Chickahominy, 7,000; and near White House, 1,500; total, 27,200. This is my latest information.... I place little reliance on reports...by deserters, stragglers, and negroes.... The moment I can get any reliable information as to the force in Richmond and Petersburg I will forward it...." (Lincoln v.5, 1953, 499)

2 Lincoln selected Nathaniel P. Banks, former governor of Massachusetts, as General Benjamin Butler's successor in Louisiana. Banks in civilian life had worked his way up from a machinist to president of the Illinois Central; in politics, his agility had made him in turn a Democrat, a Know-Nothing and a Republican; although thus far in the war his record in the Shenandoah Valley and at Cedar Mountain had evoked no raptures among informed observers. Before leaving for the New Orleans, Banks sent the War Department a requisition for supplies. Stanton, probably among the first to enjoy the nickname of "Nothing Positive" that the Army attached to Banks, sent the requisition to Lincoln. In this letter, Lincoln did little to conceal his irritation with the request. (Angle and Miers 1960, 423)

Telegram to General A. E. Burnside, Executive Mansion, Washington, November 25, 1862.[1]

Major General Burnside, Falmouth, Virginia:

If I should be in boat off Aquia Creek at dark tomorrow (Wednesday) evening, could you, without inconvenience, meet me and pass an hour or two with me?

A. Lincoln.

Telegram to General Curtis [Cipher] Washington, November 30, 1862.[2]

Major General Curtis, Saint Louis, Missouri:

Frank Blair wants Manter's Thirty-second, Curly's Twenty-seventh, Boyd's Twenty-fourth and the Ninth and Tenth Cavalry to go with him down the river. I understand it is with you to decide whether he shall have them and if so, and if also it is consistent with the public service, you will oblige me a good deal by letting him have them.

A. Lincoln.

To General S. R. Curtis, Executive Mansion, Washington, December 10, 1862.[3]

Major General Curtis, St. Louis, Missouri:

---

1 Aside from the whiskers that made him famous, Burnside had other claims to distinction. A successful gun manufacturer and railroad executive before the war, as the general who had captured Roanoke Island, as a creditable corps commander at South Mountain and Antietam. But Burnside insisted that he was not truly fitted to lead the Army of the Potomac. Lincoln did indeed journey to Aquia Creek to present his own plan for beating Lee; however, Burnside and his generals did not agree with the strategy.

2 Although Lincoln obviously supported Blair, it appears there are other than political considerations at play. As General Ulysses S. Grant notes, "General F. P. Blair joined me at Milliken's Bend a full-fledged general, without having served in a lower grade. He commanded a division in the campaign. I had known Blair in Missouri, where I had voted against him in 1858 when he ran for Congress. I knew him as a frank, positive and generous man, true to his friends even to a fault, but always a leader. I dreaded his coming; I knew from experience that it was more difficult to command two generals desiring to be leaders than it was to command one army officered intelligently and with subordination. It affords me the greatest pleasure to record now my agreeable disappointment in respect to his character. There was no man braver than he, nor was there any who obeyed all orders of his superior in rank with more unquestioning alacrity. He was one man as a soldier, another as a politician." (Grant 1952, 300)

3 In the summer of 1862 there issued from the general commanding at St. Louis an order "to assess and collect without unnecessary delay the sum of five hundred thousand dollars from the secessionists and southern sympathizers" of the city and county of St. Louis. The order stated that the money was to be "used in subsisting, clothing and arming the enrolled militia while in active service, and in providing for the support of the families of such militiamen and United States volunteers as may be destitute." It was extended to other parts of the state. The unpleasant duty of making and collecting the assessment was imposed upon half a dozen of the best known citizens of St. Louis. The assessment was begun. Collections were enforced by the military. Suddenly the board having the matter in charge suspended the work. The order countermanding the assessment came from Washington. It was terse: "As there seems to be no present military necessity for the enforcement of this assessment, all proceedings under the order will be suspended." (Stevens 1921, 791)

Please suspend, until further order, all proceeding on the order made by General Schofield, on the twenty-eighth day of August last, for assessing and collecting from secessionists and Southern sympathizers the sum of five hundred thousand dollars, etc., and in the meantime make out and send me a statement of facts pertinent to the question, together with your opinion upon it.

A. Lincoln.

Telegram to General Curtis, Executive Mansion, Washington, December 14, 1862.[1]

Major General Curtis, St. Louis, Missouri:

If my friend Dr. William Fithian, of Danville, Ill., should call on you, please give him such facilities as you consistently can about recovering the remains of a step-son, and matters connected therewith.

A. Lincoln.

Telegram to General Curtis, Executive Mansion, Washington, December 16, 1862.[2]

Major General Curtis, Saint Louis, Missouri:

N. W. Watkins, of Jackson, Mo., (who is half-brother to Henry Clay), writes me that a colonel of ours has driven him from his home at Jackson. Will you please look into the case and restore the old man to his home if the public interest will admit?

A. Lincoln.

Telegram to General Burnside, War Department, Washington City, December 16, 1862.[3]

Major General Burnside, Falmouth:

Your dispatch about General Stahel is received. Please ascertain from General Sigel and his old corps whether Stahel or Schurz is preferable and telegraph the result, and I will act immediately. After all I shall be governed by your preference.

A. Lincoln.

---

1 William Fithian, of Danville, Illinois, had served with Lincoln in the Illinois House of Representatives during the latter's first term, and in 1838 had been returned to the State Senate. (Lincoln 1930, 63)

2 Former General Nathaniel Watkins was a veteran of both the War of 1812 and the Mexican War. The colonel in question, Albert Jackson, explained that Mr. Watkins had "acted in hostility to the government" and, in fact, "had another, and better, residence in which to move." Colonel Jackson concluded that "there was no oppression or hardship in his case." Ellinghouse 2010, 63)

3 Burnside replied, "My application for the appointment of Gen Stahel is based upon the recommendation of Gen Sigel who has been a very useful and efficient officer during the time that I have had command of this army. He is decidedly of the opinion that Gen Stahel is the best man." (Lincoln v.6, 1953, 6)

Telegram to General Curtis, Executive Mansion, Washington, December 17, 1862.[1]

Major General Curtis:
Could the civil authority be reintroduced into Missouri in lieu of the military to any extent, with advantage and safety?
A. Lincoln.

Telegram to General Burnside, Executive Mansion, Washington, December 17, 1862.[2]

Major General Burnside:
George Patten says he was a classmate of yours and was in the same regiment of artillery. Have you a place you would like to put him in? And if so what is it?
A. Lincoln.

Telegram to General Curtis, Executive Mansion, Washington, December 19, 1862.[3]

Major General Curtis, Saint Louis, Mo.:
Hon. W. A. Hall, member of Congress here, tells me, and Governor Gamble telegraphs me; that quiet can be maintained in all the counties north of the Missouri River by the enrolled militia. Confer with Governor Gamble and telegraph me.
A. Lincoln.

Telegram to General A. E. Burnside, Washington, December 19, 1862.[4]

Major General Burnside:
Come, of course, if in your own judgment it is safe to do so.
A. Lincoln.

---

1 This question was doubtless based upon the notion that, even during a time of war, Missouri should be returned to civilian control as soon as circumstances permitted. Certainly, in surveying the military situation in late 1862, there seems little chance that Confederacy could ever gain military or political control over the state. (Bowman 2011, 146)

2 George Patten was an 1847 graduate of the U.S. Military Academy at West Point who served as a Pennsylvania Military Academy faculty member and administrator from the 1860s through his retirement in 1881. A veteran of both the Mexican War and the Seminole Wars in Florida, he was a South Carolinian who remained loyal to the Union during the Civil War. Patten did not see active service during the war. (Starnes 2012)

3 Curtis responded that the enrolled militia was not reliable, only skeleton formations of Federal troops were patrolling north of the river and Governor Gamble was not in St. Louis and unable to be contacted. (Keller 2012)

4 This noted was in response to a Burnside request for a personal meeting. Indeed, December, 1862, was a bad month for Major General Ambrose E. Burnside and the Army of the Potomac. On December 12, he suffered a major defeat in the battle of Fredericksburg. Further, stung by Democratic resurgence in the fall elections of 1862, the administration desperately needed to turn the tide of war. (Grant 1979, xiii)

Telegram to General Curtis, Executive Mansion, Washington, December 27, 1862.[1]

Major General Curtis, Saint Louis, Mo.:

Let the order in regard to Dr. McPheeters and family be suspended until you hear from me.

A. Lincoln.

Telegram to General A. E. Burnside, War Department, Washington City, December 30, 1862, 3:30 P.M.[2]

Major General Burnside:

I have good reason for saying you must not make a general movement of the army without letting me know.

A. Lincoln.

Telegram to General Dix, Executive Mansion, Washington, December 31, 1862.[3]

Major General Dix, Fort Monroe, Va.:

I hear not a word about the Congressional election of which you and I corresponded. Time clearly up.

A. Lincoln.

---

1 Samuel B. McPheeters, a Presbyterian minister in St. Louis, had been censured by General Curtis for preaching disloyalty to his congregation in St. Louis. (Raymond 1865, 438)

2 Burnsides' subordinates continued to question his leadership and Generals John Newton and John Cochrane, respectively division and brigade commanders, had appeared in Washington on leave the afternoon of December 30, their only mission to convince someone of importance that Burnside was incompetent and his campaign must be halted. The two officers eventually reached the White House, where they shocked the president with accounts of widespread doubt about Burnside's capacity. Though he became indignant at the insubordinate intrigue, Lincoln wrote Burnside this succinct note asking him not to make any important movements without first checking with the administration. Burnside answered immediately, if not cheerfully, that he would rescind the orders that had anticipated the intended campaign. Since the army would not be going anywhere, he said he would sail up to Washington, primarily to personally confer with Lincoln. (Marvel 1991, 209)

3 Despite his antislavery stand, Lincoln reaffirmed to Virginians his promise that districts holding congressional elections before January 1, 1863, when the Emancipation Proclamation would go into effect, would be exempted from its provisions. With northern morale plummeting and opposition to emancipation growing, Lincoln clearly placed a greater premium on Union-held elections in Virginia and elsewhere in the South than on black freedom. The Virginia Eastern Shore easily reelected Congressman Joseph Segar, and the district that included Alexandria held an election that was subsequently contested by the loser. When, on the day before he was to issue his proclamation, Lincoln had not received a report of an election in the Norfolk district, he hurriedly wired Gen. John A. Dix, the area commander this December 31 message. Dix then telegraphed Lincoln that he had just received the returns from the election, and John B. McCloud, the victor, would leave immediately for Washington to take his seat. Dix reported that the Union men of the district hoped to secure "their exemption from the penalties of disloyalty, by electing a member of Congress so as to be represented by the 1st Jany. 1863." The next day Lincoln, as he had promised, included the counties of occupied Virginia in his list of areas exempted from the provisions of the Emancipation Proclamation. (Harris 1997, 103-4)

Strategic Perspectives: The War of 1863

At the beginning of 1863, the Confederacy seemed to have a fair chance of ultimate success on the battlefield. However, during this year three great campaigns would take place that would shape the outcome of the war in favor of the North. One would see the final solution to the control of the Mississippi River. A second, concurrent with the first, would break the back of any Confederate hopes for success by invasion of the North and recognition abroad. The third slow and uncertain in its first phases would result eventually in Union control of the strategic gateway to the South Atlantic region of the Confederacy—the last great stronghold of secession and the area in which the internecine conflict would come of age as modern total war.

Confusion over Clearing the Mississippi: When Halleck went east in September 1862 to become General in Chief, his splendid army was divided between Grant and Buell. Grant, with over 60,000 men, remained in western Tennessee guarding communication lines. Buell's army of 56,000, after containing Bragg's invasion of Kentucky, had been taken over by Rosecrans, whose hard-won victory at Murfreesboro at the end of 1862 nevertheless immobilized the Army of the Cumberland for nearly half a year. To the west, only the posts at Vicksburg and Port Hudson prevented the Union from controlling the entire length of the Mississippi and splitting the Confederacy in two. Naval expeditions, under Capt. David G. Farragut, supported by the army, tried to seize Vicksburg in May and again in July 1862, but the Confederates easily repulsed the attempts. In the autumn Grant pressed Halleck to let him get on with the campaign down the Mississippi and finally received the response: "Fight the enemy where you please." But while Halleck and Grant were planning to move against Vicksburg by water and land, Lincoln and Stanton also outlined a similar move, but without consulting the military leaders.

The Chief Executive had long seen the importance of controlling the Mississippi, and in the fall of 1862 he and the Secretary of War prepared plans for a simultaneous advance northward from New Orleans and southward from Tennessee. Somewhat vague orders were drawn up giving command of the northbound expedition to Maj. Gen. Nathaniel Banks, who had replaced Butler as commander of the Department of the Gulf. Command of the southbound expedition was to go to Maj. Gen. John A. McClernand. Both officers were relatively untried, unstable, volunteer officers and politicians who often dabbled in intrigue in order to gain favors. Further, McClernand was to operate within Grant's department but independently of him. When Halleck found out about the Lincoln-Stanton plan, he persuaded the President to put Grant in command of the southbound expedition and to make McClernand one of his subordinates.[1]

Grant's Campaign Against Vicksburg:

Grant first tried a combined land and water expedition against Vicksburg in December 1862-January 1863. He sent Maj. Gen. William T. Sherman down river from Memphis, but the Confederates under Van Dorn and Forrest raided and cut the 200-mile-long line of communications. Sherman himself bogged down before Vicksburg, and Grant, perhaps also wishing to keep close rein on McClernand, who ranked Sherman, then determined on a river expedition which he would lead in person. Late in January Grant arrived before Vicksburg. He had upwards of 45,000 men, organized into three corps, the XIII Corps under McClernand, the XV Corps under Sherman, and Maj. Gen. James B. McPherson's XVII Corps. During the ensuing campaign Grant received two more corps as reinforcements to bring his total strength to 75,000 men.

Vicksburg had almost a perfect location for defense. At that point on the river, bluffs rose as high as 250 feet above the water and extended for about 100 miles from north to south. North of Vicksburg lay the Yazoo River and its delta, a gloomy stretch of watery, swampy bottom land extending 175 miles from north to south, 60 miles from east to west. The ground immediately south of Vicksburg was almost as swampy and impassable. The Confederates had fortified the bluffs from Haynes' Bluff on the Yazoo, some 10 miles above Vicksburg, to Grand Gulf at the mouth of the Big Black River about 40 miles below. Vicksburg could not be assaulted from the river, and sailing past it was extremely hazardous. The river formed a great U here, and Vicksburg's guns threatened any craft that tried to run by. For the Union troops to attack successfully, they would have to get to the high, dry ground east of town. This would put them in Confederate territory between two enemy forces. Lt. Gen. John C. Pemberton commanded some 30,000 men in Vicksburg, while the Confederate area commander, General Joseph E. Johnston (now recovered from his wound at Fair Oaks), concentrated the other scattered Confederate forces in Mississippi at Jackson, the state capital, 40 miles east of Vicksburg.

During late winter and early spring, with the rains falling, the streams high, and the roads at their wettest and muddiest, overland movement was impossible. Primarily to placate discontented politicians and a critical press, Grant

---

1 Matloff 1969, 236-237.

made four attempts to reach high ground east of Vicksburg. All four were un-successful, foiled either by Confederate resistance or by natural obstacles. One of the more spectacular efforts was digging canals. These projects had as their objective the clearing of an approach by which troops could sail to a point near the high ground without being fired on by Vicksburg's guns, and all failed. That Grant kept on trying in the face of such discouragement is a tribute to his dogged persistence, and that Lincoln supported him is a tribute to his confidence in the general. The trouble was that Grant had been on the river for two months, and by early spring, Vicksburg was no nearer falling than when he came.

On April 4 in a letter to Halleck, Grant divulged his latest plan to capture Vicksburg. Working closely with the local naval commander, Flag Officer David D. Porter, Grant evolved a stroke of great boldness. He decided to use part of his force above Vicksburg to divert the Confederates while the main body marched southward on the west side of the Mississippi, crossed to the east bank, and with only five days' rations struck inland to live off a hostile country without a line of supply or retreat. As he told Sherman, the Union troops would carry "what rations of hard bread, coffee, and salt we can and make the country furnish the balance." Porter's gunboats and other craft, which up to now were on the river north of Vicksburg, were to run past the batteries during darkness and then ferry the troops over the river. Sherman thought the campaign too risky, but the events of the next two months were to prove him wrong.

While Sherman demonstrated near Vicksburg in March, McClernand's and McPherson's corps started their advance south. The rains let up in April, the wa-ters receded slightly, and overland movement became somewhat easier. On the night of April 16 Porter led his river fleet past Vicksburg, whose guns, once the move was discovered, lit up the black night with an eerie bombardment. All but one transport made it safely, and starting on April 30, Porter's craft ferried the troops eastward over the river at Bruinsburg below Grand Gulf. The final march against Vicksburg was ready to begin.

At this time the Confederates had more troops in the vicinity than Grant had but never could make proper use of them. Grant's swift move had bewildered Pemberton. Then too, just before marching downstream, Grant had ordered a brigade of cavalry to come down from the Tennessee border, riding between the parallel north-south railroad lines of the Mississippi Central and Mobile and Ohio. Led by Col. Benjamin H. Grierson, this force sliced the length of the state, cutting railroads, fighting detachments of Confederate cavalry, and finally reach-ing Union lines at Baton Rouge, Louisiana. Most important, for the few days that counted most, it drew Pemberton's attention away from Grant and kept the Confederate general from discerning the Union's objectives.

Once more divided counsel hampered co-ordination of Confederate strategy. Johnston had been sent west by Davis to take over-all command, an imposing task, for Pemberton's army in Mississippi and Bragg's in Tennessee were widely separated. Things were further confused by Davis' directive to Pemberton to hold Vicksburg at all costs while Johnston recognized the potential trap and ordered him to move directly against Grant. In such a situation Pemberton could do little that was right. He tried to defend too wide an area; he had not concentrated but dispersed his forces at Vicksburg, the Big Black River, and along the railroad line to Jackson, where Johnston was gathering more troops.

After Grant had captured Port Gibson on May 1, and Sherman's corps had rejoined the main force, the Union commander decided that he must defeat Johnston before turning on Vicksburg. He moved northeastward and fought his way into Raymond on May 12, a move which put him squarely between Johnston and Pemberton and in a position to cut the Confederate line of communications. Next day Sherman and McPherson marched against the city of Jackson, with McClernand following in reserve, ready to hold off Pemberton. The leading corps took Jackson on May 14 and drove its garrison eastward. While Sherman occupied the state capital to fend off Johnston, the other two corps turned west against Pemberton and Vicksburg. Pemberton tried too late to catch Grant in open country. He suffered severe defeats at Champion's Hill (May 16) and Black River Bridge (May 17) and was shut up in Vicksburg. In eighteen days' Grant's army had marched 200 miles, had won four victories, and had finally secured the high ground along the Yazoo River that had been the goal of all the winter's fruitless campaigning.

Grant assaulted the Vicksburg lines on May 15 and 22, but as Sherman noted of the attacks: "The heads of columns have been swept away as chaff from the hand on a windy day." The only recourse now was a siege. Grant settled down, and removed McClernand from command after the attack of May 22 during which the corps commander sent a misleading report, then later slighted the efforts of the other corps and publicly criticized the army commander. Grant replaced him with Maj. Gen. Edward O. C. Ord, and ordered the army to implant batteries and dig trenches around the city.

The rest was now a matter of time, as Sherman easily kept Johnston away and the Federals advanced their siege works toward the Confederate fortifications. Food became scarce and the troops and civilians inside Vicksburg were soon reduced to eating mules and horses. Shells pounded the city, and the Federal lines were drawn so tight that one Confederate soldier admitted that "a cat could not have crept out of Vicksburg without being discovered." The front lines were so close that the Federals threw primitive hand grenades into the Confederate works. By July 1 the Union troops had completed their approaches and were ready for another assault. But Vicksburg was starving and Pemberton asked for terms. Grant offered to parole all prisoners, and the city surrendered on Independence Day. Since Grant was out of telegraphic contact with Washington, the news reached the President via naval channels on July 7, the day before General Banks' 15,000-man army, having advanced up river from New Orleans, captured Port Hudson. The whole river was now repossessed by the Union, the Confederacy sliced in two. Once more Grant had removed an entire Confederate army from the war—40,000 men—losing only one tenth that number in the process.[1]

Hooker Crosses the Rappahannock: Events in the Western theater in the spring and early summer of 1863 were impressive. Those in the east during the same period were fewer in number but equally dramatic. After

---

1 Matloff 1969, 237-241.

the battle of Fredericksburg, Burnside's Army of the Potomac went into winter quarters on the north bank of the Rappahannock, while the main body of Lee's Army of Northern Virginia held Fredericksburg and guarded the railway line to Richmond. During January, Burnside's subordinates intrigued against him and went out of channels to present their grievances to Congress and the President. When Burnside heard of this development, he asked that either he or most of the subordinate general officers be removed. The President accepted the first alternative, and on January 25, 1863, replaced Burnside with Maj. Gen. Joseph Hooker. The new commander had won the sobriquet of "Fighting Joe" for his intrepid reputation as a division and corps commander. He was highly favored in Washington, but in appointing him the President took the occasion to write a fatherly letter in which he warned the general against rashness and over ambition, reproached him for plotting against Burnside, and concluded by asking for victories.

Under Hooker's able administration, discipline and training improved. Morale, which had fallen after Fredericksburg, rose as Hooker regularized the furlough system and improved the flow of rations and other supplies to his frontline troops. Abolishing Burnside's grand divisions Hooker returned to the orthodox corps, of which he had seven, each numbering about 15,000 men. One of Hooker's most effective innovations was the introduction of distinctive corps and division insignia. He also took a long step toward improving the cavalry arm of the army, which up to this time had been assigned many diverse duties and was split up into small detachments. Hooker regarded cavalry as a combat arm of full stature, and he concentrated his units into a cavalry corps of three divisions under Brig. Gen. George Stoneman. On the other hand Hooker made a costly mistake in decentralizing tactical control of his artillery to his corps commanders. As a result Union artillery would not be properly massed in the coming action at Chancellorsville.

Hooker had no intention of repeating Burnside's tragic frontal assault at Fredericksburg. With a strength approaching 134,000 men, Hooker planned a double envelopment which would place strong Union forces on each of Lee's flanks. He ordered three of his infantry corps to move secretly up the Rappahannock and ford the stream, while two more corps, having conspicuously remained opposite Fredericksburg, were to strike across the old battlefield there. Two more corps were in reserve. The cavalry corps, less one division which was to screen the move up river, was to raid far behind Lee's rear to divert him. Hooker's plan was superb; his execution faulty. The three corps moved quickly up the river and by the end of April had crossed and advanced to the principal road junction of Chancellorsville. They were now in the so-called "Wilderness," a low, flat, confusing area of scrub timber and narrow dirt roads in which movement and visibility were extremely limited. Maj. Gen. John Sedgwick crossed the Rappahannock at Fredericksburg on the 29th, and the two remaining corps moved to within supporting distance of Hooker at Chancellorsville. So far everything had gone according to plan, except that Stoneman's diversion had failed to bother Lee. One of Stuart's brigades kept Stoneman under surveillance while the main body of cavalry shadowed Hooker so effectively that the Southern commander knew every move made by the Union army. By the morning of April 30, Lee was aware of what was afoot and knew that he was threatened by double envelopment. Already Hooker was sending his columns eastward toward the back door to Fredericksburg. A less bold and resolute man than Lee would have retreated southward at once, and with such ample justification that only the captious would have found fault. But the Southern general, his army numbering only 60,000, used the principles of the offensive, maneuver, economy of force, and surprise to compensate for his inferior numbers. Instead of retreating, he left a part of his army to hold the heights at Fredericksburg and started west for Chancellorsville with the main body.[1]

Chancellorsville: Lee's Finest Battle: When Lee began to move,
Hooker simply lost his courage. Over protests of his corps commanders, he ordered the troops back into defensive positions around Chancellorsville. The Federals established a line in the forest, felled trees for an abatis, and constructed earth-and-log breastworks. Their position faced generally south, anchored on the Rappahannock on the east; but in the west it was weak, unsupported, and hanging in the air. Lee brought his main body up and on May I made contact with Hooker's strong left. That day Stuart's cavalry discovered Hooker's vulnerable right flank and promptly reported the intelligence to Lee. Conferring that night with Stonewall Jackson, Lee made another bold decision. Facing an army much greater than his own, he decided to divide his forces and further envelop the envelopers. Accordingly, Lee committed about 17,000 men against Hooker's left to hold it in place while Jackson with some 26,000 men made a wide 15-mile swing to get beyond the right flank. At first glance Lee's decision might appear a violation of the principles of mass and concentration, but while Lee's two forces were initially separated their common objective was the Army of the Potomac, and their ultimate routes converged on a common center.

Jackson's force, in a 10-mile-long column, moved out at daybreak of May 2, marching southwest first, then swinging northwest to get into position. The Federals noted that something was happening off to the south but were unable to penetrate the defensive screen; Hooker soon began to think Lee was actually retreating. In late afternoon Jackson turned onto the Orange turnpike near Wilderness Tavern. This move put him west of Hooker's right flank, and since the woods thinned out a little at this point it was possible to form a line of battle. Because time was running short and the hour of the day was late, Jackson deployed in column of divisions, with each division formed with brigades abreast, the same kind of confusing formation Johnston had used at Shiloh. Shortly after 5:00 p.m. Jackson's leading division, shrieking the "rebel yell" and driving startled rabbits and deer before it, came charging out of the woods, rolling up Maj. Gen. Oliver O. Howard's XI Corps in wild rout. The Confederates pressed forward, but fresh Union troops, disorganization of his own men, and oncoming darkness stymied the impatient Jackson. While searching for a road that would permit him to cut off Hooker from United States Ford across the Rappahannock, Jackson fell prey to a mistaken ambush by his own men. The Confederate

---

1 Matloff 1969, 241-244.

leader was wounded and died eight days later. During the night of May 2, Stuart, Jackson's successor as corps commander, re-formed his lines. Against Stuart's right, Hooker launched local counterattacks which at first gained some success, but the next morning withdrew his whole line. Once more Hooker yielded the initiative at the moment he had a strong force between Lee's two divided and weaker forces.

Stuart renewed the attack during the morning as Hooker pulled his line back. Hooker was knocked unconscious when a shell struck the pillar of the Chancellor house against which he was leaning. Until the end of the battle he was dazed and incapable of exercising effective command, but he did not relinquish it nor would the army's medical director declare him unfit. Meanwhile Sedgwick, who shortly after Jackson's attack had received orders to proceed through Fredericksburg to Chancellorsville, had assaulted Marye's Heights. He carried it about noon on May 3, but the next day Lee once more divided his command, leaving Stuart with 25,000 to guard Hooker, and moved himself with 21,000 to thwart Sedgwick. In a sharp action at Salem Church, Lee forced the Federals off the road and northward over the Rappahannock. Lee now made ready for a full-scale assault against the Army of the Potomac huddled with its back against the river on May 6, but Hooker ordered retirement to the north bank before the attack. Confederate losses were approximately 13,000; Federal losses, 17,000. But Lee lost far more with the death of Jackson. Actually, Lee's brilliant and daring maneuvers had defeated only one man—Hooker—and in no other action of the war did moral superiority of one general over the other stand out so clearly as a decisive factor in battle. Chancellorsville exemplified Napoleon's maxim: "The General is the head, the whole of the army."

Hooker was a talented tactical commander with a good reputation. But in spite of Lincoln's injunction, "This time, put in all your men," he allowed nearly one-third of his army to stand idle during the heaviest fighting. Here again was a general who could effectively lead a body of troops under his own eyes, but could not use maps and reports to evaluate and control situations that were beyond his range of vision. Hooker, not the Army of the Potomac, lost the battle of Chancellorsville. Yet for the victors, Chancellorsville was a hollow triumph. It was dazzling, a set piece for the instruction of students of the military art ever since, but it had been inconclusive, winning glory and little more. It left government and army on both sides with precisely the problems they had faced before the campaign began.[1]

Lee's Second Invasion of the North: By 1863 the war had entered what Sherman called its professional phase.

The troops were well trained and had ample combat experience. Officers had generally mastered their jobs and were deploying their forces fairly skillfully in accordance with the day's tactical principles. Furthermore, the increased range and accuracy of weapons, together with the nature of the terrain, had induced some alterations in tactics, alterations which were embodied in a revised infantry manual published in 1863. Thus, by the third year of the war, battles had

---

1 Matloff 1969, 245-246.

begun to take on certain definite characteristics. The battle of Gettysburg is a case in point.

Gettysburg was, first of all, an act of fate—a 3-day holocaust, largely unplanned and uncontrollable. Like the war itself, it sprang from decisions that men under pressure made in the light of imperfect knowledge. It would someday symbolize the war with all the blunders and heroism, hopes and delusions, combativeness and blinding devotion of the American man in arms of that period. With its enormous destruction, tactical maneuvers, and use of weapons, Gettysburg was one of the most dramatic and most typical of the 2,000-odd land engagements of the Civil War.

After the great victory at Chancellorsville, the Confederate cause in the eastern theater looked exceptionally bright. If 60,000 men could beat 134,000, then the Confederacy's inferiority in manpower was surely offset by superior generalship and skill at arms. Vicksburg was not yet under siege, although Grant had ferried his army over to the east bank of the Mississippi. If Davis and Lee were overly optimistic, they could hardly be blamed. Both men favored another invasion of the North for much the same political and military reasons that led to invasion in 1862. Longstreet, on the other hand, was concerned over the Federal threats in the west. He proposed going on the defensive in Virginia and advised taking advantage of the Confederacy's railroads and interior lines to send part of the Army of Northern Virginia to Tennessee to relieve pressure on Vicksburg. But he was overruled and Lee made ready to move into Pennsylvania. By this time Union strategy in the east was clearly defined: to continue operations against Confederate seaports—an attempt to seize Fort Sumter on April 7 had failed—and to destroy Lee's army. President Lincoln's orders made clear that the destruction of the Army of Northern Virginia was the major objective of the Army of the Potomac. Richmond was only incidental.

On June 30, 1863, the Army of the Potomac numbered 115,256 officers and enlisted men, with 362 guns. It consisted of 51 infantry brigades organized into 19 divisions, which in turn formed 7 infantry corps. The cavalry corps had 3 divisions. The field artillery, 67 batteries, was assigned by brigades to the corps, except for army reserve artillery. The Army of Northern Virginia, numbering 76,224 men and 272 guns in late May, comprised 3 infantry corps, each led by a lieutenant general, and Stuart's cavalry division. (The Confederacy was much more generous with rank than was the U.S. Army.) In each corps were 3 divisions, and most divisions had 4 brigades. Of the 15 field artillery battalions of 4 batteries each, 5 battalions were attached to each corps under command of the corps' artillery chiefs.

In early June Lee began moving his units away from Fredericksburg. In his advance he used the Shenandoah and Cumberland Valleys, for by holding the east-west mountain passes he could readily cover his approach route and line of communications. Hooker got wind of the move; he noted the weakening of the Fredericksburg defenses, and on June 9 his cavalry, commanded by Brig. Gen. Alfred Pleasonton, surprised Stuart at Brandy Station, Virginia. Here on an open plain was fought one of the few mounted, saber-swinging, cut-and-thrust cavalry combats of the Civil War. Up to now the Confederate cavalry had been superior, but at Brandy Station the Union horsemen "came of age," and Stuart was lucky to hold his position.

When the Federals learned that Confederate infantrymen were west of the Blue Ridge heading north, Hooker started to move to protect Washington and Baltimore and to attempt to destroy Lee. Earlier, Lincoln had vetoed Hooker's proposal to seize Richmond while Lee went north. As the Army of Northern Virginia moved through the valleys and deployed into Pennsylvania behind cavalry screens, the Army of the Potomac moved north on a broad front to the east, crossing the Potomac on June 25 and 26. Lee, forced to disperse by the lack of supplies, had extended his infantry columns from McConnellsburg and Chambersburg on the west to Carlisle in the north and York on the east.

After Brandy Station, and some sharp clashes in the mountain passes, Stuart set forth on another dramatic ride around the Union army. With only vague instructions and acting largely on his own initiative, he proved of little use to Lee. It was only on the afternoon of July 2 with his troopers so weary that they were almost falling from their saddles, that Stuart rejoined Lee in the vicinity of Gettysburg, too late to have an important influence on the battle. His absence had deprived Lee of prompt, accurate information about the Army of the Potomac. When Lee learned from Longstreet on June 28 that Hooker's men were north of the Potomac, he ordered his widespread units to concentrate at once between Gettysburg and Cashtown.

After Chancellorsville, Lincoln, though advised to drop Hooker, had kept him in command of the Army of the Potomac on the theory that he would not throw away a gun because it has misfired once. But Hooker soon became embroiled with Halleck and requested his own relief. He was replaced by a corps commander, Maj. Gen. George G. Meade, who before dawn on June 28 received word of his promotion and the accompanying problems inherent in assuming command of a great army while it was moving toward the enemy. Meade, who was to command the Army of the Potomac for the rest of the war, started north on a broad front at once but within two days decided to fight a defensive action in Maryland and issued orders to that effect. However, not all his commanders received the order, and events overruled him.[1]

Gettysburg: Outposts of both armies clashed during the afternoon of June 30 near the quiet little Pennsylvania market town of Gettysburg. The terrain in the area included rolling hills and broad shallow valleys. Gettysburg was the junction of twelve roads that led to Harrisburg, Philadelphia, Baltimore, Washington, and the mountain passes to the west which were controlled by Lee. The rest was inevitable; the local commanders sent reports and recommendations to their superiors, who relayed them upward, so that both armies, still widely dispersed, started moving toward Gettysburg.

On July 1, Union cavalrymen fought a dismounted delaying action against advance troops of Lt. Gen. Ambrose P. Hill's corps northwest of town. By this stage of the war cavalrymen, armed with saber, pistol, and breech-loading carbine, were often deployed as mounted infantrymen, riding to battle but fighting

---

[1] Matloff 1969, 246-249.

on foot. The range and accuracy of the infantry's rifled muskets made it next to impossible for mounted men to attack foot soldiers in position. With their supe-rior speed and mobility, cavalrymen, as witnessed in the Gettysburg campaign, were especially useful for screening, reconnaissance, and advance guard actions in which they seized and held important hills, river crossings, and road junctions pending the arrival of infantry. During the morning hours of July 1, this was the role played by Union horsemen on the ridges north and west of Gettysburg.

By noon both the I and the XI Corps of the Army of the Potomac had joined in the battle, and Lt. Gen. Richard S. Ewell's Corps of Confederates had moved to support Hill. The latter, advancing from the north, broke the lines of the XI Corps and drove the Federals back through Gettysburg. The Union infantry ral-lied behind artillery positioned on Cemetery and Culp's Hills south of the town. Lee, who reached the field about 2:00 p.m. ordered Ewell to take Cemetery Hill, "if possible." But Ewell failed to press his advantage, and the Confederates set-tled into positions extending in a great curve from northeast of Culp's Hill, west-ward through Gettysburg, thence south on Seminary Ridge. During the night the Federals, enjoying interior lines, moved troops onto the key points of Culp's Hill, Cemetery Hill, Cemetery Ridge, and Little Round Top.

Meade had completed his dispositions by the morning of July 2, and his line was strong except in two places. In the confusion, Little Round Top was oc-cupied only by a signal station when the supporting cavalry was dispatched to guard the army trains and not replaced; and the commander of the III Corps, Maj. Gen. Daniel E. Sickles, on his own responsibility moved his line forward from the south end of Cemetery Ridge to higher ground near the Peach Orchard, so that his corps lay in an exposed salient. By early afternoon, seven corps were arrayed along the Union battle line.

On the Confederate side, Lee had not been able to attack early; reconnais-sance took time, and Longstreet's leading division did not arrive until afternoon. Generals in the Civil War tried to combine frontal assaults with envelopments and flanking movements, but the difficulty of timing and coordinating the move-ments of such large bodies of men in broken terrain made intricate maneuvers difficult. The action on the second day at Gettysburg graphically illustrates the problem. Lee wanted Longstreet to outflank the Federal left, part of Hill's corps was to strike the center, while Ewell's corps was to envelop the right flank of Meade's army. The attack did not start until 3:00 p.m. when Longstreet's men, having deployed on unfamiliar ground, under a corps commander that preferred to take a defensive stance, advanced toward Little Round Top. The brigade was the basic maneuver element, and it formed for the attack with regiments in a two-rank line. Divisions usually attacked in columns of brigades, the second 150 to 300 yards behind the first, the third a similar distance behind the second. Skirmishers protected the flanks if no units were posted on either side. But such textbook models usually degenerated under actual fighting conditions, and so it was with Longstreet's attack. Divisions and brigades went in piecemeal, but with savage enthusiasm. Attacks started in close order as most men were using single-shot muzzleloaders and had to stand shoulder to shoulder in order to get enough firepower and shock effect. But intervals between units soon increased under fire, troops often scattered for cover and concealment behind stone walls and trees, and thereafter units advanced by short rushes supported by fire from neighboring units. Thus, by late afternoon the smoke of battle was thick over the fields south of Gettysburg and the cries of the wounded mingled with the crash of musketry. The whole sector had become a chaos of tangled battle lines.

At this point Meade's chief engineer, Brig. Gen. Gouverneur Warren, discovering that no infantry held Little Round Top, persuaded the commander of the V Corps, Maj. Gen. George Sykes, to send two brigades and some artillery to the hill. They arrived just in time to hold the summit against a furious Confederate assault. When this attack bogged down, Longstreet threw a second division against Sickles' troops in the Peach Orchard and Wheatfield; this cracked the Federal line and drove as far as Cemetery Ridge before Meade's reserves halted it. Lee then ordered his troops to attack progressively from right to left and one of Hill's divisions assaulted Cemetery Ridge in piecemeal fashion, but was driven off. On the north Ewell attacked about 6:00 p.m. and captured some abandoned trenches, but Federals posted behind stone walls proved too strong. As the day ended the Federals held all their main positions. The Confederates had fought hard and with great bravery, but the progressive attack, which ignored the principle of-mass, never engaged the Union front decisively at any point. The assaults were delivered against stoutly defended, prepared positions; Malvern Hill and Fredericksburg had shown this tactic to be folly, although perhaps Lee's successes against prepared positions at Chancellorsville led him to over optimism.

Meade, after requesting the opinions of his corps commanders, decided to defend, rather than attack, on July 3. He also estimated that Lee, having attacked his right and left, would try for his center. He was right. Lee had planned to launch a full-scale, coordinated attack all along the line but then changed his mind in favor of a massive frontal assault by 10 brigades from 4 divisions of Longstreet's and Hill's corps against the Union center, which was held by Maj. Gen. Winfield Scott Hancock's II Corps. The assault was to be preceded by a massive artillery barrage.

The infantry's main support during the war was provided by field artillery. Rifled guns of relatively long range were available, but the soldiers preferred the 6-pounder and 12-pounder smoothbores. Rifled cannon were harder to clean; their projectiles were not as effective; their greater range could not always be effectively used because development of a good indirect fire control system would have to await the invention of the field telephone and the radio; and, finally, the rifled guns had flat trajectories, whereas the higher trajectories of the smoothbores enabled gunners to put fire on reverse slopes. Both types of cannon were among the artillery of the two armies at Gettysburg.

At 1:00 p.m. on July 3 Confederate gunners opened fire from approximately 140 pieces along Seminary Ridge in the greatest artillery bombardment witnessed on the American continent up to that time. For two hours the barrage continued, but did little more than tear up ground, destroy a few caissons, and expend ammunition. The Union artillery in the sector, numbering only 80 guns, had not been knocked out. It did stop firing in order to conserve ammunition, and the silence seemed to be a signal that the Confederates should begin their attack.

Under command of Maj. Gen. George E. Pickett, 15,000 men emerged from the woods on Seminary Ridge, dressed their three lines as if on parade, and began the mile-long, 20-minute march toward Cemetery Ridge. The assault force—47 regiments altogether—moved at a walk until it neared the Union lines, then broke into a run. Union artillery, especially 40 Napoleons on the south end of the ridge and some rifled guns on Little Round Top, opened fire, enfiladed the gray ranks, and forced Pickett's right over to the north. Despite heavy casualties the Confederates kept their formation until they came within rifle and canister range of the II Corps, and by then the lines and units were intermingled. The four brigades composing the left of Pickett's first line were heavily hit but actually reached and crossed the stone wall defended by Brig. Gen. John Gibbon's ad Division of the II Corps, only to be quickly cut down or captured. Pickett's survivors withdrew to Seminary Ridge, and the fighting was over except for a suicidal mounted charge by Union cavalry, which Longstreet's right flank units easily halted. Both sides had fought hard and with great valor, for among 90,000 effective Union troops and 75,000 Confederates there were more than 51,000 casualties. The Army of the Potomac lost 3,155 killed, 14,529 wounded, and 5,365 prisoners and missing. Of the Army of Northern Virginia, 3,903 were killed, 18,735 wounded, and 5,425 missing and prisoners. If Chancellorsville was Lee's finest battle, Gettysburg was clearly his worst; yet the reverse did not unnerve him or reduce his effectiveness as a commander. The invasion had patently failed, and he retired at once toward the Potomac. As that river was flooded, it was several days before he was able to cross. Mr. Lincoln, naturally pleased over Meade's defensive victory and elated over Grant's capture of Vicksburg, thought the war could end in 1863 if Meade launched a resolute pursuit and destroyed Lee's army on the north bank of the Potomac. But Meade's own army was too mangled, and the Union commander moved cautiously, permitting Lee to return safely to Virginia on July 13. Gettysburg was the last important action in the eastern theater in 1863. Lee and Meade maneuvered against each other in Virginia, but there was no more fighting. After Gettysburg and Vicksburg the center of strategic gravity shifted to Tennessee.[1]

The Chickamauga Campaign:
One week before the surrender of Vicksburg and the Union victory at Gettysburg, General Rosecrans moved out of Murfreesboro, Tennessee, and headed for Chattanooga, one of the most important cities in the south because of its location. It was a main junction on the rail line linking Richmond with Knoxville and Memphis. President Lincoln had long recognized the importance of railroads in this area. In 1862 he said, "To take and hold the railroad at or east of Cleveland [near Chattanooga], in East Tennessee, I think fully as important as the taking and holding of Richmond." Furthermore, at Chattanooga the Tennessee River cuts through the parallel ridges of the Appalachian Mountains and forms a natural gateway to either north or south. By holding the city, the Confederates could threaten Kentucky and prevent a Union penetration of the southeastern part of the Confederacy. If the Union

---

1 Matloff 1969, 249-254.

armies pushed through Chattanooga, they would be in position to attack Atlanta, Savannah, or even the Carolinas and Richmond from the rear. As Lincoln told Rosecrans in 1863, "If we can hold Chattanooga and East Tennessee I think the rebellion must dwindle and die."

After the spring and summer campaigns in the east, the Davis government in Richmond approved a movement by Longstreet's corps of Lee's army to the west to reinforce the hard-pressed Bragg. Longstreet's move—a 900-mile trip by rail—involving some 10,000-15,000 men and six batteries of artillery, began on September 9. But a force under Burnside, now commanding the Department of the Ohio, which was not part of Rosecrans' command, had penetrated the Cumberland Gap and driven the Confederates from Knoxville; Longstreet had to go around by way of Savannah and Augusta to Atlanta, Georgia, and did not reach Bragg until September 18. The rail network was rickety, and Longstreet's soldiers quipped that such poor rolling stock had never been intended to carry such good soldiers. Movement of Longstreet's troops from Virginia was nevertheless an outstanding logistical achievement for the Confederacy.

Rosecrans had meanwhile reached the north bank of the Tennessee River near Stevenson, Alabama, on August 20. By September 4 his forces were across and on their way toward Chattanooga. After months of delay Rosecrans had accomplished the feat of completely outmaneuvering Bragg without a major battle. He planned to get in behind Bragg from the southwest and bottle him up in Chattanooga, but the Confederate general saw through the scheme and slipped away southward, carefully planting rumors that his army was demoralized and in flight. Rosecrans then resolved to pursue, a decision that would have been wise if Bragg has been retreating in disorder.

There were few passes through the mountains and no good lateral roads. Rosecrans' army was dispersed in three columns over a 40-mile front in order to make use of the various passes. Bragg concentrated his army about September 10 at Lafayette, Georgia, some twenty miles south of Chattanooga. As his force was three times as large as any one of the Union columns, Bragg hopefully anticipated that he could defeat Rosecrans in detail. But his intelligence service failed him: he thought there were two, rather than three Union columns, and prepared plans accordingly. He first planned to strike what he thought was Rosecrans' right—actually the center—then the left, but his subordinates did not support him promptly, and the attacks were made in desultory fashion. Thus, twice in three days Bragg missed a fine opportunity to inflict a serious reverse upon the Federals because of his subordinates' failure to carry out orders.

By September 12 Rosecrans was at last aware that Bragg was not retreating in disorder but was preparing to fight. The Union commander ordered an immediate concentration, but this would take several days and in the meantime his corps were vulnerable. Although Bragg was usually speedy in executing attacks, this time he delayed, awaiting the arrival of Longstreet's corps. He intended to push Rosecrans southward away from Chattanooga into a mountain cul-de-sac where the Federals could be destroyed.

By September 17 Bragg was poised just east of Chickamauga Creek. (Chickamauga, translated from Cherokee into English, means "River of Death.") When

Longstreet's three leading brigades arrived on September 18, Bragg decided to cross the Chickamauga and attack. But the Federals, with two corps almost concentrated, defended the fords so stoutly that only a few units got over that day. During the night more Confederates slipped across, and by morning of the 19th about three-fourths of Bragg's men were over.

Rosecrans' third corps went into the line on the 19th, and now Bragg faced a much stronger force than he had expected. The heavily wooded battlefield had few landmarks, and some units had difficulty maintaining direction. Fighting continued throughout much of the day, but by nightfall the Federals still controlled the roads to Chattanooga. That night Lee's "Warhorse," Longstreet, arrived in person with two more brigades. He went looking for Bragg to report to him and lost his way in the woods. Encountering some soldiers, he asked them to identify their unit. When they replied with numbers—Confederate divisions were named for their commanders—he realized he was within Union lines, hastily rode off in the darkness, and eventually found Bragg. During the night Rosecrans regrouped and dug in.

Bragg decided to renew the attack the next day and to attack progressively from his right to left (sometimes known in military parlance as "oblique order"). He reorganized the Army of Tennessee into two wings under Polk and Longstreet with little regard for its existing corps organization. The attack began about 9:00 a.m. and hit Thomas' corps first. The Union line held until Rosecrans received an erroneous report that one of his units was not supported, and ordered another unit to move in and help. In the ensuing confusion, orders designated a unit which was already in line of battle. When this force obediently abandoned its position, Longstreet, just beginning his attack, saw the hole and drove into it at once. Thomas' right flank was bent back and most of the Union right wing simply melted from the field and streamed in rout back toward Chattanooga. Rosecrans, considering himself defeated, retired to Chattanooga to organize it for defense. Thomas, with about two-thirds of the disorganized army, stood fast and checked vicious attacks by Longstreet and Polk until nightfall. This resolute stand and the valorous performance of the U.S. 19th Infantry won for Thomas and that unit the title "Rock of Chickamauga." A Confederate remembered that afternoon how "the dead were piled upon each other in ricks, like cord wood, to make passage for advancing columns. The sluggish Chickamauga ran red with human blood."

Bragg concluded that no decisive results could be attained that day. Polk, Longstreet, and Forrest pleaded with him to push the routed Federals and recapture Chattanooga. But 18,000 casualties (the Federals had lost only 1,500 less) so unnerved Bragg that he permitted Thomas to withdraw unmolested from the field to a blocking position extending from Missionary Ridge west to Lookout Mountain. Next day Thomas retired into Chattanooga. Polk wrote to President Davis of Bragg's "criminal negligence," and Forrest a week later insubordinately told the army commander, "You have played the part of a damned scoundrel, and are a coward and if you were any part of a man I would slap your jaws." Yet nothing could erase completely the fact that the Confederates had won a great victory and had Rosecrans' army bottled up in a trap.[1]

Grant at Chattanooga:

Rosecrans' army, having started out offensively, was now shut up in Chattanooga, as Bragg took up positions on Lookout Mountain and Missionary Ridge. The Union commander accepted investment and thus surrendered his freedom of action. Burnside, at Knoxville, was too far away to render immediate aid. There were no strong Confederate units north of Chattanooga, but Rosecrans' line of communications was cut away. The Nashville and Chattanooga Railroad, instead of running directly into the city, reached the river at Stevenson, crossed at Bridgeport southwest of Chattanooga, and ran through Confederate territory into town. River steamers could get to within only eight miles of Chattanooga; beyond, the Tennessee River was swift and narrow. Supplies therefore came over the mountains in wagons, but starting September 30 Confederate cavalry under Maj. Gen. Joseph Wheeler, one of Bragg's cavalry corps commanders, raided as far north as Murfreesboro. Though heavily and effectively opposed in his effort to tear up the railroad, he managed to destroy many precious Union supply wagons. With the mountain roads breaking down under the heavy traffic in wet weather, rations within Chattanooga ran short. Men went hungry, and horses and mules began to die of starvation. Rosecrans prepared to reopen his line of communications by means of an overland route to the west. But this route was dominated by Confederate troops on Raccoon and Lookout Mountains. Additional troops to clear these strongpoints were required if the Army of the Cumberland was to survive.

Washington finally awoke to the fact that an entire Union army was trapped in Chattanooga and in danger of capture. In a midnight council meeting on September A, the President met with Secretary Stanton, General Halleck, and others to determine what could be done. As General Meade was not then active in the east, they decided to detach two corps, or about 20,000 men, from the Army of the Potomac and send them by rail to Tennessee under the command of General Hooker, who had been without active command since his relief in June. The forces selected included 10 artillery batteries with over 3,000 mules and horses. The 1,157-mile journey involved four changes of trains, owing to differing gauges and lack of track connections, and eclipsed all other such troop movements by rail up to that time. The troops began to entrain at Manassas Junction and Bealton Station, Virginia, on September 25 and five days later the first trains arrived at Bridgeport, Alabama. Not all of the troops made such good time—for the majority of the infantry the trip consumed about nine days. And movement of the artillery, horses, mules, baggage, and impedimenta was somewhat slower. Combined with a waterborne movement of 17,000 men under Sherman from Mississippi, the reinforcement of the besieged Rosecrans was a triumph of skill and planning.

Chickamauga had caused Stanton and his associates to lose confidence in Rosecrans. For some time Lincoln had been dubious about Rosecrans, who, he said, acted "like a duck hit on the head" after Chickamauga, but he did not immediately choose a successor. Finally, about mid-October, he decided to unify

---

1   Matloff 1969, 254-257.

command in the west and to vest it in General Grant, who still commanded the Army of the Tennessee. In October Stanton met Grant in Louisville and gave him orders which allowed him some discretion in selecting subordinates. Grant was appointed commander of the Military Division of the Mississippi, which embraced the Departments and Armies of the Ohio, the Cumberland, and the Tennessee, and included the vast area from the Alleghenies to the Mississippi River north of Banks' Department of the Gulf. Thomas replaced Rosecrans, and Sherman was appointed to command Grant's old army.

Now that Hooker had arrived, the line of communications, or the "cracker line" to the troops, could be reopened. Rosecrans had actually shaped the plan, and all that was needed was combat troops to execute it. On October 26 Hooker crossed the Tennessee at Bridgeport and attacked eastward. Within two days he had taken the spurs of the mountains, other Union troops had captured two important river crossings, and the supply line was open once more. Men, equipment, and food moved via riverboat and wagon road, bypassing Confederate strongpoints, to reinforce the besieged Army of the Cumberland.

In early November Bragg weakened his besieging army by sending Longstreet's force against Burnside at Knoxville. This move reduced Confederate strength to about 40,000 at about the same time that Sherman arrived with two army corps from Memphis. The troops immediately at hand under Grant— Thomas' Army of the Cumberland, two corps of Sherman's Army of the Tennessee, and two corps under Hooker from the Army of the Potomac—now numbered about 60,000. Grant characteristically decided to resume the offensive with his entire force.

The Confederates had held their dominant position for so long that they seemed to look on all of the Federals in Chattanooga as their ultimate prisoners. One day Grant went out to inspect the Union lines and he reached a point where Union and Confederate picket posts were not far apart. Not only did his own troops turn out the guard, but a smart set of Confederates came swarming out, formed a neat military rank, snapped to attention, and presented arms. Grant returned the salute and rode away. But plans were already afoot to divest the Confederates of some of their cockiness.

Grant planned to hit the ends of the Confederates' line at once. Hooker would strike at Lookout Mountain, and Sherman moving his army upstream, across the river from Chattanooga, and crossing over by pontons, would hit the upper end of Missionary Ridge. While they were breaking the Confederate flanks, Thomas' men could make limited attacks on the center, and the Army of the Cumberland's soldiers, already nursing a bruised ego for the rout at Chickamauga, realized that in the eyes of the commanding general they were second-class troops.

Hooker took Lookout Mountain on November 24. On the same day Sherman crossed the Tennessee at the mouth of Chickamauga Creek and gained positions on the north end of Missionary Ridge. The next day his attacks bogged down as he attempted to drive southward along the Ridge. To help Sherman, Grant directed the Army of the Cumberland to take the rifle pits at the foot of the west slope of Missionary Ridge. These rifle pits were the first of three lines of Confederate trenches. Thomas' troops rushed forward, seized the pits, and then, having a score to settle with the Confederates positioned above them, took control of this phase of the battle. Coming under fire from the pits above and in front of them, the Federals simply kept on going. When Grant observed this movement he muttered that someone was going to sweat for it if the charge ended in disaster. But Thomas' troops drove all the way to the top, and in the afternoon Hooker swept the southern end of the ridge. The Federals then had the unusual experience of seeing a Confederate army disintegrate into precipitate retreat and beckoned to their Northern comrades: "My God! Come and see them run!" Grant pursued Bragg the next day, but one Confederate division skillfully halted the pursuit while Bragg retired into Georgia to regroup.

The battles around Chattanooga ended in one of the most complete Union victories of the war. Bragg's army was defeated, men and materiel captured, and the Confederates driven south. The mountainous defense line which the Confederates had hoped to hold had been pierced; the rail center of Chattanooga was permanently in Union hands; and the rich, food-producing eastern Tennessee section was lost to the Confederacy. Relief had come at last for the Union sympathizers in eastern Tennessee. With Chattanooga secured as a base, the way was open for an invasion of the lower South.[1]

---

1   Matloff 1969, 257-261.

CORRESPONDENCE: 18631

To General H. W. Halleck, Executive Mansion, Washington, January 1, 1863.[2]

Major General Halleck:

Dear Sir—General Burnside wishes to cross the Rappahannock with his army, but his grand division commanders all oppose the movement. If in such a difficulty as this you do not help, you fail me precisely in the point for which I sought your assistance You know what General Burnside's plan is, and it is my

---

1 While the actual text is not included here, it should be noted that Lincoln issued the *Emancipation Proclamation* on January 1, 1863, as the nation approached its third year of bloody civil war. The proclamation declared "that all persons held as slaves" within the rebellious states "are, and henceforward shall be free." Despite this expansive wording, the Emancipation Proclamation was limited in many ways. It applied only to states that had seceded from the Union, leaving slavery untouched in the loyal border states. It also expressly exempted parts of the Confederacy that had already come under Northern control. Most important, the freedom it promised depended upon Union military victory. Although the Emancipation Proclamation did not end slavery in the nation, it captured the hearts and imagination of millions of Americans and fundamentally transformed the character of the war. After January 1, 1863, every advance of federal troops expanded the domain of freedom. Moreover, the Proclamation announced the acceptance of black men into the Union Army and Navy, enabling the liberated to become liberators. By the end of the war, almost 200,000 black soldiers and sailors had fought for the Union and freedom. (National Archives 2012)

2 In the end, Halleck's moral and official courage, however, failed the President in this emergency. He declined to give his military opinion, and asked to be relieved from further duties as general-in-chief. This left Lincoln no option, and still having need of the advice of his general-in-chief on other questions, he indorsed on his own letter, "withdrawn because considered harsh by General Halleck." The complication, however, continued to grow worse, and the correspondence more strained. Burnside declared that the country had lost confidence in both the Secretary of War and the general-in-chief; also, that his own generals were unanimously opposed to again crossing the Rappahannock. Halleck, on the contrary, urged another crossing, but that it must be made on Burnside's own decision, plan, and responsibility. (Nicolay 2008, 119)

---

wish that you go with him to the ground, examine it as far as practicable, confer with the officers, getting their judgment, and ascertaining their temper—in a word, gather all the elements for forming a judgment of your own, and then tell General Burnside that you do approve or that you do not approve his plan. Your military skill is useless to me if you will not do this.

Yours very truly,

A. Lincoln.

To General S. R. Curtis, Executive Mansion, Washington, January 2, 1863.[1]

Major General Curtis:

My Dear Sir—Yours of December 29 by the hand of Mr. Strong is just received. The day I telegraphed you suspending the order in relation to Dr. McPheeters, he, with Mr. Bates, the Attorney General, appeared before me and left with me a copy of the order mentioned. The doctor also showed me the Copy of an oath which he said he had taken, which is indeed very strong and specific. He also verbally assured me that he had constantly prayed in church for the President and government, as he had always done before the present war. In looking over the recitals in your order, I do not see that this matter of the prayer, as he states it, is negatived, nor that any violation of his oath is charged nor, in fact, that anything specific is alleged against him. The charges are all general: that he has a rebel wife and rebel relations, that he sympathizes with rebels, and that he exercises rebel influence. Now, after talking with him, I tell you frankly I believe he does sympathize with the rebels, but the question remains whether such a man, of unquestioned good moral character, who has taken such an oath as he has, and cannot even be charged with violating it, and who can be charged with no other specific act or omission, can, with safety to the government, be exiled upon the suspicion of his secret sympathies. But I agree that this must be left to you, who are on the spot; and if, after all, you think the public good requires his removal, my suspension of the order is withdrawn, only with this qualification, that the time during the suspension is not to be counted against him. I have promised him this. But I must add that the United States Government must not, as by this order, undertake to run the churches. When an individual in a church or out of it becomes dangerous to the public interest, he must be checked; but let the churches, as such, take care of themselves. It will not do for the United States to appoint trustees, supervisors, or other agents for the churches.

Yours very truly,

A. Lincoln.

P. S. The committee composed of Messrs. Yeatman and Filley (Mr. Broadhead not attending) has presented your letter and the memorial of sundry citizens. On the whole subject embraced exercise your best judgment, with a sole view to the public interest, and I will not interfere without hearing you.

A. Lincoln., January 3, 1863.

---

1 The Presbytery, the regular church authority in the matter, subsequently decided that Rev. McPheeters could not return to his pastoral duties. (Raymond 1865, 439)

To General S. L Curtis, Executive Mansion, Washington, January 5, 1863.[1]

Major General Curtis:

My Dear Sir—I am having a good deal of trouble with Missouri matters, and I now sit down to write you particularly about it. One class of friends believe in greater severity and another in greater leniency in regard to arrests, banishments, and assessments. As usual in such cases, each questions the other's motives. On the one hand, it is insisted that Governor Gamble's unionism, at most, is not better than a secondary spring of action; that hunkerism and a wish for political influence stand before Unionism with him. On the other hand, it is urged that arrests, banishments, and assessments are made more for private malice, revenge, and pecuniary interest than for the public good. This morning I was told, by a gentleman who I have no doubt believes what he says, that in one case of assessments for $10,000 the different persons who paid compared receipts, and found they had paid $30,000. If this be true, the inference is that the collecting agents pocketed the odd $20,000. And true or not in the instance, nothing but the sternest necessity can justify the making and maintaining of a system so liable to such abuses. Doubtless the necessity for the making of the system in Missouri did exist, and whether it continues for the maintenance of it is now a practical and very important question. Some days ago Governor Gamble telegraphed me, asking that the assessments outside of St. Louis County might be suspended, as they already have been within it, and this morning all the members of Congress here from Missouri but one laid a paper before me asking the same thing. Now, my belief is that Governor Gamble is an honest and true man, not less so than yourself; that you and he could confer together on this and other Missouri questions with great advantage to the public; that each knows something which the other does not; and that acting together you could about double your stock of pertinent information. May I not hope that you and he will attempt this? I could at once safely do (or you could safely do without me) whatever you and he agree upon. There is absolutely no reason why you should not agree.

Yours as ever,

A. Lincoln.

P. S. I forgot to say that Hon. James S. Rollins, member of Congress from one of the Missouri districts, wishes that, upon his personal responsibility, Rev. John M. Robinson, of Columbia, Missouri; James L. Matthews, of Boone County, Missouri; and James L. Stephens, also of Boone County, Missouri, may be allowed to return to their respective homes. Major Rollins leaves with me very strong papers from the neighbors of these men, whom he says he knows to be true men. He also says he has many constituents who he thinks are rightly exiled, but that he thinks these three should be allowed to return. Please look into the case, and oblige Major Rollins if you consistently can.

---

1 Affairs in Missouri continued to plague Lincoln. This time the question involved the peculiar practice of levying assessments on Southern sympathizers, a singular source of discord compounded by bad feelings between the governor and department commander, In this letter, Lincoln—seemingly incapable of holding grudges—seeks to engage and infuse Curtis with similar feelings. (Lincoln, Miers and Angle 1955, 528)

Yours truly,
A. Lincoln.
[Copy sent to Governor Gamble.]

Telegram to General Rosecrans, Executive Mansion, Washington, January 5, 1863.[1]

Major General W. S. Rosecrans, Murfreesborough, Tenn.:
Your dispatch announcing retreat of enemy has just reached here. God bless you and all with you! Please tender to all, and accept for yourself, the nation's gratitude for your and their skill, endurance, and dauntless courage.
A. Lincoln.

Telegram to General Dix, War Department, Washington, January 7, 1863.[2]

Major General Dix, Fort Monroe, Va.:
Do Richmond papers of 6th say nothing about Vicksburg, or if anything, what?
A. Lincoln.

To General H. W. Halleck, Executive Mansion, Washington, January 7, 1863.[3]

Major General Halleck:
My Dear Sir—What think you of forming a reserve cavalry corps of, say, 6000 for the Army of the Potomac? Might not such a corps be constituted from the cavalry of Sigel's and Slocum's corps, with scraps we could pick up here and there?
Yours truly,
A. Lincoln.

---

1 This note was in response to Rosecrans' victory at Stones River, which brought a thin gleam of cheer to the North. It blunted, temporarily, the mounting copperhead offensive against the administration's war policy. However, the Army of the Cumberland was so crippled by this "victory" that Rosecrans felt unable to renew the offensive for several months. (McPherson 1988, 583)

2 Dix responded, "The only 2 Richmond papers of the Sixth I have seen say nothing of Vicksburg but they admit & mourn over the Rebel defeat at Murfreesboro." In a later telegram, Dix references a January 6 *Richmond Examiner* entry that indicates a Confederate confidence of holding Vicksburg against any force the Federals can bring against it. However, Dix adds, "Our forces are well advised of their movements." (Lincoln v.6, 1953, 43)

3 No reply from Halleck has been found; however, on January 14, however, General Carl Schurz wrote Lincoln, "Today I went with Gen. Sigel to see Gen. Burnside, who fully agreed to it that I should command the Eleventh Corps and Gen. Stahel the Cavalry Reserve. Gen. Stahel also is very well satisfied with it. All concerned now agreeing upon that point the only thing that is wanted is that you should be kind enough to issue an order placing me in command of the Corps and Gen. Stahel in command of the Cavalry-Reserve, consisting of the cavalry now with the Grand Reserve Division and such regiments as will be attached to it."(Lincoln v.6, 1953, 43)

To Major General Burnside, Commanding, Falmouth, January 8, 1863.[1]

General Burnside:

I understand General Halleck has sent you a letter of which this is a copy. I approve this letter. I deplore the want of concurrence with you in opinion by your general officers, but I do not see the remedy. Be cautious, and do not understand that the government or country is driving you. I do not yet see how I could profit by changing the command of the Army of the Potomac; and if I did, I should not wish to do it by accepting the resignation of your commission.

A. Lincoln.

---

1   Lincoln forwards his endorsement of Halleck's January 7, 1863 letter to Burnside which states:

Major General Burnside, Commanding, etc., Falmouth:

General: Your communication of the 5th was delivered to me by your aide-de-camp at 12 M. today.

In all my communications and interviews with you since you took command of the Army of the Potomac I have advised a forward movement across the Rappahannock. At our interview at Warrenton I urged that you should cross by the fords above Fredericksburg rather than to fall down to that place; and when I left you at Warrenton it was understood that at least a considerable part of your army would cross by the fords, and I so represented to the President. It was this modification of the plan proposed by you that I telegraphed you had received his approval. When the attempt at Fredericksburg was abandoned, I advised you to renew the attempt at some other point, either in whole or in part, to turn the enemy's works, or to threaten their wings or communications; in other words, to keep the enemy occupied till a favorable opportunity offered to strike a decisive blow. I particularly advised you to use your cavalry and light artillery upon his communications, and attempt to cut off his supplies and engage him at an advantage.

In all our interviews I have urged that our first object was, not Richmond, but the defeat or scattering of Lee's army, which threatened Washington and the line of the upper Potomac. I now recur to these things simply to remind you of the general views which I have expressed, and which I still hold.

The circumstances of the case, however, have somewhat changed since the early part of November. The chances of an extended line of operations are now, on account of the advanced season, much less than then. But the chances are still in our favor to meet and defeat the enemy on the Rappahannock, if we can effect a crossing in a position where we can meet the enemy on favorable or even equal terms. I therefore still advise a movement against him. The character of that movement, however, must depend upon circumstances which may change any day and almost any hour. If the enemy should concentrate his forces at the place you have selected for a crossing, make it a feint and try another place. Again, the circumstances at the time may be such as to render an attempt to cross the entire army not advisable. In that case, theory suggests that, while the enemy concentrates at that point, advantages can be gained by crossing smaller forces at other points to cut off his lines, destroy his communication, and capture his rear-guards, outposts, etc. The great object is to occupy the enemy to prevent his making large detachments or distant raids, and to injure him all you can with the least injury to yourself. If this can be best accomplished by feints of a general crossing and detached real crossings, take that course; if by an actual general crossing, with feints on other points, adopt that course. There seem to me to be many reasons why a crossing at some point should be attempted.

It will not do to keep your large army inactive. As you yourself admit, it devolves on you to decide upon the time, place, and character of the crossing which you may attempt. I can only advise that an attempt be made, and as early as possible.

Very respectfully, your obedient servant,

H. W. Halleck, General-in-Chief. (Woodbury 1867, 241-242)

Telegram to General S. R. Curtis, Executive Mansion, Washington, January 10, 1863.[1]

Major General Curtis, St. Louis, MO.:

I understand there is considerable trouble with the slaves in Missouri. Please do your best to keep peace on the question for two or three weeks, by which time we hope to do something here toward settling the question in Missouri.

A. Lincoln.

Telegram to General Burnside, Executive Mansion, Washington, January 23, 1863.[2]

General Burnside:

Will see you any moment when you come.

A. Lincoln.

War Department, Adjutant-General's Office, Washington, D.C. January 25, 1863.[3]

I. The President of the United States has directed:

---

1 When Congress met in December for the short session the House appointed a select committee on gradual emancipation in the loyal slave-holding states. Frank P. Blair was made the Missouri member of it. On the 10th of December Senator Henderson introduced in the Senate his bill to give Missouri $20,000,000 to pay for the slaves of loyal owners. The next day Representative Noell put in his bill in the House, appropriating $10,000,000 to reimburse loyal owners of slaves in Missouri. Both bills passed by large majorities but the difference in the amounts made it necessary to compromise. The President did all he could to expedite the legislation. (Stevens 1921, 678)

2 Earlier in the day, Burnside had wired Lincoln, "I have prepared some very important orders, and I want to see you before issuing them. Can I see you alone if I am at the White House after midnight? I must be back by 8 o'clock tomorrow morning." The orders were as follows: "General Joseph Hooker, major general of volunteers and brigadier general U. S. Army, having been guilty of unjust and unnecessary criticisms of the actions of his superior officers, and of the authorities, and having, by the general tone of his conversation, endeavored to create distrust in the minds of officers who have associated with him, and having, by omissions and otherwise, made reports and statements which were calculated to create incorrect impressions, and for habitually speaking in disparaging terms of other officers, is hereby dismissed from the service of the United States as a man unfit to hold an important commission during a crisis like the present, when so much patience, charity, confidence, consideration, and patriotism are due from every soldier in the field." W. T. H. Brooks, John Newton, John Cochrane, brigadier generals, were also recommended for dismissal. Major General W. B. Franklin, Major General W. F. Smith, Brigadier General Samuel D. Sturgis, Brigadier General Edward Ferraro, being of no service to the army, were to be relieved from duty with it. (Eckenrode and Conrad 1941, 252-253)

3 Despite the fact that disloyal subordinates undermined Burnside's command, he had indeed thrown down the gauntlet—the government was obliged to support him or accept his resignation. Stanton, as well as Lincoln, had long since lost faith in him. Put in command in order to eclipse McClellan, he had dismally failed and had been, in fact, fortunate not to lose his army. Setting aside his personal opinion of Burnside being a loyal and devoted officer, Lincoln well realized that he was incapable of command and sent word to Halleck, on January 25, to meet Burnside at the White House that morning. The same day orders were issued from the War Department relieving, at his own request, Burnside from command of the army. Sumner (old and sick) was relieved of duty. Franklin was too. Hooker was assigned to Burnside's place. (Ibid, 253)

1st. That Major General A. E. Burnside, at his own request, be relieved from the command of the Army of the Potomac.

2d. That Major General E. V. Sumner, at his own request, be relieved from duty in the Army of the Potomac.

3d. That Major General W. B. Franklin be relieved from duty in the Army of the Potomac.

4th. That Major General J. Hooker be assigned to the command of the Army of the Potomac.

II. The officers relieved as above will report in person to the adjutant-general of the army.

To General J. Hooker, Executive Mansion, Washington, January 26, 1863.[1]

Major General Hooker:

General—I have placed you at the head of the Army of the Potomac. Of course I have done this upon what appear to me to be sufficient reasons, and yet I think it best for you to know that there are some things in regard to which I am not quite satisfied with you. I believe you to be a brave and skillful soldier, which of course I like. I also believe you do not mix politics with your profession, in which you are right. You have confidence in yourself, which is a valuable if not an indispensable quality. You are ambitious, which within reasonable bounds does good rather than harm; but I think that during General Burnside's command of the army you have taken counsel of your ambition and thwarted him as much as you could, in which you did a great wrong to the country and to a most meritorious and honorable brother officer. I have heard, in such a way as to believe it, of your recently saying that both the army and the government needed a dictator. Of course it was not for this, but in spite of it, that I have given you the command. Only those generals who gain successes can set up dictators. What I now ask of you is military success, and I will risk the dictatorship. The government will support you to the utmost of its ability, which is neither more nor less than it has

---

1 Although Lincoln had not selected him for this responsible place without reservation, Hooker had no sooner taken command than he began to infuse his magnetism and energy into the whole army. He abolished Burnside's organization by grand divisions and reestablished the corps system. He reorganized the cavalry and brought it into a new and greater efficiency. He improved his own favorite branch of the service, the artillery; and he set himself with great care to improve the condition and morale of the infantry. He insisted that the camps be made comfortable and sanitary. Sites were carefully selected and log foundations for the tents were made, their interstices being closed with clay. Chimneys of cross sticks and clay were erected with internal fireplaces. Orders concerning cleanliness were issued, rigid general inspections were enforced and the unheard of luxury of fresh soft bread was introduced. Clothing and blankets were also supplied, and winter quarters between the Rappahannock and the Potomac assumed an air of comfort that had theretofore been unknown. The army was promptly paid to November 1, packages of underclothing and edibles were sent from home by the boatload. "Fighting Joe" was the hero of the camp, and his men were ready to follow him anywhere. The rising spirits of the army found expression in all sorts of sports. Theaters were improvised and comical entertainments were given. Camp journals were published. Sack and meal races were run. Greased pigs were chased and oiled poles were climbed. Leaves of absence and furloughs were granted for periods of ten days, and these were increased in number for excellence in discipline. (Boyle 1903, 76-77)

done and will do for all commanders. I much fear that the spirit that you have aided to infuse into the army, of criticizing their commander and withholding confidence from him, will now turn upon you. I shall assist you as far as I can to put it down. Neither you nor Napoleon, if he were alive again, could get any good out of an army while such a spirit prevails in it. And now beware of rashness. Beware of rashness, but with energy and sleepless vigilance go forward and give us victories.

Yours very truly,
A. Lincoln.

Telegram to General Butler, Executive Mansion, Washington, January 28, 1863.[1]

Major General Butler, Lowell, Mass.:
Please come here immediately. Telegraph me about what time you will arrive.
A. Lincoln.

Telegram to General Dix, Executive Mansion, Washington, January 29, 1863.[2]

Major General Dix, Fort Monroe, Va.:
Do Richmond papers have anything from Vicksburg?
A. Lincoln.

Telegram To General Dix, War Department, Washington City, January 30, 1863, 5:45 P.M.[3]

Major General Dix, Fort Monroe, Va.:
What iron-clads, if any, have gone out of Hampton Roads within the last two days?
A. Lincoln.

Telegram to General Dix, War Department, Washington City, January 31, 1863.[4]

Major General Dix, Fort Monroe, Va.:

1 In December 1862, Lincoln replaced the controversial Butler with General Nathaniel Banks and Lincoln wished to discuss Butler's future in the Union army. In 1863, Butler was named to command the Department of Virginia and North Carolina which was subsequently designated the Army of the James, which formed the left wing of the combined forces under General Grant in 1864. (Smith 2011)

2 General Dix replied on the same day, "The Richmond papers up to and including the 27th, the latest date we have, were carefully examined and nothing about Vicksburg was noticed." (Lincoln v.6, 1953, 83)

3 General Dix replied on the same day, "No iron-clads have left for two days. The Weehawken is at Norfolk; the Patapsco is here, waiting for favorable weather, and the Nahant is at Newport News. I have just telegraphed to General Halleck our success in a fight with [Roger A.] Pryor." (Lincoln v.6, 1953, 84)

4 Irish-born Michael Corcoran, a Union General, had been captured at Bull Run; Roger A. Pryor, a member of the Confederate Congress, was a general in the Confederate army. (Hay 1998, 362)

Corcoran's and Pryor's battle terminated. Have you any news through Richmond papers or otherwise?

A. Lincoln.

Telegram to General Schenck, War Department, Washington City, January 31, 1863.[1]

Major General Schenck, Baltimore, Md.:

I do not take jurisdiction of the pass question. Exercise your own discretion as to whether Judge Pettis shall have a pass.

A. Lincoln.

Telegram to General Schenck [Cipher] War Department, Washington, February 4, 1863.[2]

Major General Schenck, Baltimore, Md.:

I hear of some difficulty in the streets of Baltimore yesterday. What is the amount of it?

A. Lincoln.

Telegram to General W. S. Rosecrans, Executive Mansion, Washington, February 12, 1863.[3]

Major General Rosecrans, Murfreesborough, Tenn.:

Your dispatch about "river patrolling" received. I have called the Secretary of the Navy, Secretary of War, and General-in-Chief together, and submitted it to them, who promise to do their very best in the case. I cannot take it into my own hands without producing inextricable confusion.

A. Lincoln.

---

1 A purported telegram from Schenck received at 4:40 P.M. on January 31, reads: "Judge Pettis desires leave tonight to visit a sick soldier at Gloucester Point. Shall he have it? A second telegram from Schenck received at 11:20 P.M., replied, "I beg to say that the telegram sent you in my name about a pass was without my authority." "Judge Pettis" was probably S. Newton Pettis, appointed associate justice in Colorado Territory in 1861, who had returned to Pennsylvania in 1862. (Lincoln v.6, 1953, 86)

2 Apparently, convalescent soldiers had taken out their frustrations by beating former slaves. There is no doubt that Schenck's command was tough on any perceived collaboration with the Confederates. Historian Robert J. Brugger noted that General Schenck had little tolerance for what he viewed as subversive actions. Brugger wrote that Schenck "went so far as to round up women who seemed to be spying on Union movements and send the ladies to Confederate lines" Brugger wrote that "on 3 July 1863 Schenck issued an order 'requesting and recommending' that every house display the American flag on the fourth. Police took down the numbers of flagless residences. After the battle of Gettysburg....Baltimoreans were forbidden to receive or entertain wounded from Lee's army." (Behn 2012)

3 General Rosecrans had telegraphed on February 11: "The enemy will direct all its operations to intercept our connection. To prevent this it is absolutely necessary to patrol the rivers. Information in possession of the commanding General and post Commanders must be promptly acted upon. It is, therefore, absolutely necessary to have the gunboats which co-operate in that work directed to report to, and receive instructions from, the general commanding, or, in his absence, the commanders along the river districts. The officers commanding gunboats express a willingness to co-operate with the department, but in order to make their aid effective and prompt, such arrangements should be made." (Lincoln v.6, 1953, 101)

Telegram to General Hooker, Executive Mansion, Washington, February 27, 1863.[1]

Major General Hooker:

If it will be no detriment to the service I will be obliged for Capt. Henry A. Marchant, of Company I, Twenty-third Pennsylvania Volunteers, to come here and remain four or five days.

A. Lincoln.

Telegram to General Hooker, Executive Mansion, Washington, March 13, 1863.[2]

Major General Hooker:

General Stahel wishes to be assigned to General Heintzelman and General Heintzelman also desires it. I would like to oblige both if it would not injure the service in your army, or incommode you. What say you?

A. Lincoln.

Telegram to General Rosecrans, Executive Mansion, Washington, March 25, 1863.[3]

Major General Rosecrans, Murfreesborough, Tenn.:

Your dispatches about General Davis and General Mitchell are received. General Davis' case is not particular, being simply one of a great many recommended and not nominated because they would transcend the number allowed by law. General Mitchell (was) nominated and rejected by the Senate and I do not think it proper for me to renominate him without a change of circumstances such as the performance of additional service, or an expressed change of purpose on the part of at least some senators who opposed him.

A. Lincoln.

---

1 Henry A. Marchant of Philadelphia was an artist who had been associated with his brother Edward D. Marchant in the painting of portraits and miniatures. During February 1863, Edward D. Marchant was engaged in painting the portrait of Lincoln. (Lincoln v.6, 1953, 118)

2 Hooker replied on March 14, "No serious loss will result to the service by the transfer of General Stahl to General Heintzelman's command, provided Colonel [Percy] Wyndham, now on duty with General H., be ordered to join his regiment [First New Jersey Cavalry]." On February 2, Samuel P. Heintzelman had been placed in command of the Twenty-second Corps and Department of Washington, and on March 17, Brigadier General Julius Stahel was assigned to command the cavalry under Heintzelman. (Lincoln v.6, 1953, 135)

3 General Rosecrans telegraphed on March 24, midnight, asking appointment of Brigadier General Jefferson C. Davis, formerly colonel of the Twenty-second Indiana Infantry, as a major general. On March 25, Rosecrans telegraphed a similar request for appointment of Brigadier General Robert B. Mitchell, formerly colonel of the Second Kansas Infantry. Neither was appointed, but Davis was brevetted major general of Volunteers as of August 8, 1864. (Lincoln v.6, 1953, 148)

Telegram to General S. A. Hurlbut, Washington, March 25, 1863.[1]

Major General Hurlbut, Memphis:

What news have you? What from Vicksburg? What from Yazoo Pass? What from Lake Providence? What generally?

A. Lincoln.

To General D. Hunter (Private) Executive Mansion, Washington, D. C April 1, 1863.[2]

Major General Hunter:

My Dear Sir— I am glad to see the accounts of your colored force at Jacksonville, Florida. I see the enemy are driving at them fiercely, as is to be expected. It is important to the enemy that such a force shall not take shape and grow and thrive in the South, and in precisely the same proportion it is important to us that it shall. Hence, the utmost caution and vigilance is necessary on our part. The enemy will make extra efforts to destroy them, and we should do the same to preserve and increase them.

Yours truly,

A. Lincoln.

Telegram to General Hooker, Executive Mansion, Washington, April 3, 1863.[3]

Major General Hooker:

---

1 Yazoo Pass was a water entry to Vicksburg and was blocked off by actions at Steele's Bayou. Lincoln, in some exasperation, sought Hurlbut's advice. But Hurlbut, although in overall charge of the base camp at Memphis, was presiding unsuccessfully over the "widely dispersed 16th Corps" in this phase of the siege. It would take a land assault by Grant to take Vicksburg, and the city would hold out until July 4, 1863. (Apperson and Roper 2001, 395)

2 In March 1862, a change in command resulted in Major General David Hunter's becoming the commander of the Department of the South. An abolitionist in conviction, Hunter declared "contrabands" in this district "free" and quietly began to recruit troops from black slave communities on the islands. His initial efforts met with little success, as blacks were suspicious of the sudden opportunity to don a uniform and arms to go to battle. He later instituted a draft of all able-bodied black men between 18 and 45 in the states of South Carolina, Georgia, and Florida. (Booker 2000, 72)

3 The *Carrie Martin*, a small steamer, left the Washington Navy Yard on the afternoon of April 4, 1863. On board were Mr. and Mrs. Lincoln, their ten-year-old son, Tad, Attorney General Bates, the President's old crony Dr. Anson G. Henry, then Surveyor General of Washington Territory, a Captain Crawford of the Overland Service, and Noah Brooks. It snowed heavily and before nightfall the wind reached gale proportions with the result that the ship put into a cove, opposite Indian Head, where the anchor was dropped until the next morning. It was still snowing when they arrived at Aquia Creek, where a special train, consisting of "a rude freight car, decorated with flags," met the President and his guests and transported them to Falmouth Station. There the President and his party were met by General Butterfield, Joe Hooker's Chief of Staff accompanied by an escort of lancers, and in carriages they rode "over a fearfully muddy road, 'the sacred soil' red and clayey" to headquarters. For lodgings they were given wall-tents, warmed by stoves and, it was noted, "real sheets" were on the beds. Mr. Lincoln seemed to enjoy the sharp contrast to the White House. Mr. Lincoln had come for relaxation, but, in the days that followed, he was as fully occupied as ever. Weather permitting, he reviewed the forces, visited hospitals, received callers. He

---

Our plan is to pass Saturday night on the boat, go over from Aquia Creek to your camp Sunday morning, remain with you till Tuesday morning, and then return. Our party will probably not exceed six persons of all sorts.

A. Lincoln.

Telegram to General Hooker, Washington, April 12, 1863.[1]

Major General Hooker:

Your letter by the hand of General Butterfield is received, and will be conformed to. The thing you dispense with would have been ready by mid-day tomorrow.

A. Lincoln.

Telegram to Admiral S. P. Dupont, Executive Mansion, Washington, April 13, 1863.[2]

Admiral Dupont:

Hold your position inside the bar near Charleston; or, if you shall have left it, return to it, and hold it until further orders. Do not allow the enemy to erect

---

was constantly on horseback and is said to have exhausted several mounts. When someone remarked that the rest was good for him, he shook his head dubiously and replied: "I don't know about the 'rest,' as you call it. I suppose it is good for the body. But the tired part of me is inside and out of reach."" (Means 1961, 105-106)

1 Hooker's letter of April 11, 1863, hand carried to Lincoln by his Chief of Staff, Major General Daniel Butterfield, read as follows: "After giving the subject my best reflection, I have concluded that I will have more chance of inflicting a serious blow upon the Enemy by turning his position to my right, and if practicable to sever his communication with Richmond with my Dragoon force, and such Batteries as it may be deemed advisable to send with them. I am apprehensive that he will retire from before me the moment I should succeed in crossing the river, and over the shortest line to Richmond, and thus escape being seriously crippled. I hope that when the Cavalry have established themselves on the line between him and Richmond, they will be able to hold him and check his retreat until I can fall on his rear, or if not that, I will compel him to fall back by the way of Culpepper, and Gordonsville over a longer line than my own with his supplies cut off. The Cavalry will probably cross the river above the Rappahannock bridge, thence to Culpepper and Gordonsville, and across to the Aquia Railroad somewhere in the vicinity of Hanover Court House. They will probably have a fight in the vicinity of Culpepper, but not one that should cause them much delay or embarrassment. I have given directions for the Cavalry to be in readiness to commence the movement on Monday morning next. While the Cavalry are moving, I shall threaten the passage of the river at various points, and after they have passed well to the Enemies rear, shall endeavor to effect the crossing. I hope Mr. President, that this plan will receive your approval. It will obviate the necessity of detaching a force from Washington in the direction of Warrenton, while I think it will enhance my chances for inflicting a heavy blow upon the enemies forces. We have no news from over the river today, the enemy refusing to let us have the newspaper. I sincerely trust that you reached home safely, and in good time yesterday. We all look back to your visit with great satisfaction." (Lincoln v.6, 1953, 169)

2 Lincoln realized that, above all things, the immense psychological value of monitors must not be dissipated. Within the month the frightened Confederates below Vicksburg had destroyed a captured ironclad when Porter's dummy monitor had come in sight. Moreover, if Du Pont abandoned the attack now, the jubilant Confederates might shift their troops elsewhere--against Grant at Vicksburg, or the Army of the Potomac in Virginia. In this note, he instructs Du Pont to hold his ground. The following day, April 14, fearing that Du Pont and General Hunter might interpret the presidential order as a reprimand, Lincoln amplified his thoughts in a private note written jointly to the two commanders. (West 1957, 237-238)

new batteries or defenses on Morris Island. If he has begun it, drive him out. I do not herein order you to renew the general attack. That is to depend on your own discretion or a further order.

A. Lincoln.

To General D. Hunter and Admiral S. F. Dupont, Executive Mansion, Washington, April 14, 1863.[3]

General Hunter and Admiral Dupont:

This is intended to clear up an apparent inconsistency between the recent order to continue operations before Charleston and the former one to remove to another point in a certain contingency. No censure upon you, or either of you, is intended. We still hope that by cordial and judicious co-operation you can take the batteries on Morris Island and Sullivan's Island and Fort Sumter. But whether you can or not, we wish the demonstration kept up for a time, for a collateral and very important object. We wish the attempt to be a real one, though not a desperate one, if it affords any considerable chance of success. But if prosecuted as a demonstration only, this must not become public, or the whole effect will be lost. Once again before Charleston, do not leave until further orders from here. Of course this is not intended to force you to leave unduly exposed Hilton Head or other near points in your charge.

Yours truly,

A. Lincoln.

P. S. Whoever receives this first, please send a copy to the other immediately. A. L.

Telegram to General S. Hooker, Washington, April 15, 1863, 10:15 P.M.[4]

Major General Hooker:

---

3 The "apparent inconsistency" to which Lincoln refers seems to be defined in Welles' April 2 communication to Du Pont: "The exigencies of the public service are so pressing in the Gulf that the Department directs you to send all the ironclads that are in a fit condition to move, after your present attack upon Charleston, directly to New Orleans, reserving to yourself only two." John Hay delivered Welles' order of April 2, and on April 16 he wrote Nicolay from Hilton Head, South Carolina, of the reception of Lincoln's order of April 13: "The General and the Admiral this morning received the orders from Washington, directing the continuance of operations against Charleston. The contrast was very great in the manner in which they received them. The General was absolutely delighted.... He said, however, that the Admiral seemed in very low spirits about it.... Whether the intention of the Government be to reduce Charleston now....or by powerful demonstration to retain a large force of the enemy here, he is equally anxious to go to work again...." Du Pont wrote Welles on April 1: "I am...painfully struck by the tenor and tone of the President's order, which seems to imply a censure, and I have to request that the Department will not hesitate to relieve me by an officer who . . . is more able to execute that service in which I have had the misfortune to fail: the capture of Charleston...." (Lincoln v.6, 1953, 173)

4 On April 17 Hooker replied to Lincoln's letter of the April 15: "I have the honor to acknowledge your communication of the night of the 15th inst. and in compliance with your request, transmit herewith a letter from Genl. Stoneman dated the 16th inst, as it will fully inform you of the circumstances attending his march up the river....The letter was this moment received. His failure, to accomplish speedily the objects of his expedition, is a source of deep regret...but I can find nothing in his conduct...requiring...censure. We cannot control the elements. From your letter I conclude that you had misapprehended the position of his ad-

---

It is now 10:15 P.M. An hour ago I received your letter of this morning, and a few moments later your dispatch of this evening. The latter gives me considerable uneasiness. The rain and mud of course were to be calculated upon. General S. is not moving rapidly enough to make the expedition come to anything. He has now been out three days, two of which were unusually fair weather, and all three without hindrance from the enemy, and yet he is not twenty-five miles from where he started. To reach his point he still has sixty to go, another river (the Rapidan) to cross, and will be hindered by the enemy. By arithmetic, how many days will it take him to do it? I do not know that any better can be done, but I greatly fear it is another failure already. Write me often. I am very anxious.

Yours truly,

A. Lincoln.

Telegram to General W. S. Rosecrans, Executive Mansion, Washington, April 23, 1863, 10:10 A.M.[1]

Major General Rosecrans, Murfreesborough, Tenn.:

Your dispatch of the 21st received. I really cannot say that I have heard any complaint of you. I have heard complaint of a police corps at Nashville, but your name was not mentioned in connection with it, so far as I remember. It may be that by inference you are connected with it, but my attention has never been drawn to it in that light.

A. Lincoln.

Telegram to General J. Hooker, Washington, April 27, 1863, 3:30 P.M.[2]

Major General Hooker:

How does it look now?

A. Lincoln.

---

vance the night of the second day out...which was on the South Side of the Rappahannock and fifty miles from this camp. I have given directions for him to remain in his present position, holding himself in readiness to march as soon, after, the roads and rivers will permit...I still hope to turn his movement to some good account....No one, Mr. President can be more anxious, than myself to relieve your cares and anxieties and you may be assured that I shall spare no labor, and suffer no opportunity to pass unimproved, for so doing. We have no reason to suppose that the enemy have any knowledge of the design of Genl. Stoneman's movement." (Lincoln v.6, 1953, 176)

1 Rosecrans had telegraphed Lincoln on April 21 as follows: "Thrice has notice directly come to me that some complaint has been lodged in the minds of persons high in authority or in records in the War office against the working of my army policy or that there was a conflict of authority between the civil & military each time I have stated that I know of none & asked for the specification that I might remedy the evil No reply has been given No information of what this all means. Can there be anything wrong I want to know it & appeal to you to please order the complaints to be communicated to me fully. If the Fox is unearthed, I will promise to skin him or pay for his hide." (Lincoln v.6, 1953, 186)

2 Hooker replied at 5 P.M.: "I am not sufficiently advanced to give an opinion. We are busy. Will tell you all as soon as I can, and have it satisfactory." (Lincoln v.6, 1953, 188)

Telegram to General D. Butterfield, Washington, May 3, 1863, 4:35 P.M.[1]

Major General Butterfield:
Where is General Hooker? Where is Sedgwick? Where is Stoneman?
A. Lincoln.

Telegram to General J. Hooker, Washington, May 4, 1863, 3:10 P M.[2]

Major General Hooker:
We have news here that the enemy has reoccupied heights above Fredericks-burg. Is that so?
A. Lincoln.

Telegram to General Burnside, Executive Mansion, Washington, May 4, 1863.[3]

Major General Burnside, Cincinnati, O.:
Our friend General Sigel claims that you owe him a letter. If you so remember please write him at once. He is here.
A. Lincoln.

Telegram to General Hooker, Washington, May 6, 1863, 11:00 A.M.[4]

Major General Hooker:
The great storm of yesterday and last night, has interrupted the telegraph; so that we think fit to send you Gen. Dix despatch of the contents of Richmond papers. I need not repeat the contents. We also try to get it to you by Telegraph. We have nothing from your immediate whereabouts since your short despatch to me, of the 4th. We hear many rumors, but do not exactly know what has be-come of Sedgwick. We have heard no word of Stoneman, except what is in Dix's despatch about Col. Davis which looks well. It is no discourgement that you have already fought the bulk of Longstreet's force, nor that Jackson is severely wounded. And now, God bless you, and all with you. I know you will do your best. Waste no time unnecessarily, to gratify our curiosity with despatches.
A. Lincoln.

---

1 Butterfield replied to Lincoln's query at 4:40 P.M., "General Hooker is at Chancellorsville. General Sedgwick, with 15,000 to 20,000 men, at a point 3 or 4 miles out from Fredericksburg, on the road to Chancellorsville. Lee is between. Stoneman has not been heard from. This is the situation at this hour from latest reports, 4.30 p.m." (Lincoln v.6, 1953, 196)

2 Hooker replied, "I am informed that it is so, but attach no importance to it." (Lincoln v.6, 1953, 196)

3 German-born Major General Franz Sigel commanded units that included the German XI Corps of the Army of the Potomac. Although he had graduated from Germany's military academy, Sigel was a weak leader who had the habit of snapping his fingers at shellbursts and shouting orders in his native language to his amazed non-German troops. After being defeated on May 15, 1864, by Major General John Breckinridge at New Market, Virginia, Sigel was relieved of his command. (Wright 2001, 154-155)

4 For Hooker's reply, see note to Lincoln's telegram of 12:30 P.M.

Telegram to General Hooker, Washington, May 6, 1863, 12:30 P.M. [1]

Major General Hooker:

Just as I telegraphed you contents of Richmond papers showing that our cavalry has not failed, I received General Butterfield's of 11 A.M. yesterday. This, with the great rain of yesterday and last night securing your right flank, I think puts a new face upon your case; but you must be the judge.

A. Lincoln.

Telegram to General Hooker, Washington, May 6, 1863, 2:25 P.M. [2]

Major General Hooker:

We have through General Dix the contents of Richmond papers of the 5th. General Dix's dispatch in full is going to you by Captain Fox of the navy. The substance is General Lee's dispatch of the 3d (Sunday), claiming that he had beaten you and that you were then retreating across the Rappahannock, distinctly stating that two of Longstreet's divisions fought you on Saturday, and that General [E. F.] Paxton was killed, Stonewall Jackson severely wounded, and Generals Heth and A. P. Hill slightly wounded. The Richmond papers also stated, upon what authority not mentioned, that our cavalry have been at Ashland, Hanover Court-House, and other points, destroying several locomotives and a good deal of other property, and all the railroad bridges to within five miles of Richmond.

A. Lincoln.

---

1 General Butterfield's despatch to Lincoln: "General Hooker is not at this moment able, from pressing duties, to write of the condition of affairs. He deems it his duty that you should be fully and correctly advised. He has intrusted it to me. These are my words, not his. 'Of his plans you were fully aware. The cavalry, as yet learned, have failed in executing their orders. [William W.] Averell's division returned; nothing done; loss of 2 or 3 men. [John] Buford's Regulars not heard from. General [John] Sedgwick failed in the execution of his orders, and was compelled to retire, and crossed the river at Banks' Ford last night; his losses not known. The First, Third, Fifth, Eleventh, Twelfth, and two divisions of Second Corps are now on south bank of Rappahannock, intrenched between Hunting Run and Scott's Dam. Trains and Artillery Reserve on north bank of Rappahannock. Position is strong, but circumstances, which in time will be fully explained, make it expedient, in the general's judgment, that he should retire from this position to the north bank of the Rappahannock for his defensible position. Among these is danger to his communication by possibility of enemy crossing river on our right flank and imperiling this army, with present departure of two-years' and three months' [nine-months'] troops constantly weakening him. The nature of the country in which we are prevents moving in such a way as to find or judge position or movements of enemy. He may cross to night, but hopes to be attacked in this position." (Ibid, 200)

2 Hooker replied at 4:30 P.M., "Have this moment returned to camp. On my way received your telegrams of 11 a.m. and 12:30. The army had previously recrossed the river, and was on its return to camp. As it had none of its trains of supplies with it, I deemed this advisable. Above, I saw no way of giving the enemy a general battle with the prospect of success which I desire. Not to exceed three corps, all told, of my troops have been engaged. For the whole to go, there is a better place nearer at hand. Will write you at length to-night. Am glad to hear that a portion of the cavalry have at length turned up. One portion did nothing." (Lincoln v.6, 1953, 199-200)

To General J. Hooker, Headquarters Army of the Potomac, May 7, 1863.[1]

Major General Hooker:

My Dear Sir—The recent movement of your army is ended without effecting its object, except, perhaps, some important breakings of the enemy's communications. What next? If possible, I would be very glad of another movement early enough to give us some benefit from the fact of the enemy's communication being broken; but neither for this reason nor any other do I wish anything done in desperation or rashness. An early movement would also help to supersede the bad moral effect of there certain, which is said to be considerably injurious. Have you already in your mind a plan wholly or partially formed? If you have, prosecute it without interference from me. If you have not, please inform me, so that I, incompetent as I may be, can try and assist in the formation of some plan for the army.

Yours as ever,

A. Lincoln.

Telegram to General J. Hooker, Washington, D. C. May 8, 1863, 4 P.M.[2]

Major General Hooker:

The news is here of the capture by our forces of Grand Gulf—a large and very important thing. General Willich, an exchanged prisoner just from Richmond, has talked with me this morning. He was there when our cavalry cut the roads in that vicinity. He says there was not a sound pair of legs in Richmond, and that our men, had they known it, could have safely gone in and burned everything and brought in Jeff Davis. We captured and paroled 300 or 400 men. He says as he came to City Point there was an army three miles long (Longstreet's, he thought) moving toward Richmond.

Muroy has captured a dispatch of General Lee, in which he says his loss was fearful in his last battle with you.

A. Lincoln.

---

1 On May 5, the Army of the Potomac had begun to cross back to the north bank of the Rappahannock, the Chancellorsville Campaign a depressing failure. A Confederate army of sixty thousand had fought a Federal army twice its size to a standstill and, at one point, the evening of May 2, had it on the ragged edge of disaster. By the evening of May 6, the baffled Union army, its numbers reduced by seventeen thousand casualties, was back in the camps it had left in confidence a few days earlier. On the evening of the same day, after receiving the report that Hooker was recrossing the Rappahannock, Lincoln's first words were, "My God! My God! What will the country say?" But despite disappointments and failures, the war had to go on, and in two years of thwarted hopes Lincoln had learned that whatever the shortcomings of his army commanders might be, the past was irretrievable, and he, more than anyone else, had to look ahead. And so, on May 7, he queried Hooker as to his plans for the future. (Starr 1979, 366)

2 August von Willich, born in Prussia, the orphaned son of a Napoleonic officer, receiving a military education and, at age eighteen, he was commissioned in the Royal Prussian Army. Willich commanded a regiment on the second day at Shiloh, and was appointed brigadier general of volunteers in July 1862. He commanded 1st Brigade, 2nd Division, Right Wing, at Stones River, where he was captured on December 31, 1862 (Furqueron and Nofi 1998, 278-279)

Telegram to General J. A. Dix, War Department, May 9, 1863.[1]

Major General Dix:

It is very important for Hooker to know exactly what damage is done to the railroads at all points between Fredericksburg and Richmond. As yet we have no word as to whether the crossings of the North and South Anna, or any of them, have been touched. There are four of these Crossings; that is, one on each road on each stream. You readily perceive why this information is desired. I suppose Kilpatrick or Davis can tell. Please ascertain fully what was done, and what is the present condition, as near as you can, and advise me at once.

A. Lincoln.

Telegram to General Dix, War Department, Washington City, May 11, 1863.[2]

Major General Dix:

Do the Richmond papers have anything about Grand Gulf or Vicksburg?

A. Lincoln.

Telegram to General Butterfield [Cipher] War Department, Washington City, May 11, 1863.[3]

Major General Butterfield:

About what distance is it from the observatory we stopped at last Thursday to the line of enemies' works you ranged the glass upon for me?

A. Lincoln.

To General J. Hooker, Executive Mansion, Washington, D.C. May 14, 1863.[4]

Major General Hooker, Commanding:

My Dear Sir—When I wrote on the 7th, I had an impression that possibly by an early movement you could get some advantage from the supposed facts that the enemy's communications were disturbed and that he was somewhat

---

1 In response to this dispatch Dix replied: "Mr. Ould says neither of the two bridges over the South Anna nor the bridge over the North Anna was destroyed. The railroad communication is uninterrupted...."(French 1906. 339)

2 Dix replied: "I had but a moment to examine the papers. I have enclosed them to the Secretary of War. I saw nothing of Grand Gulf or Vicksburg." (Lincoln v.6, 1953, 210)

3 General Butterfield replied at 6:15 P.M. "About two miles in a direct line." (Ibid, 209)

4 Hooker had once again developed plans to move south of the Rappahannock River and, on May 13, he notified Lincoln that he was going to move on the following day. Alarmed that the move might be premature, Lincoln called Hooker to Washington. Upon Hooker's arrival on the following day, Lincoln handed him this letter giving him his objectives. Thus, by the end of May, Lee was preparing the Army of Northern Virginia for an invasion of the North, while Hooker maintained the Army of the Potomac in its positions along the Rappahannock. Lee intended to gather supplies, threaten some major northern cities, promote the northern peace movement, draw the Army of the Potomac away from the Rappahannock River, and fight a battle somewhere at some time. Hooker had his orders: keep Lee out of mischief and rebuild his army. (Krause and Cody 2005, 353)

deranged in position. That idea has now passed away, the enemy having re-established his communications, regained his positions, and actually received reinforcements. It does not now appear probable to me that you can gain anything by an early renewal of the attempt to cross the Rappahannock. I therefore shall not complain if you do no more for a time than to keep the enemy at bay and out of other mischief by menaces and occasional cavalry raids, if practicable, and to put your own army in good condition again. Still, if in your own clear judgment you can renew the attack successfully, I do not mean to restrain you. Bearing upon this last point, I must tell you that I have some painful intimations that some of your corps and division commanders are not giving you their entire confidence. This would be ruinous, if true, and you should therefore, first of all, ascertain the real facts beyond all possibility of doubt.

Yours truly,

A. Lincoln.

Telegram to General W. S. Rosecrans, Washington, May 20, 1863.[1]

Major General Rosecrans:

Yours of yesterday in regard to Colonel Haggard is received. I am anxious that you shall not misunderstand me. In no case have I intended to censure you or to question your ability. In Colonel Haggard's case I meant no more than to suggest that possibly you might have been mistaken in a point that could [be] corrected. I frequently make mistakes myself in the many things I am compelled to do hastily.

A. Lincoln.

Telegram to General W. S. Rosecrans, Washington, May 21, 1863, 4:40 P.M.[2]

Major General Rosecrans:

---

1 Rosecrans' telegram of May 19 is as follows: "The autograph letter of your Excellency dated May first . . . respecting the case of Col. David R. Haggard has just been handed me by the colonel. It seems to me . . . that my action . . . is not properly understood. My duty as comdr of troops is to see that they are kept at their maximum of efficiency . . . officers exist only to effect this . . . this duty is just recognized . . . by Genl Order Number one hundred war Dept. of 1862 which requires . . . commanders to report all officers who by reason of ill health or other cause have been absent from duty over sixty days. This was Col. Haggard's case when I assumed the command of this Dept. but he was in ill health when I saw him. He continued in ill health & absent . . . more than sixty days & I reported the facts to the War Dept. . . . the War Dept. dismissed him instead of mustering him out . . . now the Col. appears here & has not a doubt of his health & physical ability to command his Regiment. . . . His former place has not as yet been filled. . . . I have no objection whatever to the revocation of the order whereby he was mustered out. . . . I have thought it proper & due to you as well as to my official action to say this much in this case because the note of your Excellency seemed to imply that his being mustered out of the service was an official mistake of the Comdr. of this Dept. . . ." (Lincoln v.6, 1953, 224) No further reference has been found to the case of Colonel David R. Haggard of the Fifth Kentucky Cavalry, and Lincoln's letter to Rosecrans of May 1 has not been located. (Ibid, 225)

2 This letter relates to a plan by Lincoln to suborn Confederate newspapers and in the continuing propaganda war within the Confederacy. In this instance, the clergy was enlisted.

For certain reasons it is thought best for Rev. Dr. Jaquess not to come here. Present my respects to him, and ask him to write me fully on the subject he has in contemplation.

A. Lincoln.

Telegram to General S. A. Hurlbut, Washington, May 22, 1863.[1]

Major General Hurlbut, Memphis, Tenn.:

We have news here in the Richmond newspapers of 20th and 21st, including a dispatch from General Joe Johnston himself, that on the 15th or 16th—a little confusion as to the day—Grant beat Pemberton and [W. W.] Loring near Edwards Station, at the end of a nine hours' fight, driving Pemberton over the Big Black and cutting Loring off and driving him south to Crystal Springs, twenty-five miles below Jackson. Joe Johnston telegraphed all this, except about Loring, from his camp between Brownsville and Lexington, on the 18th. Another dispatch indicates that Grant was moving against Johnston on the 18th.

A. Lincoln.

Methodist minister James F. Jaquess, who was also a colonel in the Union army, was apparently put into contact with the administration through his superior officer, Brigadier General James A. Garfield, with the view of having Jaquess use his contacts within the Southern branch of the church. It is not clear Lincoln expected Jaquess to accomplish as he traveled throughout the South in 1863. Possibly, he was to seek out peace sentiments within his Southern brethren, but he also might have been attempting to sow discontent among Southern clergy. In any event, Lincoln was careful to disconnect himself from Jaquess and there seem to have been some in Washington who deemed Jaquess a spy. (Heidler et al. 2000, 511) On May 28, Lincoln provided Rosecrans with some additional thoughts: "I have but a slight personal acquaintance with Col. Jaquess, though I know him very well by character. Such a mission as he proposes I think promises good, if it were free from difficulties, which I fear it cannot be. First, he cannot go with any government authority whatever. This is absolute and imperative. Secondly, if he goes without authority, he takes a great deal of personal risk—he may be condemned, and executed as a spy. If, for any reason, you think fit to give Col. Jaquess a Furlough, and any authority from me, for that object, is necessary, you hereby have it for any length of time you see fit." (Lincoln v.6, 1953, 236)

1 Hurlbut replied on May 23: "I forward the following, just received from Col. John A. Rawlins, assistant adjutant-general, rear of Vicksburg, 20th....The Army of the Tennessee landed at Bruinsburg on 30th April....On 1st May, fought battle of Port Gibson; defeated rebels under [John S.] Bowen, whose loss in killed, wounded, and prisoners was at least 1,500; loss in artillery, five pieces....On 12th May, at the battle of Raymond, rebels were defeated, with a loss of 800....On the 14th, defeated Joseph E. Johnston, captured Jackson, with loss to the enemy of 400, besides immense stores and manufactories, and seventeen pieces artillery.... On the 16th, fought the bloody and decisive battle of Baker's Creek, in which the entire Vicksburg force, under [John C.] Pemberton, was defeated, with loss of twenty-nine pieces of artillery and 4,000 men....On the 17th, defeated same force at Big Black Bridge, with loss of 2,600 men and eleven pieces of artillery....On the 18th, invested Vicksburg closely. To-day General [Frederick] Steele carried the rifle-pits on the north of the city. The right of the army rests on the Mississippi above Vicksburg....I learn further that there are from 15,000 to 20,000 men in Vicksburg, and that Pemberton lost nearly all his field artillery; that the cannonading at Vicksburg ceased about 3 p.m. of 20th. Grant has probably captured nearly all." (Lincoln v.6, 1953, 226)

Telegram to General Burnside, War Department, Washington, May 26, 1863.[1]

Major General Burnside, Cincinnati, O.:
Your dispatch about Campbell, Lyle, and others received and postponement ordered by you approved. I will consider and telegraph you again in a few days.
A. Lincoln.

Telegram to General Schenck, Executive Mansion, Washington, May 27, 1863.[2]

Major General Schenck, Baltimore, Md.:
Let the execution of William B. Compton be respited or suspended till further order from me, holding him in safe custody meanwhile. On receiving this notify me.
A. Lincoln.

Telegram to General W. S. Rosecrans, War Department, May 27, 1863.[3]

Major General Rosecrans, Murfreesborough, Tenn.:
Have you anything from Grant? Where is Forrest's headquarters?
A. Lincoln.

To General Schofield, Executive Mansion, Washington, May 27, 1863.[4]

General John M. Schofield:
My Dear Sir—Having relieved General Curtis and assigned you to the command of the Department of the Missouri, I think it may be of some advantage for me to state why I did it. I did not relieve General Curtis because of any full

---

1 Burnside's despatch of May 26 stated: "The extension of time to [Thomas M.] Campbell and [John R.] Lyle in justice requires the same extension to the others condemned to be hung on Johnson's Island next Friday, and I have therefore ordered that the executions be postponed one week till I can hear more definitely from you." (Ibid, 231) Campbell and Lyle were Confederate spies.

2 Later references to William B. Compton in the Official Records indicate that he was still in confinement at Fort McHenry in January, 1865. (Ibid, 234)

3 Rosecrans replied at 10:15 P.M., "According to our latest news, Forrest's headquarters were at Spring Hill yesterday, and moved to Riggs' cross-roads, 18 miles southwest of here, to-day. The latest from Grant we have is of the rebel dispatch last night, saying that Johnston had crossed Big Black north of him with 20,000 men. they were not jubilant at 2 o'clock to-day, when our provost-marshal was on their front, talking to Dr. [Benjamin F.] Avent Bragg's chief surgeon." (Ibid, 233)

4 General Samuel R. Curtis had suppressed the Rev. Samuel S. McPheeters from preaching because of the minister's Southern sympathies and, while civilians were difficult enough to control, disciplining the military could be equally troublesome. Lincoln's policy was wherever possible to expand and protect the number of friends of the Union. This meant trying to patch up differences where possible and removing obstacles where necessary. Eventually, Lincoln decided that the situation in Missouri required a change in command and appointed General John M. Schofield to replace Curtis and wrote Schofield this personal advisory. (Behn 2013)

conviction that he had done wrong by commission or omission. I did it because of a conviction in my mind that the Union men of Missouri, constituting, when united, a vast majority of the whole people, have entered into a pestilent factional quarrel among themselves—General Curtis, perhaps not of choice, being the head of one faction and Governor Gamble that of the other. After months of labor to reconcile the difficulty, it seemed to grow worse and worse, until I felt it my duty to break it up somehow; and as I could not remove Governor Gamble, I had to remove General Curtis. Now that you are in the position, I wish you to undo nothing merely because General Curtis or Governor Gamble did it, but to exercise your own judgment, and do right for the public interest. Let your military measures be strong enough to repel the invader and keep the peace, and not so strong as to unnecessarily harass and persecute the people. It is a difficult role, and so much greater will be the honor if you perform it well. If both factions, or neither, shall abuse you, you will probably be about right. Beware of being assailed by one and praised by the other.

Yours truly,

A. Lincoln.

Telegram to General Hooker, Washington, May 27, 1863, 11 P.M.[1]

Major General Hooker:

Have you Richmond papers of this morning? If so, what news?

A. Lincoln.

Telegram to General W. S. Rosecrans, Washington, May 28, 1863.[2]

Major General Rosecrans, Murfreesborough, Tenn.:

I would not push you to any rashness, but I am very anxious that you do your utmost, short of rashness, to keep Bragg from getting off to help Johnston against Grant.

A. Lincoln.

---

1   Hooker replied at 11:20 P.M., "I have received your telegram of 11 p.m. Rumors, and reports of rumors indicate that important changes are being made by them. Nothing, however, so far as I know, is sufficiently developed to determine what these changes are. The Richmond paper of yesterday I have, but it contains no news. I will keep you fully advised." (Lincoln v.6, 1953, 233)

2   Rosecrans curtly dismissed the president's prodding. "Dispatch received," he wired back. "I will attend to it." Then on June 2 Halleck telegraphed, "If you can do nothing yourself, a portion of your troops must be sent to Grant's relief." Rosecrans blandly promised action at some unspecified future date and polled his corps and division commanders in hopes of finding support for his continued inaction. He was not disappointed. The fifteen generals were virtually unanimous in declaring their belief that Bragg had detached no substantial forces to Johnston, though Rosecrans almost undoubtedly knew better. They also agreed that an advance by the Army of the Cumberland would not likely prevent such a transfer. Most of all, they agreed that an immediate advance was not a good idea. The only dissenter was Rosecrans's new chief of staff, Brig. Gen. James A. Garfield. The thirty-one-year-old Garfield was correct in pointing out the opportunity for an immediate advance, but he usually had a keen eye for politics and may well have been most concerned with the impression his statement would make in Washington. (Woodworth 1998, 17)

Telegram to General A. E. Burnside, Washington, May 29, 1863.[1]

Major General Burnside, Cincinnati, O.:

Your dispatch of today received. When I shall wish to supersede you I will let you know. All the Cabinet regretted the necessity of arresting, for instance, Vallandigham, some perhaps doubting there was a real necessity for it; but, being done, all were for seeing you through with it.

A. Lincoln.

Telegram to General U. S. Grant, War Department, June 2, 1863.[2]

Major General Grant, Vicksburg, via Memphis:

Are you in communication with General Banks? Is he coming toward you or going farther off? Is there or has there been anything to hinder his coming directly to you by water from Alexandria?

A. Lincoln.

Telegram to Major General Hooker [Cipher] Executive Mansion, Washington, June 4, 1863.[3]

Major General Hooker:

Let execution of sentences in the cases of Daily, Margraf, and Harrington be respited till further orders from me, they remaining in close custody meanwhile.

A. Lincoln.

Telegram to General Butterfield, War Department, Washington, June 4, 1863.[4]

Major General Butterfield:

---

1 Clement Laird Vallandigham, a Peace Democrat who was considered the foremost Copperhead, was probably Lincoln's toughest critic. A major constitutional confrontation occurred after Vallandigham was detained, tried by a military tribunal, and exiled to the Confederacy for his bitter political speeches against Lincoln and his administration. (Williams 2002, 67)

2 Grant telegraphed on June 8 that Banks, "has Port Hudson closely invested," and that he would forward by mail a letter from Banks of June 4. Banks' letter of June 4 reads in part: "It seems to me that I have no other course than to carry my object here thus crippling the enemy, and to join you with my whole strength as soon as possible This I hope to accomplish in a few days...." (Lincoln v.6, 1953, 244)

3 Privates Enos Daily, Philip Margraff, and Carlos Harrington of the One Hundred Forty-sixth New York Volunteers, were all sentenced to be shot for desertion. Hooker's telegram acknowledging receipt of Lincoln's order was received at 9:20 P.M., June 4. (Ibid, 248)

4 On June 4, General Butterfield telegraphed: "Richmond Sentinel June 3d. says, "Jackson June 1st. Grant demanded the surrender of Vicksburg on Thursday giving three days to Pemberton to consider the demand. Pemberton replied that he did not want 15 minutes & that his troops would die in the trenches before they would surrender. The federal troops are demoralized & refused to renew the attack on Saturday. The enemys Gunboats are firing hot shot at the City the federal loss is estimated at 25,000 or 30,000.... Port Hudson is invested. Nothing in Enquirer of June 4." (Ibid, 247)

The news you send me from the Richmond Sentinel of the 3d must be greatly if not wholly incorrect. The Thursday mentioned was the 28th, and we have dispatches here directly from Vicksburg of the 28th, 29th, 30th, and 31st; and, while they speak of the siege progressing, they speak of no assault or general fighting whatever, and in fact they so speak as to almost exclude the idea that there can have been any since Monday the 25th, which was not very heavy. Neither do they mention any demand made by Grant upon Pemberton for a surrender. They speak of our troops as being in good health, condition, and spirits. Some of them do say that Banks has Port Hudson invested.

A. Lincoln.

Telegram to General Hooker, Washington, June 5, 1863.[1]

Major General Hooker:

Yours of today was received an hour ago. So much of professional military skill is requisite to answer it that I have turned the task over to General Halleck. He promises to perform it with his utmost care. I have but one idea which I think worth suggesting to you, and that is, in case you find Lee coming to the north of the Rappahannock, I would by no means cross to the south of it. If he should leave a rear force at Fredericksburg, tempting you to fall upon it, it would fight in entrenchments and have you at advantage, and so, man for man, worst you at that point, while his main force would in some way be getting an advantage of you northward. In one word, I would not take any risk of being entangled up on the river like an ox jumped half over a fence and liable to be torn by dogs front and rear without a fair chance to gore one way or to kick the other.

If Lee would come to my side of the river I would keep on the same side and fight him, or act on the defensive, according as might be my estimate of his strength relatively to my own. But these are mere suggestions, which I desire to be controlled by the judgment of yourself and General Halleck.

A. Lincoln.

Telegram to General Dix, War Department, Washington, June 6, 1863.[2]

Major General Dix, Fort Monroe, Va.:

By noticing the news you send from the Richmond Dispatch of this morning you will see one of the very latest dispatches says they have nothing reliable from Vicksburg since Sunday. Now we here have a dispatch from there Sunday and others of almost every day preceding since the investment, and while they show

---

1 Both armies remained generally inactive till the 5th of June, when General Hooker wrote a lengthy letter to Lincoln detailing his reasons as to why appearances indicated an potential advance by Lee. (Raymond 1865, 769)

2 As the siege of Vicksburg progressed, Grant received a steady stream of reinforcements from his own department and departments farther afield. The arrival of all these reinforcements raised Grant's strength from 50,000 at the end of May to 77,000 in mid-June. This enabled him to split his command in two, half to continue the siege of Vicksburg and the other half to keep an eye on Johnston's growing army at Jackson. Grant assigned command of this new force to his trusted lieutenant, William T. Sherman. (Martin 1994, 193)

the siege progressing they do not show any general fighting since the 21st and 22d. We have nothing from Port Hudson later than the 29th when things looked reasonably well for us. I have thought this might be of some interest to you.

A. Lincoln.

Telegram to General Dix, Executive Mansion, Washington, June 8, 1863.[1]

Major General Dix, Fort Monroe:

We have dispatches from Vicksburg of the 3d. Siege progressing. No general fighting recently. All well. Nothing new from Port Hudson.

A. Lincoln.

Telegram to General Dix, War Department, Washington, June 8, 1863.[2]

Major General Dix, Fort Monroe:

The substance of news sent of the fighting at Port Hudson on the 27th we have had here three or four days, and I supposed you had it also, when I said this morning, "No news from Port Hudson." We knew that General Sherman was wounded, but we hoped not so dangerously as your dispatch represents. We still have nothing of that Richmond newspaper story of Kirby Smith crossing and of Banks losing an arm.

A. Lincoln.

Telegram to General Hooker, Washington, June 9, 1863.[3]

Major General Hooker:

I am told there are 50 incendiary shells here at the arsenal made to fit the 100 pounder Parrott gun now with you. If this be true would you like to have the shells sent to you?

A. Lincoln.

---

1 Dix telegraphed at 3 P.M. in reply to both of Lincoln's June 8 messages, "Steamer *Cahawba* has just arrived from New Orleans with the 6th N.Y. Vols. Left on 2nd June Port Hudson was attacked on the (27th) twenty seventh. Gen Sherman was brought to New Orleans severely wounded and little hopes of his recovery. He was speechless when Col [William] Wilson saw him...." (Lincoln v.6, 1953, 254) Note: The reports of General Sherman's condition were somewhat exaggerated.

2 Ibid.

3 The Parrott gun, a rifled artillery weapon, was named after its inventor, a West Pointer named Robert P. Parrott. He had resigned from the Army in 1836 to become superintendent of the Cold Spring Foundry, which was the most important Northern munitions factory during the war. There the Parrott gun was produced in large quantities. (Dupuy 1956, 218)

Telegram to General Hooker, Washington, June 10, 1863.[1]

Major General Hooker:

Your long dispatch of today is just received. If left to me, I would not go south of the Rappahannock upon Lee's moving north of it. If you had Richmond invested today you would not be able to take it in twenty days; meanwhile your communications, and with them your army, would be ruined. I think Lee's army, and not Richmond, is your true objective point. If he comes towards the upper Potomac, follow on his flank, and on the inside track, shortening your lines while he lengthens his. Fight him, too, when opportunity offers. If he stay where he is, fret him and fret him.

A. Lincoln.

Telegram to General Hooker [Cipher] Executive Mansion, Washington, June 12, 1863.[2]

Major General Hooker:

If you can show me a trial of the incendiary shells on Saturday night, I will try to join you at 5 P.M. that day Answer.

A. Lincoln.

Telegram to General Kelley, Washington, June 14, 1863, 1:27 P.M.[3]

Major General Kelley, Harper's Ferry:

Are the forces at Winchester and Martinsburg making any effort to get to you?

A. Lincoln.

Telegram to General R. C. Schenck, War Department, June 14, 1863.[4]

Major General Schenck:

---

1 Earlier in June, upon discerning signs of Lee's movement, Hooker had again displayed his obsession with attacking Richmond. In this letter, Lincoln is again forced to reiterate the headquarters doctrine as to the futility of attacking the city and, instead, directs him to pursue Lee. (Hattaway and Jones, 1991, 399)

2 Hooker replied, "It will give me great pleasure to have the gun on exhibition at 5 P.M. tomorrow. I have some good targets in the shape of rebel camps which the gun will enfilade." (Lincoln v.6, 1953, 270)

3 Kelley replied, "Dispatch received. I am not advised that the forces at Winchester, under General Milroy, are falling back on this place. The forces of my command at Martinsburg are ordered to fall back on me, if assailed by overpowering numbers." (Lincoln v.6, 1953, 274)

4 Schenck replied, "I am doing all I can to get Milroy back toward Harper's Ferry on the railroad. He sent down a courier in the night to say that, if he could not fall back, he could sustain himself, and hold his position five days, but I have no force to support him. The rebels appear to have pushed on beyond him rapidly and impetuously, and are reported approaching Martinsburg." (Ibid, 274)

Get General Milroy from Winchester to Harper's Ferry, if possible. He will be "gobbled up" if he remains, if he is not already past salvation.

A. Lincoln, President, United States.

Telegram to General Tyler, War Department, June 14, 1863.[1]

General Tyler, Martinsburg:
Is Milroy invested so that he cannot fall back to Harper's Ferry?
A. Lincoln.

Telegram to General Tyler, War Department, June 14, 1863.[2]

General Tyler, Martinsburg:
If you are besieged, how do you dispatch me? Why did you not leave before being besieged?
A. Lincoln.

Telegram to General Hooker, Washington, June 14, 1863, 3:50 P.M.[3]

Major General Hooker:
So far as we can make out here, the enemy have Muroy surrounded at Winchester, and Tyler at Martinsburg. If they could hold out a few days, could you help them? If the head of Lee's army is at Martinsburg and the tail of it on the plank-road between Fredericksburg and Chancellorsville, the animal must be very slim somewhere; could you not break him?
A. Lincoln.

Telegram to General Meagher, War Department, Washington, June 16, 1863.[4]

General T. Francis Meagher, New York:

---

1 Tyler replied at 3 P.M., "General Milroy is in a tight place. If he gets out, it will be by good luck and hard fighting. Not a straggler from his army is yet in; it is neck or nothing. We are besieged here; have had a little skirmish. I imagine our rebel friends are waiting for grub and artillery." (Ibid, 275)

2 No reply has been located, but Tyler fell back to Harper's Ferry.

3 At this point, the Army of Northern Virginia became mysteriously elongated, advance guard splashing across the Potomac shallows above Harpers Ferry, rear guard lingering near Fredericksburg, other elements strung out between. In this letter, Lincoln advises Hooker that so long an animal must be very slim somewhere, and suggests that it might be broken in half if the thinnest spot could just be found. But War Department distrust of Hooker was too solid by now, and Hooker could not take the initiative; he was crippled by the Chancellorsville failure, and neither he nor anyone else could prevent what was coming. (Catton 1956, 247)

4 Thomas Francis Meagher, an Irish revolutionary sentenced to be hanged, drawn, and quartered by the British government, became the darling of Irish-America in the Civil War years. His death sentence was commuted to banishment for life in Tasmania. After making an escape by sea in 1852, he landed in New York City to the cheers of the immigrant Irish. Meagher then set about making a new life, marrying the daughter of a rich New York

Your dispatch received. Shall be very glad for you to raise 3000 Irish troops if done by the consent of and in concert with Governor Seymour.

A. Lincoln.

Telegram to General Hooker, Washington, June 16, 1863, 10 P.M.[1]

Major General Hooker:

To remove all misunderstanding, I now place you in the strict military relation to General Halleck of a commander of one of the armies to the general-in-chief of all the armies. I have not intended differently, but as it seems to be differently understood I shall direct him to give you orders and you to obey them.

A. Lincoln.

Telegram to General Hooker, War Department, Washington, June 17, 1863.[2]

Major General Hooker:

Mr. Eckert, superintendent in the telegraph office, assures me that he has sent and will send you everything that comes to the office.

A. Lincoln.

Telegram to General Dingman, War Department, Washington, June 18, 1863.[3]

General A. Dingman, Belleville, C. W.:

Thanks for your offer of the Fifteenth Battalion. I do not think Washington is in danger.

A. Lincoln.

---

merchant, editing an Irish-American newspaper, practicing law, exercising his oratorical powers, and involving himself in a number of Central American adventures. Like so many other restless Americans, he found new opportunities in the Civil War. As captain in the 69th New York State Militia, he added to his earlier laurels a martial reputation earned at the Battle of Bull Run. (Kohl 1994, xi)

1   As the Army of the Potomac moved northward to counter the Confederate threat, a long, slow-burning animosity between Hooker and Halleck flared. For some time Hooker had bypassed Halleck and communicated directly with the President. Halleck protested that such action threatened the efficiency of the army. In this note, Lincoln sought to clarify the relationships. (Thomas 1952, 382)

2   Hooker had telegraphed Lincoln on the 16th and Halleck on the 17th of his need for "correct information concerning the enemy on the north side of the Potomac." (Lincoln v.6, 1953, 284)

3   A telegram signed "A. Dingman, Brig. Genl. Vols. Canada," from Belleville, C. W. [Ontario], was received in cipher from New York on June 18, as follows: "If Washington is in danger the fifteenth battalion is at your service to drive Lee back to Richmond. Hurrah for the Union...answer." (Ibid, 285)

To General J. M. Schofield, Executive Mansion, Washington, June 22, 1863.[1]

General John M. Schofield:

My Dear Sir—Your dispatch, asking in substance whether, in case Missouri shall adopt gradual emancipation, the General Government will protect slave owners in that species of property during the short time it shall be permitted by the State to exist within it, has been received. Desirous as I am that emancipation shall be adopted by Missouri, and believing as I do that gradual can be made better than immediate for both black and white, except when military necessity changes the case, my impulse is to say that such protection would be given. I cannot know exactly what shape an act of emancipation may take. If the period from the initiation to the final end should be comparatively short, and the act should prevent persons being sold during that period into more lasting slavery, the whole would be easier. I do not wish to pledge the General Government to the affirmative support of even temporary slavery beyond what can be fairly claimed under the Constitution. I suppose, however, this is not desired, but that it is desired for the military force of the United States, while in Missouri, to not be used in subverting the temporarily reserved legal rights in slaves during the progress of emancipation. This I would desire also. I have very earnestly urged the slave States to adopt emancipation; and it ought to be, and is, an object with me not to overthrow or thwart what any of them may in good faith do to that end. You are therefore authorized to act in the spirit of this letter in conjunction with what may appear to be the military necessities of your department. Although this letter will become public at some time, it is not intended to be made so now.

Yours truly,

A. Lincoln.

---

1 On June 20, Schofield had advised Lincoln, "The action of the Missouri state convention upon the question of Emancipation will depend very much upon whether they can be assured that the action will be sustained by the General Government & the people protected in their slave property during the short time that slavery is permitted to exist. Am I authorized in any manner directly or indirectly to pledge such support & protection? This question is of such vital importance to the peace of Missouri that I deem it my duty to lay it before your Excellency." (Ibid, 289) Note: Although the Emancipation Proclamation did not apply to Missouri, the question of the abolition of slavery in the State entered largely into the local politics of the day. At the election held in November, 1862, for members of the General Assembly, a majority of emancipationists were returned, though they were unable to take any definite action in the matter, owing to the exhausted condition of the state treasury, and to the constitutional provision, which forbade the emancipation of slaves without the consent of the owners, or the payment of a full equivalent for the slaves so freed. Satisfied that the people of the State were in favor of doing away with slavery, the legislature indicated it so plainly that Governor Gamble summoned the convention to meet on June 15, 1863, for the purpose of acting upon the question. After a prolonged debate, an ordinance was adopted which provided for gradual emancipation, and the convention then adjourned sine die. (Carr 1888, 363)

Telegram to General Couch, War Department, June 24, 1863.[1]

Major General Couch, Harrisburg, Pa.:

Have you any reports of the enemy moving into Pennsylvania? And if any, what?

A. Lincoln.

Telegram to General Dix, Washington, June 24, 1863.[2]

Major General Dix, Yorktown, Va.:

We have a dispatch from General Grant of the 19th. Don't think Kirby Smith took Milliken's Bend since, allowing time to get the news to Joe Johnston and from him to Richmond. But it is not absolutely impossible. Also have news from Banks to the 16th, I think. He had not run away then, nor thought of it.

A. Lincoln.

Telegram to General Peck, War Department, Washington, June 25, 1863.[3]

General Peck, Suffolk, Va.:

Colonel Derrom, of the Twenty-fifth New Jersey Volunteers, now mustered out, says there is a man in your hands under conviction for desertion, who formerly belonged to the above named regiment, and whose name is Templeton—Isaac F. Templeton, I believe. The Colonel and others appeal to me for him. Please telegraph to me what is the condition of the case, and if he has not been executed send me the record of the trial and conviction.

A. Lincoln.

---

1 Although Lincoln's telegram to Couch might sound as if, along with everyone else in Washington, he was overly concerned with the situation in Pennsylvania, his true beliefs were revealed in an exchange of letters with Governor Joel Parker of New Jersey. Parker wrote on June 29, 1863, "The people of New Jersey are apprehensive." The governor insisted on telling the president what to do. McClellan should be reinstated as commander of the Army of the Potomac and "the enemy should be driven from Pennsylvania." Lincoln responded on the day before the commencement of the battle at Gettysburg with the exact opposite opinion. "I really think the attitude of the enemies' army in Pennsylvania presents us the nest opportunity we have had since the war began." Lincoln, almost alone, saw Lee's invasion not as a dire tragedy, but as an opportunity. Lincoln was also fully aware that he was placing Meade in command of a recently twice-beaten army whose morale from fighting for so long in Virginia, was fragile. His basic concern was that Meade's Army of the Potomac needed to fulfill two functions at once: protect Washington and Baltimore, and strike at Lee and the Army of Northern Virginia as they entered Pennsylvania. (White 2009, 576)

2 No response from Dix has been identified.

3 Brigadier General Michael Corcoran replied to Lincoln's telegram at 3 P.M., "Isaac Templeton . . . has not yet been executed. The proceedings were reviewed by Maj Genl Dix and the record is in his hands. I will advise him that you wish it sent to you. Genl Peck is absent." (Lincoln v.6, 1953, 295)

Telegram to General Slocum, War Department, Washington, June 25, 1863.[1]

Major General Slocum, Leesburg, Va.:

Was William Gruvier, Company A, Forty-sixth, Pennsylvania, one of the men executed as a deserter last Friday?

A. Lincoln.

Telegram to General Burnside [Cipher] Washington, June 26. 1863.[2]

Major General Burnside Cincinnati, O.:

What is the case of "Willie Waller" at Maysville, Kentucky?

A. Lincoln.

Telegram to General Hooker, War Department, Washington, June 27, 1863, 8 A.M.[3]

Major General Hooker:

It did not come from the newspapers, nor did I believe it, but I wished to be entirely sure it was a falsehood.

A. Lincoln.

Telegram to General Burnside, Executive Mansion, Washington, June 28, 1863.[4]

Major General Burnside, Cincinnati, O.:

There is nothing going on in Kentucky on the subject of which you telegraph, except an enrolment. Before anything is done beyond this, I will take care to understand the case better than I now do.

A. Lincoln.

---

1 No reply has been located, but the roster of the Forty-sixth Pennsylvania lists William Gruver, enlisted September 2, 1861; deserted June 4, 1863, and executed at Leesburg, Virginia, June 19, 1863. (Ibid)

2 William Waller had been convicted as a spy and sentenced to be hanged. The court recommended clemency, and Burnside telegraphed Lincoln on June 27, recommending commutation to imprisonment for duration of the war. On June 30, Lincoln endorsed Burnside's telegram, writing, "Let the sentence be commuted as Gen. Burnside recommends." (Ibid, 296)

3 Someone had reported to Lincoln a rumor that Hooker had slipped in and out of Washington during the night of the twenty-fifth, probably for the purpose of drinking at his favorite haunts. Learning that Lincoln was concerned as to the "visit," Hooker had written, "My compliments to the President, and inform him that I had not that honor.... Was it from the newspapers that you received a report, or an idea, that I was in Washington last night?" Lincoln made his opinion on the matter clear in this June 27 note. (Wheeler 1987, 92)

4 Burnside had telegraphed Lincoln on June 26, "I am satisfied from my knowledge of [Kentucky] that it would be very unwise to enroll the free negroes of that State. It would not add materially to our strength and I assure you it would cause much trouble I sincerely hope this embarrassment to the interests of the public service will not be placed in our way. Please answer at once." (Lincoln v.6, 1953, 299)

Telegram to General Schenck, War Department, Washington, June 28, 1863.[1]

Major General Schenck, Baltimore, Md.:

Every place in the Naval school subject to my appointment is full, and I have one unredeemed promise of more than half a year's standing.

A. Lincoln.

Telegram to General Couch [Cipher] Washington City, June 30, 1863, 3:23 P.M.[2]

Major General Couch, Harrisburg, Pa.:

I judge by absence of news that the enemy is not crossing or pressing up to the Susquehanna. Please tell me what you know of his movements.

A. Lincoln.

To General D. Hunter, Executive Mansion, Washington, June 30, 1863.[3]

Major General Hunter:

My Dear General—I have just received your letter of the 25th of June. I assure you, and you may feel authorized in stating, that the recent change of commanders in the Department of the South was made for no reasons which convey any imputation upon your known energy, efficiency, and patriotism; but for causes which seemed sufficient, while they were in no degree incompatible with the respect and esteem in which I have always held you as a man and an officer.

I cannot, by giving my consent to a publication of whose details I know nothing, assume the responsibility of whatever you may write. In this matter your own sense of military propriety must be your guide, and the regulations of the service your rule of conduct.

I am very truly your friend,

A. Lincoln.

---

1 On June 13, General Schenck had telegraphed Lincoln "I see appointment of Midshipmen at large announced in papers today. I trust mine for my brother Lieut. Schencks orphan son is not too late...." On June 28, Schenck telegraphed again, "I am very sorry that I can get no reply to my application for an appointment at large at the Naval Academy for the Son of my deceased Brother Lieut. Schenck who died in the service" (Ibid)

2 At 9 P.M. Couch replied to Lincoln's telegram, "The rebel infantry force left Carlisle early this morning, on the Baltimore pike. Cavalry still on this side of that town. Early, with 8,000, left York this morning; went westerly or northwesterly. Rebels at York and Carlisle yesterday a good deal agitated about some news they had received. I telegraphed news to General Meade, care of the Secretary of War." (Ibid, 310)

3 Hunter had been relieved of his command of the Department of the South on June 3, 1863. He would principally serve on courts of inquiry until he assumed command of the Department of West Virginia on May 19, 1864. (Ibid, 311)

Telegram to General Burnside, War Department, Washington, July 3, 1863.[1]

Major General Burnside, Cincinnati, Ohio:

Private Downey, of the Twentieth or Twenty-sixth Kentucky Infantry, is said to have been sentenced to be shot for desertion today. If so, respite the execution until I can see the record.

A. Lincoln.

Telegram to General French. [Cipher] War Department, Washington, July 5, 1863.[2]

Major General French, Fredericktown, Md.:

I see your dispatch about destruction of pontoons. Cannot the enemy ford the river?

A. Lincoln.

Telegram to General H. W. Halleck, Soldiers' Home, Washington, July 6, 1863, 7 P.M.[3]

Major General Halleck:

I left the telegraph office a good deal dissatisfied. You know I did not like the phrase—in Orders, No. 68, I believe—"Drive the invaders from our soil." Since that, I see a dispatch from General French, saying the enemy is crossing his wounded over the river in flats, without saying why he does not stop it, or even intimating a thought that it ought to be stopped. Still later, another dispatch from General Pleasonton, by direction of General Meade, to General French, stating that the main army is halted because it is believed the rebels are concentrating "on the road towards Hagerstown, beyond Fairfield," and is not to move until it is ascertained that the rebels intend to evacuate Cumberland Valley.

These things appear to me to be connected with a purpose to cover Baltimore and Washington and to get the enemy across the river again without a further

---

1 While no reply has been located, on August 5, 1863, Private John Downey, Company G, Twenty-sixth Kentucky Volunteers, was pardoned by Lincoln and ordered to return to duty. (Ibid, 313)

2 Major-General William French had pushed his cavalry force to Williamsport and Falling Waters, where they destroyed the Confederate pontoon bridge and captured its guard. (Meade 1863, 53)

3 Lincoln continued to be focused on getting General Meade to pursue Lee. As usual, the president considered the recent battle an opportunity to destroy armies—not win possession of ground. Meade, like too many Union generals before him, did not appear to share this viewpoint. On the Fourth of July, the same day that Vicksburg fell, the general issued an order to his officers that compared the Rebels to foreigners but offered no plans for pursuit beyond the Potomac. "Our task is not yet accomplished," he wrote, "and the commanding general looks to the army for greater efforts to drive from our soil every vestige of the presence of the invader." To the president's ears, this comparison sounded defeatist. "Will our Generals never get that idea out of their heads?" he complained to John Hay. "The whole country is our soil." Two days after Meade's directive, Lincoln's frustration boiled over. On Monday evening, July 6, he left the War Department and headed out to the Soldiers' Home for the evening. He had just received word that Lee's army was beginning to cross the Potomac River. This time, however, he could not restrain himself and sent this biting message to Halleck. (Pinsker 2003, 104)

collision, and they do not appear connected with a purpose to prevent his crossing and to destroy him. I do fear the former purpose is acted upon and the latter rejected.

If you are satisfied the latter purpose is entertained, and is judiciously pursued, I am content. If you are not so satisfied, please look to it.

Yours truly,

A. Lincoln.

Telegram to General Thomas, War Department, Washington, July 8, 1863, 12:30 P.M.[1]

General Lorenzo Thomas, Harrisburg, Pa.:

Your dispatch of this morning to the Secretary of War is before me. The forces you speak of will be of no imaginable service if they cannot go forward with a little more expedition. Lee is now passing the Potomac faster than the forces you mention are passing Carlisle. Forces now beyond Carlisle to be joined by regiments still at Harrisburg, and the united force again to join Pierce somewhere, and the whole to move down the Cumberland Valley, will in my unprofessional opinion be quite as likely to capture the "man in the moon" as any part of Lee's army.

A. Lincoln.

Telegram to General Schenck [Cipher] War Department, Washington City, July 11, 1863.[2]

Major General Schenck, Baltimore, Md.:

How many rebel prisoners captured within Maryland and Pennsylvania have reached Baltimore within this month of July?

A. Lincoln.

To General Grant, Executive Mansion, Washington, July 13, 1863.[3]

Major General Grant:

My Dear General—I do not remember that you and I ever met personally. I write this now as a grateful acknowledgment of the almost inestimable service you have done the Country. I write to say a word further. When you first reached the vicinity of Vicksburg, I thought you should do what you finally did—march

---

1 Upon receiving Lincoln's telegram, Thomas telegraphed Stanton, "Telegram of the President received. It is a slow business to organize militia and put them in march. I am afraid the President supposed the troops in advance were to delay until those behind came up, but not so, as the orders are to press forward...." (Lincoln v.6, 1953, 322)

2 General Schenck replied at 5:30 P.M., "Have received in this month of July at Fort McHenry six thousand one hundred and forty two (6142) prisoners of war captured in Maryland and Pennsylvania." At 12:30 A.M. on July 12, Schenck telegraphed, "Add to the number of prisoners I reported . . . six hundred & fifty three, more received at Fort Delaware by way of Philadelphia. Those in hospitals here are not included." (Ibid, 323-324)

3 This letter clearly indicates Lincoln's admiration for an officer who possessed the initiative and boldness to successfully take the battle to the Confederate forces. (Browne 1974, 220)

the troops across the neck, run the batteries with the transports, and thus go below; and I never had any faith except a general hope that you knew better than I, that the Yazoo Pass expedition and the like could succeed. When you dropped below, and took Port Gibson, Grand Gulf, and vicinity, I thought you should go down the river and join General Banks; and when you turned northward, east of the Big Black, I feared it was a mistake. I now wish to make the personal acknowledgment that you were right and I was wrong.

Yours very truly,

A. Lincoln.

Telegram to General J. M. Schofield, War Department, Washington, July 13, 1863.[1]

General Schofield, St. Louis, Mo.:

I regret to learn of the arrest of the *Democrat* editor. I fear this loses you the middle position I desired you to occupy. I have not learned which of the two letters I wrote you it was that the *Democrat* published, but I care very little for the publication of any letter I have written. Please spare me the trouble this is likely to bring.

A. Lincoln.

To General Lane, Executive Mansion, Washington, July 17, 1863.[2]

Hon. S. H. Lane:

My Dear Sir—Governor Carney has not asked to [have] General Blunt removed, or interfered with, in his military operations. He has asked that he, the Governor, be allowed to commission officers for troops raised in Kansas, as other governors of loyal States do; and I think he is right in this.

He has asked that General Blunt shall not take persons charged with civil crimes out of the hands of the courts and turn them over to mobs to be hung; and I think he is right in this also. He has asked that General Ewing's department be extended to include all Kansas; and I have not determined whether this is right or not.

Yours truly,

A. Lincoln.

---

1 This letter refers to the arrest of St Louis newspaper editor William McKee. In general, Lincoln suspected that arrests of reporters and editors needlessly polarized opposition to the war by attempting to suppress language from the legitimate party opposition that worked no palpable harm on the U.S. military. Lincoln maintained this position throughout the war. (Neely 1991, 28)

2 On June 5, the War Department had appointed James G. Blunt special recruiting commissioner for Kansas, with authority to enlist a regiment of white cavalry and one of Negro infantry. It also empowered him to name the officers of these regiments. Those of the white regiment would be commissioned by the Governor of Kansas on Blunt's application, those of the Negro regiment by the Secretary of War. Carney's protest resulted in a modification of Blunt's instructions. On June 26 the War Department informed Blunt that henceforth he was not to nominate officers for the Fourteenth Kansas, as the white regiment was designated, that instead all the officers would be elected by the regiment itself and then commissioned by the Governor. (Castel 1958, 119)

To General Schofield, Executive Mansion, Washington, July 20, 1863.[1]

Major General John M. Schofield:

My Dear General—I have received and read your letter of the 14th of July. I think the suggestion you make, of discontinuing proceedings against Mr. McKee, a very proper one. While I admit that there is an apparent impropriety in the publication of the letter mentioned, without my consent or yours, it is still a case where no evil could result, and which I am entirely willing to overlook.

Yours truly,

A. Lincoln.

To General Oliver O. Howard, Executive Mansion, Washington, July 21, 1863.[2]

Major General Oliver Howard:

My dear General Howard—Your letter of the 18th. is received. I was deeply mortified by the escape of Lee across the Potomac, because the substantial destruction of his army would have ended the war, and because I believed, such destruction was perfectly easy, believed that Gen. Meade and his noble army had expended all the skill, and toil, and blood, up to the ripe harvest, and then let the crop go to waste. Perhaps my mortification was heightened because I had always believed—making my belief a hobby possibly—that the main rebel army going North of the Potomac, could never return, if well attended to; and because I was so greatly flattered in this belief, by the operations at Gettysburg. A few days having passed, I am now profoundly grateful for what was done, without criticism for what was not done. Gen. Meade has my confidence as a brave and skillful officer, and a true man.

Yours very truly,

A. Lincoln

---

1 From Lincoln's perspective, this letter seeks to resolve the matter of St Louis newspaper editor William McKee's arrest.

2 In the days after Gettysburg, Meade's cautious pursuit of Lee stirred dissatisfaction throughout the country, from the President on down. Howard's reaction was typical. The few letters written between the close of the battle and Lee's final evacuation of Maryland on July 14 hint that he would have welcomed another fight. There was frequent contact with Lee's rear guard and cavalry yet never a major engagement. On the twelfth, Meade was close enough for a general assault on Lee's position around Williamsport on the Potomac above Harpers Ferry, but at a meeting of corps commanders Howard was one of the few who voted to attack. On the thirteenth Howard requested permission to make a reconnaissance very early on the morning of the next day, and according to one reporter's account, Meade refused the request. This refusal was supposed to have permitted Lee to escape unnoticed and brought a sharp newspaper attack on Meade. Actually, there had been reconnaissance the previous day and more were ordered for the fourteenth of which the newspapers took no account. Howard, ever loyal to his superiors, believed that it was his duty to acquaint President Lincoln with the correct story and on July 18 wrote him a letter absolving Meade of all blame. (Carpenter 1999, 56-57)

Telegram to General J. M. Schofield, Washington, July 22, 1863.[1]

Major General Schofield, St. Louis, Mo.:

The following dispatch has been placed in my hands. Please look to the subject of it. Lexington, Mo., July 21, 1863 Hon. S C. Pomeroy: Under Orders No.63 the sheriff is arresting slaves of rebels inside our lines, and returning them in great numbers.

Can he do it? Answer.

A. Lincoln.

To General G. G. Meade [Private] Executive Mansion, Washington, July 27, 1863.[2]

Major General Meade:

I have not thrown General Hooker away; and therefore I would like to know whether it would be agreeable to you, all things considered, for him to take a corps under you, if he himself is willing to do so. Write me in perfect freedom, with the assurance that I will not subject you to any embarrassment by making your letter or its contents known to any one. I wish to know your wishes before I decide whether to break the subject to him. Do not lean a hair's breadth against your own feelings, or your judgment of the public service, on the idea of gratifying me.

Yours truly,

A. Lincoln.

Telegram to General A. B. Burnside, War Department, Washington, July 27, 1863.[3]

Major General Burnside, Cincinnati, O.:

Let me explain. In General Grant's first dispatch after the fall of Vicksburg, he said, among other things, he would send the Ninth Corps to you. Thinking

---

1 Schofield's reply was received at 8 P.M.: "Your dispatch relative to arrest of slaves of rebels is received. I will attend to the matter immediately." (Lincoln v.6, 1953, 344)

2 Although Hooker had been relegated to that select group of major generals who had failed to lead the Army of the Potomac to victory, Lincoln was not inclined to discard him. Fighters were scarce and must be put to use. Here, Lincoln asks Meade if he would consider having Hooker under him as a corps commander. Meade resorted to the expedient of not actually asking for Hooker but of not objecting if the General were ordered to serve under him. Lincoln misconstrued this to mean that Meade really wanted him. When Lincoln asked if Hooker should be sent at once, Meade set the record straight by replying that he had never expressed or entertained any such desire. In a letter home, he stated his true feelings: "It would be very difficult for Hooker to be quiet under me or anyone else, and I sincerely trust some independent command will be found for him." As an aside, Hooker had known of the proposal to return him to his old corps and naturally resented the turn things took. (Hebert 1999, 248)

3 On June 4, the Ninth Corps was sent to reinforce Grant at Vicksburg, and after Vicksburg the corps took part in the campaign against Jackson, Mississippi. Halleck notified Burnside, 11:20 A.M., July 25, that "whether the Ninth Corps will be returned to your department or sent to General Rosecrans will depend upon the enemy's movements." On July 31, Grant ordered the corps returned to its former command at Cincinnati. (Lincoln v.6, 1953, 350)

it would be pleasant to you, I asked the Secretary of War to telegraph you the news. For some reasons never mentioned to us by General Grant, they have not been sent, though we have seen outside intimations that they took part in the expedition against Jackson. General Grant is a copious worker and fighter, but a very meager writer or telegrapher. No doubt he changed his purpose in regard to the Ninth Corps for some sufficient reason, but has forgotten to notify us of it.

A. Lincoln.

To General H. W. Halleck, Executive Mansion, July 29, 1863.[1]

Major General Halleck:

Seeing General Meade's dispatch of yesterday to yourself causes me to fear that he supposes the Government here is demanding of him to bring on a general engagement with Lee as soon as possible. I am claiming no such thing of him. In fact, my judgment is against it; which judgment, of course, I will yield if yours and his are the contrary. If he could not safely engage Lee at Williamsport, it seems absurd to suppose he can safely engage him now, when he has scarcely more than two thirds of the force he had at Williamsport, while it must be that Lee has been reinforced. True, I desired General Meade to pursue Lee across the Potomac, hoping, as has proved true, that he would thereby clear the Baltimore and Ohio Railroad, and get some advantages by harassing him on his retreat.

These being past, I am unwilling he should now get into a general engagement on the impression that we here are pressing him, and I shall be glad for you to so inform him, unless your own judgment is against it.

Yours truly,

A. Lincoln.

To General S. A. Hurlbut, Executive Mansion, Washington, July 31, 1863.[2]

My Dear General Hurlbut:

---

1 General Meade had telegraphed Halleck at 3 P.M. on July 28: "I am making every effort to prepare this army for an advance.... I am in hopes to commence the movement to-morrow, when I shall first throw over a cavalry force to feel for the enemy, and cross the infantry as fast as possible....No reliable intelligence of the position of the enemy has been obtained. He pickets the Rappahannock from Fredericksburg to Rappahannock Station. These pickets, however, seem to be mere 'lookouts,' to warn him of my approach.... "Contradictory reports . . . place the main body, some at Gordonsville, others say at Staunton and Charlottesville, and some assert the retreat has been extended to Richmond. My own expectation is that he will be found behind the line of the Rapidan...."P.S. 4 p.m. —A scout just returned...reports the enemy have repaired the railroad bridge across the Rapidan, and are using the road to Culpeper Courthouse; that Lee has been reinforced by D. H. Hill, reported with 10,000 men, and that he intends to make a stand at Culpeper or in its vicinity." At 10 A.M., Halleck communicated Lincoln's note to Meade. (Ibid, 354)

2 The Emancipation Proclamation drew much criticism, North as well as South, not to mention challenges to its legality. In this letter to General S.A. Hurlburt, who had expressed a wish to resign, Lincoln reaffirmed the inviolability of the proclamation, and his belief that it was lawful. Note: Although, in 1961, Lincoln had wanted Hurlbut's resignation, he was not inclined to accept it at this point in the war. (Cuomo and Holzer 2004, 285)

Your letter by Mr. Dana was duly received. I now learn that your resignation has reached the War Department. I also learn that an active command has been assigned you by General Grant. The Secretary of War and General Halleck are very partial to you, as you know I also am. We all wish you to reconsider the question of resigning; not that we would wish to retain you greatly against your wish and interest, but that your decision may be at least a very well-considered one.

I understand that Senator [William K.] Sebastian, of Arkansas, thinks of offering to resume his place in the Senate. Of course the Senate, and not I, would decide whether to admit or reject him. Still I should feel great interest in the question. It may be so presented as to be one of the very greatest national importance; and it may be otherwise so presented as to be of no more than temporary personal consequence to him.

The Emancipation Proclamation applies to Arkansas. I think it is valid in law, and will be so held by the courts. I think I shall not retract or repudiate it. Those who shall have tasted actual freedom I believe can never be slaves or quasi-slaves again. For the rest, I believe some plan substantially being gradual emancipation would be better for both white and black. The Missouri plan recently adopted, I do not object to on account of the time for ending the institution; but I am sorry the beginning should have been postponed for seven years, leaving all that time to agitate for the repeal of the whole thing. It should begin at once, giving at least the new-born a vested interest in freedom which could not be taken away. If Senator Sebastian could come with something of this sort from Arkansas, I, at least, should take great interest in his case; and I believe a single individual will have scarcely done the world so great a service. See him if you can, and read this to him; but charge him not to make it public for the present. Write me again.

Yours very truly,

A. Lincoln.

To General N. P. Banks, Executive Mansion, Washington, August 5, 1863.[1]

My Dear General Banks:

While I very well know what I would be glad for Louisiana to do, it is quite a different thing for me to assume direction of the matter. I would be glad for her to make a new constitution, recognizing the emancipation proclamation, and adopting emancipation in those parts of the State to which the proclamation does not apply. And while she is at it, I think it would not be objectionable for her to adopt some practical system by which the two races could gradually live themselves out of their old relation to each other, and both come out better pre-

---

1 When, from 1863 onwards, Louisiana and Tennessee were discussing the possibility of forming new governments in order to reenter the Union, and were actually taking steps towards this end, there was still lacking any definite proposal as to the way in which the broken threads might be retied. Lincoln, cautiously, so that he might avoid all semblance of the authoritarianism of which the individual States and the Congress of the Union were apt to complain, set to work wherever he could, diplomatically advising on the processes. This August 1863 letter to Nathaniel Banks provides considerable insight into Lincoln's thoughts on the matter. (Ludwig, Eden and Cedar 1930, 433)

pared for the new. Education for young blacks should be included in the plan. After all, the power or element of "contract" may be sufficient for this probationary period, and by its simplicity and flexibility may be the better.

As an antislavery man, I have a motive to desire emancipation which proslavery men do not have but even they have strong enough reason to thus place themselves again under the shield of the Union, and to thus perpetually hedge against the recurrence of the scenes through which we are now passing.

Governor Shepley has informed me that Mr. Durant is now taking a registry, with a view to the election of a constitutional convention in Louisiana. This, to me, appears proper. If such convention were to ask my views, I could present little else than what I now say to you. I think the thing should be pushed forward, so that, if possible, its mature work may reach here by the meeting of Congress.

For my own part, I think I shall not, in any event, retract the emancipation proclamation: nor, as executive, ever return to slavery any person who is free by the terms of that proclamation, or by any of the acts of Congress.

If Louisiana shall send members to Congress, their admission to seats will depend, as you know, upon the respective Houses, and not upon the President.

Yours very truly,

A. Lincoln.

To General U. S. Grant, Executive Mansion Washington, August 9, 1863.[1]

My Dear General Grant:

I see by a dispatch of yours that you incline quite strongly toward an expedition against Mobile. This would appear tempting to me also, were it not that in view of recent events in Mexico I am greatly impressed with the importance of re-establishing the national authority in western Texas as soon as possible. I am not making an order, however; that I leave, for the present at least, to the general-in-chief.

A word upon another subject: General Thomas has gone again to the Mississippi Valley, with the view of raising colored troops. I have no reason to doubt that you are doing what you reasonably can upon the same subject. I believe it is a resource which if vigorously applied now will soon close the contest. It works doubly, weakening the enemy and strengthening us. We were not fully ripe for it until the river was opened. Now, I think at least one hundred thousand can and ought to be rapidly organized along its shores, relieving all white troops to serve

---

1 Lincoln's concern about Texas derived from a troubling turn in Mexico. Napoleon III had invaded, defeated the Mexican armies and set up a pro-Confederate puppet government in Mexico City. Lincoln wanted a stronger U.S. presence in Texas to discourage the French from turning their eyes upon Texas. The president, however, did not translate that concern into an order. Micromanaging was not his style in dealing with Grant. He did not have to, as he did with some of his other generals. But Grant caught his drift. He telegraphed back: "After the fall of Vicksburg I did incline very much to an immediate move on Mobile....I see however the importance of a movement into Texas just at this time." As shown by their telegraphic interactions, Lincoln and Grant tended to sing from the same page. Lincoln propounded the strategy objectives, which focused primarily on the destruction of the Confederate forces, and left the execution to Grant and the generals under him. (Johnson 2006)

elsewhere. Mr. Dana understands you as believing that the Emancipation Proc-lamation has helped some in your military operations. I am very glad if this is so.

Did you receive a short letter from me dated the 13th of July?

Yours very truly,

A. Lincoln.

To General W. S. Rosecrans, Executive Mansion, Washington, August 10, 1863.[1]

My Dear General Rosecrans:

Yours of the 1st was received two days ago. I think you must have inferred more than General Halleck has intended, as to any dissatisfaction of mine with you. I am sure you, as a reasonable man, would not have been wounded could you have heard all my words and seen all my thoughts in regard to you. I have not abated in my kind feeling for and confidence in you. I have seen most of your dis-patches to General Halleck—probably all of them. After Grant invested Vicks-burg I was very anxious lest Johnston should overwhelm him from the outside, and when it appeared certain that part of Bragg's force had gone and was going to Johnston, it did seem to me it was exactly the proper time for you to attack Bragg with what force he had left. In all kindness let me say it so seems to me yet. Finding from your dispatches to General Halleck that your judgment was differ-ent, and being very anxious for Grant, I, on one occasion, told General Halleck I thought he should direct you to decide at once to immediately attack Bragg or to stand on the defensive and send part of your force to Grant. He replied he had already so directed in substance. Soon after, dispatches from Grant abated my anxiety for him, and in proportion abated my anxiety about any movement of yours. When afterward, however, I saw a dispatch of yours arguing that the right time for you to attack Bragg was not before, but would be after, the fall of Vicksburg, it impressed me very strangely, and I think I so stated to the Secretary of War and General Halleck. It seemed no other than the proposition that you could better fight Bragg when Johnston should be at liberty to return and assist him than you could before he could so return to his assistance.

Since Grant has been entirely relieved by the fall of Vicksburg, by which Johnston is also relieved, it has seemed to me that your chance for a stroke has been considerably diminished, and I have not been pressing you directly or indi-rectly. True, I am very anxious for East Tennessee to be occupied by us; but I see and appreciate the difficulties you mention. The question occurs, Can the thing be done at all? Does preparation advance at all? Do you not consume supplies as fast as you get them forward? Have you more animals today than you had at the

---

1 Beginning June 24, in nine days, during which there occurred a succession of violent storms, Rosecrans executed a series of rapid and brilliant movements that culminated in expel-ling Bragg from Tennessee. The Confederate general withdrew to Chattanooga. Rosecrans was slow to follow him up and attack him. Although the bridges and railroad tracks were repaired by July 18, he delayed his movement against Chattanooga almost a month longer, complaining to Washington of lack of horses and supplies, and of the disaffection of the Administration towards him. Accordingly, on August 10, the President wrote him this very frank letter, telling exactly the feeling he had toward him, and criticizing his past and pres-ent inaction. (Lincoln 1909, 224)

battle of Stone's River? And yet have not more been furnished you since then than your entire present stock? I ask the same questions as to your mounted force.

Do not misunderstand: I am not casting blame upon you; I rather think by great exertion you can get to East Tennessee; but a very important question is, Can you stay there? I make no order in the case—that I leave to General Halleck and yourself.

And now be assured once more that I think of you in all kindness and confidence, and that I am not watching you with an evil eye.

Yours very truly,

A. Lincoln.

To General J. A. McClernand, Executive Mansion, Washington, August 12, 1863.[1]

Major General McClernand:

My Dear Sir—Our friend William G. Greene has just presented a kind letter in regard to yourself, addressed to me by our other friends Yates, Hatch, and Dubois.

I doubt whether your present position is more painful to you than to myself. Grateful for the patriotic stand so early taken by you in this life-and-death struggle of the nation, I have done whatever has appeared practicable to advance you and the public interest together. No charges, with a view to a trial, have been preferred against you by any one; nor do I suppose any will be. All there is, so far as I have heard, is General Grant's statement of his reasons for relieving you. And even this I have not seen or sought to see; because it is a case, as appears to me, in which I could do nothing without doing harm. General Grant and yourself have been conspicuous in our most important successes; and for me to interfere and thus magnify a breach between you could not but be of evil effect. Better leave it where the law of the case has placed it. For me to force you back upon General Grant would be forcing him to resign. I cannot give you a new command, because we have no forces except such as already have commanders.

I am constantly pressed by those who scold before they think, or without thinking at all, to give commands respectively to Frémont, McClellan, Butler, Sigel, Curtis, Hunter, Hooker, and perhaps others, when, all else out of the way, I have no commands to give them. This is now your case; which, as I have said, pains me not less than it does you. My belief is that the permanent estimate of what a general does in the field is fixed by the "cloud of witnesses" who have

---

1 McClernand's dismissal came after he wrote an order of congratulations to the XIII Corps success in battle which, with some help from his headquarters, got into the papers. This violated a standing War Department regulation to submit such papers to army headquarters before publication; worse, McClernand had implied in the order that the XIII Corps alone had been responsible for the success of the campaign. Sherman bitterly remarked that the order was really addressed "to a constituency in Illinois, and McPherson said it was designed "to impress the public mind with the magnificent strategy, superior tactics, and brilliant deeds" of McClernand. Grant asked McClernand if the order as published was genuine. McClernand said it was and he was prepared to stand by it. Grant finally decided to act and on June 18 relieved McClernand. Lincoln, in this note, endorses Grant's decision. (Ambrose 1997, 40)

been with him in the field, and that, relying on these, he who has the right needs not to fear.

Your friend as ever,

A. Lincoln.

Telegram to General Meade, Executive Mansion, Washington, August 21, 1863.[1]

Major General Meade, Warrenton, Va.:

At this late moment I am appealed to in behalf of William Thompson of Company K, Third Maryland Volunteers, in Twelfth Army Corps, said to be at Kelly's Ford, under sentence to be shot today as a deserter. He is represented to me to be very young, with symptoms of insanity. Please postpone the execution till further order.

A. Lincoln.

Telegram to General Schofield, Washington, August 22, 1863.[2]

General Schofield, Saint Louis, Mo.:

Please send me if you can a transcript of the record in the case of McQuin and Bell, convicted of murder by a military commission. I telegraphed General Strong for it, but he does not answer.

A. Lincoln.

Telegram to General J. M. Schofield, Washington, August 27, 1863, 8:30 P.M.[3]

General Schofield, St. Louis:

---

1 Meade replied the same day, "In compliance with your instructions, I will at once direct that the execution . . . be suspended until further orders from you." (Lincoln v.6, 1953, 400)

2 The records in the case have not been found. On August 31, Colonel John F. Philips of the Seventh Cavalry, Missouri State Militia, wrote Lincoln about the case. David Bell, a sergeant in Company B of Philips' regiment, and one McGuire, were convicted of the murder of William Major, a citizen of Pettis County, Missouri. On furlough at the time, Bell was drunk and blamed the murder on McGuire. (Ibid, 402)

3 The dispatch which Lincoln forwarded was received from Representative Abel C. Wilder and Senator James H. Lane on August 26 at 8:45 P.M., and read: "The result of the massacre at Lawrence having excited feelings amongst our people, which makes a collision between them & the military probable, the imbecility & incapacity of Schofield is most deplorable. Our people unanimously demand the removal of Schofield, whose policy has opened Kansas to invasion & butchery." On August 28, General Schofield replied to Lincoln, "Since the capture of Vicksburg a considerable portion of the rebel army in the Mississippi Valley has disbanded, and large numbers of men have come back to Missouri....some....under instructions to carry on guerrilla warfare, and others, men of the worst character, become marauders on their own account.... Under instructions from the rebel authorities, as I am informed and believe, considerable bands, called Border Guards, were organized in the counties of Missouri bordering on Kansas, for the ostensible purpose of protecting those counties from inroads from Kansas, and preventing slaves of rebels from escaping from Missouri into Kansas....Upon the representation of General Ewing and others.... I became satisfied there could be no cure for the evil short of the removal from those counties of all slaves entitled to their freedom, and of the families of all men known to belong to these bands, and oth-

I have just received the dispatch which follows, from two very influential citizens of Kansas, whose names I omit. The severe blow they have received naturally enough makes them intemperate even without there being any just cause for blame. Please do your utmost to give them future security and to punish their invaders.

A. Lincoln.

Telegram to General G. G. Meade, War Department, Washington, August 27, 1863, 9 A.M.[1]

Major General Meade, Warrenton, Va.:

Walter, Rionese, Folancy, Lai, and Kuhn appealed to me for mercy, without giving any ground for it whatever. I understand these are very flagrant cases, and that you deem their punishment as being indispensable to the service. If I am not mistaken in this, please let them know at once that their appeal is denied.

A. Lincoln.

---

ers who were known to sympathize with them. Accordingly I directed General Ewing to adopt and carry out the policy he had indicated, warning him, however, of the retaliation which might be attempted.... Almost immediately after it became known that such policy had been adopted, [William C.] Quantrill secretly assembled from several of the border counties of Missouri about 300 of his men. They met at a preconcerted place...near the Kansas line, at about sunset, and immediately marched for Lawrence, which place they reached at daylight the next morning. They sacked and burned the town and murdered the citizens in the most barbarous manner. It is easy to see that any unguarded town in a country where such a number of outlaws can be assembled is liable to a similar fate, if the villains are willing to risk the retribution which must follow.... I am officially informed that a large meeting has been held at Leavenworth, in which a resolution was adopted to the effect that the people would assemble at a certain place on the border, on the 8th of September, for the purpose of entering Missouri to search for their stolen property. Efforts have been made by the mayor of Leavenworth to get possession of the ferry at that place for the purpose of crossing armed parties of citizens into Northern Missouri. I have strong reasons for believing that the authors of the telegram to you are among those who introduced and obtained the adoption of the Leavenworth resolution, and who are endeavoring to organize a force for the purpose of general retaliation upon Missouri. Those who so deplore my `imbecility and incapacity' are the very men who are endeavoring to bring about a collision between the people of Kansas and the troops under General Ewing's command. I have not the `capacity' to see the wisdom or justice of permitting an irresponsible mob to enter Missouri for the purpose of retaliation even for so grievous a wrong as that which Lawrence has suffered. I have increased the force upon the border...and no effort will be spared to punish the invaders of Kansas and to prevent such acts in future...." (Ibid, 415-416)

1 Meade responded, "Walter, Rionese, Folancy, Lai, and Kuhn were to have been executed yesterday. Their execution was postponed by my order till Saturday, the 29th, that time might be given to procure the services of a Roman Catholic priest to assist them in preparing for death. They are substitute conscripts who enlisted for the purpose of deserting after receiving the bounty; and being the first of this class whose cases came before me, I believed that humanity, the safety of this army, and the most vital interests of the country required their prompt execution as an example, the publicity given to which might, and, I trust in God will, deter others from imitating their bad conduct. In view of these circumstances, I shall, therefore, inform them their appeal to you is denied." The executions were effected on August 29, 1863. (Davis 1894, 266)

Telegram to General Foster, War Department, Washington, August 28, 1863.[1]

Major General Foster, Fort Monroe, Va.:

Please notify, if you can, Senator Bowden, Mr. Segar, and Mr. Chandler, all or any of them, that I now have the record in Dr. Wright's case, and am ready to hear them. When you shall have got the notice to them, please let me know.

A. Lincoln.

Telegram to General Crawford, Executive Mansion, Washington, August 28, 1863.[2]

General Crawford, Rappahannock Station, Va.:

I regret that I cannot be present to witness the presentation of a sword by the gallant Pennsylvania Reserve Corps to one so worthy to receive it as General Meade.

A. Lincoln.

To General W. S. Rosecrans, Executive Mansion, Washington, August 31, 1863.[3]

My Dear General Rosecrans:

Yours of the 22d was received yesterday. When I wrote you before, I did not intend, nor do I now, to engage in an argument with you on military questions. You had informed me you were impressed through General Halleck that I was dissatisfied with you, and I could not bluntly deny that I was without unjustly

---

1 David M. Wright, a Norfolk, Virginia, white physician murdered a black army officer, a lieutenant named Sandborn. Wright pleaded insanity, claiming he had experienced a transient psychosis. The lieutenant had marched a company of black troops through the main streets of the city on the day of the homicide. Wright became upset by this news when he was informed of it by his family. Although he did nothing immediately, he later accosted the officer and shot him. Lincoln requested a psychiatric examination that eventually determined that Wright was sane at the time of the crime. (Colaizzi 1989, 57)

2 Brigadier General Samuel W. Crawford wrote Lincoln on August 20: "The honor of your company is requested at the presentation of a sword to Major General Meade, by the Officers of the Penna. Res. Corps, at the Head Quarters near Rappahannock Station, on Friday, the 28th inst; at 5 o'clock." (Lincoln v.6, 1953, 418)

3 On August 22, Rosecrans replied to Lincoln's communication of August 10: "Permit me to assure you that I am not and have not been touched with any of that official pride which desires to have its own way. It has been a principle and a characteristic of my life to take advice and learn both from superiors and inferiors. When great interests are confided to my care this principle becomes even more imperative. On the question of moving against Bragg every division and corps commander gave his written opinion adversely to an immediate or early move....But I am sure when you consider we have but a single line of rail road from Louisville, that we are three hundred miles from that base that we have crossed by three days march the formidable barrier of the Cumberland mountains that we have in front a swift river from five to eight hundred yards wide and seventy miles of mountains in front of us to reach the fertile regions of northern Georgia you see that few armies have been called upon to attempt a more arduous campaign. Thanking you for your kindness may I ask you when impulsive men suppose me querrulous to believe I am only straight forward and in earnest and that you may always rely upon my using my utmost efforts to do what is best for our country and the lives and honor of the soldiers of my command, I remain very respectfully...." This is Lincoln's response to Rosecrans' August 22 letter. (Ibid, 425)

---

implicating him. I therefore concluded to tell you the plain truth, being satisfied the matter would thus appear much smaller than it would if seen by mere glimpses. I repeat that my appreciation of you has not abated. I can never forget whilst I remember anything, that about the end of last year and the beginning of this, you gave us a hard-earned victory, which, had there been a defeat instead, the nation could hardly have lived over. Neither can I forget the check you so opportunely gave to a dangerous sentiment which was spreading in the North.

Yours, as ever,

A. Lincoln.

To General H. W. Halleck, Executive Mansion, Washington, August 31, 1863.[1]

Major General Halleck:

It is not improbable that retaliation for the recent great outrage at Lawrence, in Kansas, may extend to indiscriminate slaughter on the Missouri border, unless averted by very judicious action. I shall be obliged if the general-in-chief can make any suggestions to General Schofield upon the subject.

A. Lincoln.

Telegram to General Meade, Executive Mansion, Washington, September 9, 1863.[2]

Major General Meade, Warrenton, Va.:

It would be a generous thing to give General Wheaton a leave of absence for ten or fifteen days, and if you can do so without injury to the service, please do it.

A. Lincoln.

Telegram to General Wheaton, Washington, September 10, 1863.[3]

General Wheaton, Army of Potomac:

Yesterday at the instance of Mr. Blair, senator, I telegraphed General Meade asking him to grant you a leave of absence, to which he replied that you had not applied for such leave, and that you can have it when you do apply. I suppose it is proper for you to know this.

A. Lincoln.

---

1 Halleck telegraphed General Schofield on September 2: "You will please report whether measures are being taken to prevent hostile collisions on the Kansas border; also whether General Ewing's order to depopulate certain counties in Missouri has been approved or disapproved by you.' Schofield replied from Leavenworth City, Kansas, at 8 P.M.: "Your dispatch is just received. I came here to prevent the trouble you refer to. Shall go to Kansas City to-morrow, and remain on the border until the difficulty is over. I believe I can prevent any collision. As yet I have neither approved nor disapproved General Ewing's order. I think it must be modified, but will not do it until I see him." (Ibid, 423-424)

2 Meade replied at once, "Gen. Wheaton, has made no application for a leave of absence. There will be no difficulty in his obtaining one, when he does apply." (Ibid, 437)

3 Ibid.

Telegram to General A. E. Burnside, Washington, September 11, 1863.[1]

Major General Burnside, Cumberland Gap:

Yours received. A thousand thanks for the late successes you have given us. We cannot allow you to resign until things shall be a little more settled in East Tennessee. If then, purely on your own account, you wish to resign, we will not further refuse you.

A. Lincoln.

Telegram to General Meade, Executive Mansion, Washington, September 11, 1863.[2]

Major General Meade, Warrenton, Va.:

It is represented to me that Thomas Edds, in your army, is under sentence of death for desertion, to be executed next Monday. It is also said his supposed desertion is comprised in an absence commencing with his falling behind last winter, being captured and paroled by the enemy, and then going home. If this be near the truth, please suspend the execution till further order and send in the record of the trial.

A. Lincoln.

Telegram to General Meade, Washington, September 12, 1863.[3]

Major General Mead, Warrenton, Va.:

The name is "Thomas Edds" not "Eddies" as in your dispatch. The papers left with me do not designate the regiment to which he belongs. The man who gave me the papers, I do not know how to find again. He only told me that Edds is in the Army of the Potomac, and that he fell out of the ranks during Burnside's mud march last winter. If I get further information I will telegraph again.

A. Lincoln.

---

1 Burnside had telegraphed Lincoln on September 10: "You will remember that I some time ago told you that I wished to retire to private life. The rebellion now seems pretty well checked & the work I am doing can no doubt be as well or better performed by someone else so that I can now conscientiously ask to be allowed to resign if you think the good of service will permit. I shall be here tomorrow & will be glad to get an answer I look upon East Tennessee as one of the most loyal sections of the U.S." Burnside replied to this note from Lincoln on September 17: "Thank you for your dispatch & I desire to stay as long as you think necessary but am very anxious to look after my private affairs as soon as the public service will allow." (Lincoln v.6, 1953, 439)

2 See note 238.

3 Meade replied the same day, "There is no man of the name of 'Edds' under sentence of death. Twelve men are sentenced to be executed next Friday Sept 18th but no case approximates either in date or circumstances to the one you specify." Thomas Edds has not been identified. (Ibid, 442-443)

To General H. W. Halleck, Executive Mansion, Washington, September 13, 1863.[1]

Major General Halleck:

If I did not misunderstand General Meade's last dispatch, he posts you on facts as well as he can, and desires your views and those of the Government as to what he shall do. My opinion is that he should move upon Lee at once in manner of general attack, leaving to developments whether he will make it a real attack. I think this would develop Lee's real condition and purposes better than the cavalry alone can do. Of course my opinion is not to control you and General Meade.

Yours truly,

A. Lincoln.

Telegram to General Meade, Executive Mansion, Washington, September 16, 1863.[2]

Major General Meade, Warrenton, Va.:

Is Albert Jones of Company K, Third Maryland Volunteers, to be shot on Friday next? If so please state to me the general features of the case.

A. Lincoln.

Telegram to General Meade, Executive Mansion, Washington, September 17, 1863.[3]

Major General Meade, Headquarters Army of Potomac:

Yours in relation to Albert Jones is received. I am appealed to in behalf of Richard M. Abrams of Company A, Sixth New Jersey Volunteers, by Governor Parker, Attorney General Frelinghuysen, Governor Newell, Hon. Mr. Middleton, M. C., of the district, and the marshal who arrested him. I am also appealed to in behalf of Joseph S. Smith, of Company A, Eleventh New Jersey Volunteers, by Governor Parker, Attorney General Frelinghuysen, and Hon. Marcus C. Ward. Please state the circumstances of their cases to me.

A. Lincoln.

---

1 Until now, the administration had not pressed Meade to advance against Lee. According to Secretary of the Navy Gideon Welles, the president had complained to him about the inaction, saying: "It is...the same old story of this Army of the Potomac. Imbecility, inefficiency—don't want to do—is defending the capital....it is terrible, terrible, this weakness, this indifference of our Potomac generals, with such armies of good and brave men." But neither Lincoln nor Halleck proposed any offensive movement. The replies from Halleck and Lincoln must have made Meade wonder. Halleck responded with two telegrams the next day, recommending "a sudden raid" that might "if possible, to cut off some portion" of Lee's army. The president addressed his suggestion to Halleck, writing this note, although adding, "Of course, my opinion is not to control you and General Meade." The army marched within twenty-four hours, crossing the Rappahannock and moving toward the Rapidan into the area occupied by John Pope's Army of Virginia in the summer of 1862; but the advance stalled. (Wert 2005, 313)

2 While no reply has been discovered, Lincoln's September 17 letter to Meade suggests that Meade had indeed responded.

3 The roster of Company K, Third Maryland Volunteers, lists Albert Jones as "killed, September 18, 1863." Richard M. Abrahams is listed on the roster as dishonorably discharged at Fort Jefferson, Florida, June 12, 1864, and released from confinement July 3, 1865. Joseph S. Smith is listed as transferred to Company A, Twelfth New Jersey Volunteers, returned to duty May 20, 1865, and mustered out July 15, 1865. (Lincoln v.6, 1953, 461)

Telegram to General Schenck, Executive Mansion, Washington, September 17, 1863.[1]

Major General Schenck, Baltimore, Md.:

Major Haynor left here several days ago under a promise to put down in writing, in detail, the facts in relation to the misconduct of the people on the eastern shore of Virginia. He has not returned. Please send him over.

A. Lincoln.

To General H. W. Halleck, Executive Mansion, Washington D.C. September 19, 1863.[2]

Major General Halleck:

By General Meade's dispatch to you of yesterday it appears that he desires your views and those of the government as to whether he shall advance upon the enemy. I am not prepared to order, or even advise, an advance in this case, wherein I know so little of particulars, and wherein he, in the field, thinks the risk is so great and the promise of advantage so small.

And yet the case presents matter for very serious consideration in another aspect. These two armies confront each other across a small river, substantially midway between the two capitals, each defending its own capital, and menacing the other. General Meade estimates the enemy's infantry in front of him at not less than 40,000. Suppose we add fifty per cent. to this for cavalry, artillery, and extra-duty men stretching as far as Richmond, making the whole force of the enemy 60,000.

General Meade, as shown by the returns, has with him, and between him and Washington, of the same classes, of well men, over 90,000. Neither can bring the whole of his men into a battle; but each can bring as large a percentage in as the other. For a battle, then, General Meade has three men to General Lee's two. Yet, it having been determined that choosing ground and standing on the defensive

---

1 A thirty-page report submitted on September 10, 1863, by Major Henry Z. Hayner, aide-de-camp on General Schenck's staff, indicates that the difficulties on the Eastern Shore of Virginia were twofold. Several hundred citizens formerly in the "39th Rebel Regiment" had accepted amnesty offered by General Dix on the simple provision that they lay down their arms. Later, upon being required by Schenck to take an oath of allegiance, or (1) to be regarded as prisoners of war and put up for exchange, or (2) to be sent beyond Union lines; they objected to the oath on grounds of conscience, regarding themselves as still bound by their oath of allegiance to the Confederacy. The second phase of the difficulty concerned the destruction of a lighthouse by unknown persons. Two hundred and twenty-one residents of Northampton were assessed $20,000 on the grounds that the community was responsible, and collections were made from one hundred and sixty-one, over their violent protests. Hayner's report indicates that the order suspending the oath and assessments were received in a spirit of triumph over the government. (Ibid, 427)

2 In mid-September, the two armies were again facing one another back on the Rappahannock line. Lee had sent Longstreet to reinforce Bragg near Chattanooga, but one division of Meade's had gone to New York to quell draft riots, another to the South Carolina coast. Meade could not make up his mind what to do. He had asked for orders. Halleck laid the case before Lincoln. Lincoln's September 19 reply is illuminating. It reveals the workings of a logical—though unmilitary—mind, which, having weighed the pros and cons of military strategy, could come to a correct conclusion through that process of arguably homespun philosophy. (Dupuy 1956, 271)

---

gives so great advantage that the three cannot safely attack the two, the three are left simply standing on the defensive also.

If the enemy's 60,000 are sufficient to keep our 90,000 away from Richmond, why, by the same rule, may not 40,000 of ours keep their 60,000 away from Washington, leaving us 50,000 to put to some other use? Having practically come to the mere defensive, it seems to be no economy at all to employ twice as many men for that object as are needed. With no object, certainly, to mislead myself, I can perceive no fault in this statement, unless we admit we are not the equal of the enemy, man for man. I hope you will consider it.

To avoid misunderstanding, let me say that to attempt to fight the enemy slowly back into his entrenchments at Richmond, and then to capture him, is an idea I have been trying to repudiate for quite a year.

My judgment is so clear against it that I would scarcely allow the attempt to be made if the general in command should desire to make it. My last attempt upon Richmond was to get McClellan, when he was nearer there than the enemy was, to run in ahead of him. Since then I have constantly desired the Army of the Potomac to make Lee's army, and not Richmond, its objective point. If our army cannot fall upon the enemy and hurt him where he is, it is plain to me it can gain nothing by attempting to follow him over a succession of intrenched lines into a fortified city.

Yours truly,

A. Lincoln.

To General H. W. Halleck, Executive Mansion, Washington, September 21, 1863.[1]

Major General Halleck:

I think it very important for General Rosecrans to hold his position at or about Chattanooga, because if held from that place to Cleveland, both inclusive, it keeps all Tennessee clear of the enemy, and also breaks one of his most important railroad lines. To prevent these consequences is so vital to his cause that he cannot give up the effort to dislodge us from the position, thus bringing him to us and saving us the labor, expense, and hazard of going farther to find him, and also giving us the advantage of choosing our own ground and preparing it to fight him upon.

The details must, of course, be left to General Rosecrans, while we must furnish him the means to the utmost of our ability. If you concur, I think he would better be informed that we are not pushing him beyond this position; and that, in fact, our judgment is rather against his going beyond it. If he can only maintain this position, without more, this rebellion can only eke out a short and feeble existence, as an animal sometimes may with a thorn in its vitals.

Yours truly,

A. Lincoln.

---

1 Lincoln, who saw the Chickamauga battle for the resounding defeat it was, recognized that it would be an empty victory for the South so long as the Union army held Chattanooga. In the uncertain aftermath of the battle, when Rosecrans's grasp on the city appeared tenuous at best, Lincoln shared his thoughts on the scenario with Halleck in this September 21 letter. (Cozzens 1992, 281)

Telegram to General W. S. Rosecrans, Washington, September 21, 1863, 12:55 P.M.[1]

Major General Rosecrans, Chattanooga:
Be of good cheer. We have unabated confidence in you, and in your soldiers and officers. In the main you must be the judge as to what is to be done. If I were to suggest, I would say, save your army by taking strong positions until Burnside joins you, when, I hope, you can turn the tide. I think you had better send a courier to Burnside to hurry him up. We cannot reach him by telegraph. We suppose some force is going to you from Corinth, but for want of communication we do not know how they are getting along. We shall do our utmost to assist you. Send us your present positions.
A. Lincoln.

Telegram to General A. E. Burnside, Executive Mansion, Washington, September 21, 1863.[2]

General Burnside, Greenville, Tenn.:
If you are to do any good to Rosecrans it will not do to waste time with Jonesboro. It is already too late to do the most good that might have been done, but I hope it will still do some good. Please do not lose a moment.
A. Lincoln.

Telegram to General A. E. Burnside, War Department, September 21, 1863, 11 A.M.[3]

General Burnside, Knoxville, Tenn.:
Go to Rosecrans with your force without a moment's delay.
A. Lincoln.

Telegram to General W. S. Rosecrans [Cipher] War Department, September 22, 1863, 8:30 A.M.[4]

Major General Rosecrans, Chattanooga, Tenn.:

---

1 While Lincoln might have retained some measure of confidence in Rosecrans, for the moment at least, he was sorely disgusted with Burnside. As the crisis had developed in north Georgia over the past ten days, amid growing Federal knowledge of the transfer of Confederate troops to that sector, Lincoln had waited for Burnside to unite with Rosecrans; but the commander of the Army of the Ohio had had been preoccupied in East Tennessee and had not gone. Now, on September 21, after sending his encouraging message to Rosecrans, Lincoln twice reiterated his desires to Burnside in the plainest possible form, culminating with: "Go to Rosecrans with your force without a moment's delay." (Woodworth 1991, 131)
2 Ibid.
3 Ibid.
4 On the evening of September 20, Rosecrans had written Halleck: "We have met with a serious disaster; extent not yet ascertained. . . . [The] enemy overwhelmed us." The next morning he sent a telegram to Lincoln from Chattanooga, officially breaking the news and saying sadly that "after two days of the severest fighting I ever witnessed, our left and center were beaten. The left held its position until sunset. . . . Our loss is heavy and our troops worn down. . . . We have no certainty of holding our position here." Greatly alarmed, as indicated in September 20 note to Halleck, Lincoln stressed the importance of holding Chattanooga;

We have not a word here as to the whereabouts or condition of your army up to a later hour than sunset, Sunday, the 20th. Your dispatches to me of 9 A.M., and to General Halleck of 2 P. M., yesterday, tell us nothing later on those points. Please relieve my anxiety as to the position and condition of your army up to the latest moment.

A. Lincoln.

Telegram to General W. S. Rosecrans, Washington, September 23, 1863, 9:13 A.M.[1]

Major General Rosecrans, Chattanooga, Tenn.:

Below is Bragg's dispatch as found in the Richmond papers. You see he does not claim so many prisoners or captured guns as you were inclined to concede. He also confesses to heavy loss. An exchanged general of ours leaving Richmond yesterday says two of Longstreet's divisions and his entire artillery and two of Pickett's brigades and Wise's legion have gone to Tennessee. He mentions no other.

"Chicamauga River, September 20.

"General Cooper, Adjutant General:

"After two days' hard fighting we have driven the enemy, after a desperate resistance, from several positions, and now hold the field; but he still confronts us. The loses are heavy on both sides, especially in our officers....

"Braxton Bragg"

A. Lincoln.

Telegram to General W. S. Rosecrans, War Department, September 24, 1863, 10 A.M.[2]

Major General Rosecrans, Chattanooga, Term.:

---

he did not consider any advance from there necessary, Rosecrans in a defensive position would so embarrass the Confederates that "the rebellion can only eke out a short and feeble existence, as an animal sometimes may with a thorn in his vitals." This, however, was predicated on the assumption that Rosecrans could hold even a defensive position at Chattanooga, which was by no means certain. Here, Lincoln telegraphed Rosecrans for more information, pleading: "Please relieve my anxiety as to the position and condition of your army up to the latest moment." Rosecrans replied, none too reassuringly: "We are about 30,000 brave and determined men; but our fate is in the hands of God, in whom I hope." (Horn 1941, 277)

1 The assertions of the commanders on both sides, that they everywhere met superior forces of the enemy, prove only that there was but slight disparity of numbers; and that the fighting was at all points, except for the break on the Union right, unusually obstinate and determined. (Nicolay and Hay 1909, 105)

2 John B. Hood lost a leg at Chickamauga, but survived. Of these only Preston Smith, Ben Hardin Helm, and James Deshler were killed; William T. Wofford and Edward C. Walthall survived. William Preston, Patrick R. Cleburne, and John Gregg were not killed. Henry L. Benning was not killed and no generals by the other names have been identified as killed. (Lincoln v.6, 1953, 480) When ordered by Lincoln to go to Rosecrans in the wake of the battle, Burnside replied that he would do so at once...that is, as soon as he finished an operation he was planning against Jonesboro, Tennessee. However, despite additional urgings from Washington, he continued replied with excuses, delays, and questions, conclusively demonstrating his unfitness for independent command and sorely trying the patience of his

Last night we received the rebel accounts, through Richmond papers, of your late battle. They give Major General Hood as mortally wounded, and Brigadiers Preston Smith, Wofford, Walthall, Helm of Kentucky, and DesMer killed, and Major Generals Preston, Cleburne, and Gregg, and Brigadier Generals Benning, Adams, Bunn, Brown, and John [B. H.] Helm wounded. By confusion the two Helms may be the same man, and Bunn and Brown may be the same man. With Burnside, Sherman, and from elsewhere we shall get to you from forty to sixty thousand additional men.

A. Lincoln.

Telegram to General McCallum, War Department, Washington, September 25, 1863.[1]

General McCallum, Alexandria, Va.:

I have sent to General Meade, by telegraph, to suspend the execution of Daniel Sullivan of Company F, Thirteenth Massachusetts, which was to be today, but understanding there is an interruption on the line, may I beg you to send this to him by the quickest mode in your power?

A. Lincoln.

Telegram to General Meade, War Department, Washington, September 25, 1863.[2]

Major General Meade, Army of Potomac:

Owing to the press in behalf of Daniel Sullivan, Company E, Thirteenth Massachusetts, and the doubt; though small, which you express of his guilty intention, I have concluded to say let his execution be suspended till further order, and copy of record sent me.

A. Lincoln.

Telegram to General W. S. Rosecrans, War Department, September 28, 1863, 8 A.M.[3]

Major General Rosecrans, Chattanooga., Tenn.:

You can perhaps communicate with General Burnside more rapidly by sending telegrams directly to him at Knoxville. Think of it. I send a like dispatch to him.

A. Lincoln.

---

superiors. "I telegraphed him fifteen times to [reinforce Rosecrans]," Halleck later stated. (Woodworth 1998, 136)

1 Daniel Sullivan of Company E, Thirteenth Massachusetts, drafted and mustered August 4, 1863, was sentenced to be shot for desertion. His sentence was commuted to imprisonment for six months. (Lincoln v.6, 1953, 478)

2 Ibid.

3 Obviously frustrated with the lack of communication, Lincoln sarcastically sent an identical telegram to Burnside. No response has been located from either officer. (Lincoln v.6, 1953, 485-486)

To General W. S. Rosecrans, Executive Mansion, Washington, September 25, 1863.[1]

My Dear General Rosecrans:

We are sending you two small corps, one under General Howard and one under General Slocum, and the whole under General Hooker.

Unfortunately the relations between Generals Hooker and Slocum are not such as to promise good, if their present relative positions remain. Therefore, let me beg—almost enjoin upon you—that on their reaching you, you will make a transposition by which General Slocum with his Corps, may pass from under the command of General Hooker, and General Hooker, in turn receive some other equal force. It is important for this to be done, though we could not well arrange it here. Please do it.

Yours very truly,
A. Lincoln.

Telegram to General Schofield, Executive Mansion, Washington, D. C, September 30, 1863.[2]

General Schofield, Saint Louis, Mo.:

Following dispatch just received:

"Union Men Driven out of Missouri."

"Leavenworth, September 29, 1863.

"Governor Gamble having authorized Colonel Moss, of Liberty, Missouri, to arm the men in Platte and Clinton Counties, he has armed mostly the returned rebel soldiers and men wider bonds. Moss's men are now driving the Union men out of Missouri. Over one hundred families crossed the river today. Many of the wives of our Union soldiers have been compelled to leave. Four or five Union men have been murdered by Colonel Moss's men."

Please look to this and, if true, in main or part, put a stop to it.
A. Lincoln.

Telegram to General Erastus B. Tyler, War Department, Washington, October 1, 1863.[3]

General Tyler, Baltimore:

---

1 On September 25, General Henry W. Slocum had telegraphed Lincoln, "'I have just been informed that I have again been placed under command of Maj Gen Jos. Hooker. My opinion of Gen Hooker both as an Officer & a gentleman is too well known to make it necessary for me to refer to it in this communication. The public service cannot be promoted by placing under his command an Officer who has so little confidence in his ability as I have. Our relations are such that it would be degrading in me to accept any position under him. I have the honor therefore to respectfully tender the resignation of my commission as Maj Genl of volunteers." (Lincoln v.6, 1953, 486)

2 On October 2, Schofield replied to Lincoln's telegram, "I find ...that the report from Leavenworth...is a gross misrepresentation and exaggeration. A few men who claim to be loyal, but who have been engaged in murder, robbery, and arson, have been driven out....It is a base attempt of my enemies to influence your action."(Lincoln v.6, 1953, 489)

3 Before the Civil War began, George Vickers was a Maryland lave owner. According to the Kent County slave statistics, Vickers owned 23 slaves. Of those 23 slaves, he was com-

Take care of colored troops in your charge, but do nothing further about that branch of affairs until further orders. Particularly do nothing about General Vickers of Kent County.

A. Lincoln.

Send a copy to Colonel Birney. A. L.

To General Schofield, Executive Mansion, Washington, October 1, 1863.[1]

General John M. Schofield:

There is no organized military force in avowed opposition to the General Government now in Missouri, and if any shall reappear, your duty in regard to it will be too plain to require any special instruction. Still, the condition of things, both there and elsewhere, is such as to render it indispensable to maintain, for a time, the United States military establishment in that State, as well as to rely upon it for a fair contribution of support to that establishment generally. Your immediate duty in regard to Missouri now is to advance the efficiency of that establishment, and to so use it, as far as practicable, to compel the excited people there to let one another alone.

Under your recent order, which I have approved, you will only arrest individuals, and suppress assemblies or newspapers, when they may be working palpable injury to the military in your charge; and in no other case will you interfere with the expression of opinion in any form, or allow it to be interfered with violently by others. In this you have a discretion to exercise with great caution, calmness, and forbearance.

With the matter of removing the inhabitants of certain counties en masse, and of removing certain individuals from time to time, who are supposed to be mischievous, I am not now interfering, but am leaving to your own discretion.

Nor am I interfering with what may still seem to you to be necessary restrictions upon trade and intercourse. I think proper, however, to enjoin upon you the following: Allow no part of the military under your command to be engaged in either returning fugitive slaves or in forcing or enticing slaves from their homes; and, so far as practicable, enforce the same forbearance upon the people.

---

pensated $100 for each of his five slaves that enlisted in the Civil War. One of his former slaves, William Hales, enlisted in Company F of the 7th U.S. colored troops regiment on September 27, 1863. After providing a sworn affidavit proving the slaves were under his ownership, Vickers was then entitled to his $100 compensation. (Usilton 1994, 143)

1 Secession was avoided in Missouri, but otherwise it proved to be the locus of many serious problems for the Lincoln administration. The president could devise no better way to state his policy goals there, once regular Confederate forces had been driven from the state, than that the army should "compel the excited people there to leave one another alone." From Missouri would come incidents and practices that would continue to tarnish Lincoln's historical reputation. Missouri saw the origin of trials by military commission, and the use of these by the Lincoln administration would lead shortly after the war to sharp condemnation by the United States Supreme Court in *Ex parte Milligan*. That decision, in turn, dealt a blow to Lincoln's reputation as a steward of the Constitution from which he never recovered, while the disproportionately large numbers of civilians arrested in Missouri only added to a dismal record of failure of administration policy in the state. (Neely 1991, 49)

Report to me your opinion upon the availability for good of the enrolled militia of the State. Allow no one to enlist colored troops, except upon orders from you, or from here through you.

Allow no one to assume the functions of confiscating property, under the law of Congress, or otherwise, except upon orders from here.

At elections see that those, and only those, are allowed to vote who are entitled to do so by the laws of Missouri, including as of those laws the restrictions laid by the Missouri convention upon those who may have participated in the rebellion.

So far as practicable, you will, by means of your military force, expel guerrillas, marauders, and murderers, and all who are known to harbor, aid, or abet them. But in like manner you will repress assumptions of unauthorized individuals to perform the same service, because under pretense of doing this they become marauders and murderers themselves.

To now restore peace, let the military obey orders, and those not of the military leave each other alone, thus not breaking the peace themselves.

In giving the above directions, it is not intended to restrain you in other expedient and necessary matters not falling within their range.

Your obedient servant,

A. Lincoln.

Telegram to General S. M. Schofield, Washington, October 2, 1863[1]

Major General Schofield:

I have just seen your dispatch to Halleck about Major General Blunt. If possible, you better allow me to get through with a certain matter here, before adding to the difficulties of it. Meantime supply me the particulars of Major General Blunt's case.

A. Lincoln.

Telegram to General W. S. Rosecrans, War Department, October 4, 1863, 11:30 A.M.[2]

Major General Rosecrans, Chattanooga, Tenn.:

---

1 While on their way to spend the winter in Texas, William C. Quantrill's guerrilla band unsuccessfully attacked a Union fort at Baxter Springs. The fort was held by a company of about 25 black soldiers of the 2nd Kansas Colored Infantry Regiment and two companies of the 3rd Wisconsin Cavalry Regiment. Near Baxter Springs Union Major General James G. Blunt and an escort of 100 men were on their way to Fort Smith, Arkansas, where General Blunt was about to take over his new command. The escort included Company I of the 3rd Wisconsin Cavalry Regiment, a portion of the 14th Kansas Infantry Regiment, and a Union band of 15 unarmed musicians and a drummer. Quantrill's guerrillas, dressed mostly in captured Union uniforms, were mistaken by Blunt's party for Union troops from Baxter Springs coming to escort them to the fort. Blunt and his men realized their mistake too late as Quantrill's Confederate guerrillas rode with pistols blazing through the Union troops. In a few minutes, 80 Union soldiers and civilians were killed and 18 wounded. General James G. Blunt's military reputation was forever destroyed. (Gaines 1999, 64)

2 Rosecrans' telegram of October 3 noted: "If we can maintain this position in such strength that the enemy are obliged to abandon their position, and the Elections in the great States

Yours of yesterday received. If we can hold Chattanooga and East Tennessee, I think the rebellion must dwindle and die. I think you and Burnside can do this, and hence doing so is your main object. Of course to greatly damage or destroy the enemy in your front would be a greater object, because it would include the former and more, but it is not so certainly within your power. I understand the main body of the enemy is very near you, so near that you could "board at home," so to speak, and menace or attack him any day. Would not the doing of this be your best mode of counteracting his raid on your communications? But this is not an order. I intend doing something like what you suggest whenever the case shall appear ripe enough to have it accepted in the true understanding rather than as a confession of weakness and fear.

A. Lincoln.

Telegram to General J. M. Schofield, Washington, October 4, 1863[1]

Major General Schofield, St. Louis, Mo.:
I think you will not have just cause to complain of my action.
A. Lincoln.

Telegram to General Meade, War Department, Washington, October 8, 1863. [2]

Major General Meade, Army of Potomac:
I am appealed to in behalf of August Blittersdorf, at Mitchell's Station, Va., to be shot tomorrow as a deserter. I am unwilling for any boy under eighteen to be shot, and his father affirms that he is yet under sixteen. Please answer. His regiment or company not given me.
A. Lincoln.

Telegram to General Meade, Executive Mansion, Washington, October 8, 1863.[3]

Major General Meade, Army of Potomac:
The boy telegraphs from Mitchell's Station, Va. The father thinks he is in the One hundred and nineteenth Pennsylvania Volunteers. The father signs the name "Blittersdorf." I can tell no more.
A. Lincoln.

---

go favorably, would it not be well to offer a general amnesty to all officers and soldiers in the Rebellion? It would give us moral strength and weaken them very much." (Lincoln v.6, 1953, 498)

1 Schofield had telegraphed Lincoln on October 3: "I have just read the address presented to you by the Radical Delegation from Missouri. So far as it refers to me, it is not only untrue in spirit but most of it is literally false. If an answer or explanation from me is on any account desirable I shall be glad to make it." (Ibid, 1953, 498-499)

2 No reply from Meade or other communications about Blittersdorf have been found, and there seems to be no record of the name in the General Orders, Army of the Potomac. (Lincoln v.6, 1953, 506)

3 Ibid.

Telegram to General Meade, Executive Mansion, Washington, October 8, 1863.[1]

Major General Meade, Army of Potomac:

I am appealed to in behalf of John Murphy, to be shot tomorrow. His Mother says he is but seventeen. Please answer.

A. Lincoln.

Telegram to General Meade, Executive Mansion, Washington, October 8, 1863.[2]

Major General Meade, Army of Potomac:

If there is any reason to believe that this boy was under eighteen when he deserted, suspend his execution until further order.

A. Lincoln.

Telegram to General Meade, Executive Mansion, Washington, October 12, 1863.[3]

Major General Meade, Army of Potomac:

The father and mother of John Murphy, of the One hundred and nineteenth Pennsylvania Volunteers, have filed their own affidavits that he was born June 22, 1846, and also the affidavits of three other persons who all swear that they remembered the circumstances of his birth and that it was in the year 1846, though they do not remember the particular day. I therefore, on account of his tender age, have concluded to pardon him, and to leave it to yourself whether to discharge him or continue him in the service.

A. Lincoln.

Telegram to W. S. Rosecrans [Cipher] War Department, October 12, 1863, 8:35 A.M.[4]

Major General Rosecrans, Chattanooga, Tenn.:

As I understand, Burnside is menaced from the west, and so cannot go to you without surrendering East Tennessee. I now think the enemy will not attack Chattanooga, and I think you will have to look out for his making a concentrated drive at Burnside. You and Burnside now have him by the throat, and he must break your hold or perish I therefore think you better try to hold the road up to Kingston, leaving Burnside to what is above there. Sherman is coming to you,

---

1 No reply from Meade has been located. Army of the Potomac, General Orders No. 93, October 2, 1863, announced sentence of John Murphy, unassigned recruit, One Hundred Nineteenth Pennsylvania Volunteers, to be shot October 9 for desertion. (Ibid)

2 No reply has been located.

3 No reply has been located.

4 Rosecrans responded at 3 P.M., "Line from here to Kingston is long; our side is barren mountain; rebel side has railroad. Our danger is subsistence. We cannot bring up Hooker to cover our left against a crossing above us, for want of means to transport provisions and horsefeed. Enemy's side of valley full of corn. Every exertion will be made to hold what we have and gain more, after which we must put our trust in God, who never fails those who truly trust." (Lincoln v.6, 1953, 511)

though gaps in the telegraph prevent our knowing how far he is advanced. He and Hooker will so support you on the west and northwest as to enable you to look east and northeast. This is not an order. General Halleck will give his views.

A. Lincoln.

Telegram to General G. G. Meade, Washington, October 12, 1863, 9 A.M.[1]

Major General Meade:

What news this morning? A dispatch from Rosecrans, leaving him at 7.30 P.M. yesterday, says:

"Rebel rumors that head of Ewell's column reached Dalton yesterday." I send this for what it is worth.

A. Lincoln.

Telegram to General Foster, War Department, Washington, October 15, 1863.[2]

Major General Foster, Fort Monroe, Va.:

Postpone the execution of Dr. Wright to Friday the 23d instant (October). This is intended for his preparation and is final.

A. Lincoln.

Telegram to General Meade, Executive Mansion, Washington, October 15, 1863.[3]

Major General Meade, Army of Potomac:

On the 4th instant you telegraphed me that Private Daniel Hanson, of Ninety-seventh New York Volunteers, had not yet been tried. When he shall be, please notify me of the result, with a brief statement of his case, if he be convicted. Gustave Blittersdorf, who you say is enlisted in the One hundred and nineteenth Pennsylvania Volunteers as William Fox, is proven to me to be only fifteen years old last January. I pardon him, and you will discharge him or put him in the ranks at your discretion. Mathias Brown, of Nineteenth Pennsylvania Volunteers, is proven to me to be eighteen last May, and his friends say he is convicted on an enlistment and for a desertion both before that time. If this last be true he is pardoned, to be kept or discharged as you please. If not true suspend his execution and report the facts of his case. Did you receive my dispatch of 12th pardoning John Murphy?

A. Lincoln.

---

1 Meade responded, "We took yesterday some fifty prisoners. . . . There is no doubt but that up to yesterday the whole of Hill's and Ewell's Corps' were here, and some say reinforced by . . . troops from Richmond. "Lee never would have made the movements he has, leaving a strong position, if he was weakened by the detachment of any portion of Ewell's and Hill's Corps."(Ibid, 510)

2 See footnote 230.

3 No reply from Meade has been located.

To General H. W. Halleck, Executive Mansion, Washington, October 16, 1863.[1]

Major General Halleck:

I do not believe Lee can have over 60,000 effective men.

Longstreet's corps would not be sent away to bring an equal force back upon the same road; and there is no other direction for them to have come from.

Doubtless, in making the present movement, Lee gathered in all available scraps, and added them to Hill's and Ewell's corps; but that is all, and he made the movement in the belief that four corps had left General Meade; and General Meade's apparently avoiding a collision with him has confirmed him in that belief. If General Meade can now attack him on a field no worse than equal for us, and will do so now with all the skill and courage which he, his officers, and men possess, the honor will be his if he succeeds, and the blame may be mine if he fails.

Yours truly,

A. Lincoln.

Telegram to General Foster, War Department, Washington, October 17, 1863.[2]

Major General Foster, Port Monroe, Va.:

It would be useless for Mrs. Dr. Wright to come here. The subject is a very painful one, but the case is settled.

A. Lincoln.

Telegram to General W. S. Rosecrans, War Department, October 19, 1863, 9 A.M.[3]

Major General Rosecrans, Chattanooga, Tenn.:

There has been no battle recently at Bull Run. I suppose what you have heard a rumor of was not a general battle, but an "affair" at Bristow Station on the railroad, a few miles beyond Manassas Junction toward the Rappahannock, on Wednesday, the 14th. It began by an attack of the enemy upon General Warren, and ended in the enemy being repulsed with a loss of four cannon and from four to seven hundred prisoners.

A. Lincoln.

---

1 At this juncture, Meade was rapidly retiring before Lee, and yet reporting that as soon as he could find Lee he would attack him. Matters were not at all satisfactory to President Lincoln, and he wrote Halleck this pointed letter. (Baylor 1900, 175)

2 President Lincoln approved of the findings of the court, and Wright was sentenced to be hanged. The execution took place at the Norfolk fair grounds, in the middle of the racetrack, on October 23, 1863. (Wertenbaker 1962, 221)

3 At Bristow Station, Union forces had captured a battery of six guns, two battle-flags, killed two Confederate colonels, and captured one colonel and about 750 prisoners. (Conyngham 1994, 422)

Telegram to General R. C. Schenck, Executive Mansion, Washington, October 21, 1863, 2:45 P.M.[1]

Major General Schenck, Baltimore, Md.:

A delegation is here saying that our armed colored troops are at many, if not all, the landings on the Patuxent River, and by their presence with arms in their hands are frightening quiet people and producing great confusion. Have they been sent there by any order, and if so, for what reason?

A. Lincoln.

Telegram to General R. C. Schenck, Executive Mansion, Washington, October 22, 1863, 1:30 P.M.[2]

Major General Schenck, Baltimore, Md.:

Please come over here. The fact of one of our officers being killed on the Patuxent is a specimen of what I would avoid. It seems to me we could send white men to recruit better than to send negroes and thus inaugurate homicides on punctilio.

Please come over.

A. Lincoln.

To General H. W. Halleck, Executive Mansion, Washington, October 24, 1863.[3]

Major General Halleck:

Taking all our information together, I think it probable that Ewell's corps has started for East Tennessee by way of Abingdon, marching last Monday, say from Meade's front directly to the railroad at Charlottesville.

First, the object of Lee's recent movement against Meade; his destruction of the Alexandria and Orange Railroad, and subsequent withdrawal without more motive, not otherwise apparent, would be explained by this hypothesis.

---

1 General Schenck replied at 6:45 P.M.: "The delegation from St. Mary's County have grossly misrepresented matters. Col. [William] Birney went under my orders to look for the site of a camp of instruction and rendezvous for colored troops. See his report, this day forwarded to the Adjutant General. He took with him a recruiting squad, who were stationed, each with an officer at Mill Stone, Spencers, Saint Leonards, Dukes, Forest Grove & Benedict landings on the Patuxent. They are under special instructions, good discipline and have harmed no one. "The only disorder or violence has been that two secessionists, named Southeron [John H. Sothoron and son] have killed second Lieut. White [Eben White, Seventh U.S. Colored Troops] at Benedict, but we hope to arrest the murderers. The officer was a white man. The only danger of confusion must be from the citizens, not the soldiers... but Col. Birney himself visited all the landings, talked with the citizens, and the only apprehension they expressed was that their slaves might leave them. It is a neighborhood of rabid secessionists. I beg that the President will not intervene and thus embolden them." (Lincoln v.6, 1953, 530)
2 General Schenck's reply was received at 4:05 P.M.: "I will be with you by 10 Oclock tomorrow AM. We had discovered this man Sothern engaged in raising & sending off recruits to the rebel army & were about to send to arrest him when this murder was reported." (Ibid, 532)
3 Graham is probably Michael Graham, a secret service agent; while Imboden is doubtless Confederate General John D. Imboden. (Ibid, 535)

Secondly, the direct statement of Sharpe's men that Ewell has gone to Tennessee.

Thirdly, the Irishman's [Northern Spy in Richmond] statement that he has not gone through Richmond, and his further statement of an appeal made to the people at Richmond to go and protect their salt, which could only refer to the works near Abingdon.

Fourthly, Graham's statement from Martinsburg that Imboden is in retreat for Harrisonburg. This last matches with the idea that Lee has retained his cavalry, sending Imboden and perhaps other scraps to join Ewell. Upon this probability what is to be done?

If you have a plan matured, I have nothing to say. If you have not, then I suggest that, with all possible expedition, the Army of the Potomac get ready to attack Lee, and that in the meantime a raid shall, at all hazards, break the railroad at or near Lynchburg.

Yours truly,

A. Lincoln.

To General Schofield [Private and Confidential] Executive Mansion, Washington, October 28, 1863.[1]

General John M. Schofield:

---

1 Schofield, in an arguably self-serving missive, replied to Lincoln on November 9: "I have the honor to acknowledge the receipt of your confidential letter dated Oct. 28th, and containing the names of men enlisted in the militia of northwest Missouri who are said to have been disloyal. On my visit to Kansas and northwest Missouri during the troubles there in September last, I examined personally into the difficulties in Platte, Buchanan, and other western counties, and learned fully their nature and origin. I at once ordered the reorganization of the militia, which created so much commotion for a time, but which has restored that portion of the State to a condition of profound peace. I have watched the progress of affairs there closely, and have kept myself fully advised of all the facts. It is true that about twice as many former rebels as were named by your informants are in the militia organization, amounting to from five to ten per cent, of the whole. It is also true that a very much larger number of returned Missouri rebels have enlisted in the Kansas Volunteers, and, so far as I know, are faithful, good soldiers. The rule I established for the militia organization in northwest Missouri was that the officers should be of undoubted loyalty, original Union men, and that both officers and privates, as far as possible, should be men of wealth and respectability, whose all depended upon the preservation of peace. The former sufferings of these men from the lawlessness which has so long existed on the border made them willing to do military duty to save them from destruction or loss what property they had left. I have yet to hear the first report of a murder, robbery, or arson in that whole region since this new organization was made. The late election was conducted in perfect peace and good order. There is not the slightest pretense from any source of any interference or other misconduct on the part of any of the troops. I have not deemed it necessary to be very particular about the antecedents of troops that are producing such good results. If I can make a repentant rebel of more service to the government than a man who never had any political sins to repent of, I see no reason for not doing so. Indeed, I take no little satisfaction in making these men guard the property of their more loyal neighbors, and in holding their own property responsible for their fidelity. I have the satisfaction of reporting to you that the late election in all parts of the State passed off in perfect quiet and good order. I have heard of no disturbance of any kind anywhere. The aggregate vote, I think, shows that the purity of the ballot box was preserved in a remarkable degree. If the loyal people all voted, few or no rebels did. The prospects of future peace in this State are highly encouraging." (Schofield 1897, 105-106)

There have recently reached the War Department, and thence been laid before me, from Missouri, three communications, all similar in import and identical in object. One of them, addressed to nobody, and without place or date, but having the signature of (apparently) the writer, is a letter of eight closely written foolscap pages. The other two are written by a different person, at St. Joseph, Mo., and of the dates, respectively, October 12 and 13, 1863, and each inclosing a large number of affidavits. The general statements of the whole are that the Federal and State authorities are arming the disloyal and disarming the loyal, and that the latter will all be killed or driven out of the State unless there shall be a change. In particular, no loyal man who has been disarmed is named, but the affidavits show by name forty-two persons as disloyal who have been armed. They are as follows: [The names are omitted.]

A majority of these are shown to have been in the rebel service. I believe it could be shown that the government here has deliberately armed more than ten times as many captured at Gettysburg, to say nothing of similar operations in East Tennessee. These papers contain altogether thirty—one manuscript pages, and one newspaper *in extenso*, and yet I do not find it anywhere charged in them that any loyal man has been harmed by reason of being disarmed, or that any disloyal one has harmed anybody by reason of being armed by the Federal or State Government. Of course, I have not had time to carefully examine all; but I have had most of them examined and briefed by others, and the result is as stated. The remarkable fact that the actual evil is yet only anticipated—inferred—induces me to suppose I understand the case; but I do not state my impression, because I might be mistaken, and because your duty and mine is plain in any event. The locality of nearly all this seems to be St. Joseph and Buchanan County. I wish you to give special attention to this region, particularly on election day. Prevent violence from whatever quarter, and see that the soldiers themselves do no wrong.

Yours truly,

A. Lincoln.

Telegram to General Meade Executive Mansion, Washington, November 3, 1863.[1]

Major General Meade, Army of Potomac:

Samuel Wellers, private in Company B, Forty-ninth Pennsylvania Volunteers, writes that he is to be shot for desertion on the 6th instant. His own story is rather a bad one, and yet he tells it so frankly, that I am somewhat interested in him. Has he been a good soldier except the desertion? About how old is he?

A. Lincoln.

---

1 Ruckman and Kincaid systematically examined Lincoln's approach to clemency and found considerable evidence that he employed pardoning power in a strategic manner. Further, their study of the rationales provided in clemency decisions revealed an impressive effort on the part of Lincoln to provide explicit justifications for each decision and an unprecedented willingness to extend clemency upon recommendation of both prominent individuals and mass public opinion. (Ruckman and Kincaid 1999, 1)

Telegram to General Meade, Executive, Mansion Washington, November 5, 1863.[1]

Major General Meade, Army of Potomac:

Please suspend the execution of Samuel Wellers, Forty-ninth Pennsylvania Volunteers, until further orders.

A. Lincoln.

Telegram to General A. E. Burnside. War Department, Washington, November 9, 1863, 4 P.M.[2]

Major General Burnside, Knoxville, Tenn.:

Have seen dispatch from General Grant about your loss at Rogersville. Per contra, about the same time, Averell and Duffle got considerable advantage of the enemy at and about Lewisburg, Virginia: and on Saturday, the seventh, Meade drove the enemy from Rappahannock Station and Kelly's Ford, capturing eight battle-flags, four guns, and over 1800 prisoners, with very little loss to himself. Let me hear from you.

A. Lincoln.

Telegram to General G. G. Meade, Washington, November 9, 1863, 7:30 P.M.[3]

Major General Meade:

I have seen your dispatches about operations on the Rappahannock on Saturday, and I wish to say, "Well done!" Do the 1500 prisoners reported by General

---

1 Samuel Wellers' sentence was commuted to imprisonment in Dry Tortugas. (Lincoln v.6, 1953, 561)

2 Burnside replied at 1 A.M. on November 12: "Your dispatch received. The Telegraph lines have been down since Saturday night, so that we could not communicate with Genl Grant. Our loss at Rogersville was about five hundred (500) old troops and one hundred & fifty (150) new troops. Four (4) pieces of artillery and thirty six (36) wagons with all the baggage & ammunition of two (2) Regts & a battery the principal loss was in the Second Tennessee mounted Infantry. The Seventh Ohio Cavalry lost about one hundred (100) men & Phillips Illinois Battery about forty (40). The force at that point consisted of these two (2) Regts & the Phillips Battery with some recruits for a new Tennessee Regt. The rebel attacking force amounted to thirty five hundred (3500) mounted men under Gen Sam Jones. They captured about six hundred horses & equipment & as many stand of small arms. An investigation is being made as to the cause of defeat. I at first thought it was the result of carelessness on the part of the Comdg Officer Col Garrard & want of steadiness on the part of the men but as the Investigation progresses I am becoming satisfied that it is result of the necessity for holding so long a line between two formidable forces of the Enemy. It seems to be impossible to be sufficiently watchful to prevent trouble when so many points are assailable. We were holding the line from Washn. on the Tenn. River to the Watauga. The troops of this command have behaved so well that I shall be glad to find that no one was censurable for the defeat. I send you a cipher dispatch. We were all rejoiced to hear of the Successes in Western Virginia & in the Army of the Potomac." (Lincoln v.7, 1953, 6)

3 No reply has been located. Meade's telegram to Halleck of 8 P.M., November 8 stated that "Major-General Sedgwick reports officially the capture of ... over 1,500 prisoners. Major-General French took over 400 prisoners ..." However, official figures for Confederate losses to Sedgwick at Rappahannock Station on November 7 were 1674 lost, captured and missing; at Kelly's Ford, Confederate losses to French were 359 captured and missing. (Ibid, 7)

Sedgwick include the 400 taken by General French, or do the Whole amount to 1900?

A. Lincoln.

Telegram to General Schofield, War Department, Washington, November 10, 1863.[1]

General Schofield, Saint Louis, Mo.:

I see a dispatch here from Saint Louis, which is a little difficult for me to understand. It says "General Schofield has refused leave of absence to members in military service to attend the legislature. All such are radical and administration men. The election of two Senators from this place on Thursday will probably turn upon this thing." what does this mean? Of course members of the legislation must be allowed to attend its sessions. But how is there a session before the recent election returns are in? And how is it to be at "this place"—and that is Saint Louis?

Please inform me.

A. Lincoln.

Telegram to General Schofield, War Department, Washington, November 11, 1863.[2]

General Schofield, Saint Louis, Mo.:

I believe the Secretary of War has telegraphed you about members of the legislation. At all events, allow those in the service to attend the session, and we can afterward decide whether they can stay through the entire session.

A. Lincoln.

Telegram to General W. S. Rosecrans, War Department, Washington, November 14, 1863, 12:15 P.M.[3]

Major General Rosecrans, Cincinnati, Ohio:

---

1 General Schofield replied the same day, "The legislature meets at Jefferson City today. The recent election was not for members of the Legislature except perhaps to fill vacancies. I have not authority to grant leaves of absence to officers except in case of sickness. The orders of the War Dept. expressly forbid it. I have informed members of the Legislature who are in the Military service that I will accept their resignations to enable them to attend the session of the Legislature. There are but few of them & they are about equally divided between radicalls [sic] & conservatives. If authorized to do so I will grant the leaves of absence long enough to elect senators but I would not think it proper for them to be absent all winter and still retain their commissions in the army." (Ibid, 8)

2 No telegram from Stanton to Schofield about members of the legislature has been located. (Ibid, 10)

3 General Orders No. 337, October 16, 1863, created the Military Division of the Mississippi, incorporating the Departments of the Ohio, Cumberland, and Tennessee, under General Grant, and replaced Rosecrans with General George H. Thomas. Rosecrans telegraphed Lincoln from Cincinnati on November 13, "Will you permit me to publish a certified copy of my official report of the Battle of Chicamauga, also those of Generals Thomas, McCook, Crittenden & Granger. It is an act of justice I solicit from one in whose justice I confide." (Ibid, 14)

I have received and considered your dispatch of yesterday. Of the reports you mention, I have not the means of seeing any except your own. Besides this, the publication might be improper in view of the court of inquiry which has been ordered. With every disposition, not merely to do justice, but to oblige you, I feel constrained to say I think the publications better not be made now.

A. Lincoln.

Telegram to General Burnside, War Department, Washington City, November 16, 1863.[1]

Major General Burnside, Knoxville, Tenn.:
What is the news?
A. Lincoln.

Telegram to General Meade, Executive Mansion, Washington, November 20, 1863.[2]

Major General Meade, Army of Potomac:
If there is a man by the name of King under sentence to be shot, please suspend execution till further order, and send record.

A. Lincoln.

Telegram to General Meade, Executive Mansion, Washington, November 20, 1863.[3]

Major General Meade, Army of Potomac:
An intelligent woman in deep distress, called this morning, saying her husband, a lieutenant in the Army of Potomac, was to be shot next Monday for desertion, and putting a letter in my hand, upon which I relied for particulars, she left without mentioning a name or other particular by which to identify the case. On opening the letter I found it equally vague, having nothing to identify by, except her own signature, which seems to be "Mrs. Anna S. King." I could not again find her. If you have a case which you shall think is probably the one intended, please apply my dispatch of this morning to it.

A. Lincoln.

---

1 On November 17 Burnside replied to Lincoln's telegram: "Longstreet crossed the Tennessee River on Saturday at Huff's Ferry six miles below Loudon with about 15,000 men. We have resisted the advance steadily repulsing every attack, holding on, till our position was turned by superior numbers, and then retiring in good order....He attacked us yesterday about eleven o'clock at Campbell's Station and heavy fighting has been going on all day, in which we have held our own and inflicted serious loss on the enemy....No fighting since dark. We commenced retiring, and the most of the command is now within the lines of Knoxville...." (Ibid)

2 No reply either to this communication or Lincoln's the follow-up telegram of the same date has been located. The sentence of First Lieutenant Edward King, Company H, Sixty-sixth New York Infantry, was commuted to imprisonment on the Dry Tortugas, May 13, 1864. Additional correspondence associated with this file relate how Mrs. King was swindled by "an officer who gave his name as Captain Parker Co. M. 12th Pa Cavalry, who promised for $300 to get her husband pardoned...claimed to know [Lincoln] & got all the money the poor creature had." (Ibid, 25)

3 Ibid.

Telegram to General Grant, Washington, November 25, 1863, 8:40 A.M.[1]

Major General U. S. Grant:
Your dispatches as to fighting on Monday and Tuesday are here. Well done! Many thanks to all. Remember Burnside.
A. Lincoln.

Telegram to General U. S. Grant, Washington, December 8, 1863.[2]

Major General Grant:
Understanding that your lodgment at Chattanooga and Knoxville is now secure, I wish to tender you, and all under your command, my more than thanks, my profoundest gratitude, for the skill, courage, and perseverance with which you and they, over so great difficulties, have effected that important object. God bless you all!
A. Lincoln.

Telegram to General Butler, Executive Mansion, Washington, December 10, 1863.[3]

Major General Butler, Fort Monroe, Va.:
Please suspend execution in any and all sentences of death in your department until further order.
A. Lincoln.

Telegram to General Meade, Executive Mansion, Washington, December 11, 1863.[4]

Major General Meade, Army of The Potomac:

---

1 The "Well done!" notwithstanding, Grant understood that the authorities in Washington were getting more and more impatient about the situation in Knoxville, where Burnside was still semi-besieged by Longstreet. Halleck had plainly stated that he did not think Burnside was going to be able to hold out much longer unless Grant did something about the situation. Clearly, Grant's superiors expected decisive action here at Chattanooga as a prelude to a march to relieve Burnside, and they expected that decisive action to begin at once. It was just as clear to Grant, as he watched Sherman's men scrambling back down the slopes of Tunnel Hill with Cleburne's Confederates in hot pursuit, that nothing decisive was likely to happen unless he came up with a new idea or two. (Woodworth 1999, 77)

2 Grant, with the victory at Chattanooga, not only secured a permanent base of operations at that point; but also was well positioned to defend East-Tennessee against all Confederate assaults. Upon the recommendation of the President, Congress passed a resolution of thanks, and voted a medal to Grant for his victories. The resolution became a law during the session of the Congress of 1863 and 1864. (Moore 1864, 133)

3 On December 8 General Butler telegraphed, "Do you see any reason for delaying any longer the execution in the cases referred to you by Col Shaffer my Chief of Staff." A notation on the telegram, not Lincoln's, gives the names Peter Donnelley, John Flinn, and Charles Leach. (Lincoln v.7, 1953, 59)

4 No reply has been located; however, the roster of the Thirty-ninth Pennsylvania Volunteers (Tenth Reserve) lists Lieutenant Colonel James B. Knox as resigned, seemingly for health reasons, on November 23, 1863. (Lincoln v.7, 1953, 61)

Lieut. Col. James B. Knox, Tenth Regiment Pennsylvania Reserves, offers his resignation under circumstances inducing me to wish to accept it. But I prefer to know your pleasure upon the subject. Please answer.

A. Lincoln.

Telegram to General Hurlbut [Cipher] Executive Mansion, Washington, December 17, 1863.[1]

Major General Hurlbut, Memphis, Tenn.:

I understand you have under sentence of death, a tall old man, by the name of Henry F. Luckett. I personally knew him, and did not think him a bad man. Please do not let him be executed unless upon further order from me, and in the meantime send me a transcript of the record.

A. Lincoln.

Telegram to General U. S. Grant, War Department, Washington, December 19, 1863.[2]

General Grant, Chattanooga, Tennessee:

The Indiana delegation in Congress, or at least a large part of them, are very anxious that General Milroy shall enter active service again, and I share in this feeling. He is not a difficult man to satisfy, sincerity and courage being his strong traits. Believing in our cause, and wanting to fight for it, is the whole matter with him. Could you, without embarrassment, assign him a place, if directed to report to you?

A. Lincoln.

To General N. P. Banks, Executive Mansion, Washington, December 29, 1863.[3]

Major General Banks:

---

1   While most agreed that Henry Luckett was undoubtedly guilty of smuggling percussion caps to the enemy, other suggested he was insane. After Lincoln pardoned him, Luckett wrote to thank him for his clemency, noting that "it has been by your grace that I have been delivered from the Lion's paw." (Holzer 2011, 230)

2   No reply from Grant has been located; however, *Special Orders No. 169*, dated May 6, 1864, assigned Milroy to Nashville, Tennessee, to report to General George H. Thomas for duty in receiving and organizing militia regiments, and for assignment to the command of Indiana troops when organized. (Lincoln v.7, 1953, 80)

3   Lincoln had issued his Proclamation of Amnesty and Reconstruction on December 8, 1863. The executive order offered a full pardon and restoration of all rights to persons within the Confederacy who reaffirmed their allegiance by taking an oath of future loyalty. The program represented Lincoln's first attempt at comprehensive reconstruction designed to bring the rebellious south back into the Union by giving its civilian population the opportunity to come home voluntarily. Lincoln's proclamation also provided a way to shorten the war by undermining civilian enthusiasm and support in areas occupied by the Union army and to prepare the South for the emancipation of slaves. Known as the *Ten Percent Plan*, Lincoln's executive order allowed any state whose loyal members, equaling at least 10 percent of the 1860 registered voters, to form a new state government that would be entitled to federal representation in Washington. (Weitz 2000, 36) In Louisiana, under the auspices of Lincoln's plan, free black leaders had already petitioned the military governor and sent a delegation to President Lincoln in a quest for "the rights of franchise and of citizenship in this country." They had some cause for optimism. General Nathaniel P. Banks, who had replaced Benjamin Butler over a year earlier as commander of the Department of the Gulf,

Yours of the sixteenth is received, and I send you, as covering the ground of it, a copy of my answer to yours of the sixth, it being possible the original may not reach you. I intend you to be master in every controversy made with you.

Yours truly,

A. Lincoln.

Telegram to General Butler, Executive Mansion, Washington, December 30, 1863.[1]

Major General Butler, Fort Monroe, Va.:

Jacob Bowers is fully pardoned for past offence, upon condition that he re-turns to duty and re-enlists for three years or during the war.

A. Lincoln.

---

1 General Butler telegraphed Lincoln on December 30: "Jacob Bowers was sentenced to impris-onment for life by Genl. Order No. 37, from these Head Qrs which sentence was approved by me Nov. 24th. for desertion. I now believe that he simply acted under a misapprehension of his duty, being a German not understanding his duty. Please permit me to remit this sentence if he returns to duty and re enlists during the war. I suppose I have the power now to do so but the papers are in Washington. This is the first time I have ever asked you to pardon anybody." (Lincoln v.7, 1953, 98)

STRATEGIC PERSPECTIVES: THE WAR OF 1864–1865

From Bull Run to Chattanooga, the Union armies had fought their battles without benefit of either a grand strategy or a supreme field commander. During the final year of the war the people of the North grew restless, and as the election of 1864 approached, many of them advocated a policy of making peace with the Confederacy. President Lincoln never wavered. Committed to the policy of destroying the armed power of the Confederacy, he sought a general who could pull all the threads of an emerging strategy together, and then concentrate the Union armies and their supporting naval power against the secessionists. After Vicksburg in July 1863, Lincoln leaned more and more toward Grant as the man whose strategic thinking and resolution would lead the Union armies to final victory.

Strategy of Annihilation and Unity of Command: Acting largely as his own General in Chief after McClellan's removal in early 1862, Mr. Lincoln had watched the Confederates fight from one ephemeral victory to another inside their cockpit of northern Virginia. In the western theater, Union armies, often operating independently of one another, had scored great victories at key terrain points. But their hold on the communications base at Nashville was always in jeopardy as long as the elusive armies of the Confederacy could escape to fight another day at another key point. The twin, uncoordinated victories at Gettysburg and Vicksburg, 900 airline miles apart, only pointed up the North's need for an over-all strategic plan and a general who could carry it out.

Having cleared the Mississippi River, Grant wrote to Halleck and the President about the opportunities now open to his army. Grant first called for the consolidation of the autonomous western departments and the coordination of

---

seemed receptive to the idea of qualified black suffrage and, in this note, Lincoln quietly offered Banks his encouragement. Banks may in fact have considered permitting a few people of color to participate in the February 1864 election for governor and other state officials, though in the end thought better of it. (Hahn 205, 104)

their individual armies. After this great step, he proposed to isolate the area west of the line Chattanooga-Atlanta-Montgomery-Mobile. Within this region, Grant urged a "massive rear attack" that would take Union armies in the Gulf Department under Maj. Gen. Nathaniel P. Banks and Grant's Army of the Tennessee to Mobile and up the Alabama River to Montgomery. The U.S. Navy would play a major role in this attack. Simultaneously, Rosecrans was to advance overland through Chattanooga to Atlanta. All military resources within this isolated area would be destroyed.

Lincoln vetoed Grant's plan in part by deferring the Mobile-Montgomery phase. The President favored a demonstration by Banks up the Red River to Shreveport in order to show the American flag to Napoleon III's interlopers in Mexico, and Banks' Department of the Gulf was left out of the consolidation of the other western commands under Grant in October 1863.

After his own victory at Chattanooga in November, Grant wasted few hours in writing the President what he thought the next strategic moves should be. As a possible winter attack, Grant revived the touchy Mobile campaign while the Chattanooga victors were gathering strength for a spring offensive to Atlanta. Grant reasoned that Lee would vacate Virginia and shift strength toward Atlanta. For the Mobile-Montgomery plan, Grant asked for Banks' resources in the Gulf Department. Lincoln again balked because the Texas seacoast would be abandoned. Grant's rebuttal explained that Napoleon III would really be impressed with a large Army–Navy operation against Mobile Bay. The Red River campaign, Grant believed, would not deter Napoleon III. The President told Grant again that he had to heed the demands of Union diplomacy, but at the same time he encouraged Grant to enlarge his strategic proposals to include estimates for a grand Federal offensive for the coming spring of 1864.

Grant's plan of January 1864 projected a four-pronged continental attack. In concert, the four armies were to move on Atlanta, on Mobile—after Banks took Shreveport—on Lee's communications by a campaign across the middle of North Carolina on the axis New Bern-Neuse River-Goldsboro-Raleigh-Greensboro, and on Lee's Army of Northern Virginia in the hope of defeating it in an open battle. Lincoln opposed the North Carolina phase, fearing that Grant's diversion of 60,000 effective bayonets from formations covering Washington was too dangerous. Lincoln knew that Lee's eyes were always fixed on the vast amount of supplies in the depots around the Washington area.

Though Lincoln scuttled some of Grant's professional schemes, he never lost his esteem for Grant's enthusiasm and intelligence. In February 1864 Congress revived Scott's old rank of lieutenant general, to which Grant was promoted on March 9. Lincoln relieved Halleck as General in Chief, ordered Grant to Washington to assume Halleck's post, and during March the President, the new General in Chief, and the Secretary of War ironed out toplevel command arrangements which had plagued every President since the War of 1812. Lincoln and Stanton relinquished powerful command, staff, and communications tools to Grant. Stanton, greatly impressed with Grant's public acclaim, cautioned his General Staff Bureau chiefs to heed Grant's needs and timetables.

In twentieth century terms, Grant was a theater commander. As General in Chief, he reported directly to the President anti Secretary of War, keeping them informed about the broad aspects of his strategic plans and telling them in advance of his armies' needs. Grant removed himself from the politics of Washington and established his headquarters in northern Virginia. Though he planned to go quickly to troubled spots, Grant elected to accompany Meade's Army of the Potomac in order to assess Lee's moves and their effects on the other columns of the Union Army. By rail or steamboat, Grant was never far from Lincoln, and in turn the President visited Grant frequently. To tie his far-flung commands together, Grant employed a vast telegraph system.

In a continental theater of war larger than Napoleon's at its zenith, Grant's job, administratively, eventually embraced four military divisions, totaling seventeen subcommands, wherein 500,000 combat soldiers would he employed. At Washington, Halleck operated a war room for Grant and eased his heavy burden of studying the several Army commanders' detailed field directives by preparing brief digests, thus saving the General in Chief many hours of reading detailed reports. Bearing the then nebulous title of "Chief of Staff, U.S. Army," Halleck had a major job in keeping Grant informed about supply levels at base depots and advance dumps in Nashville, St. Louis, City Point, Washington, Philadelphia, Louisville, and New York City. Under Stanton, Quartermaster General Montgomery C. Meigs, the most informed logistician and supply manager of his day, dispatched men and munitions to Grant's subcommands according to a strategic timetable. As the spring offensive progressed, Stanton, Halleck, and Meigs gave Grant a rear-area team that grasped the delicate balance between theater objectives and the logistical support required to achieve them.

Grant spent the month of April on the Rapidan front developing his final strategic plan for ending the war. In essence, he recapped all of his views on the advantages to be gained from his victories in the western theater. He added some thoughts about moving several Federal armies, aided by naval power when necessary, toward a common center in a vast, concentrated effort. He planned to stop the Confederates from using their interior lines. He intended to maneuver Lee away from the Rapidan Wilderness and defeat the Army of Northern Virginia in open terrain by a decisive battle. Another Union force collected from the Atlantic seaport towns of the deep South was to cut the James-Appomattox River line to sever Lee's rail and road links with the other parts of the Confederacy. Simultaneously, Sherman's group of armies would execute a wide wheeling movement through the South to complete the envelopment of the whole country east of the Mississippi. Banks was still scheduled to make the attack through Mobile. As Lincoln described the plan, "Those not skinning can hold a leg."

By mid-April 1864 Grant had issued specific orders to each commander of the four Federal armies that were to execute the grand strategy. In round numbers the Union armies were sending 300,000 combat troops against 150,000 Confederates defending the invasion paths. Meade's Army of the Potomac and Burnside's independent IX Corps, a combined force of 120,000 men, constituted the major attack column under Grant's over-all direction. The enemy had 63,000 troops facing Grant along the Rapidan. Two subsidiary thrusts were to support

Meade's efforts. Commanding a force of 33,000 men, Butler with his Army of the James was to skirt the south bank of the James, menace Richmond, take it if possible, and destroy the railroads below Petersburg. Acting as a right guard in the Shenandoah Valley, Maj. Gen. Franz Sigel's 23,000 Federals were to advance on Lee's rail hub at Lynchburg, Virginia. With the northern Virginia triangle under attack, in the continental center of the line Sherman's 100,000 men were to march on Atlanta, annihilating Joseph E. Johnston's 65,000 soldiers, and devastating the resources of central Georgia. On the continental right of the line, Banks was to disengage as soon as possible along the Red River and with Rear Adm. David C. Farragut's blockading squadron in the Gulf of Mexico make a limited amphibious landing against Mobile. The day for advance would be announced early in May.

In rising from regimental command to General in-Chief, Grant had learned much from experience, and if he sometimes made mistakes he rarely repeated them. Not a profound student of the literature of warfare, he had become, by the eve of his grand campaign, one of those rare leaders who combine the talents of the strategist, tactician, and logistician and who marry those talents to the principle of the offensive. His operations, especially the "rear mass attack," were models of the execution of the principles of war. He was calm in crisis; reversals and disappointments did not unhinge his cool judgment. He mastered the dry-as-dust details of a logistical system and used common sense in deciding when to use the horse-drawn wagon, the railroad, or the steamboat in his strategic moves. Above all, Grant understood and applied the principle of modern war that the destruction of the enemy's economic resources is as necessary as the annihilation of the enemy's armies.[1]

Lee Cornered at Richmond:

On the morning of May 4, 1864, Meade and Sherman moved out to execute Grant's grand strategy. The combat strength of the Army of the Potomac, slimmed down from seven unwieldy corps, consisted of three infantry corps of 25,000 rifles each and a cavalry corps. Commanding the 12,000-man cavalry corps was Maj. Gen. Philip H. Sheridan, an energetic leader brought east by Grant on Halleck's recommendation. Meade again dispersed his cavalry, using troopers as messengers, pickets, and train guards, but young Sheridan, after considerable argument, eventually succeeded in concentrating all of his sabers as a separate combat arm. Grant reorganized Burnside's IX Corps of 20,000 infantrymen, held it as a strategic reserve for a time, and then assigned the IX Corps to Meade's army. Lee's army, now 70,000 strong, was also organized into a cavalry and three infantry corps.

Grant and Lee were at the height of their careers and this was their first contest of wills. Having the initiative, Grant crossed the Rapidan and decided to go by Lee's right, rather than his left. First, Grant wanted to rid himself of the need to use an insecure railroad with limited capacity back to Alexandria, Virginia. Second, he wanted to end the Army of the Potomac's dependence on a train of 4,000 wagons; the Army's mobility was hobbled by having to care for 60,000 animals. Finally, Grant wanted to use the advantages of Virginia's tidewater riv-

---

1 Matloff 1969, 262-265.

ers and base his depots on the Chesapeake Bay. He was willing to accept the risk inherent in moving obliquely across Lee's front in northern Virginia.

With little room for maneuver, Grant was forced to advance through the Wilderness, where Hooker had come to grief the year before. As the army column halted near Chancellorsville to allow the wagon trains to pass the Rapidan, on May 5 Lee struck at Meade's right flank. Grant and Meade swung their corps into line and hit hard. The fighting in the battle of the Wilderness, consisting of assault, defense, and counterattack, was close and desperate in tangled woods and thickets. Artillery could not be brought to bear. The dry woods caught fire and some of the wounded died miserably in the flame and smoke. On May 6 Lee attacked again. Longstreet's I Corps, arriving late in battle but as always in perfect march order, drove the Federals back. Longstreet himself received a severe neck wound, inflicted in error by his own men, that took him out of action until October 1864. Lee, at a decisive moment in the battle, his fighting blood aroused to a white heat, attempted to lead an assault in person; but men of the Texas brigade with whom Lee was riding persuaded the Southern leader to go to the rear and direct the battle as their Army commander. On May 7 neither side renewed the battle.

Now came the critical test of Grant's execution of strategy. He had been worsted, though not really beaten, by Lee, a greater antagonist than Bragg, Joseph E. Johnston, and Pemberton. After an encounter with Lee, each of the former Army of the Potomac commanders, McClellan, Burnside, and Hooker, had retired north of the Rappahannock River and postponed any further clashes with that great tactician. But Grant was of a different breed. He calmly ordered his lead corps to move south toward Spotsylvania as rapidly as possible to get around Lee's flank and interpose the Army of the Potomac between Lee and Richmond.

Lee detected Grant's march and, using roads generally parallel to Grant's, also raced toward the key road junction at Spotsylvania. J.E.B. Stuart's cavalry harassed and slowed Grant; Lee arrived first and quickly built strong earth-and-log trenches over commanding ground which covered the roads leading to Richmond. In this crossroads race, Sheridan's cavalry would have been useful, but Meade had dissipated the cavalry corps' strength by deploying two divisions of horse to guard his already well-protected trains. Sheridan and Meade argued once again over the use of cavalry, and the General in Chief backed Sheridan, allowing him now to concentrate his cavalry arm. Grant gave Sheridan a free hand in order to stop Stuart's raids. Leading his corps southward in a long ride toward Richmond, its objective a decisive charge against Stuart, Sheridan did the job. He fought a running series of engagements that culminated in a victory at Yellow Tavern, in which the gallant Stuart was mortally wounded. The South was already short of horses and mules, and Sheridan's 16-day raid ended forever the offensive power of Lee's mounted arm.

For four days beginning May 9 Meade struck repeatedly at Lee's roadblock at Spotsylvania but was beaten back. Twice tile Federals broke through the trenches and divided Lee's army, but in each case the attackers became disorganized. Supporting infantry did not or could not close in, and Confederate counterattacks were delivered with such ferocity that the breakthroughs could be neither exploited nor held. On the morning of the 11th, Grant wrote Halleck: "I propose to fight it out on this line if it takes all summer." On May 20, having decided the entrenchments were too strong to capture, Grant side slipped south again, still trying to envelop Lee's right flank.

With smaller numbers, Lee skillfully avoided Grant's trap and refused to leave entrenched positions and be destroyed in open battle. Lee retired to the North Anna River and dug in. Grant then continued to move south, to his left, in a daring and difficult tactical maneuver. Butler had meanwhile advanced up the peninsula toward Richmond, but Beauregard outmaneuvered him in May and bottled up Butler's men at Bermuda Hundred between the James and Appomattox Rivers. Eventually Butler and Banks, who did not take Mobile, were removed from command for their failure to carry out their assignments in the grand strategy.

Lee easily made his way into the Richmond defenses with his right flank on the Chickahominy and his center at Cold Harbor, the site of the Gaines' Mill action in 1862. The front extended for eight miles. On June 3 Grant assaulted Lee's center at Cold Harbor. Though bravely executed, the attack was badly planned. The Confederates repulsed it with gory efficiency, and Grant later regretted that he had ever made the attempt. Cold Harbor climaxed a month of heavy fighting in which Grant's forces had casualties totaling about 55,000 as against about 32,000 for those of Lee. After Cold Harbor, Grant executed a brilliant maneuver in the face of the enemy. All Union corps were on the north bank of the deep, wide James by June 14 and crossed over a 2,100-foot ponton bridge, the longest up to that time in modern history. Having established a new and modern base depot at City Point, complete with a railroad line to the front, Grant on June 18, 1864, undertook siege operations at Petersburg below Richmond, an effort which continued into the next year.

After forty-four days of continuous fighting, Lee was fixed finally in position warfare, a war of trenches and sieges, conducted ironically enough by two masters of mobile warfare. Mortars were used extensively, and heavy siege guns were brought up on railway cars. Grant still sought to get around Lee's right and hold against Lee's left to prevent him from shortening his line and achieving a higher degree of concentration. When Lee moved his lines to counter Grant, the two commanders were, in effect, maneuvering their fortifications.

Now that Lee was firmly entrenched in front of Grant, and could spare some men, he decided to ease the pressure with one of his perennial raids up the Shenandoah Valley toward Washington. Confederate Maj. Gen. Jubal A. Early's corps in early July advanced against Maj. Gen. David Hunter, who had replaced Sigel. Hunter, upon receiving confused orders from Halleck, retired up the valley. When he reached the Potomac, he turned west into the safety of the Appalachians and uncovered Washington. Early saw his chance and drove through Maryland. Delayed by a Union force on July 9 near Frederick, he reached the northern outskirts of Washington on July 11 and skirmished briskly in the vicinity of Fort Stevens. Abraham Lincoln and Quartermaster General Meigs were interested spectators. At City Point, Grant had received the news of Early's raid calmly. Using his interior waterway, he embarked the men of his VI Corps for the capital, where they landed on the 11th. When Early realized he was engaging troops from the Army of the Potomac, he managed to escape the next day.

Grant decided that Early had eluded the Union's superior forces because they had not been under a single commander. He abolished four separate departments and formed them into one, embracing Washington, western Maryland, and the Shenandoah Valley. In August, Sheridan was put in command with orders to follow Early to the death. Sheridan spent the remainder of the year in the valley, employing and coordinating his infantry, cavalry, and artillery in a manner that has won the admiration of military students ever since. He met and defeated Early at Winchester and Fisher's Hill in September and shattered him at Cedar Creek in October. To stop further raids and prevent Lee from feeding his army on the crops of that fertile region, Sheridan devastated the Shenandoah Valley.[1]

Sherman's Great Wheel to the East:

On March 17, 1864, Grant had met with Sherman at Nashville and told him his role in the grand strategy. Sherman, like Grant, held two commands. As Division of the Mississippi commander, he was responsible for the operation and defense of a vast logistical system that reached from a communications zone at St. Louis, Louisville, and Cincinnati to center on a large base depot at Nashville. Strategically, Nashville on the Cumberland River rivaled Washington, D.C., in importance. A 90-mile military railroad, built and operated by Union troops, gave Nashville access to steamboats plying the Tennessee River. Connected with Louisville by rail, Nashville became one vast storehouse and corral. If the city was destroyed, the Federal forces would have to fall back to the Ohio River line. Wearing his other hat, Sherman was a field commander, with three armies under his direction.

With the promise of the return of his two crack divisions from the Red River expedition by May 1864 and with a splendid administrative system working behind him, Sherman was ready to leave Chattanooga in the direction of Atlanta. His mission was to destroy Johnston's armies and capture Atlanta, which after Richmond was the most important industrial center in the Confederacy. With 254 guns, Sherman matched his three small armies, and a separate cavalry command—a total force of more than 100,000 men—against Joseph E. Johnston's Army of Tennessee and the Army of Mississippi including Wheeler's cavalry, consisting of 65,000 men.

Sherman moved out on May 4, 1864, the same day the Army of the Potomac crossed the Rapidan. Johnston, realizing how seriously he was outnumbered, decided to go on the defensive, preserve his forces intact, hold Atlanta, and delay Sherman as long as possible. There was always the hope that the North would grow weary of the costly struggle and that some advocate of peaceful settlement might defeat Abraham Lincoln in the election of 1864. From May 4 through mid-July, the two forces maneuvered against each other. There were daily fights but few large-scale actions. As Sherman pushed south, Johnston would take up a strong position and force Sherman to halt, deploy, and reconnoiter. Sherman would then outflank Johnston, who in turn would retire to a new line and start the process all over again. On June 27 Sherman, unable to maneuver because the

---

1 Matloff 1969, 266-270.

roads were muddy and seriously concerned by the unrest in his armies brought about by constant and apparently fruitless marching, decided to assault Johnston at Kennesaw Mountain. This attack against prepared positions, like the costly failure at Cold Harbor, was beaten back. Sherman returned to maneuver and forced Johnston back to positions in front of Atlanta.

Johnston had done his part well. He had accomplished his missions and had so slowed Sherman that Sherman covered only 100 miles in 74 days. Johnston, his forces intact, was holding strong positions in front of Atlanta, his main base; but by this time Jefferson Davis had grown impatient with Johnston and his tactics of cautious delay. In July he replaced him with Lt. Gen. John B. Hood, a much more impetuous commander.

On July 20, while Sherman was executing a wide turning movement around the northeast side of Atlanta, Hood left his fortifications and attacked at Peach Tree Creek. When Sherman beat him off, Hood pulled back into the city. While Sherman made ready to invest, Hood attacked again and failed again. Sherman then tried cavalry raids to cut the railroads, just as Johnston had during the advance from Chattanooga, but Sherman's raids had as little success as Johnston's. Sherman then began extending fortifications on August 31. Hood, who had dissipated his striking power in his assaults, gave up and retired to northwest Alabama, and Sherman marched into Atlanta on the first two days of September. Sherman hoped that Mobile had fallen, and a shorter line for his supplies by way of Montgomery, Alabama, or still better by the lower Chattahoochee to Columbus, Georgia, was open. Admiral Farragut had entered Mobile Bay on August 5, 1864, but had no troops to take Mobile itself.

The fall of Atlanta gave President Lincoln's campaign for reselection in 1864 a tremendous boost. In addition, the psychological lift given the Union by Admiral Farragut's personal heroism in the battle of Mobile Bay greatly added to Lincoln's prestige.

Atlanta was only a halfway point in Sherman's vast wheel from the western theater toward the rear of Lee's Army of Northern Virginia. Abandoning the idea of catching up with Hood, Sherman by telegraph outlined his next strategic move to Lincoln and Grant in early September 1864. Sherman's two proposals proved him an able strategist as well as a consummately bold and aggressive commander. To defend Nashville, he suggested that he send two corps, 30,000 men, back to Thomas, where that commander would raise and train more men and be in position to hold Tennessee if Hood came north. To carry the offensive against the economic heart of the Confederacy, Sherman recommended that he himself take four corps—62,000 men—cut his own communications, live off the country, and march to the seacoast through Georgia, devastating and laying waste all farms, railways, and storehouses in his path. Whether he arrived at Pensacola, Charleston, or Savannah, Sherman reasoned he could hold a port, make contact with the U.S. Navy, and be refitted by Stanton and Meigs. Meigs promised to do the logistical job, and Lincoln and Grant, though their reaction to the plan was less than enthusiastic, accepted it in a show of confidence in Sherman.

Before marching out of Atlanta, Sherman's engineers put selected buildings to the torch and destroyed all railroads in the vicinity. On November 12, moving away from the Nashville depots toward Savannah, the Division of the Mississippi troops broke telegraphic contact with Grant. They had twenty days' emergency rations in their wagons, but planned to replenish them by living off the country. Operating on a 60-mile-wide front, unimpeded by any Confederate force, Sherman's army systematically burned and destroyed what it did not need. The march became something of a rowdy excursion. Sherman's campaign, like Sheridan's in the Shenandoah, anticipated the economic warfare and strategic aerial bombardments of the twentieth century. Yet the victims of his methods could hardly be blamed if they regarded Sherman's strategy as an excuse for simple thievery. On December 10 Sherman, having broken the classic pattern by moving away from his logistical base, arrived in front of Savannah. Confederate forces evacuated the seaport on December 21 and Sherman offered it to the nation as a Christmas present. Awaiting him offshore was Meigs' floating seatrain, which enabled him to execute the last phase of Grant's strategy, a thrust north toward the line of the James River.[1]

Thomas Protects the Nashville Base: Sherman, as the western theater commander, did not learn of Nashville's fate until he reached Savannah. He had planned Nashville's defense well enough by sending his IV and XXII Corps under Maj. Gen. John M. Schofield to screen Hood's northward move from Florence, Alabama. Schofield was to allow Thomas some time to assemble 50,000 men and strengthen Nashville. The aggressive Hood with his 30,000 men had lost a golden opportunity to trap Schofield at Spring Hill, Tennessee, on November 29, 1864. Unopposed, the Union troops made a night march across Hood's front to escape capture. Bitterly disappointed, Hood overtook Schofield the next day at Franklin.

Grant's continental timetable could have at this point been upset by Hood. Booty at Nashville might carry Hood to the Ohio or allow him to concentrate with Lee before Richmond. But Franklin turned into one of the Confederacy's most tragic battles. It commenced about 3:30 p.m. on November So and ended at dusk as Hood threw 18,000 of his veterans against a solidly entrenched force of Federals. Like Pickett's charge at Gettysburg, Hood's frontal assault gained nothing. He lost over 6,000 men, including 13 general officers. At nightfall Schofield brought his troops in behind Thomas' defenses at Nashville.

Hood was in a precarious position. He had been far weaker than Thomas to begin with; the battle of Franklin had further depleted his army; and, even worse, his men had lost confidence in their commander. The Federals in Nashville were securely emplaced in a city which they had been occupying for three years. Hood could do little more than encamp on high ground a few miles south of Nashville and wait. He could not storm the city; his force was too small to lay siege; to sidestep and go north was an open invitation to Thomas to attack his flank and rear; and to retreat meant disintegration of his army. He could only watch Thomas' moves.

Thomas, the Rock of Chickamauga, belonged to the last bootlace school of soldiering. In comparison with Grant and Sherman, he was slow; but he was also thorough. He had gathered and trained men and horses and was prepared to

---

1 Matloff 1969, 270-274.

attack Hood on December 10, but an ice storm the day before made move- ment impossible. Grant and his superiors in Washington fretted at the delay, and the General in Chief actually started west to remove Thomas. But on December 15 Thomas struck like a sledgehammer in an attack that militarily students have regarded as virtually faultless.

Thomas' tactical plan was a masterly, coordinated attack. His heavily weighted main effort drove against Hood's left flank while a secondary attack aimed simultaneously at Hood's right. Thomas provided an adequate reserve and used cavalry to screen his flank and extend the envelopment of the enemy left. Hood, on the other hand, was overextended and his thin line was concave to the enemy, denying him the advantage of interior lines. Hood's reserve was inadequate, and his cavalry was absent on a minor mission. The two-day battle proceeded according to Thomas' plan as the Federals fixed Hood's right while slashing savagely around the Confederate left flank. They broke Hood's first line on December 15, forcing the Southerners to retire to a new line two miles to the rear. The Federals repeated their maneuver on the 16th, and by nightfall the three-sided battle had disintegrated into a rout of Hood's army. Broken and defeated, it streamed southward, protected from hotly pursuing Union cavalry only by the intrepid rear-guard action of Forrest's horsemen. The shattered Army of the Tennessee reached Tupelo, Mississippi, on January 10, 1865. It no longer existed as an effective fighting force; Hood was relieved of command and his scattered units were assigned to other areas of combat. The decisive battle of Nashville had eliminated one of the two great armies of the Confederacy from a shrinking chessboard.[1]

Lee's Last 100 Days:

President Lincoln was delighted with Savannah as a Christmas present, and in his congratulatory letter to Sherman and Grant the Commander in Chief said that he would leave the final phases of the war to his two leading professional soldiers. Accordingly, from City Point, Grant directed Sherman, on December 27, 1864, to march overland toward Richmond. At 3:00 p.m. on December 31, Sherman agreed to execute this last phase of Grant's continental sweep. In the final 100 days of the war, the two generals would clearly demonstrate the art of making principles of warfare come alive and prove that each principle was something more than a platitude. Each commander had a common objective: Grant and Meade would continue to hammer Lee. Sherman was to execute a devastating invasion northward through the Carolinas toward a juncture with Meade's Army of the Potomac, then on the line of the James River. Their strategy was simple. It called for the massing of strength and exemplified an economy of force. It would place Lee in an unmaneuverable position, cutting him off from all other Confederate commanders. Surprise would be achieved by reuniting all of Sherman's original corps when Schofield, moving from central Tennessee by rail, river, and ocean transport, arrived at the Carolina capes. Solidly based on a centralized logistical system with protected Atlantic sea trains at their side, Grant and Sherman were ready to end Lee's stay in Richmond.

---

1 Matloff 1969, 274-275.

Robert E. Lee, the master tactician, divining his end, wrote to Davis that the Confederates would have to concentrate their forces for a last-ditch stand. In February 1865 the Confederate Congress conferred supreme command of all Confederate armies on Lee, but it was an empty honor. Lee could no longer control events. Sherman moved through Columbia, South Carolina, in February, took Wilmington, North Carolina, the Confederacy's last port, then pushed on. Johnston, newly reappointed to a command, had the mission of stopping Sherman's forces, but could not. At Richmond and Petersburg toward the end of March, Grant renewed his efforts along a thirty-eight-mile front to get at Lee's right (west) flank. By now Sheridan's cavalry and the VI Corps had returned from the Shenandoah Valley, and the total force immediately under Grant numbered 101,000 infantry, 14,700 cavalry, and 9,000 artillery. Lee had 46,000 infantry, 6,000 cavalry, and 5,000 artillery.

On March 29 Grant began his move to the left. Sheridan and the cavalry pushed out ahead by way of Dinwiddie Court House in order to strike at Burke's Station, the intersection of the Southside and Danville Railroads, while Grant's main body moved to envelop Lee's right. But Lee, alerted to the threat, moved west. General A.P. Hill, who never stood on the defense if there was a chance to attack, took his corps out of its trenches and assaulted the Union left in the swampy forests around White Oak Road. He pushed General Warren's V Corps back at first, but Warren counterattacked and by March 31 had driven Hill back to his trenches. Next day Sheridan advanced to Five Forks, a road junction southwest of Petersburg, and there encountered a strong Confederate force under General Pickett—cavalry plus two infantry divisions—which Lee had dispatched to forestall Sheridan. Pickett attacked and drove Sheridan back to Dinwiddie Court House, but there Sheridan dug in and halted him. Pickett then entrenched at Five Forks instead of pulling back to make contact with Hill, whose failure to destroy Warren had left a gap between him and Pickett, with Warren's corps in between. Sheridan, still formally the commander of the Army of the Shenandoah, had authority from Grant to take control of any nearby infantry corps of the Army of the Potomac. He wanted Warren to fall upon Pickett's exposed rear and destroy him, but Warren moved too slowly, and Pickett consolidated his position. Next day Sheridan attacked again but failed to destroy Pickett because Warren had moved his corps too slowly and put most of it in the wrong place. Sheridan, another devotee of the offensive principle who would not tolerate failure to engage the enemy, summarily relieved Warren of command.

Grant renewed his attack against Lee's right on April 2. The assault broke the Confederate line and forced it back northward. The Federals took the line of the Southside Railroad, and the Confederates withdrew toward Petersburg. Lee then pulled Longstreet's corps away from the shambles of Richmond to hold the line, and in this day's action Hill was killed. With his forces stretched thin, Lee had to abandon Richmond and the Petersburg fortifications. He struck out and raced west toward the Danville Railroad, hoping to get to Lynchburg or Danville, break loose, and eventually join forces with Johnston. But Grant had him in the open at last. He pursued relentlessly and speedily, with troops behind (east of) Lee and south of him on his left flank, while Sheridan dashed ahead with the cavalry to head Lee off. A running fight ensued from April 2 through 6. Ewell's corps was surrounded and captured at Sayler's Creek. Lee's rations ran out; his men began deserting and straggling. Finally, Sheridan galloped his men to Appomattox Court House, squarely athwart Lee's line of retreat.

Lee resolved that he could accomplish nothing more by fighting. He met Grant at the McLean House in Appomattox on April 9, 1865. The handsome, well-tailored Lee, the very epitome of Southern chivalry, asked Grant for terms. Reserving all political questions for his own decision, Lincoln had authorized Grant to treat only on purely military matters. Grant, though less impressive in his bearing than Lee, was equally chivalrous. He accepted Lee's surrender, allowed 28,356 paroled Confederates to keep their horses and mules, furnished rations to the Army of Northern Virginia, and forbade the soldiers of the Army of the Potomac to cheer or fire salutes in celebration of victory over their old antagonists. Johnston surrendered to Sherman on April 26, twelve days after the assassination of the President. The last major trans-Mississippi force gave up the struggle on May 26, and the grim fighting was over.[1]

---

1 Matloff 1969, 275-277.

CORRESPONDENCE: 1864–1865

Telegram to General Sullivan, War Department, Washington, January 1, 1864, 3:30 P.M.[1]

General Sullivan, Harper's Ferry:

Have you anything new from Winchester, Martinsburg or thereabouts?

A. Lincoln.

Telegram to General Butler, Executive Mansion, Washington, January 2, 1864.[2]

Major General Butler:

Sir—The Secretary of War and myself have concluded to discharge of the prisoners at Point Lookout the following classes: First, those who will take the oath prescribed in the proclamation of December 8, and issued by the consent of General Marston, will enlist in our service. Second, those who will take the oath and be discharged and whose homes lie safely within our military lines.

I send by Mr. Hay this letter and a blank-book and some other blanks, the way of using which I propose for him to explain verbally better than I can in writing.

---

1 On December 31, 1863, Sullivan had reported to General Benjamin F. Kelley that General Jubal Early would attack within twenty four hours. His reply to Lincoln's telegram was received at 5:30 P.M. on January 1, 1864: "I have ordered a force to Winchester strong enough to develop anything that may be there. I believe the reports from Martinsburg this morning were premature. I am now leaving for Martinsburg to see for myself." (Lincoln v.7, 1953, 103)

2 Point Lookout, Maryland, with over 52,000 total prisoners, was the largest Union prison, and probably the largest on either side, exceeding the 45,613 held at Andersonville. Researchers have suggested that over 4,000 Confederates may have died at the Point Lookout camp. (Chesson 1996, 474) "Blank-books" were the mechanism for formally recording oaths of allegiance. (Randall and Current 2000, 25)

Yours, very truly,

A. Lincoln.

Telegram to General Meade, Executive Mansion, Washington, January 5, 1864.[1]

Major General Meade:

If not inconsistent with the service, please allow General William Harrow as long a leave of absence as the rules permit with the understanding that I may lengthen it if I see fit. He is an acquaintance and friend of mine, and his family matters very urgently require his presence.

A. Lincoln.

To General Q. A. Gillmore, Executive Mansion, Washington, January 13, 1864.[2]

Major General Gillmore:

I understand an effort is being made by some worthy gentlemen to reconstruct a legal State government in Florida. Florida is in your Department, and it is not unlikely you may be there in person. I have given Mr. Hay a commission of major, and sent him to you, with some blank-books and other blanks, to aid in the reconstruction. He will explain as to the manner of using the blanks, and also my general views on the subject. It is desirable for all to co-operate, but if irreconcilable differences of opinion shall arise, you are master. I wish the thing done in the most speedy way, so that when done it be within the range of the late proclamation on the subject. The detail labor will, of course, have to be done by others; but I will be greatly obliged if you will give it such general supervision as you can find consistent with your more strictly military duties.

A. Lincoln.

To General P. Steele, Executive Mansion, Washington, January 20, 1864.[3]

Major General Steele:

---

1 General William Harrow rode the Eighth Judicial Circuit in Illinois with Lincoln. He stumped Indiana during Lincoln's campaign for the presidency, and was his close friend for many years. (U.S. Writers' Program 1941, 403)

2 Major General Quincy Gillmore replied from Hilton Head, South Carolina, on January 21, 1864: "I have received your letter of the 13th inst. by Major Hay, & the matter therein referred to will receive my hearty support. There will not be an hour's delay after the major is ready. I understand from him that his blanks have not arrived here yet.....What I propose to do for Florida will render it necessary for me to be there in person to inaugurate the work. I have every confidence in the success of the enterprise." (Lincoln v.7, 1953, 126)

3 In Arkansas, where a decided Union feeling had existed from the outbreak of the rebellion, the appearance of the proclamation was the signal for a movement to bring the State back into the Union. On the 20th of January, a delegation of citizens from Arkansas had an interview with the President, in which they urged "the adoption of certain measures for the re-establishment of a legal state government, and especially the ordering of an election for governor. In consequence of this application, and in substantial compliance with their request, the President, while leaving certain dates unspecified, wrote to General Steele, who commanded in that Department, and ordered the election. (Raymond 1865, 490-491)

Sundry citizens of the State of Arkansas petition me that an election may be held in that State, at which to elect a Governor; that it be assumed at that election, and thenceforward, that the constitution and laws of the State, as before the rebellion, are in full force, except that the constitution is so modified as to declare that there shall be neither slavery nor involuntary servitude, except in the punishment of crimes whereof the party shall have been duly convicted; that the General Assembly may make such provisions for the freed people as shall recognize and declare their permanent freedom, and provide for their education, and which may yet be construed as a temporary arrangement suitable to their condition as a laboring, landless, and homeless class; that said election shall be held on the 28th of March, 1864, at all the usual places of the State, or all such as voters may attend for that purpose, that the voters attending at eight o'clock in the morning of said day may choose judges and clerks of election for such purpose; that all persons qualified by said constitution and laws, and taking the oath presented in the President's proclamation of December 8, 1863, either before or at the election, and none others, may be voters; that each set of judges and clerks may make returns directly to you on or before the —th day of — next; that in all other respects said election may be conducted according to said constitution and laws: that on receipt of said returns, when five thousand four hundred and six votes shall have been cast, you can receive said votes, and ascertain all who shall thereby appear to have been elected; that on the —th day of — next, all persons so appearing to have been elected, who shall appear before you at Little Rock, and take the oath, to be by you severally administered, to support the Constitution of the United States and said modified Constitution of the State of Arkansas, may be declared by you qualified and empowered to enter immediately upon the duties of the offices to which they shall have been respectively elected.

You will please order an election to take place on the 28th of March, 1864, and returns to be made in fifteen days thereafter.

A. Lincoln.

Telegram to General Foster, War Department, Washington, January 27, 1864.[1]

Major General Foster, Knoxville, Tenn.:

---

1 At the beginning of January, 1864, some spicy but courteous correspondence occurred between Generals Foster and Longstreet, concerning the circulation of handbills among the soldiers of the latter, containing a copy of President Lincoln's Amnesty Proclamation. It was having a powerful effect, and Longstreet found the number of desertions from his army rapidly increasing. Whereupon he wrote to Foster, saying he supposed the immediate object of such a circulation was to induce desertions and win his men to the taking of an oath of allegiance to the National Government. He suggested that it would be more proper to make any communications to his soldiers on the subject of peace and reconciliation through the commanding general, rather than by handbills. Foster replied that he was right in supposing that the object of the handbills was to induce men in rebellion against their government to lay down their arms and become good citizens, and he sent twenty copies of the Amnesty Proclamation to Longstreet, so that he might himself, in accordance with his own suggestion, show his desire for peace, by circulating them among his officers and men. (Lossing 1877, 282)

Is a supposed correspondence between General Longstreet and yourself about the amnesty proclamation, which is now in the newspapers, genuine?
A. Lincoln.

To General H. W. Halleck, Executive Mansion, Washington, January 28, 1864. [1]

Major General Halleck:
Some citizens of Missouri, vicinity of Kansas City, are apprehensive that there is special danger of renewed troubles in that neighborhood, and thence on the route toward New Mexico. I am not impressed that the danger is very great or imminent, but I will thank you to give Generals Rosecrans and Curtis, respectively, such orders as may turn their attention thereto and prevent as far as possible the apprehended disturbance.
Yours truly,
A. Lincoln.

Telegram to General Sickles, Executive Mansion, Washington, January 29, 1864.[2]

Major General Sickles, New York:
Could you, without it being inconvenient or disagreeable to yourself, immediately take a trip to Arkansas for me?
A. Lincoln.

---

1 General Samuel R. Curtis had been assigned to command the Department of Kansas on January 1, 1864, and General William S. Rosecrans had been assigned to command the Department of the Missouri on January 22. On January 29, Halleck sent the following despatch to each: "Some citizens of Missouri having represented to the President that there is special danger of renewed troubles in the neighborhood of Kansas City and on the route toward New Mexico, he directs that your attention be called to the matter, so that, if necessary, measures may be taken to prevent the apprehended disturbance." (Lincoln v.7, 1953, 158)

2 General Sickles wrote Lincoln on January 27, 1864, that he could walk without crutches by use of an artificial leg and was anxious for duty. On January 29 he replied to Lincoln's telegram, "Your telegram received this afternoon. I am ready to go at once. Shall I wait here for orders or proceed to Washington?" (Ibid, 160) Follow-up orders defined Sickles' assignment: "I wish you to make a tour for me (principally for observation and information) by way of Cairo and New-Orleans, and returning by the Gulf and Ocean. All Military and Naval officers are to facilitate you with suitable transportation, and by conferring with you, and imparting, so far as they can, the information herein indicated, but you are not to command any of them. You will call at Memphis, Helena, Vicksburg, New-Orleans, Pensacola, Key-West, Charleston-Harbor, and such intermediate points as you may think important. Please ascertain at each place what is being done, if anything, for reconstruction...how the Amnesty proclamation works, if at all...what practical hitches, if any, there are about it... whether deserters come in from the enemy, what number has come in at each point since the Amnesty, and whether the ratio of their arrival is any greater since than before the Amnesty...what deserters report generally, and particularly, whether, and to what extent, the Amnesty is known within the rebel lines. Also learn what you can as to the colored people...how they get along as soldiers, as laborers in our service, on leased plantations, and as hired laborers with their old masters, if there be such cases. Also, learn what you can about the colored people within the rebel lines. Also get any other information you may consider interesting, and, from time to time, send me what you may deem important to be known here at once, and be ready to make a general report on your return." (Ibid, 185)

Telegram to General Sedgwick, Executive Mansion, Washington, February 11, 1864.[1]

Major General Sedgwick, Army of Potomac:
Unless there be some strong reason to the contrary, please send General Kilpatrick to us here, for two or three days.
A. Lincoln.

Telegram to General Steele, Executive Mansion, Washington, February 17, 1864.[2]

Major General Steele, Little Rock, Arkansas:
The day fixed by the convention for the election is probably the best, but you on the ground, and in consultation with gentlemen there, are to decide. I should have fixed no day for an election, presented no plan for reconstruction, had I known the convention was doing the same things. It is probably best that you merely assist the convention on their own plan, as to election day and all other matters I have already written and telegraphed this half a dozen times.
A. Lincoln.

Telegram to General Rosecrans, War Department, Washington, February 22, 1864.[3]

Major General Rosecrans, Saint Louis, Mo.:

---

1 This appears to be associated with Lincoln's endorsement of the Kilpatrick-Dahlgren Raid which was designed primarily to release the Federal prisoners in Richmond. On February 28, 1864, General Judson Kilpatrick and Colonel Ulric Dahlgren at the head of four thousand picked troopers left Stevensburg and made direct for Richmond. The raid—though it penetrated to within five miles of Richmond— failed. By a series of accidents—chief of which was the treachery of Dahlgren's guide—the two forces, after separating for the attack, lost each other and were never able to unite. Tuesday, March 1st, found both Kilpatrick and Dahlgren—widely separated—in retreat, and riding hard for the Peninsula. But that night, in the storm that raged, Dahlgren and his advance (about one hundred men) with whom he rode became lost from the remainder of his little command . Dahlgren was subsequently killed by Confederate forces (Beymer 2003, 73-74)

2 Lincoln's impatience with Steele is clearly reflected in this telegram. And, indeed, he had instructed Steele on numerous occasions to "assist" the state authorities. One example is a January 30, 1864 noted: "Seeing still further accounts of the action of the convention in Arkansas, induces me to write you yet again. They seem to be doing so well, that possibly the best you can do would be to help them on their own plan...but of this, you must confer with them, and be the judge. Of all things, avoid if possible, a dividing into cliques among the friends of the common object. Be firm and resolute against such as you can perceive would make confusion and division." (Lincoln v.7, 1953, 161)

3 Since the outbreak of the war, there had existed in the North a minority of sympathizers with the Rebellion who organized a secret society, with lodges, ritual, and ramifications after the pattern of the revolutionists in Continental Europe. They called themselves the Knights of the Golden Circle, and they had several aliases (the Order of American Knights, the Order of the Star, and the Sons of Liberty, etc.) to use in case of discovery. They intended to undermine the Union sentiment in the Northern States, by enrolling as many members as possible, who pledged themselves, not merely not to support the Union cause by enlisting in it, but actively to aid the rebels by giving them information and other help. Where they safely could, they assailed the property and lives of loyal citizens. They collected arms and ammunition, they formed military bodies and drilled, and they prepared for a vast exhibition of their powers when the right hour should strike. Till then, they worked underground. The

Colonel Sanderson will be ordered to you today, a mere omission that it was not done before. The other questions in your dispatch I am not yet prepared to answer.

A. Lincoln.

To General F. Steele, War Department, Washington, February 25, 1864.[1]

Major General Steele, Little Rock, Arkansas:

General Sickles is not going to Arkansas. He probably will make a tour down the Mississippi and home by the gulf and ocean, but he will not meddle in your affairs.

At one time I did intend to have him call on you and explain more fully than I could do by letter or telegraph, so as to avoid a difficulty coming of my having made a plan here, while the convention made one there, for reorganizing Arkansas; but even his doing that has been given up for more than two weeks. Please show this to Governor Murphy to save me telegraphing him.

A. Lincoln.

Telegram to General Thomas, War Department, Washington, February 28, 1864.[2]

General L. Thomas, Louisville, Kentucky:

Northern High Priest of the Knights was Clement L. Vallandigham; the Southern head was Sterling Price, a general in the Confederate Army. Vallandigham claimed that at its height the order numbered half a million, and though he probably exaggerated, the organization was large enough to be formidable. It flourished in Ohio, Indiana, Illinois, Kentucky, and Missouri, where its members, by voting in concert, might turn the scale in a close election. Their secrecy added tenfold to their presumed strength. At this point, in the spring of 1864, General Rosecrans, commanding in Missouri, having unearthed the secrets of the Knights, imparted them to Governor Yates, of Illinois, who joined him in urging the President to allow Colonel Sanderson, of Rosecrans' staff, to go to Washington with the evidence. With some reluctance, Lincoln sent Sanderson; but he suspected also that Rosecrans wished by this ruse to embroil the President with Secretary Stanton; and therefore he also dispatched Major John Hay, a personal secretary, to St. Louis to ascertain the real impact of the revelations. (Thayer 1915, 168)

1 On February 24, Provisional Governor Isaac Murphy telegraphed Lincoln, "I hope you will not send General Sickles here, and if an order has been made to that effect that it may be revoked. His coming here would only be an annoyance and will do no good. Everything is working well. General Steele is doing everything that can be done."A second telegram of the same date signed by Murphy and Freeman Warner, chairman of the Executive Committee of Arkansas, reiterated the request. (Lincoln v.7, 1953, 205)

2 In late 1863, Chase tried to inaugurate a new freedmen's policy in the Mississippi Valley and enlarge Treasury Department jurisdiction over freedmen's affairs. Criticizing the assignment of freedmen to particular plantations, he proposed a higher wage scale for blacks and a policy of leasing land to freedmen either in groups or as individuals. He also hoped to be able to induce landlords to sell land in small parcels to former slaves. Motivated by a desire to improve conditions for blacks and perhaps also to create an issue on which he might challenge Lincoln for the Republican nomination in 1864, Chase promised the freedmen paternal guidance, humanitarian care, and a limited program of land reform. Chase attempted to effect these important changes by administrative actions under existing legislation, but Lincoln refused to go along with them. Probably because he regarded the immediate question of post-emancipation policy as inextricably linked to military matters, he ordered General Lorenzo Thomas in February 1864, after a series of conflicts between

I see your dispatch of yesterday to the Secretary of War.

I wish you would go to the Mississippi River at once, and take hold of and be master in the contraband and leasing business. You understand it better than any other man does. Mr. Miller's system doubtless is well intended, but from what I hear I fear that, if persisted in, it would fall dead within its own entangling details. Go there and be the judge. A Mr. Lewis will probably follow you with something from me on this subject, but do not wait for him. Nor is this to induce you to violate or neglect any military order from the General-in-Chief or Secretary of War.

A. Lincoln.

To General Thomas, Executive Mansion Washington, March 1, 1864.[1]

General L. Thomas:

This introduces Mr. Lewis, mentioned in my dispatch sent you at Louisville some days ago. I have but little personal acquaintance with him; but he has the confidence of several members of Congress here who seem to know him well. He hopes to be useful, without charge to the government, in facilitating the introduction of the free-labor system on the Mississippi plantations. He is acquainted with, and has access to, many of the planters who wish to adopt the system. He will show you two letters of mine on this subject, one somewhat General, and the other relating to named persons; they are not different in principle. He will also show you some suggestions coming from some of the planters themselves. I desire that all I promise in these letters, so far as practicable, may be in good faith carried out, and that suggestions from the planters may be heard and adopted, so far as they may not contravene the principles stated, nor justice, nor fairness, to laborers. I do not herein intend to overrule your own mature judgment on any point.

Yours truly,
A. Lincoln.

Telegram to General Steele, War Department, Washington, March 3, 1864.[2]

Major General Steele, Little Rock, Ark.:

Treasury agents and military officers had occurred, to take control of "the contraband and leasing business." Lincoln thought the proposed Treasury system was well intentioned, but he believed it would not work because of its "entangling details." Thereafter, Thomas tightened the existing labor regulations in the Mississippi Valley and extended them to plantations that Treasury officials had tried to operate. This development did not end the political and administrative conflict between the Treasury Department and the army over freedmen's policy, but it transferred the struggle to Congress where freedmen's bureau bills were being formulated. For the time being, however, Lincoln had decided the issue in favor of military control. (Belz 2000, 47)

1 Ibid.
2 The text of Steele's address to the people of Arkansas concerning the vote on the new state constitution was contained in a telegram of March 2. Also included in that same message was Steele's recommendation that "Willard M Randolph late Attorney Genl of the Confederate states for the Eastern district of Ark be pardoned, he only accepted office to

Yours including address to people of Arkansas is received. I approve the address and thank you for it. Yours in relation to William M. Randolph also received. Let him take the oath of December 8, and go to work for the new constitution, and on your notifying me of it, I will immediately issue the special pardon for him.

A. Lincoln.

Telegram to General Butler, Executive Mansion, Washington, March 4, 1864.[1]

Major General Butler, Fort Monroe, Va.:

Admiral Dahlgren is here, and of course is very anxious about his son. Please send me at once all you know or can learn of his fate.

A. Lincoln.

Address to General Grant, March 9, 1864. [2]

General Grant:

The expression of the nation's approbation of what you have already done, and its reliance on you for what remains to do in the existing great struggle, is now presented with this commission constituting you Lieutenant General of the Army of the United States.

With this high honor, devolves on you an additional responsibility. As the country herein trusts you, so, under God, it will sustain you. I scarcely need add, that with what I here speak for the country, goes my own hearty personal concurrence.

A. Lincoln.

Order Assigning U. S. Grant Command of the Armies of the United States, Executive Mansion, Washington, March 10, 1864.[3]

Under the authority of an act of Congress to revive the grade of Lieutenant General in the United States Army, approved February 29, 1864, Lieutenant

---

keep out the rebel army. He is a man of talent...will be true to the U.S. He will assist in the election." (Lincoln v.7, 1953, 222)

1 As indicated in footnote 307, Union Colonel Ulric Dahlgren was killed in a failed attempt to release the Federal prisoners in Richmond. Documents found on Dahlgren's body detailed plans to burn Richmond, Virginia, and assassinate Confederate President Jefferson Davis and his cabinet. These plans were part of a speech intended for Dahlgren's troops and were used as anti-Union propaganda by the Confederate leadership. (Wright 2001, 81)

2 General Grant replied: Mr. President—I accept this commission, with gratitude for the high honor conferred.

With the aid of the noble armies that have fought on so many fields for our common country, it will be my earnest endeavor not to disappoint your expectations. I feel the full weight of the responsibilities now devolving on me, and I know that if they are met, it will be due to those armies; and above all, to the favor of that Providence which leads both nations and men. (Raymond 1865, 476)

3 Grant left Washington shortly after receiving the appointment of Lieutenant-General, and was at Nashville at the time that Lincoln's order was issued promoting him to the supreme command. He proceeded at once to reorganize the army and, with no disparagement to

General Ulysses S. Grant, United States Army, is assigned to the command of the Armies of the United States.

A. Lincoln.

Telegram to General U. S. Grant [Private] Executive Mansion, Washington, March 15, 1864.[1]

Lieutenant-General Grant, Nashville, Tenn.:

General McPherson having been assigned to the command of a department, could not General Frank Blair, without difficulty or detriment to the service, be assigned to command the Corps he commanded a while last autumn?

A. Lincoln.

Telegram to General Butler, Executive Mansion, Washington, March 22, 1864.[2]

Major General Butler, Fort Monroe, Va.:

Hon. W. R. Morrison says he has requested you by letter to effect a special exchange of Lieut. Col. A. F. Rogers, of Eightieth Illinois Volunteers, now in Libby Prison, and I shall be glad if you can effect it.

A. Lincoln.

Correspondence with General C. Schurz [Private] Washington, March 13, 1864.[3]

Major General Schurz:

My Dear Sir—Yours of February 29 reached me only four days ago; but the delay was of little consequence, because I found, on feeling around, I could not invite you here without a difficulty which at least would be unpleasant, and perhaps would be detrimental to the public service. Allow me to suggest that if you wish to remain in the military service, it is very dangerous for you to get temporarily out of it; because, with a Major General once out, it is next to impossible for even the President to get him in again. With my appreciation of your ability and correct principle, of course I would be very glad to have your service for the

---

certain commanders who were removed or transferred upon his suggestion, he judiciously replaced them with those he considered better suited for independent command. (Coppée 1866, 277-279)

1 Although normally critical of most "political" generals, both Grant and Sherman, rated Blair—brother of the Postmaster-general—one of the more proficient military leaders of the war. He had been instrumental in saving Missouri for the Union and was later to win a further military reputation in the Western campaigns. (Chase 1954, 298)

2 General Butler replied on the same day: "I had supposed that I had effected the exchange of Lieut Col [Andrew F.] Rogers of the 80th. Illinois, but when the prisoner came down, it was the wrong Col Rogers. However I will try again."(Lincoln v.7, 1953, 261)

3 At this juncture, Schurz had been suffering a litany of medical issues. At Sperryville, Virginia, he was sick for severaldays in August 1862 but participated in the Second Bull Run campaign. He had jaundice in March 1863 and returned first to Washington and then to Philadelphia to recuperate. He was at Chancellorsville and Gettysburg. Early in September he had "camp fever" and went on sick leave. During the first of 1864 he was sick with fever while camped near Lookout Mountain. Toward the end of February 1864, Schurz had diarrhea and went to New York on leave. (Welsh 1996, 292)

country in the approaching political canvass; but I fear we cannot properly have it without separating you from the military.

Yours truly,

A. Lincoln.

To General G. G. Meade, Executive Mansion, Washington, March 29, 1864.[1]

Major General Meade:

My Dear Sir—Your letter to Colonel Townsend, inclosing a slip from the "Herald," and asking a court of inquiry, has been laid before me by the Secretary of War, with the request that I would consider it. It is quite natural that you should feel some sensibility on the subject; yet I am not impressed, nor do I think the country is impressed, with the belief that your honor demands, or the public interest demands, such an inquiry. The country knows that at all events you have done good service; and I believe it agrees with me that it is much better for you to be engaged in trying to do more, than to be diverted, as you necessarily would be, by a court of inquiry.

Yours truly,

A. Lincoln.

Telegram to General U. S. Grant, Executive Mansion, Washington, March 29, 1864.[2]

Lieutenant-General Grant, Army of the Potomac:

Captain Kinney, of whom I spoke to you as desiring to go on your staff, is now in your camp, in company with Mrs. Senator Dixon. Mrs. Grant and I, and some others, agreed last night that I should, by this dispatch, kindly call your attention to Captain Kinney.

A. Lincoln.

---

1 On March 15, 1864, General Meade wrote Assistant Adjutant General Edward D. Townsend: "I inclose herewith a slip from the New York Herald, containing a communication signed 'Historicus,' purporting to give an account of the battle of Gettysburg. . . . For the past fortnight the public press . . . has been teeming with articles, all having for their object assaults upon my reputation as an officer, and tending to throw discredit upon my operations at Gettysburg. . . . "I have not noticed any of these attacks, and should not now . . . but that the character of the communication . . . bears such manifest proofs that it was written either by someone present at the battle, or dictated . . . and having access . . . to confidential papers that were never issued to the army, much less made public. "I cannot resist the belief that this letter was either written or dictated by Maj. Gen. D. E. Sickles. . . . "I have to ask, therefore, that the Department will take steps to ascertain whether . . . Sickles has authorized or indorses this communication, and, in the event of his replying in the affirmative, I have to request of the President . . . a court of inquiry. . . ." The three-column clipping from the *New York Herald* of March 12, 1864, criticized errors in Meade's report of the Gettysburg operations and particularly referred to his failure to heed advice of his corps commanders. (Lincoln v.7, 1953, 273-274)

2 On the same day, Grant telegraphed Lincoln. "Your dispatch suggesting Capt. Kennedy for a staff appointment just recd. I would be glad to accommodate Capt. Kennedy but in the selection of my staff I do not want any one whom I do not personally know to be qualified for the position assigned them." (Grant 1982, 221)

Telegram to General Butler, Executive Mansion, Washington, April 12, 1864.[1]

Major General Butler, Fort Monroe, Va.:

I am pressed to get from Libby, by special exchange, Jacob C. Hagenbuek, first lieutenant, Company H, Sixty-seventh Pennsylvania Volunteers. Please do it if you can without detriment or embarrassment.

A. Lincoln.

Telegram to General Meade, Executive Mansion, Washington, April 17, 1864.[2]

Major General Meade, Army of the Potomac:

Private William Collins of Company B, of the Sixty-ninth New York Volunteers, has been convicted of desertion, and execution suspended as in numerous other cases. Now Captain O'Neill, commanding the regiment, and nearly all its other regimental and company officers, petition for his full pardon and restoration to his company. Is there any good objection?

A. Lincoln.

Telegram to General Dix, Executive Mansion, Washington, April 21, 1864.[3]

Major General Dix, New York:

Yesterday I was induced to telegraph the officer in military command at Fort Warren, Boston Harbor, Massachusetts, suspending the execution of Charles Carpenter, to be executed tomorrow for desertion. Just now, on reaching your order in the case, I telegraphed the same officer withdrawing the suspension, and leave the case entirely with you. The man's friends are pressing me, but I refer them to you, intending to take no further action myself.

A. Lincoln.

---

1 Butler replied on the same day that he would "endeavor to effect the proposed exchange." The roster of the Sixty-seventh Pennsylvania Volunteers lists Jacob C. Hagenbuch as mustered out at the expiration of his term on March 24, 1865. (Lincoln v.7, 1953, 297)

2 No reply or further reference has been located. Captain Bernard S. O'Neill of the Sixty-ninth New York Volunteers was killed at Petersburg, Virginia, June 16, 1864. (Lincoln v.7, 1953, 301)

3 The *New York* Tribune (April 26, 1864) reported the execution of Carpenter and his accomplice as follows: "Privates Charles Carpenter and Matthew Riley . . . two unassigned recruits of the Vermont volunteers, suffered the extreme penalty of military law on Friday last [April 22], at Fort Warren, Boston Harbor, for the crime of desertion. They deserted the service in December, 1863. Carpenter after deserting, disguised himself, and commenced business as a bounty or substitute broker.... They were convicted and sentenced to be shot... before a general court martial that met on January 30...which sentence was approved by Gen. Dix. Maj. Cabot was charged with the execution of this order....." (Ibid, 306)

Telegram to General Butler, Executive Mansion, Washington, April 23, 1864.[1]

Major General Butler, Fort Monroe, Va.:

Senator Ten Eyck is very anxious to have a special exchange of Capt. Frank J. McLean, of Ninth Tennessee Cavalry now, or lately, at Johnson's Island, for Capt. T. Ten Eyck, Eighteenth U. S. Infantry, and now at Richmond. I would like to have it done. Can it be?

A. Lincoln.

Telegram to General Meade, War Department, Washington City, April 25, 1864.[2]

Major General Meade, Army of Potomac:

A Mr. Corby brought you a note from me at the foot of a petition I believe, in the case of Dawson, to be executed today. The record has been examined here, and it shows too strong a case for a pardon or commutation, unless there is something in the poor man's favor outside of the record, which you on the ground may know, but I do not. My note to you only means that if you know of any such thing rendering a suspension of the execution proper, on your own judgment, you are at liberty to suspend it. Otherwise I do not interfere.

A. Lincoln.

Telegram to General Thomas, Executive Mansion, Washington, April 26, 1864.[3]

Major General Thomas, Chattanooga, Tenn.:

Suspend execution of death sentence of young Perry, of Wisconsin, condemned for sleeping on his post, till further orders, and forward record for examination.

A. Lincoln.

To General U. S. Grant, Executive Mansion, Washington, April 30, 1864.[4]

---

1 The imprisoned Union captain was the son of New Jersey senator John C, Ten Eyck, and neither the senator nor the president balked at privately arranging the younger Ten Eyck's freedom even as they publicly professed support for the official administration policy of prohibiting such exchanges. (Sanders 2005, 315)

2 Chaplain William Corby, Eighty-eighth New York Volunteers, had telegraphed Lincoln on April 24: "General Meade has not the official proceedings relative to the Court Martial of L Dawson who is under sentence of death to take place 25th instant therefore cannot act Please say what will be done." General Meade replied to Lincoln's telegram the same day: "I duly received your note by Mr Corby & after examining the case of Dawson could see nothing to justify my recommending a mitigation. The only point is the fact that he has been awaiting sentence for a long period & may have deluded himself into the belief that he would escape. Unless you intervene he will be executed." (Lincoln v.7, 1953, 315)

3 No reply from Thomas has been found, and "Perry from Wisconsin" has not been satisfactorily identified. The court-martial files contain an incomplete record of Private Charles O. Perry, Company B, Third Maine Volunteers, sentenced to death for sleeping on post, but it is uncertain that this is the same soldier. (Ibid, 317)

4 As we have observed, by the time of the American Civil War, the telegraph enabled the US president to keep in close touch with his senior commanders. And, while some have criticized Lincoln for abusing this new capability, he nonetheless understood completely the

Lieutenant-General Grant:

Not expecting to see you before the spring campaign opens, I wish to express in this way my entire satisfaction with what you have done up to this time, so far as I understand it.

The particulars of your plans I neither know nor seek to know. You are vigilant and self-reliant; and, pleased with this, I wish not to obtrude any restraints or constraints upon you. While I am very anxious that any great disaster or capture of our men in great number shall be avoided, I know that these points are less likely to escape your attention than they would be mine. If there be anything wanting which is within my power to give, do not fail to let me know it.

And now, with a brave army and a just cause, may God sustain you.

Yours very truly,

A. Lincoln.

Telegram to General W. T. Sherman, Washington, May 4, 1864.[1]

Major General Sherman, Chattanooga, Tenn.:

I have an imploring appeal in behalf of the citizens who say your Order No.8 will compel them to go north of Nashville. This is in no sense an order, nor is it even a request that you will do anything which in the least shall be a drawback upon your military operations, but anything you can do consistently with those operations for those suffering people I shall be glad of.

A. Lincoln.

Telegram to General Lew Wallace, War Department, Washington, May 10, 1864.[2]

Major General Wallace, Baltimore:

---

different roles of politicians and generals, as suggested by this letter to Grant. (Horner 2000, 142)

1 Sherman's General Orders No. 8, April 19, 1864, read in part: "Provisions will no longer be issued to citizens at military posts south of Nashville. When citizens cannot procure provisions in the country there is no alternative but they must remove to the rear. . . . It is idle for us to be pushing forward subsistence stores if they are lavished and expended on any persons except they belong to the army proper." On May 5, 1864, Sherman replied to Lincoln's telegram: "We have worked hard with the best talent of the country & it is demonstrated that the railroad cannot supply the army & the people too. One or the other must quit & the army don't intend to unless Joe Johnston makes us. The issues to citizens have been enormous & the same weight of corn or oats would have saved thousands of the mules whose carcasses now corduroy the roads and which we need so much. We have paid back to East Tenn. ten for one of provisions taken in war. I will not change my order and I beg of you to be satisfied that the clamor is partly a humbug & for effect, & to test it I advise you to tell the bearers of the appeal to hurry to Kentucky & make up a caravan of cattle & wagons & to come over by Cumberland Gap and Somerset to relieve their suffering friends on foot as they used to do before a railroad was built. Tell them they have no time to lose. We can relieve all actual suffering by each company or regiment giving of their savings. Every man who is willing to fight and work gets all rations & all who won't fight or work should go away and we offer them free transportation" (Lincoln v.7, 1953, 330-331)

2 The case of Dr. Francis L. Hawks, rector of Christ Church in Baltimore, was reported by Wallace the following day: "Your telegram touching 'the trouble with Dr. Hawks,' and requesting me to ask Bishop Whittingham to give you his view . . . reached me so late . . . that

Please tell me what is the trouble with Dr. Hawks. Also please ask Bishop Whittington to give me his view of the case.

A. Lincoln.

Telegram to General W. S. Rosecrans, Executive Mansion, Washington, May 11, 1864.[1]

Major General Rosecrans, St. Louis, Missouri:

Complaints are coming to me of disturbances in Canoll, Platte, and Buchanan counties. Please ascertain the truth, correct what is found wrong, and telegraph me.

A. Lincoln.

Telegram to General B. P. Butler [Cipher] Washington, May 18, 1864.[2]

Major General Butler, Bermuda Hundred, Va.:

Until receiving your dispatch of yesterday, the idea of commissions in the volunteers expiring at the end of three years had not occurred to me. I think no trouble will come of it; and, at all events, I shall take care of it so far as in me lies. As to the Major Generalships in the regular army, I think I shall not dispose of another, at least until the combined operations now in progress, under direction

---

I could do nothing . . . until this morning. Knowing that Bp. W. knew nothing of the affair, I carried yr. request to him in person. After a full expose, he wrote you a letter in reply, which I have the honor to forward. . . .Dr. H. came to Baltimore . . . from New York, imported by the disloyalists. . . . Today his congregation . . . are sympathisers of the highest social caste. Publicly the Revd gentleman never says anything exceptionable; hence, his loyal people defend him, and even carry their entreaties to yr. Excellency. They honestly believe him all right, while I feel a positive assurance that he is all wrong. . . .I waited patiently till I became satisfied and assured of his dangerous character, abilities, and operations, then directed my Provt. Marshal to notify him that he must either take the oath of allegiance . . . or leave the city within twenty four hours. Would a Union Man hesitate about the alternative to take? . . . .The Provt. Marshal found him absent in New York. He is not yet returned; probably on account of notice of the order. . . .I beg you to support my action. . . .I laid my order at his door, because, being leader among the disaffected Ministers, I hoped his example would, for the present, at least, admonish the rest." Protestant Episcopal Bishop William R. Whittingham's letter, enclosed by Wallace, reads in part: "There are very strong reasons, personal and official, why I should desire to remain totally unconnected with the case. Nevertheless, I could not, in duty, decline to hear Gen. Wallace's statement of the grounds upon which he acted, nor can I refuse to the President the expression of my conviction, upon hearing that statement, that he had sufficient reasons. . . ." (Ibid, 335-336)

1 General Alfred Pleasonton replied on May 12, 1864: "Maj Genl Rosecrans is absent. . . . Your dispatch Recd in reference to Disturbances. . . . Brig Genl Clinton B Fisk Commanding that District telegraphs as follows: St Joseph Mo, May 12, 1864 The President of the U S may be assured that there is less disturbance in Carroll Putnam & Buchanan counties in this state than at any previous time during the Rebellion. The Citizens of this this [sic] district are very generally engaging earnestly in their legitimate pursuits. I wish the President would give us the source of information he has received." (Ibid, 337)

2 On May 17 Butler had telegraphed: "On the 16th of May 1861, I was honored by your kindness with a commission as Major General United States Volunteers I have heard that such commission expires by limitation of three years. I by no means desire to quit the service till the war is done. Do you think I have time enough to entitle me to one of the vacant commissions in the army to date from May 16th 61? Otherwise, I should prefer my present one if you think me fit to hold either and I can hold on to it." (Ibid, 347)

---

of General Grant, and within which yourself and command are included, shall be terminated.

Meanwhile, on behalf of yourself, officers, and men, please accept my hearty thanks for what you and they have so far done.

A. Lincoln.

Telegram to General Meade, Executive Mansion, Washington, May 25, 1864.[1]

Major General Meade, Army of Potomac:

Mr. J. C. Swift wishes a pass from me to follow your army to pick up rags and cast-off clothing. I will give it to him if you say so, otherwise not.

A. Lincoln.

Telegram to General Meade, Executive Mansion, Washington, June 6, 1864.[2]

Major General Meade, Army of the Potomac:

Private James McCarthy, of the One-hundred and fortieth New York Volunteers, is here under sentence to the Dry Tortugas for an attempt to desert. His friends appeal to me and if his colonel and you consent, I will send him to his regiment. Please answer.

A. Lincoln.

Telegram to General L. Thomas, Executive Mansion, Washington, June 13, 1864.[3]

Major General Thomas, Louisville, Kentucky:

Complaint is made to me that in the vicinity of Henderson, our militia is seizing negroes and carrying them off without their own consent, and according to no rules whatever, except those of absolute violence. I wish you would look into this and inform me, and see that the making soldiers of negroes is done according to the rules you are acting upon, so that unnecessary provocation and irritation be avoided.

A. Lincoln.

---

1 On March 4 and March 9, 1864, John C. Swift had written Lincoln offering to pay $200 per month to the Sanitary Commission for the exclusive privilege of picking up clothing cast off by Grant's army. (Ibid, 362)

2 Fort Jefferson in the Dry Tortugas, off Florida, was one of the most isolated of American prisons and certainly one of the most unhealthy. (Fetherling 2001, 269)

3 Thomas replied on the same day: "Telegram of this date recd. I have no doubt there has been ground for complaint in the vicinity of Henderson, Ky, but I will take immediate measures to prevent a recurrence of any acts of violence on the person of officers engaged in recruiting colored troops in Ky." (Lincoln v.7, 1953, 390)

Telegram to General U. S. Grant, Washington, June 15, 1864, 7 A.M.[1]

Lieutenant-General Grant, Headquarters Army of the Potomac:

I have just received your dispatch of 1 P.M. yesterday. I begin to see it: you will succeed. God bless you all.

A. Lincoln.

Telegram to General W. S. Rosecrans, Washington, June 24, 1864.[2]

Major General Rosecrans, St. Louis, Missouri:

Complaint is made to me that General Brown does not do his best to suppress bushwhackers. Please ascertain and report to me.

A. Lincoln.

To General P. Steele, Executive Mansion, Washington, June 29, 1864[3]

Major General Steele:

I understand that Congress declines to admit to seats the persons sent as Senators and Representatives from Arkansas. These persons apprehend that, in consequence, you may not support the new State government there as you otherwise would. My wish is that you give that government and the people there the same support and protection that you would if the members had been admitted,

---

1 This in response to Grant's June 14, 1864 note to Halleck that advised, "Our forces will commence crossing the James to-day. The enemy show no signs yet of having brought troops to the south side of Richmond. I will have Petersburg secured, if possible, before they get there in much force. Our movement from Cold Harbor to the James River has been made with great celerity and so far without loss or accident." (Ibid, 393)

2 Brigadier General Egbert B. Brown was in command of the District of Central Missouri. On August 5, Rosecrans replied to Lincoln's telegram: "I have carefully examined into the administration and conduct of General E. B. Brown...and...I conclude... that General Brown is a zealous, honest, earnest officer, diligent and painstaking, but not remarkably quick of apprehension, not without some bias against all active innovations on the old order of things. But his strong sense of justice operates to check his bias and has given to his administration on the whole the character of a success for the cause of the Nation.... I have no one but General Pleasonton to take his place.... Should Your Excellency conclude to send me an able general officer, I could give General Brown the presidency of a general court-martial which we have constantly in session here. General Brown's wishes and his health would both favor this change." (Ibid, 407)

3 Congress had passed a bill to guarantee certain states which had seceded from the Union by usurpation, as Arkansas had without a statewide vote, a method of coming back into the Union. The bill had been presented to Lincoln an hour before Adjournment Sine Die of Congress. Lincoln vetoed it because he thought the Congress was unfair to Arkansas and Louisiana (Louisiana having made the same preparations to come into the Union as Arkansas). Lincoln said the way he presented the re-admittance of seceded states back to the Union in his Proclamation of 1863 wasn't the only way to accomplish coming back into the Union but the bill passed by Congress was unfair to the two states who had in good faith complied with the Proclamation. Lincoln believed the two states were not being allowed to join the Union because Congress felt it would hamper the chances of the passage of the abolishment of slavery amendment to the Constitution of the United States. (Pollan 1982, 20)

because in no event, nor in any view of the case, can this do any harm, while it will be the best you can do toward suppressing the rebellion.

Yours truly,

A. Lincoln.

Telegram to General Grant, Executive Mansion, Washington, June 29, 1864.[1]

Lieutenant-General Grant, City Point:

Dr. Worster wishes to visit you with a view of getting your permission to introduce into the army "Harmon's Sandal Sock." Shall I give him a pass for that object?

A. Lincoln.

Telegram to General U. S. Grant, Washington City, July 10, 1864, 2 P.M.[2]

Lieutenant-General Grant, City Point, Va.:

Your dispatch to General Halleck, referring to what I may think in the present emergency, is shown me. General Halleck says we have absolutely no force here fit to go to the field. He thinks that with the hundred-day men and invalids we have here we can defend Washington, and, scarcely, Baltimore. Besides these there are about eight thousand, not very reliable, under Howe, at Harper's Ferry with Hunter approaching that point very slowly, with what number I suppose you know better than I. Wallace, with some odds and ends, and part of what came up with Ricketts, was so badly beaten yesterday at Monocacy, that what is left can attempt no more than to defend Baltimore. What we shall get in from Pennsylvania and New York will scarcely be worth counting, I fear. Now, what I think is, that you should provide to retain your hold where you are, certainly, and bring the rest with you personally, and make a vigorous effort to destroy the enemy's forces in this vicinity. I think there is really a fair chance to do this, if the movement is prompt. This is what I think upon your suggestion, and is not an order.

A. Lincoln.

---

1   No reply has been discovered. Harmon's sandal-socks were of "wash leather," designed to be worn with another pair of ordinary socks. On April 13, 1864, J. Rutherford Worster had sent Lincoln a pair of the socks together with numerous testimonials and requested: "Mr. President, if you will please endorse me to Genl. Grant...with your views of the utility of the sandal, for the preservation of the feet, on long marches...and the prevention of straggling &c. I will put a pair on the Genl. as I am going out to the front this evening...." (Lincoln v.7, 1953, 416)

2   The day after writing this letter reminding Grant of Jubal Early's threat to Washington, Lincoln ventured out to Ft. Stevens near his summer residence at the Soldiers' Home where he himself came under confederate fire. (Holzer 2011, 246)

Telegram to General U. S. Grant, Washington, July 11, 1864, 8 A.M.[1]

Lieutenant-General Grant, City Point, Va.:

Yours of 10.30 P.M. yesterday received, and very satisfactory. The enemy will learn of Wright's arrival, and then the difficulty will be to unite Wright and Hunter south of the enemy before he will recross the Potomac. Some firing between Rockville and here now.

A. Lincoln.

Telegram to General U. S. Grant, Washington, July 12, 1864, 11:30 A.M.[2]

Lieutenant-General Grant, City Point, Va.:

Vague rumors have been reaching us for two or three days that Longstreet's corps is also on its way [to] this vicinity. Look out for its absence from your front.

A. Lincoln.

Telegram to General U. S. Grant, Washington, July 17, 1864, 11:25 A.M.[3]

Lieutenant-General Grant, City Point, Va.:

In your dispatch of yesterday to General Sherman, I find the following, to wit: "I shall make a desperate effort to get a position here, which will hold the enemy without the necessity of so many men."

---

1 This in response to Grant's telegram of July 10 concerning the defense of Washington: "I have sent from here a whole corps commanded by an excellent officer, besides over three thousand other troops. One Division of the Nineteenth Corps, six thousand strong is now on its way to Washington. One Steamer loaded with these troops having passed Ft. Monroe today. They will probably reach Washington tomorrow night. This force under [Horatio G.] Wright will be able to compete with the whole force with [Richard S.] Ewell. Before more troops can be sent from here [David] Hunter will be able to join Wright in rear of the Enemy, with at least ten thousand men, besides a force sufficient to hold Maryland Heights. I think on reflection it would have a bad effect for me to leave here, and with Genl [Edward O. C.] Ord at Baltimore and Hunter and Wright with the forces following the enemy up, could do no good. I have great faith that the enemy will never be able to get back with much of his force." (Grant 1984, 203)

2 To reassure Lincoln, Grant telegraphed Halleck on July 13: "Summary of evidence gathered from deserters, scouts, and cavalry reconnaissance by [David M.] Gregg on our left show that none of [Ambrose P.] Hill's or Longstreet's corps have left our front...." (Lincoln v.7, 1953, 438)

3 Grant's telegram to Sherman of July 16 reported that: "The attempted invasion of Maryland having failed to give the enemy a firm foothold North, they are now returning, with possibly 25,000 troops.... It is not improbable, therefore, that you will find in the next fortnight re-enforcements in your front to the number indicated above. I advise, therefore, that if you can get to Atlanta you set about destroying the railroads as far to the east and south of you as possible; collect all the stores of the country for your own use, and select a point that you can hold until help can be had. I shall make a desperate effort to get a position here which will hold the enemy without the necessity of so many men. If successful, I can detach from here for other enterprises, looking as much to your assistance as anything else." (Van Horne and Ruger 1875, 120)

Pressed as we are by lapse of time I am glad to hear you say this; and yet I do hope you may find a way that the effort shall not be desperate in the sense of great loss of life.

A. Lincoln, President.

Telegram to General D. Hunter, Washington July 17, 1864.[1]

Major General Hunter, Harper's Ferry, West Va.:

Yours of this morning received. You misconceive. The order you complain of was only nominally mine, and was framed by those who really made it with no thought of making you a scapegoat. It seemed to be General Grant's wish that the forces under General Wright and those under you should join and drive at the enemy under General Wright. Wright had the larger part of the force, but you had the rank. It was thought that you would prefer Crook's commanding your part to your serving in person under Wright. That is all of it. General Grant wishes you to remain in command of the department, and I do not wish to order otherwise.

A. Lincoln.

Telegram to General W. T. Sherman, Executive Mansion, Washington, July 18, 1864, 11:25 A.M.[2]

Major General Sherman, Chattahoochee River, Georgia:

I have seen your dispatches objecting to agents of Northern States opening recruiting stations near your camps. An act of Congress authorizes this, giving the appointment of agents to the States, and not to the Executive Government. It is not for the War Department, or myself, to restrain or modify the law, in its execution, further than actual necessity may require. To be candid, I was for the passage of the law, not apprehending at the time that it would produce such inconvenience to the armies in the field as you now cause me to fear. Many of the States were very anxious for it, and I hoped that, with their State bounties, and active exertions, they would get out substantial additions to our colored forces, which, unlike white recruits, help us where they come from, as well as where they go to. I still hope advantage from the law; and being a law, it must be treated as such by all of us. We here will do what we consistently can to save you from difficulties arising out of it. May I ask, therefore, that you will give your hearty co-operation.

A. Lincoln.

---

1 Hunter had telegraphed Lincoln from Harper's Ferry earlier on the same day: "I[again] most earnestly request to be relieved from the command of this department. Your order, conveyed through Genl Halleck, has entirely destroyed my usefulness. When an officer is selected as the scapegoat to cover up the blunders of others, the best interests of the country require that he should at once be relieved from command." (Lincoln v.7, 1953, 445)

2 Lincoln was concerned about Sherman's harsh handling of the recruiters sent from Northern states to enlist freed slaves into the Union army Sherman saw these agents as another civilian nuisance and put obstacles in their way every chance he had. Lincoln asked for his cooperation, and Sherman reluctantly agreed. (Marszalek 2002, 71)

Telegram to General U. S. Grant, Executive Mansion, Washington, July 20, 1864, 4:30 P.M.[1]

Lieutenant-General Grant, City Point, Va.:

Yours of yesterday, about a call for three hundred thousand, is received. I suppose you had not seen the call for five hundred thousand, made the day before, and which, I suppose, covers the case. Always glad to have your suggestions. A. Lincoln.

Telegram to General D. Hunter [Cipher] War Department, July 23, 1864.

Major General Hunter, Harper's Ferry, West Va.:[2]

Are you able to take care of the enemy, when he turns back upon you, as he probably will on finding that Wright has left? A. Lincoln.

Telegram to General W. T. Sherman, Washington, July 26, 1864, 2:30 P.M.[3]

Major General Sherman, Near Atlanta:

I have just seen yours complaining of the appointment of Hovey and Osterhaus. The point you make is unquestionably a good one, and yet please hear a word from us. My recollection is that both General Grant and yourself recom-

---

1 On July 19 Grant telegraphed Lincoln: "In my opinion there ought to be an immediate call for, say, 300,000 men to be put in the field in the shortest possible time. The presence of this number of re-enforcements would save the annoyance of raids, and would enable us to drive the enemy from his present front, particularly from Richmond, without attacking fortifications. The enemy now have their last man in the field. Every depletion of their army is an irreparable loss. Desertions from it are now rapid. With the prospect of large additions to our force the desertions would increase. The greater number of men we have the shorter and less sanguinary will be the war. I give this entirely as my views and not in any spirit of dictation, always holding myself in readiness to use the material given me to the best advantage I know how." (Lincoln v.7, 1953, 453)

2 Hunter responded, "My force is not strong enough to hold the enemy, should he return upon us with his whole force." But he added that the information of Crook and the reconnaissance of Averell tended to show that Early was falling back. (Pond 1883, 98)

3 On July 27, Sherman replied to Lincoln's telegram, "Your dispatch of yesterday is received. I beg you will not regard me as fault-finding, for I assert that I have been well sustained in every respect.... I did not suppose my dispatches could go outside the office at the War Department.... Hovey and Osterhaus are both worthy men and had they been promoted on the eve of the Vicksburgh campaign it would have been natural and well accepted but I do think you will admit that their promotion coming to us when they had been to the rear the one offended because I could not unite in the same division five Infantry and five cavalry regiments; and the other for temporary sickness, you can see how ambitious aspirants for military fame regard these things; and they come to me and point them out as evidence that I am wrong in encouraging them in a silent, patient discharge of duty. I assure you that every General of my army has spoken of it and referred to it as evidence that promotion results from importunity and not from actual services. I have refrained from recommending any thus far in the campaign and think we should reach some stage in the game before stopping to balance accounts or writing history I assure you that I do think you have conscienciously acted throughout the war with marked skill in ...military appointments, and that as few mistakes have been made as could be expected. I will furnish all my army and Division commanders with a copy of your dispatch, that they may feel reassured." (Lincoln v.7, 1953, 464)

mended both H[ovey] and O[sterhaus] for promotion, and these, with other strong recommendations, drew committals from us which we could neither honorably or safely disregard. We blamed H[ovey] for coming away in the manner in which he did, but he knew he had apparent reason to feel disappointed and mortified, and we felt it was not best to crush one who certainly had been a good soldier. As to O[sterhaus], we did not know of his leaving at the time we made the appointment, and do not now know the terms on which he left.

Not to have appointed him, as the case appeared to us at the time, would have been almost, if not quite, a violation of our word. The word was given on what we thought was high merit and somewhat on his nationality. I beg you to believe we do not act in a spirit of disregarding merit. We expect to await your programme for further changes and promotions in your army. My profoundest thanks to you and your whole army for the present campaign so far.

A. Lincoln.

Telegram to General U, S. Grant [Cipher] Washington, August 3, 1864.[1]

Lieutenant-General Grant, City Point, Va.:

I have seen your dispatch in which you say, "I want Sheridan put in command of all the troops in the field, with instructions to put himself south of the enemy, and follow him to the death. Wherever the enemy goes, let our troops go also."

This, I think, is exactly right as to how our forces should move; but please look over the dispatches you may have received from here, ever since you made that order, and discover, if you can, that there is any idea in the head of any one here of "putting our army south of the enemy," or of following him to the "death," in any direction. I repeat to you, it will neither be done nor attempted, unless you watch it every day and hour, and force it.

A. Lincoln.

To General S. O. Burbridge, Washington, August 8, 1864.[2]

Major General Burbridge, Lexington, Ky.:

Last December Mrs. Emily T. Helm, half-sister of Mrs. Lincoln, and widow of the rebel general, Ben Hardin Helm, stopped here on her way from Georgia to Kentucky, and I gave her a paper, as I remember, to protect her against the mere fact of her being General Helm's widow. I hear a rumor today that you recently sought to arrest her, but were prevented by her presenting the paper from me. I do not intend to protect her against the consequences of disloyal words or acts,

---

1 This letter seems to have brought Grant to a sense of his real responsibilities. He went north himself, put Sheridan in Hunter's place, and gave him authority over the 30,000 troops in the area. He then returned to Petersburg, without seeing the President. (Ballard 1952, 212)

2 No reply or further reference has been found, but following the publication of the dispatch in 1895, Emily Todd Helm addressed an open letter to *Century Magazine* (June, 1895) in which she noted, "This despatch is a surprise to me, since I was never arrested and never had any trouble with the United States authorities...." (Lincoln v.7, 1953, 485)

spoken or done by her since her return to Kentucky, and if the paper given her by me can be construed to give her protection for such words and acts, it is hereby revoked *pro tanto*. Deal with her for current conduct just as you would with any other.

A. Lincoln.

Telegram to General U. S. Grant, Washington, August 14, 1864, 1:30 P.M.[1]

Lieutenant-General Grant, City Point, Va.:

The Secretary of War and I concur that you had better confer with General Lee, and stipulate for a mutual discontinuance of house-burning and other destruction of private property. The time and manner of conference and particulars of stipulation we leave, on our part, to your convenience and judgment.

A. Lincoln.

Telegram to General W. T. Sherman, Executive Mansion, Washington, August 15, 1864.[2]

Major General Sherman, Near Atlanta, Ga.:

If the Government should purchase, on its own account, cotton northward of you, and on the line of your communications, would it be an inconvenience to you, or detriment to the military service, for it to come to the north on the railroad?

A. Lincoln.

---

1 Grant replied on August 17: "I have thought over your dispatch relative to an arrangement between Gen. Lee and myself for the suppression of insindiaryism [sic] by the respective Armies. Experience has taught us that agreements made with rebels are binding upon us but are not observed by them longer than suits their convenience. On the whole, I think the best that can be done is to publish a prohibitory order against burning private property except where it is a Military necessity or in retaliation for like acts by the enemy. When burning is done in retaliation, it must be done by order of a Dept. or Army Commander and the order for such burning to set forth the particular act it is in retaliation for. Such an order would be published and would come to the knowledge of the rebel Army. I think this course would be much better than any agreement with Gen. Lee. I could publish the order or it could be published by you. This is respectfully submitted for your consideration and I will then act as you deem best." (Ibid, 493)

2 No reply from Sherman has been discovered, but that he telegraphed on August 17 in regard to the transportation of cotton is indicated by a note of Rufus K. Williams written on Executive Mansion stationery, August 26, as follows: "I have seen Hon Secty Treas and proposed that Dr W. A. Turner my son-in-law, a devoted political friend of yours, should be appointed special agent to purchase this 1200 bales of cotton, that an order be issued to Genl Sherman, according to his own suggestions by Telegraph of 17th Inst. to transport it to Nashville. That it be sold at Nashville and liberal freights be retained by the Government, and if desired three fourths of the proceeds be invested in Government securities. This is strictly within the 8 Sect of Act of July 1864." (Ibid. 495-496)

Telegram to General U. S. Grant, Executive Mansion, Washington, August 17, 1864.[1]

Lieutenant-General Grant, City Point, Va.:

I have seen your dispatch expressing your unwillingness to break your hold where you are. Neither am I willing. Hold on with a bulldog grip, and chew and choke as much as possible.

A. Lincoln.

Telegram to General Butler, Executive Mansion, Washington, August 20, 1864.[2]

Major General Butler, Bermuda Hundred, Va.:

Please allow Judge Snead to go to his family on Eastern Shore, or give me some good reason why not.

A. Lincoln.

To General U. S. Grant, Executive Mansion, Washington, September 12, 1864.[3]

Lieutenant-General Grant:

Sheridan and Early are facing each other at a dead-lock. Could we not pick up a regiment here and there, to the number of say ten thousand men, and quietly but suddenly concentrate them at Sheridan's camp and enable him to make a strike?

This is but a suggestion.

Yours truly,

A. Lincoln.

---

1 On the evening of August 17, Grant was sitting in front of his headquarters, with several staff-officers about him, when the telegraph operator came over from his tent and handed him this dispatch. He opened it, and as he proceeded with the reading his face became suffused with smiles. After he had finished it, he broke into a hearty laugh and remarked, "The President has more nerve than any of his advisers. This is what he says after reading my reply to Halleck's dispatch." He then read to note aloud to his staff. (Porter 2000, 279)

2 Butler candidly replied on August 21: "I have never hindered...E K Snead...from going to his family on the Eastern Shore I had supposed he was there until I saw in the New York *Tribune* of the nineteenth a scurrilous article by him dated at Alexandria.... The trouble is Snead is a liar, has deceived the President.... Of such are the restored Govt of Virginia." (Lincoln v.7, 1953, 508)

3 A week later Sheridan launched his aggressive campaign up the Shenandoah Valley. His actions at Opequon Creek and Fisher's Hill sent Early reeling southward. Grant was determined that Lee should never again use the Valley either as a corridor to the North or as a storehouse of supplies. "Nothing should be left to invite the enemy to return," he instructed Sheridan. "Take all provisions, forage, and stock wanted for the use of your command; such as cannot be consumed destroy.... The people should be informed that so long as an army can subsist among them recurrences of these raids must be expected, and we are determined to stop them at all hazards." (Thomas 1952, 446)

Telegram to General W. T. Sherman. Washington, September 17, 1864.[1]

Major General Sherman, Atlanta, Georgia:

I feel great interest in the subjects of your dispatch mentioning corn and sorghum, and the contemplated visit to you.

A. Lincoln, President of the United States.

To General W. T. Sherman, Executive Mansion, Washington, September 19, 1864.[2]

Major General Sherman:

The State election of Indiana occurs on the 11th of October, and the loss of it to the friends of the Government would go far towards losing the whole Union cause. The bad effect upon the November election, and especially the giving the State government to those who will oppose the war in every possible way, are too much to risk if it can be avoided. The draft proceeds, notwithstanding its strong tendency to lose us the State. Indiana is the only important State voting in October whose soldiers cannot vote in the field. Anything you can safely do to let her soldiers or any part of them go home and vote at the State election will be greatly in point. They need not remain for the Presidential election, but may return to you at once. This is in no sense an order, but is merely intended to impress you with the importance to the Army itself of your doing all you safely can, yourself being the judge of what you can safely do.

Yours truly,

A. Lincoln.

Telegram to General P. Sheridan, Executive Mansion, Washington, September 20, 1864.[3]

Major General Sheridan, Winchester, Va.:

---

1 On September 15, 1864, Sherman had telegraphed Halleck: "My report is done, and will be forwarded as soon as I get a few more of the subordinate reports. I am awaiting a courier from General Grant.... Governor Brown has disbanded his militia, to gather the corn and sorghum of the State. I have reason to believe that he and Stephens want to visit me, and I have sent them a hearty invitation. I will exchange 2,000 prisoners with Hood, but no more." The visit of Governor Joseph E. Brown and Alexander H. Stephens did not materialize. (Lincoln v.8, 1953, 9-10)

2 Neely suggests that the celebration of the survival of the two-party system during the Civil War ignores the point of view of the Civil War generation itself. Lincoln, in his only explicit endorsement of the two-party system, in 1852, revealed that he shared the era's uncertainty about the role of political parties. "A free people," Lincoln had said, "in times of peace and quiet, when pressed by no common danger, naturally divide into parties. At such times, the man who is of neither party, is not, cannot be, of any consequence." Lincoln and his age generally accepted the inevitability of parties in peacetime but were by no means certain that parties were natural in times of war. Moreover, it would have come as news to Lincoln, let alone more partisan Republicans, to learn, as some maintain, "Lincoln's leadership of the Union war effort was [not] severely and dangerously hampered by political partisanship." Neely's conclusion is reflected in this letter to Sherman, when he was trying to persuade the general to furlough Indiana troops to vote in the Indiana state election. (Neely 1996, 197)

3 On September 19 Sheridan had telegraphed Grant: "I have the honor to report that I attacked the forces of Genl Early over the Berryville Pike at the crossing of Opequan Creek, and

Have just heard of your great victory. God bless you all, officers and men. Strongly inclined to come up and see you.

A. Lincoln.

To General Hitchcock, Executive Mansion, Washington, September 21, 1864.[1]

General Hitchcock:

Please see the bearer, Mr. Broadwell, on a question about a mutual supplying of clothes to prisoners.

Yours truly,

A. Lincoln.

To General U. S. Grant, Executive Mansion, Washington, September 22, 1864.[2]

Lieutenant-General Grant:

I send this as an explanation to you, and to do justice to the Secretary of War. I was induced, upon pressing application, to authorize the agents of one of the districts of Pennsylvania to recruit in one of the prison depots in Illinois; and the thing went so far before it came to the knowledge of the Secretary that, in my judgment, it could not be abandoned without greater evil than would follow its going through. I did not know at the time that you had protested against that class of thing being done; and I now say that while this particular job must be completed, no other of the sort will be authorized, without an understanding with you, if at all. The Secretary of War is wholly free of any part in this blunder.

Yours truly,

A. Lincoln.

Telegram to General W. T. Sherman, Washington, September 27, 1864.[3]

Major General Sherman, Atlanta, Georgia:

---

after a most stubborn and sanguinary engagement...completely defeated him...driving him through Winchester, capturing about twenty five hundred (2500) prisoners, five (5) of artillery, nine (9) Army flags, and most of their wounded...." (Lincoln v.8, 1953, 13)

1 On September 12, 1864, M. M. Broadwell, of New York City, wrote to Colonel William Hoffman, commissary general of prisoners: "I propose to effect an arrangement by which both the Federal and rebel prisoners shall be furnished with blankets and clothing....My personal relations with most of the rebel officials, and my family connections with some, enable me to negotiate this matter with the rebel authorities. I propose, therefore,... to go to Richmond and get the consent of the rebel authorities to receive and distribute such blankets and clothing as the United States Government will furnish to the prisoners now held at the South....." (Lincoln v.8, 1953, 16)

2 On September 25 Stanton telegraphed Grant substantially the same information contained in this letter of September 22, and Grant replied on the same day: "Your dispatch in relation to the organization of troops from prisoners of war is just received. I would advise that they be placed all in one regiment, and be put on duty either with Pope, or sent to New Mexico." (Ibid, 17)

3 Sherman had telegraphed Halleck on September 26: "I have re-enforced my line back as far as Chattanooga; but in Middle Tennessee we are weak.... I would like to have any regiments in

You say Jefferson Davis is on a visit to Hood. I judge that Brown and Stephens are the objects of his visit.

A. Lincoln.

Telegram to General U. S. Grant, Washington, September 29, 1864.[1]

Lieutenant-General Grant, City Point, Va.:

I hope it will have no constraint on you, nor do harm any way, for me to say I am a little afraid lest Lee sends reinforcements to Early, and thus enables him to turn upon Sheridan.

A. Lincoln.

To General U. S. Grant, Executive Mansion, Washington, October 5, 1864.[2]

Lieutenant-General Grant:

I inclose you a copy of a correspondence in regard to a contemplated exchange of naval prisoners through your lines, and not very distant from your headquarters. It only came to the knowledge of the War Department and of myself yesterday, and it gives us some uneasiness. I therefore send it to you with the

---

Indiana or Ohio sent to Nashville.... Jeff. Davis is on a visit to [John B.] Hood at Palmetto." On September 28, he replied to Lincoln: "I have positive knowledge that Jeff Davis made a speech at Macon on the 22nd.... It was bitter against [Joseph E.] Johnston & Govr Brown. The militia is now on furlough. Brown is at Milledgeville trying to get a legislature to meet next month but he is afraid to act unless in concert with other Governors. Judge Wright of Rome has been here and Messrs [Joshua] Hill and [Thomas A.R.] Nelson former members of our Congress are also here now and will go to meet Wright at Rome and then go back to Madison and Milledgeville. Great efforts are being made to re-enforce Hood's army and to break up my Railroads, and I should have at once a good reserve force at Nashville. It would have a bad effect if I were to be forced to send back any material part of my army to guard roads so as to weaken me to an extent that I could not act offensively if the occasion calls for it." (Ibid, 27)

1 Here, once again, it can be seen that the President did not pretend to thrust military advice upon his commander, but only modestly suggested his views. Grant replied immediately: "Your dispatch just received. I am taking steps to prevent Lee sending reinforcements to Early, by attacking him here." Grant closed with an account of the successes of the morning. (Porter 2000, 303)

2 Gideon Welles, Lincoln's Secretary of the Navy, offers some background with respect to the exchange of naval prisoners. "Late in the afternoon [October 4] the President called upon me to inquire respecting arrangements for a proposed exchange of naval prisoners which was making some disturbance at the War Department and with General Butler. For some fifteen months our naval officers and men who had been captured remained in Rebel prisons. Their number was not large, but the omission to exchange, whether from neglect or design, was justly causing dissatisfaction. For more than a year I had, at various times, made inquiry of the Secretary of War and at the War Department, generally oral, but sometimes by letter, and received evasive answers—of difficulties on account of remoteness, of unusual prisoners, of refusal by the Rebels to exchange negroes — but with assurances that matters would be soon adjusted. Some of our men we had learned were in irons and in close confinement, with slight prospect of relief. I gave the President briefly the facts, that there had been no exchange of naval prisoners for fourteen or fifteen months, that in the exchanges going on no naval prisoners were embraced, that appeals earnest and touching had been made to me by our prisoners and by theirs, but I had been able to afford no relief." (Welles 1911, 168)

statement that, as the numbers to be exchanged under it are small, and so much has already been done to effect the exchange, I hope you may find it consistent to let it go forward under the general supervision of General Butler, and particularly in reference to the points he holds vital in exchanges. Still, you are at liberty to arrest the whole operation if in your judgment the public good requires it.

Yours truly,

A. Lincoln.

Telegram to General U. S. Grant. Washington, October 12, 1864.[1]

Lieutenant-General Grant, City Point, Va.:

Secretary of War not being in, I answer yours about election. Pennsylvania very close, and still in doubt on home vote. Ohio largely for us, with all the members of Congress but two or three. Indiana largely for us,—Governor, it is said, by fifteen thousand, and eight of the eleven members of Congress. Send us what you may know of your army vote.

A. Lincoln.

Telegram to General P. H. Sheridan, Executive Mansion, Washington, October 22, 1864.[2]

Major General Sheridan:

With great pleasure I tender to you and your brave army the thanks of the nation, and my own personal admiration and gratitude, for the month's operations in the Shenandoah Valley; and especially for the splendid work of October 19, 1864.

Your obedient servant,

A. Lincoln.

---

1 Ohio, Pennsylvania, and Indiana held state elections in October. The outcome would be important to the party and as a forecast of results in November. Ohio and Pennsylvania allowed soldiers to cast ballots in the field, but Indiana, with twenty-nine regiments and two batteries serving with Sherman, had made no provision for the soldier vote. So Lincoln sent instructions suggesting: "Anything you [Sherman] can safely do to let her soldiers, or any part of them, go home and vote at the State election will be greatly in point. They need not remain for the Presidential election, but may return to you at once." Sherman granted wholesale furloughs to his Hoosier troops. Generals Frank Blair and John A. Logan, on Lincoln's authority, made speeches in Indiana. Soldier ballots swelled the Republican pluralities, and *Harper's Weekly* commented: "The October elections show that unless all human foresight fails, the election of Abraham Lincoln and Andrew Johnson is assured." (Thomas 1952, 450)

2 When Sheridan retraced his steps down the Shenandoah Valley the second week in October, Early shadowed him to the vicinity of Middletown. On October 19, the Confederates delivered a brilliant surprise attack at Cedar Creek that routed two-thirds of the much larger Federal army. Hesitation on Early's part, exhaustion and hunger among the Southern troops that led them to fall out of ranks to pillage Union camps, and Sheridan's rallying of his soldiers combined to bring the third ignominious defeat in a month to the Army of the Valley. Cedar Creek essentially ended major military activity in the Valley. (Gallagher 1991, 15)

Telegram to General G. H. Thomas, Washington, October 23, 1864, 5 P.M.[1]

Major General Thomas, Nashville, Tennessee:

I have received information today, having great appearance of authenticity, that there is to be a rebel raid into Western Kentucky; that it is to consist of four thousand infantry and three thousand cavalry, and is to start from Corinth, Mississippi, On the fourth day of November.

A. Lincoln., President.

Send copy to General Washburn at Memphis. A. L.

Telegram to General Burbridge, Executive Mansion, Washington, November 4, 1864.[2]

Major General Burbridge, Lexington, Ky.:

Suspend execution of all the deserters ordered to be executed on Sunday at Louisville, until further order, and send me the records in the cases. Acknowledge receipt.

A. Lincoln.

Telegram to General S. O. Burbridge, Washington, November 10, 1864.[3]

Major General Burbridge, Lexington, Ky.:

I have just received a telegram from Governor Bramlette saying: "General John B. Houston, a loyal man and prominent citizen, was arrested, and yesterday, started off by General Burbridge, to be sent beyond our lines by way of Catlettsburg, for no other offense than opposition to your re-election," and I have answered him as follows below, of which please take notice and report to me.

A. Lincoln.

To General S. A. Hurlbut [Private] Executive Mansion, Washington, November 14, 1864. [4]

Major General Hurlbut:

---

1 General George Thomas telegraphed Halleck at 9:30 P.M.: "The dispatch of the President of to-day, concerning the threatened raid into Western Kentucky, has been received. I will gain all the information I can about the rumor, and prepare to prevent its being carried into execution...." (Lincoln v.8, 1953, 74)

2 Burbridge replied on the same day: "Your dispatch received and orders issued in conformity thereto. The record will be forwarded at once." (Ibid, 89)

3 Burbridge replied on November 11: "Gov Bramlette is wrong in saying that Jno B Huston was arrested for no other offence than opposition to your reelection. Hustons influence & speeches have been of a treasonable character & he persisted in making the latter after several warnings of what the consequences would be He has been allowed however to return from Covington under oath & bond not again to oppose his Govt. A vigorous policy against rebel sympathizers in this State must be pursued & if I have erred I fear I have made too few arrests instead of too many." (Ibid, 99)

4 From Washington, Lincoln continued to press for the restoration of loyal civil governments across the South; he remained committed to his efforts aimed at "moulding society for durability in the Union" throughout the South by eradicating slavery by any available means.

Few things since I have been here have impressed me more painfully than what, for four or five months past, has appeared a bitter military opposition to the new State government of Louisiana. I still indulged some hope that I was mistaken in the fact; but copies of a correspondence on the subject between General Canby and yourself, and shown me today, dispel that hope. A very fair proportion of the people of Louisiana have inaugurated a new State government, making an excellent new constitution—better for the poor black man than we have in Illinois. This was done under military protection, directed by me, in the belief, still sincerely entertained, that with such a nucleus around which to build we could get the State into position again sooner than otherwise. In this belief a general promise of protection and support, applicable alike to Louisiana and other States, was given in the last annual message. During the formation of the new government and constitution they were supported by nearly every loyal person, and opposed by every secessionist. And this support and this opposition, from the respective standpoints of the parties, was perfectly consistent and logical. Every Unionist ought to wish the new government to succeed; and every disunionist must desire it to fail. Its failure would gladden the heart of Slidell in Europe, and of every enemy of the old flag in the world. Every advocate of slavery naturally desires to see blasted and crushed the liberty promised the black man by the new constitution. But why General Canby and General Hurlbut should join on the same side is to me incomprehensible.

Of course, in the condition of things at New Orleans, the military must not be thwarted by the civil authority; but when the Constitutional Convention, for what it deems a breach of privilege, arrests an editor in no way connected with the military, the military necessity for insulting the convention and forcibly discharging the editor is difficult to perceive. Neither is the military necessity for protecting the people against paying large salaries fixed by a legislature of their own choosing very apparent. Equally difficult to perceive is the military necessity for forcibly interposing to prevent a bank from loaning its own money to the State. These things, if they have occurred, are, at the best, no better than gratuitous hostility. I wish I could hope that they may be shown not to have occurred. To make assurance against misunderstanding, I repeat that in the existing condition of things in Louisiana, the military must not be thwarted by the civil authority; and I add that on points of difference the commanding general must be judge and master. But I also add that in the exercise of this judgment and control, a purpose, obvious, and scarcely unavowed, to transcend all military necessity, in order to crush out the civil government, will not be overlooked.

Lifting the blockade from ports under Union occupation, he hoped to smooth the way to reunion by placating the impoverished. And yet some of the very reasons that impelled him to move forward before November 1864 were now absent. He no longer had to worry about hurrying along the process of emancipation and reconstruction in case he failed of reelection. Although he remained committed to using the erection of new civil governments and the restoration of trade as ways to weaken the Confederacy, he did not need to worry about tipping the military balance before the election. Abolition by constitutional amendment would obviate questions about the continued viability of the Emancipation Proclamation after the termination of hostilities and would hasten the process in the loyal border states, especially Kentucky and Delaware, where efforts to spark state initiated emancipation had failed. (Simpson 2001, 81)

Yours truly,
A. Lincoln.

Telegram to General Rosecrans. Executive Mansion, Washington, November 26, 1864.[1]

Major General Rosecrans:

Please telegraph me briefly on what charge and evidence Mrs. Anna B. Martin has been sent to the penitentiary at Alton.

A. Lincoln.

Telegram to General G. H. Thomas. Washington, December 16, 1864.[2]

Major General Thomas, Nashville, Tennessee:

Please accept for yourself, officers, and men, the nation's thanks for your good work of yesterday. You made a magnificent beginning; a grand consummation is within your easy reach. Do not let it slip.

A. Lincoln.

To General W. T. Sherman, Executive Mansion, Washington, December 26, 1864.[3]

My Dear General Sherman:

Many, many thanks for your Christmas gift, the capture of Savannah.

When you were about leaving Atlanta for the Atlantic coast, I was anxious, if not fearful; but feeling that you were the better judge, and remembering that "nothing risked, nothing gained," I did not interfere. Now, the undertaking being a success, the honor is all yours; for I believe none of us went further than to acquiesce.

And taking the work of General Thomas into the count, as it should be taken, it is indeed a great success. Not only does it afford the obvious and immediate military advantages; but in showing to the world that your army could be divided, putting the stronger part to an important new service, and yet leaving enough

---

1 General Rosecrans responded on November 30, 1864: "Annie B. Martin on her written request & in accordance with instructions from War Dept date of April twenty fourth eighteen sixty three sent beyond the lines not to return during the war under pain of imprisonment during the war she returned during the war under pain of imprisonment during the war she returned without authority was tried by Military Commission & sentenced to imprisonment during the war in her examination she states she is disloyal & if released would return south." (Lincoln v.8, 1953, 122)

2 On December 15, General Thomas had telegraphed General Halleck from Nashville, " I attacked the enemy's left this morning and drove it... about eight miles. Have captured ... a ... train of about 20 wagons with between 800 and 1,000 prisoners and 16 pieces of artillery. I shall attack the enemy again to-morrow...." (McMurry 2002, 35)

3 Three days before Christmas Sherman presented the city of Savannah to Lincoln. The Northern press proudly declared that no American would ever buy a gift for his child, sweetheart, or wife without remembering "the great soldier who has given this grandest of Christmas gifts to the country." The New York Herald even predicted that when Lee's soldiers learned that Thomas had annihilated Hood and that Sherman was in Georgia with sixty thousand men, there would be rebellion throughout the Army of Northern Virginia and the government would crumble. Hood's "wild goose chase" had failed, and the blame would fall squarely on President Davis: "...the "grand rebellion will collapse like a big balloon with all the gas let out at once." (Bailey 2000. 169)

to vanquish the old opposing force of the whole,—Hood's army,—it brings those who sat in darkness to see a great light. But what next?

I suppose it will be safe if I leave General Grant and yourself to decide.

Please make my grateful acknowledgments to your whole army of officers and men.

Yours very truly,

A. Lincoln.

Telegram to General U. S. Grant, Washington, December 28, 1864, 5:30 P.M.[1]

Lieutenant-General Grant, City Point, Va.:

If there be no objection, please tell me what you now understand of the Wilmington expedition, present and prospective.

A. Lincoln.

Telegram to General Butler, Executive Mansion, Washington, December 29, 1864.[2]

Major General Butler:

There is a man in Company I, Eleventh Connecticut Volunteers, First Brigade, Third Division, Twenty-fourth Army Corps, at Chapin's Farm, Va.; under the assumed name of William Stanley, but whose real name is Frank R. Judd, and who is under arrest, and probably about to be tried for desertion. He is the son of our present minister to Prussia, who is a close personal friend of Senator Trumbull and myself. We are not willing for the boy to be shot, but we think it as well that his trial go regularly on, suspending execution until further order from me and reporting to me.

A. Lincoln.

To General U. S. Grant, Executive Mansion, Washington, January 5, 1865.[3]

Lieutenant-General Grant, City Point, Va.:

---

1 Grant replied on the same day: "The Wilmington expedition has proven a gross and culpable failure. Many of the troops are now back here. Delays and free talk of the object of the expedition enabled the enemy to move troops to Wilmington to defeat it. After the expedition sailed from Fort Monroe three days of fine weather was squandered, during which the enemy was without a force to protect himself. Who is to blame I hope will be known." Note: The joint expedition under Admiral David D. Porter and General Benjamin F. Butler was abandoned on December 25 when Butler and General Godfrey Weitzel decided that Fort Fisher at Wilmington, North Carolina, could not be carried by assault. (Lincoln v.8, 1953, 188)

2 The case of Frank R. Judd is tangled. Following his enlistment in the Eighth Illinois Cavalry on February 6, 1864, he was appointed to West Point, where he reported on June 4, 1864, but left without taking his entrance examination. He enlisted as Frank Judson in the Third Massachusetts Cavalry on July 15, 1864, and was listed as a deserter on September 30, 1864. He enlisted in the Eleventh Connecticut Volunteers under the name of William Stanley on November 26, 1864. (Ibid, 190)

3 Lieutenant-Governor Richard T. Jacob, of Kentucky, had been banished by the Federals and was temporarily living with Confederate General John Breckinridge's military family.

Richard T. Jacob, Lieutenant-Governor of Kentucky, is at the Spotswood House, in Richmond, under an order of General Burbridge not to return to Kentucky. Please communicate leave to him to pass our lines, and come to me here at Washington.

A. Lincoln.

Telegram to General Grant, Executive Mansion, Washington, January 6, 1865.[1]

Lieutenant-General Grant, City Point:

If there is a man at City Point by the name of Waterman Thornton who is in trouble about desertion, please have his case briefly stated to me and do not let him be executed meantime.

A. Lincoln.

Telegram to General B. F. Butler, Executive Mansion, Washington, January 10, 1865.[2]

Major General Butler, Fort Monroe, Va.:

No principal report of yours on the Wilmington expedition has ever reached the War Department, as I am informed there. A preliminary report did reach here, but was returned to General Grant at his request. Of course, leave to publish cannot be given without inspection of the paper, and not then if it should be deemed to be detrimental to the public service.

A. Lincoln.

Telegram to General B. F. Butler, Executive Mansion, Washington, January 13, 1865. [3]

Major General Butler, Fort Monroe, Va.:

Lincoln had not been consulted prior to the banishment. (Mosgrove 1999, 231)

1 Grant replied on January 7: "In reply to your dispatch of this morning I have to state that Genl Griffin commanding 2nd Division 9th Army Corps telegraphs me that private Waterman Thornton one hundred seventy ninth (179) New York Volunteers was executed yesterday... for desertion to the enemy" (Lincoln v.8, 1953, 203)

2 On January 8, General Butler was relieved from command of the Department of Virginia and North Carolina and replaced by General Edward O. C. Ord. On January 9, he had telegraphed Lincoln: "I have telegraphed to the Secretary of War for leave to publish my report of the Wilmington affair. I have received no answer. He is absent; in his absence I respectfully ask your leave to publish it. It is but justice...." (Ibid, 207)

3 Basler suggests that the most negative effect of all congressional activity of the War was brought to bear on Lincoln's administration by the Joint Committee on the Conduct of the War, established as the result of a resolution of December 2, 1861, calling for investigations of the military disasters at Bull Run and Ball's Bluff. Senators Benjamin F. Wade of Ohio, Zachariah Chandler of Michigan, and Andrew Johnson of Tennessee were joined by four representatives: D. W. Gooch of Massachusetts, George W. Julian of Indiana, John Covode of Pennsylvania, and Moses F. Odell of New York. As has been known to happen with other investigative committees, the Joint Committee became the political tool of its more ambitious members, Wade and Chandler, who undertook to use it as a lever for achieving Radical Republican ends. Its investigations were partisan to the point of persecuting, on the one hand, able Democratic generals such as Charles P. Stone (for the Ball's Bluff episode) and General George B. McClellan, and, on the other hand, whitewashing and prais-

Yours asking leave to come to Washington is received. You have been summoned by the Committee on the Conduct of the War to attend here, which, of
course, you will do.

A. Lincoln.

Telegram to General G. M. Dodge, Executive Mansion, Washington, January 15, 1865.[1]

Major General Dodge, St. Louis, Missouri:

It is represented to me that there is so much irregular violence in northern
Missouri as to be driving away the people and almost depopulating it. Please
gather information, and consider whether an appeal to the people there to go to
their homes and let one another alone recognizing as a full right of protection for
each that he lets others alone, and banning only him who refuses to let others
alone may not enable you to withdraw the troops, their presence itself [being] a
cause of irritation and constant apprehension, and thus restore peace and quiet,
and returning prosperity. Please consider this and telegraph or write me.

A. Lincoln.

To General Grant, Executive Mansion, Washington, January 19, 1865.[2]

Lieutenant-General Grant:

Please read and answer this letter as though I was not President, but only
a friend. My son, now in his twenty-second year, having graduated at Harvard,
wishes to see something of the war before it ends. I do not wish to put him in
the ranks, nor yet to give him a commission, to which those who have already

---

ing such Republican favorites as Generals Benjamin F. Butler and John C. Frémont, whose
considerably worse military lapses were offset (among Radicals) by their abolitionism and
avowed vindictiveness toward the South. The major result of the Joint Committee's actions
was to constrain Lincoln to appoint or retain officers of dubious ability or proved incom-
petence, for purely political reasons, far beyond Lincoln's own established predilection in
such matters. (Basler 1967, 58)

1 On January 16, General Dodge replied: "I have the honor to acknowledge the receipt of your
telegram of the 15th inst. Since I assumed command here the troubles in North Missouri
have increased from the fact that the troops that were in those Counties, infested by gueril-
la bands, were nearly all withdrawn...to send to General Thomas; but there is no doubt that
this country is now more quiet than it has been before for three years. Where these troubles
exist the people are to a great extent disloyal and it is the protection, aid, and sympathy
that they give to the enemy and to outlaws that causes these troubles....Allow me to assure
you that the course you propose would be protested against by the State authorities, the
legislature, the convention and by nearly every undoubtedly loyal man in North Missouri,
while it would receive the sanction of nearly every disloyal, semi-loyal, and non-committed
person there, all such could, under that course live and should want to stay in that country,
while every loyal man would have to leave these counties when the disloyal sentiment is in
the ascendancy...." (Lincoln v.8, 1953, 217)

2 Robert Lincoln graduated from Harvard in 1864, and pled to be allowed to join the army, only
to meet with Mary Lincoln's adamant refusal to allow another son to be put at risk. While
this spoke favorably of Mary's maternal instincts, her husband realized it was a political
mistake, with so many of the country's other sons volunteering or being drafted, and in
1865 Lincoln persuaded Mary to allow Robert to join Grant's personal staff with the rank
of captain. (Guelzo 1999, 388)

served long are better entitled and better qualified to hold. Could he, without embarrassment to you, or detriment to the service, go into your military family with some nominal rank, I, and not the public, furnishing his necessary means? If no, say so without the least hesitation, because I am as anxious and as deeply interested that you shall not be encumbered as you can be yourself.

Yours truly,

A. Lincoln.

Telegram to General Dodge, Executive Mansion, Washington, January 19, 1865.[1]

Major General Dodge, Saint Louis, Mo.:

If Mrs. Beattie, alias Mrs. Wolff, shall be sentenced to death, notify me, and postpone the execution till further order.

A. Lincoln.

Telegram to General Ord, Executive Mansion, Washington, January 19, 1864.[2]

Major General Ord:

You have a man in arrest for desertion passing by the name of Stanley. William Stanley, I think, but whose real name is different. He is the son of so close a friend of mine that I must not let him be executed. Please let me know what is his present and prospective condition.

A. Lincoln.

Telegram to General G. M. Dodge, Executive Mansion, Washington, January 24, 1865.[3]

Major General Dodge, St. Louis, Mo.:

It is said an old lady in Clay County, Missouri, by name Mrs. Winifred B. Price, is about being sent South. If she is not misbehaving let her remain.

A. Lincoln.

---

1 General Dodge replied on the same day: "Mrs. Beattie has been sent to her friends in the rebel lines." In a second telegram of the same date he queried: "'Have you any orders for Maj Wolfe Had he not better be sent to Johnsons Island for exchange" The identity of Mrs. Beattie is not clarified but is indicated in an item appearing in the St. Louis Missouri Republican, November 22, 1864: "Mrs. Kate Beattie -A good deal of local interest has been excited within a few days past, in regard to a woman professing to be Mrs. Wolff, wife of the rebel Major condemned to be shot in retaliation for the murder of Maj. Wilson. All our readers know that she is now a prisoner, but the following advertisement from Memphis... will be of interest: "Information Wanted: Fifty dollars reward will be given for information as to the whereabouts of Mrs. Kate Beattie, wife of Capt. Tuck. Beattie, of Lexington, Mo.... Mrs. Beattie is about five feet four inches tall, has light blue eyes, hair closely shingled, and a scar upon the right cheek. She is rather eccentric, intelligent, and prepossessing in manners." (Lincoln v.8, 1953, 223)

2 No reply from General Ord has been located.

3 General Dodge replied on January 26: "No order has been issued from these Head Quarters banishing Mrs Winfred E Price nor from any subordinate that I can learn of." (Lincoln v.8, 1953, 234)

Telegram to General Grant, Executive Mansion, Washington, January 25, 1865.[1]

Lieutenant-General Grant, City Point:
If Newell W. Root, of First Connecticut Heavy Artillery, is under sentence of death, please telegraph me briefly the circumstances.
A. Lincoln.

Telegram to General Grant, War Department, Washington, January 25, 1865.[2]

Lieutenant-General Grant, City Point, Va.:
Having received the report in the case of Newell W. Root, I do not interfere further in the case.
A. Lincoln.

Telegram to General U. S. Grant, Executive Mansion, Washington, January 31, 1865.[3]

Lieutenant-General Grant, City Point, Va.:
A messenger is coming to you on the business contained in your dispatch. Detain the gentlemen in comfortable quarters until he arrives, and then act upon the message he brings, as far as applicable, it having been made up to pass through General Ord's hands, and when the gentlemen were supposed to be beyond our lines.
A. Lincoln.

---

1 On January 25, 1865, Captain and Judge Advocate P.T. Whitehead telegraphed: "I have the honor to report in regard to Private Newell W. Root alias Geo H Harris Co H 1st Conn Heavy Artillery, that he was tried by this Court on Dec 19th 1864 & convicted of 'deserting to the Enemy' & sentenced to be hung. His sentence is approved by General Meade & ordered to be carried into effect at City Point on Friday 27th inst.... Root deserted to the enemy near Dutch Gap & gave himself up to the rebels as a union deserter; was released... and on making his way through... Ky represented himself as a rebel deserter for the purpose of getting out of the service. He gave the name of Harris & came to City Point in arrest under that name...." (Ibid, 235)

2 Newell W. Root was hanged on January 27, 1865. (Ibid, 237)

3 The messenger was Major Thomas Eckert, who bore with him a letter of the Secretary of War to General Grant, that stated, "The President desires that you will please procure for the bearer, Major Thomas T. Eckert, an interview with Messrs. [Alexander] Stephens, [Robert M. T.] Hunter, and [John A.] Campbell and if on his return to you he requests it pass them through our lines to Fortress Monroe by such route and under such military precautions as you may deem prudent, giving them protection and comfortable quarters while there, and that you let none of this have any effect upon your movements or plans." (Lincoln 1926, 444) Early in 1865, the President of the Confederacy was influenced by Francis Preston Blair, Senior, to appoint a peace commission for informal conference with the Federal government. President Lincoln, having directed Secretary Seward to meet the southern representatives, Messrs. Stephens, Hunter, and Campbell, at Fortress Monroe, handed him written instructions which read: "You will make known to them that three things are indispensable, to wit: first, The restoration of the national authority throughout all the States; second, No receding by the Executive of the United States on the slavery question from the position assumed thereon in the late annual message to Congress, and in preceding documents; third, No cessation of hostilities short of an end of the war, and the disbanding of all forces hostile to the government. You will inform them that all propositions of theirs, not inconsistent with the above, will be considered and passed upon in a spirit of sincere liberality. You will hear all they may choose to say and report it to me. You will not assume to definitely consummate anything." (Rothschild 1906, 153)

Telegram to General U. S. Grant, Washington, February 1, 1865.[1]

Lieutenant-General Grant, City Point:

Let nothing which is transpiring change, hinder, or delay your military movements or plans.

A. Lincoln.

Telegram to General U. S. Grant, Washington, February 2, 1865.[2]

Lieutenant-General Grant, City Point, Va.:

Say to the gentlemen I will meet them personally at Fortress Monroe as soon as I can get there.

A. Lincoln.

Telegram to General U. S. Grant. Executive Mansion, Washington, February 8, 1865.[3]

Lieutenant-General Grant, City Point. Va.:

I am called on by the House of Representatives to give an account of my interview with Messrs. Stephens, Hunter, and Campbell, and it is very desirable to me to put your dispatch of February 1, to the Secretary of War, in which, among other things, you say: "I fear now their going back without any expression from any one in authority will have a bad influence." I think the dispatch does you credit, while I do not see that it can embarrass you. May I use it?

A. Lincoln.

Telegram to General S. Pope, Executive Mansion, Washington, February 12, 1865.[4]

Major General Pope, St. Louis, Missouri:

---

1 While Lincoln had agreed to a conference with the Confederate peace delegates, Alexander Stephens, Robert M. Hunter, and John A. Campbell, he also made it clear to Grant that this should not interfere with any of the general's plans, insisting that Grant fight while the negotiations proceeded. He reiterated his point in this February 1 telegram. Grant promised that there would be no armistice. (Stoker 2010, 397)

2 Lincoln and Secretary of State Seward met Alexander H. Stephens, Vice-President of the Confederacy, and the other Confederate representatives on February 2, 1865, on the *River Queen*, at Fortress Monroe. While Lincoln had a friendly conference, he nonetheless presented his ultimatum: that the one and only condition of peace was that Confederates "must cease their resistance." (Browne 1974, 290)

3 Grant replied on the same day: "By all means use my dispatch, referred to in yours of this date, if you desire to do so. It was marked 'confidential' in contra distinction to official dispatches but not to prevent such use being made of it as you or the Secretary of War might think proper." (Lincoln v.8, 1953, 270)

4 General John Pope had been placed in command of the Department of the Missouri to succeed General Samuel R. Curtis who was transferred to the Department of the Northwest. He replied on February 13: "Dispatch recd & attended to Provost Marshal system in Mo is oppressive and absurd I am examining into & will correct the whole matter." (Ibid, 293)

I understand that provost-marshals in different parts of Missouri are assuming to decide that the conditions of bonds are forfeited, and therefore are seizing and selling property to pay damages. This, if true, is both outrageous and ridiculous. Do not allow it. The courts, and not provost-marshals, are to decide such questions unless when military necessity makes an exception. Also excuse John Eaton, of Clay County, and Wesley Martin, of Platte, from being sent South, and let them go East if anywhere.

A. Lincoln.

Telegram to General J. Pope, Executive Mansion, Washington, February 14, 1865. [1]

Major General Pope, St. Louis, Missouri:

Yours of yesterday about provost-marshal system received. As part of the same subject, let me say I am now pressed in regard to a pending assessment in St. Louis County. Please examine and satisfy yourself whether this assessment should proceed or be abandoned; and if you decide that it is to proceed, please examine as to the propriety of its application to a gentleman by the name of Charles McLaran.

A. Lincoln.

Telegram to General Pope, Executive Mansion, Washington February 15, 1865. [2]

Major General Pope, St. Louis, Missouri:

Please ascertain whether General Fisk's administration is as good as it might be, and answer me.

A. Lincoln.

---

1 On February 24, General Grenville M. Dodge, in command of the Division of the Missouri, reported to Pope's adjutant, Captain Joseph M. Bell: "I have the honor to report in relation to the assessment in Saint Louis that when I assumed command here I found a large number of refugees being supported here by the Government. Houses over the city for their occupation had been seized and rents accumulating that the Government would have to pay.... General Halleck... instructed that where the local authorities would not protect and support . . . refugees the disloyal should be assessed to do it.... The Sanitary Commission proposed to take charge...provided I would fix up the old Lawson Hospital.... This was done at a cost of about $10,000.... This assessment of $10,000 was made to reimburse the quartermaster's department . . . and if stopped will bring the whole matter back on Government.... The assessment on Colonel McLaran I considered too much, and have ordered it reduced $1,500. He was colonel of the Minute Men when the war commenced...." (Ibid, 298)

2 Pope replied from Milwaukee on February 20: "Your dispatch asking about General Fisk met me here, where I had come to meet General Curtis. I return to Saint Louis to-morrow, and will endeavor to answer your inquiry. I have not been long enough in command to find out fully about men and their proceedings, but shall find out soon." Note: No report from Pope on General Clinton B. Fisk has been found. (Ibid, 300)

Telegram to General U. S. Grant, Washington, February 24, 1865.[1]

Lieutenant-General Grant, City Point, Virginia:
I am in a little perplexity. I was induced to authorize a gentleman to bring Roger A. Pryor here with a view of effecting an exchange of him; but since then I have seen a dispatch of yours showing that you specially object to his exchange. Meantime he has reached here and reported to me. It is an ungracious thing for me to send him back to prison, and yet inadmissible for him to remain here long. Cannot you help me out with it? I can conceive that there may be difference to you in days, and I can keep him a few days to accommodate on that point. I have not heard of my son's reaching you.
A. Lincoln.

Telegram to General Pope, Executive Mansion, Washington, February 24, 1865.[2]

Major General Pope, Saint Louis, Mo.:
Please inquire and report to me whether there is any propriety of longer keeping in Gratiott Street Prison a man said to be there by the name of Riley Whiting.
A. Lincoln.

Telegram to General U. S. Grant, Washington, February 25, 1865.[3]

Lieutenant-General Grant, City Point, Virginia:
General Sheridan's dispatch to you, of today, in which he says he "will be off on Monday," and that he "will leave behind about two thousand men," causes the Secretary of War and myself considerable anxiety. Have you well considered whether you do not again leave open the Shenandoah Valley entrance to Maryland and Pennsylvania, or, at least, to the Baltimore and Ohio Railroad?
A. Lincoln.

---

1 Grant replied on February 25: "Send Pryor on here and we will exchange him; He can do us no harm now. Capt Lincoln reported on the 22nd and was assigned to duty at my Head Quarters." (Ibid, 314) Pryor, who rose to the rank of general early in the war, lost his Confederate brigade due to political-military issues. He subsequently joined the 3rd Virginia Cavalry, Company E, as a private but carried his general officer's title out of military tradition and courtesy. (Hubard 2007, xxvi)

2 No reply has been found.

3 On 27 February 1865, Sheridan rode out from Winchester with two cavalry divisions. He had orders from Grant to break the Virginia Central Railroad at Staunton, continue down the Shenandoah Valley, cross the Blue Ridge and capture Lynchburg. There Sheridan would break up the South Side Railroad. Afterward, he would continue down into North Carolina, where he would rendezvous with Sherman. (Horn 1999, 209) Grant realized that Lincoln has misinterpreted Sherman's direction and Grant replied on February 26: "Two thousand cavalry and that to be increased to three thousand, besides all his Infantry is what Genl. Sheridan means. His movement is in the direction of the enemy & the tendency will be to protect the B. & O. road and to prevent an attempt to invade Maryland and Penna." (Lincoln v.8, 1953, 317)

Telegram to General U. S. Grant, Washington, February 27, 1865.[1]

Lieutenant-General Grant, City Point, Virginia:

Subsequent reflection, conference with General Halleck, your dispatch, and one from General Sheridan, have relieved my anxiety; and so I beg that you will dismiss any concern you may have on my account, in the matter of my last dispatch.

A. Lincoln.

Telegram to General U. S. Grant, Washington, March 2, 1865.[2]

Lieutenant-General Grant, City Point, Va.:

You have not sent contents of Richmond papers for Tuesday or Wednesday. Did you not receive them? If not, does it indicate anything?

A. Lincoln.

Telegram to General John Pope, Executive Mansion, Washington, March 7, 1865.[3]

Major General Pope, St. Louis, Missouri:

Please state briefly, by telegraph, what you concluded about the assessments in St. Louis County. Early in the war one Samuel B. Churchill was sent from St. Louis to Louisville, where I have quite satisfactory evidence that he has not misbehaved. Still I am told his property at St. Louis is subjected to the assessment, which I think it ought not to be. Still I wish to know what you think.

A. Lincoln.

To General U. S. Grant. Washington, March 8, 1865.[4]

Lieutenant-General Grant, City Point, Va:

---

1 No response from Grant has been found.

2 Grant replied the same day: "Richmond papers received daily. No bulletins were sent Tuesday or Wednesday because there was not an item of either good or bad news in them. There is every indication that Genl Sherman is perfectly safe. I am looking every day for direct news from him." (Lincoln v.8, 1953, 329)

3 Pope replied on March 8: "I wrote fully concerning assessment to the Secy of War on the twenty sixth 26 Feby. I submitted the question to War Dept, as the authority for assessment originated in Washington & the order was made before I came here there are strong reasons given for making it given me by Genl Dodge which are communicated in my letter.... That letter must be in War Dept and I respectfully invite your attention to it." Note: Pope's letter of February 26 has not been found. (Ibid, 343-344)

4 On March 8, Grant telegraphed Stanton at 11:30 A.M.: "We have got supplies going out by Norfolk to the rebel army stopped, but information received shows that large amounts still go by way of the Black-water. They no doubt go on the Treasury permits heretofore given under Act of Congress regulating trade with states in insurrection. I would respectfully recommend that orders be sent to the Army and Navy everywhere, to stop supplies going to the interior and annulling all permits for such trade heretofore given." A second telegram from Grant to Stanton stated: "I believe Genl [James W.] Singleton should be ordered to return from Richmond and all permits he may have should be revoked. Our friends in Richmond... send word that Tobacco is being exchanged on the Potomac for Bacon, and

Your two dispatches to the Secretary of War, one relating to supplies for the enemy going by the Blackwater, and the other to General Singleton and Judge Hughes, have been laid before me by him. As to Singleton and Hughes, I think they are not in Richmond by any authority, unless it be from you. I remember nothing from me which could aid them in getting there, except a letter to you, as follows, to wit: *Executive Mansion, Washington City, February 7, 1865. Lieutenant-General Grant, City Point, Va.: General Singleton, who bears you this, claims that he already has arrangements made, if you consent, to bring a large amount of Southern produce through your lines. For its bearing on our finances, I would be glad for this to be done, if it can be, without injuriously disturbing your military operations, or supplying the enemy. I wish you to be judge and master on these points. Please see and hear him fully, and decide whether anything, and, if anything, what, can be done in the premises. Yours truly,*

A. Lincoln.

I believe I gave Hughes a card putting him with Singleton on the same letter. However this may be, I now authorize you to get Singleton and Hughes away from Richmond, if you choose, and can. I also authorize you, by an order, or in what form you choose, to suspend all operations on the Treasury trade permits, in all places southeastward of the Alleghenies. If you make such order, notify me of it, giving a copy, so that I can give corresponding direction to the Navy.

A. Lincoln.

Telegram to General J. Pope, Executive Mansion, Washington, March 19, 1865.[1]

Major General Pope, St. Louis, Missouri:

they believe Singleton to be at the bottom of it. I am also of the opinion that all permits issued to Judge [James] Hughes should be cancelled. I think the same of all other permits heretofore granted, but in the case of Singleton and Judge Hughes, I believe there is a deep laid plan for making millions and they will sacrifice every interest of the country to succeed. I do not know Hughes personally never having seen him but once, but the conviction here expressed is forced upon me." (Ibid, 344)

1 On March 2, Governor Thomas C. Fletcher had written Pope for his views as to "the best uses of the military forces in this Department, and their relation to the present and prospective condition of this State." Pope's lengthy reply of March, in substance, sets forth that the civil authority should recognize its responsibilities and perform its duties. On March 8, Pope had written Lincoln: "I...transmit...a printed copy [clipping from the *Missouri Republican*, March 8, 1865] of a letter addressed by me to the Governor of Missouri.... In addition to what is set forth in the letter...I...submit for your consideration a few...suggestions, which it was perhaps well not to make public in my letter to Gov. Fletcher. I ask your consideration of these suggestions and of those contained in the printed letter, and if they meet your approval I...request that I may be so notified.... It is...desirable that...the General Government be relieved from all concern in the civil affairs of the State, and be required only to defend it against armed invasion. So long as United States troops remain in Missouri . . . they will be a constant source of embarrassment and a difficult obstacle to the renewal of civil administration.... So long as the troops remain and.... Martial Law obtains the people will feel a constant desire to appeal from the State Executive and the Civil laws, to the Military Authorities and to the General Government; and no step will be taken toward a resumption of local civil administration.... Remove that source of difficulty, and they will soon learn, that they must depend upon themselves and their state government, as their final resort for justice. I do not propose to change the present condition of the military suddenly, but... cautiously and gradually, as follows. 'The term of the Missouri State Militia...paid by the

Understanding that the plan of action for Missouri contained in your letter to the Governor of that State, and your other letter to me, is concurred in by the Governor, it is approved by me, and you will be sustained in proceeding upon it. A. Lincoln.

Telegram to General W. S. Hancock, Washington, March 22, 1865.[1]

Major General Hancock, Winchester, Va.:

Seeing your dispatch about General Crook, and fearing that through misapprehension something unpleasant may occur, I send you below two dispatches of General Grant, which I suppose will fully explain General Crook's movements. A. Lincoln.

General Government and...under officers of the United States is about to expire....Under no circumstances should these troops be reorganized or employed in the same manner.... No authority should be given to raise troops for service in Missouri. If these recommendations be adopted, we shall be left...within a few months, with nothing but a few regiments of Volunteers from other States. These...I will push down to the Southern border of the State.... In many counties...the civil courts are in full operation. In those...I propose to suspend Martial law, not by any public order, but simply by private instructions to commanding officers to withdraw their Provost Marshals and to refrain...from any interference with citizens.... Slowly, county by county, the military forces of the United States can thus be withdrawn from all connection with the...civil affairs of the State. If troops or Martial Law are afterwards required...let the Governor take the responsibility of declaring Martial Law and enforcing it by his State Militia.... There is a loyal State executive and civil officers and a large loyal majority in the State and I cannot see why it is not abundantly able to settle all controversies between its own citizens, without referring them to the Administration at Washington. . . .'" (Ibid, 365-366)

1 Major General George Crook had been in command of the Department of West Virginia when he was captured at Cumberland on February 21, 1865. On March 20, Edward D. Townsend notified Crook: "Your exchange has been effected. The general-in-chief directs that you immediately return to command of your department...." On March 21, Major General Winfield S. Hancock telegraphed Halleck: "I learn to-night...that Major-General Crook has assumed command of the Department of West Virginia, with headquarters at Cumberland. The headquarters of the department are at this place, and I am in command by the assignment of the President. I have no other official knowledge of General Crook's being in this division. I have ordered him, if he has assumed command, to replace matters as he found them, and report at Frederick, Md., in arrest, and will prefer charges against him as soon as practicable." Townsend replied to Hancock on the same day: "The Secretary of War directs that Maj. Gen. George Crook be immediately relieved from command of the Department of the Cumberland and ordered to report in person without delay to Lieutenant-General Grant for assignment to a command...." Crook relinquished command on March 22, and Hancock ordered him in obedience to orders from the Secretary of War to report to Grant. The two telegrams from Grant which Lincoln forwarded to Hancock as indicated above were: (1) to Townsend, March 18: "Please notify General Crook that his exchange has been effected, and order him back to his department. As soon as he goes on duty I will have him relieved and ordered at once to command the cavalry of the Army of the Potomac;" and (2) to Stanton, March 21: "I would recommend relieving Crook from command of his department and ordering him to command the cavalry of the Army of the Potomac...." Hancock's reply to Lincoln's telegrams was received at 11:20 A.M. on March 22: "There can be no trouble in Genl Crook's case if he has observed my order to restore matters as he found them and to proceed to Frederick in arrest. Where my order suspending his arrest, and ordering him to report to Lt Genl Grant will reach him. According to just military principle I could pursue no other course, & there will be no delay on my part in the execution of the order of the Department to send General Crook to City Point." (Ibid, 371)

Telegram to General U. S. Grant, City Point, April 1, 1865.[1]

Lieutenant-General Grant:

Yours to Colonel Bowers about the Secretary of War is shown to me. He is not here, nor have I any notice that he is coming. I presume the mistake comes of the fact that the Secretary of State was here. He started back to Washington this morning. I have your two dispatches of this morning, and am anxious to hear from Sheridan.

A. Lincoln.

Telegram to General U. S. Grant, City Point, April 1, 1865.[2]

Lieutenant-General Grant:

Yours showing Sheridan's success of today is just received and highly appreciated. Having no great deal to do here, I am still sending the substance of your dispatches to the Secretary of War.

---

1 Grant telegraphed Colonel Theodore S. Bowers from Dabney's Mill at 11:10 A.M.: "I understand the Secretary of War is at City Point. Present my respects to him, and say we would have had Petersburg before this but for the rain which unfortunately set in the first night we were out." (Ibid, 379)

2 Three telegrams were received from Grant on April 1, the first at 9:15 A.M.: "Yesterday as reported the left of the 5th Corps attempted to push north so as to cross the White Oak Road about W Dabneys House but were driven back Sheridan at the same time was pushing up the right branch of the 2 Roads from J. Boisseaus North to the same Road he was at the same time holding Dinwiddie C H & the line of Chamberlain Creek he was met by all the Enemys Cavalry & four or five brigades of Infantry & gradually forced back until at 8 P.M. last Evening he was holding a line from Chamberlain Creek to the Boydton Road probably not more than one mile from the C.H. after [the] falling back of two Divisions of the 5th Corps they again pushed forward and gained the position on the White Oak road first sought finding however the situation Sheridan was in, orders were sent to [Gouverneur K.] Warren after dark to leave the position he held & to push two (2) Divisions down by J Boisseaus & one down the Boydton Road to his relief I had much hopes of destroying the force detached by the Enemy so far to our rear I have not yet heard the result but I know that Sheridan took the offensive this A.M. Ord yesterday pushed the Enemys pickets from the left of his (Ords) line next to Hatchers Run Capturing 189 men & 2 officers with but very little loss to us this puts Ord so close to the Enemy that he cannot put out pickets in front this Morning before day the Enemy attempted to drive him from this position but was repulsed without loss on our side and leaving over 60 prisoners in our hands." The second telegram was received at 11:24 A.M.: "In my dispatch this morning I made a mistake in saying Ord lost nothing in the attack made on him this AM his casualties were about 30 killed & wounded he reported no casualties in [John W.] Turners Division which led me into the Errer. The quicksand of this section exceeds anything I have ever seen roads have to be corduroyed in front of teams and Artillery as they advance We were 56 hours moving 600 teams 5 miles with 1200 men to help them through the woods when it is perfectly dry for infantry horses will go through so deep as to scarcely be able to extricate themselves I have nothing special to report at this hour." The third was received at 5:05 P.M.: "The following dispatch is just recd from Col [Horace] Porter of my staff who was sent to communicate with Gen Sheridan. You remember I told you the 5th Corps was sent to him last evening.... Divens [Thomas C. Devin's] Div of Cavalry has just carried the barricade at the five forks held by [George E.] Pickett's Div capturing about two hundred prisoners. The enemy now seem to hold a line across the ford & White Oak roads The whole 5th Corps is now moving from here up to five forks & Gen S. will attack the enemy with every thing the Head of Warrens column is now about a mile & a half from five forks moving up rapidly Our men have never fought better. All are in excellent spirits and anxious to go in The enemy is said by all the officers to be fighting badly giving away constantly before our dismounted Cavy The enemy's loss yesterday was very heavy many of their dead are lying in the woods I [saw?] several old men with heads perfectly bald. The enemy threw away many arms in their retreat & seem to have been pretty much demoralized." (Ibid, 379-380)

A. Lincoln.

Telegram to General U. S. Grant, City Point, April 2, 1865.[1]

Lieutenant-General Grant:

Allow me to tender to you and all with you the nation's grateful thanks for this additional and magnificent success. At your kind suggestion I think I will meet you tomorrow.

A. Lincoln.

Telegram to General U. S. Grant, Headquarters Armies of the United States, City Point, April 6, 1865.[2]

Lieutenant-General Grant, in the field:

Secretary Seward was thrown from his carriage yesterday and seriously injured. This, with other matters, will take me to Washington soon. I was at Richmond yesterday and the day before, when and where Judge Campbell, who was with Messrs. Hunter and Stephens in February, called on me, and made such representations as induced me to put in his hands an informal paper, repeating the propositions in my letter of instructions to Mr. Seward, which you remember, and adding that if the war be now further persisted in by the rebels, confiscated property shall at the least bear the additional cost, and that confiscation shall be remitted to the people of any State which will now promptly and in good faith withdraw its troops and other support from resistance to the Government.

Judge Campbell thought it not impossible that the rebel legislature of Virginia would do the latter if permitted; and accordingly I addressed a private letter to General Weitzel, with permission to Judge Campbell to see it, telling him (General Weitzel) that if they attempt this, to permit and protect them, unless they attempt something hostile to the United States, in which case to give them notice and time to leave, and to arrest any remaining after such time.

I do not think it very probable that anything will come of this, but I have thought best to notify you so that if you should see signs you may understand them.

From your recent dispatches it seems that you are pretty effectually withdrawing the Virginia troops from opposition to the Government. Nothing

---

1 In this note, Lincoln congratulated Grant on the operational successes reflected in Grant's April 2, 1865 dispatch: "We are now up and have a continuous line of troops, and in a few hours will be intrenched from the Appomattox below Petersburg to the river above. Heth's and Wilcox's divisions, such part of them as were not captured, were cut off from town, either designedly on their part or because they could not help it. Sheridan with the cavalry and 5th corps is above them. Miles's division, 2d corps, was sent from the White Oak Road to Sutherland Station on the South Side Railroad, where he met them, and at last accounts was engaged with them. Not knowing whether Sheridan would get up in time, General Humphreys was sent with another division from here. The whole captures since the army started out gunning will amount to not less than twelve thousand men, and probably fifty pieces of artillery. I do not know the number of men and guns accurately however." (Grant 1952, 538)

2 No response from Grant has been found.

that I have done, or probably shall do, is to delay, hinder, or interfere with your work.

Yours truly,

A. Lincoln.

Telegram to General G. Weitzel, Headquarters Armies of The United States, City Point, April 6, 1865.[1]

Major General Weitzel, Richmond, Va.:

It has been intimated to me that the gentlemen who have acted as the legislature of Virginia in support of the rebellion may now desire to assemble at Richmond and take measures to withdraw the Virginia troops and other support from resistance to the General Government. If they attempt it, give them permission and protection, until, if at all, they attempt some action hostile to the United States, in which case you will notify them, give them reasonable time to leave, and at the end of which time arrest any who remain. Allow Judge Campbell to see this, but do not make it public.

A. Lincoln.

Telegram to General U. S. Grant, Headquarters Armies of the United States, City Point, April 7, 1865. [2]

Lieutenant-General Grant:

Gen. Sheridan says: "If the thing is pressed I think that Lee will surrender." Let the thing be pressed.

A. Lincoln.

---

1 In pursuance of this liberal offer and an additional verbal suggestion by Lincoln, Campbell matured plans and issued a call for the members of the 1861 Virginia Legislature to reassemble, to undo the secession ordinance and to remove the State from rebellion. Such was the status of affairs on April 7, when Lincoln left the captured Confederate capital. (Milton 1930, 155)

2 Learning the Confederates had evacuated Richmond in a sudden collapse of Confederate resistance, Lincoln determined to go there the next day. "I will take care of myself," he promised the solicitous Stanton. With six sailors ahead of him and six behind he walked Richmond streets to Union headquarters, visited the fled Confederate president's office and sitting down, remarked, "This must have been President Davis's chair." The Stars and Stripes replaced the Stars and Bars over the Virginia capitol. Blacks in the city hailed the emancipator. White residents, on the other hand, keenly resented seeing their city held mainly by black troops. Lee's abandonment of Petersburg and Richmond was followed by his westward flight toward Lynchburg, from where he hoped to transport his men to North Carolina and unite with General Joseph E. Johnston who was resisting Sherman's advance. His plan went awry when Sheridan, who had arrived after his victorious Shenandoah Valley campaign, attacked him and pushed on with both cavalry and infantry. "If the thing is pressed," he telegraphed Grant, "I think Lee will surrender." Lincoln, now back at City Point, read the telegram on April 7 and ordered, "Let the thing be pressed." His forces diminishing, his rations running low, Lee on April 9 at Appomattox Court House unconditionally surrendered to Grant his Army of Northern Virginia. That same day, improved in health, Lincoln returned to Washington at sundown. He learned that around one o'clock in the afternoon Grant had accepted Lee's surrender. The streets were full of cheering people; bonfires were blazing. (Rawley 2003, 214)

Telegram to General G. H. Gordon, Executive Mansion, Washington, April 11, 1865.[1]

Brig. Gen. G. H. Gordon, Norfolk, Va.:

Send to me at once a full statement as to the cause or causes for which, and by authority of what tribunal George W. Lane, Charles Whitlock, Ezra Baler, J. M. Renshaw, and others are restrained of their liberty. Do this promptly and fully.
A. Lincoln.

Telegram to General G. Weitzel, Washington, April 12, 1865.[2]

Major General Weitzel, Richmond, Va.:

I have seen your dispatch to Colonel Hardie about the matter of prayers. I do not remember hearing prayers spoken of while I was in Richmond; but I have no doubt you have acted in what appeared to you to be the spirit and temper manifested by me while there. Is there any sign of the rebel legislature coming to-

---

1   On March 31, Charles Whitlock and Ezra Baker and associates petitioned Lincoln for return of goods seized by military authorities, release from arrest, and trial before a civil tribunal. No reply from Gordon has been found. (Lincoln v.8, 1953, 395)

2   On April 9, Charles A. Dana had telegraphed Stanton from Richmond: "On Friday evening I asked Weitzel...what he was going to do about opening the churches on Sunday. He answered that all were to be allowed to be opened on condition that no disloyalty should be uttered and that the Episcopal ministers would be required to read the prayer for the President.... I told him this was all right. Last evening he sent [George F.] Shepley to me to ask that this order might be relaxed, so that the clergy would only be required not to pray for Jeff. Davis. Shepley said this was what had been determined on by...Weitzel before I gave orders to the contrary. I answered I had given no orders at all... and that Weitzel must act in the matter entirely on his own judgment. It appears that Judge Campbell thought it very desirable that a loyal prayer should not be exacted, and that Weitzel had consented to it; but when I asked him the question...he gave me an answer opposite to the reality. I report the fact, confessing that it shakes a good deal my confidence in Weitzel...." Stanton then telegraphed Weitzel: "It has just been reported to this Department that you have, at the instance of Mr. Campbell, consented that service should be performed in the Episcopal churches of Richmond to-day without the usual prayer said in loyal churches of that denomination for the President... and that you have even agreed to waive that condition. If such has been your action it is strongly condemned by this Department...you are directed immediately to report by telegraph your action in relation to religious services in Richmond...and also to state what took place between you and Mr. Campbell on the subject...." Weitzel replied the next day: "The orders in relation to religious services in Richmond were verbal, and were applicable alike to all religious denominations.... They were, in substance, that no expression would be allowed in any part of the church service... which in any way implied a recognition of any other authority than that of the United States.... No orders were given as to what would be preached or prayed for, but only as to what would not be permitted.... I have had personally but three interviews with Judge Campbell---two of them in the presence of, and the other by the written command of, the President. In neither of these interviews was any question discussed in relation to church or prayers...." On April 11, James A. Hardie telegraphed Weitzel: "The Secretary of War directs me to say that your explanation...is not satisfactory.... The Secretary also directs me to instruct you that officers commanding in Richmond are expected to require from all religious denominations in that city, in regard to their rituals and prayers, no less respect for the President...than they practiced toward the rebel chief...before he was driven from the capital." Weitzel's reply to Lincoln's telegram of April 12 was received at 3 P.M.: "You spoke of not pressing little points. You said you would not order me, but if you were in my place you would not press them. The passports have gone out for the legislature, and it is common talk that they will come together." (Ibid, 405-406)

---

gether on the understanding of my letter to you? If there is any such sign, inform me what it is; if there is no such sign, you may withdraw the offer.

A. Lincoln.

Telegram to General G. Weitzel, Washington, April 12, 1865.[1]

Major General Weitzel, Richmond, Va.:

I have just seen Judge Campbell's letter to you of the 7th. He assumes, as appears to me, that I have called the insurgent legislature of Virginia together, as the rightful legislature of the State, to settle all differences with the United States. I have done no such thing. I spoke of them, not as a legislature, but as "the gentlemen who have acted as the legislature of Virginia in support of the rebellion." I did this on purpose to exclude the assumption that I was recognizing them as a rightful body. I deal with them as men having power de facto to do a

---

1 Stanton, later, in his May 18, 1867 testimony before the House Judiciary Committee, provided his version of the events of this period, specificallythe course pursued by Lincoln and the influence under which he acted. "President Lincoln went to the city of Richmond, after its capture, and some intercourse took place between him and Judge Campbell, formerly of the Supreme Court of the United States, and General Weitzel, which resulted in the call of the rebel Legislature to Richmond. Mr. Lincoln on his return to Washington reconsidered that matter. The policy of undertaking to restore the government, through the medium of rebel organizations, was very much opposed by many persons and very strongly and vehemently opposed by myself.... I had several earnest conversations with Mr. Lincoln on the subject and advised that any effort to reorganize the Government should be under the Federal authority solely, and to treat the rebel organizations as absolutely null and void. The day preceding his death, a conversation took place between him, the Attorney-General, and myself, upon the subject, at the Executive Mansion. An hour or two afterwards and about the middle of the afternoon, Mr. Lincoln came over to the War Department and renewed the conversation. After I had repeated my reasons against allowing rebel Legislatures to assemble, or rebel authorities to have any participation whatever in the business of reorganization, he sat down at my desk, took a piece of paper, and wrote a telegram to General Weitzel and handed it to me. 'There,' said he; 'I think that will suit you.' I told him no, it did not go quite far enough; that members of the rebel Legislature would probably come to Richmond, and that General Weitzel ought to be directed to prohibit their assembling. He took up his pen again and made that addition to the telegram and signed it. He handed it to me. I said I thought that was exactly right. It was transmitted immediately to General Weitzel and was the last act ever performed by Mr. Lincoln in the War Department." It does not appear that Judge Campbell saw Lincoln's dispatch of April 12 to General Weitzel. However, this dispatch, read in the light of Mr. Stanton's statement, contains several significant sentences. He says that Judge Campbell assumes that I have called the insurgent Legislature of Virginia together, as the rightful Legislature of the State to settle all differences with the United States. I have done no such thing. I spoke of them, not as the Legislature, but as "the gentlemen who have acted as the Legislature of Virginia in support of the rebellion." I did this on purpose to exclude the assumption that I was recognizing them as a rightful body. I dealt with them as men having power de facto to do a specific thing, to-wit, to withdraw the Virginia troops and other support from resistance to the general Government for which, in the paper handed to Judge Campbell, I promised a special equivalent, to-wit, a remission to the people of the State, except in certain cases, of the confiscation of their property. Inasmuch as Judge Campbell misconstrued this, and is still pressing for an armistice contrary to the explicit statement of the paper I gave him, and particularly as General Grant has since captured the Virginia troops, so that giving consideration for their withdrawal is no longer applicable, I wish my letter to you and the paper to Judge Campbell, both to be withdrawn or countermanded and he be notified of it. Stanton says that the following words were, at his request, added: "Do not allow them to assemble, but if any have come, allow them safe return to their homes." (Connor 1920, 182-184)

---

specific thing, to wit: "To withdraw the Virginia troops and other support from resistance to the General Government," for which, in the paper handed Judge Campbell, I promised a specific equivalent, to wit: a remission to the people of the State, except in certain cases, of the confiscation of their property. I meant this, and no more. Inasmuch, however, as Judge Campbell misconstrues this, and is still pressing for an armistice, contrary to the explicit statement of the paper I gave him, and particularly as General Grant has since captured the Virginia troops, so that giving a consideration for their withdrawal is no longer applicable, let my letter to you and the paper to Judge Campbell both be withdrawn, or countermanded, and he be notified of it. Do not now allow them to assemble, but if any have come, allow them safe return to their homes.

A. Lincoln.

To General Van Alen, Executive Mansion, Washington, April 14, 1865.[1]

General Van Allen:

I intend to adopt the advice of my friends and use due precaution. I thank you for the assurance you give me that I shall be supported by conservative men like yourself, in the efforts I may make to restore the Union, so as to make it, to use your language, a Union of hearts and hands as well as of States.

Yours truly,

A. Lincoln.

---

1 The original text of this letter has never been found, nor has the note that inspired it, a plea from a New York general that Lincoln take special precautions against assassination. This reply was published in the *Sunday Morning Chronicle* on April 23, but, by then, Lincoln had been dead a week, just as Van Alen had feared, the victim of an assassin. (Lincoln 2004, 349) But, while no trace of the original letter has been found, and the text in the source is open to question, a footnote in the source is as follows: "General Van Alen wrote Lincoln, requesting him, for the sake of his friends and the nation, to guard his life and not expose it to assassination as he had by going to Richmond. Note that the above, April 14, 1865 reply, was written on the very day Lincoln was assassinated. (Lincoln v.8, 1953, 413)

Epilogue

When we consider Abraham Lincoln, what generally comes to mind is his preservation of the Union and the abolition of slavery. Or, perhaps, we recall his *Emancipation Proclamation*, or the *Gettysburg Address*, or maybe, rarely, the *Second Inaugural Address* where he envisions binding up the nation's wounds with malice toward none and charity for all. And then there is the tragedy of Ford's Theatre on that fateful evening of April 14, 1865—arguably the most durable echo of Lincoln's presidency. But what, perhaps, does not occur so freely to us is that all of these impressions of Lincoln are connected directly with his role as commander- in- chief of the army and navy. Without the war, and without the Union victory in the war under Lincoln's hands-on leadership as commander-in-chief, none of these things would have happened. Indeed, without the war, we would probably remember Lincoln—if we remembered him at all—as one of the obscure nineteenth-century presidents, in the same category, say, with Franklin Pierce or Benjamin Harrison.[1]

From the beginning to the end, Abraham Lincoln tenaciously held a single aim: to save the Union. His major acts consistently announced his purpose: repudiating secession, waging war for the Union, emancipating and arming blacks, and extending amnesty and a moderate plan of reconstruction. He embraced the concept of employing war as "politics by other means," as Europeans defined war, and he never softened his steady position that the war would end solely with restoration of national unity. War, he knew, was indeed absolute, and the man remembered for his absence of malice and charity for all instructed his generals to destroy the enemy army. He was unwavering in his belief that the Southern states had not formed a separate nation, that two countries were not at war, rather *one* country fought to subdue insurgents or rebels within that country. Surrender would be unconditional as to reunion—compromise on this point was

---

1 McPherson, 2002, 1.

impossible. There could be no treaty with rebels; as he declared in his last public address, "there is no authorized organ for us to treat with." States, once accepting defeat, and abandoning the root cause of the war—slavery—and promising loyalty, should be restored to their "proper practical relation" as quickly as possible. And to achieve his aim Lincoln's tasks were daunting: to administer a military defeat of a powerful, determined army; to root out the cause of national disunity; to open the way for the restoration of popular government; and all the while to maintain Northern unity and commitment to his aim.[1]

Lincoln's presidency became—along with Thomas Jefferson's and Franklin Roosevelt's—one of the "hinge" presidencies of American history. He reoriented the relationship of government and business through public financing of a transcontinental railroad, protective tariffs, a new national banking system, and "homestead" legislation that converted vast stretches of the public lands in the West to commercial development. In Lincoln's hands, government became a supportive ally of business rather than an uncooperative neutral party. He became the first president to embrace the use of "war powers" by a commander-in-chief, thereby beginning a debate over the meaning and extent of those powers that continues to this day. Too, he emerged as a jealous guardian of executive privilege and rebuffed with equal firmness attempts by his cabinet, Radical Republicans in Congress, and his generals to seize decision making from his hands. Caleb Blood Smith, Lincoln's first secretary of the interior, complained that "Mr. Lincoln doesn't treat a Cabinet as other Presidents—that he decides the most important questions without consulting his cabinet." Smith was not exaggerating. For the previous six decades, zealous cabinet secretaries had acquired increasing amounts of discretion and initiative, while executive authority languished. Lincoln decisively subordinated his cabinet secretaries to his own dictate as president, and thus laid down the outlines of cabinet-style administration that we live with yet. But, to have done all this, while at the same time directing a four-year-long civil war, emancipating 3.5 million slaves, and deflecting bitter, almost-treacherous opposition from his critics, seems enough to persuade even his harshest critics that Lincoln's election might have been, as some have suggested, "accidental," it is clear that the man himself was not.[2]

As commander-in-chief, Lincoln never deferred his judgment to others in choosing generals. But he was willing to discard his judgment of what was good strategy and take the opinion of any general whom he considered to be able. He was willing to yield the power to direct strategic operations to any general who could demonstrate that he was competent to frame and execute strategy. Lincoln sensed that there was something wrong in the command system. Somewhere, he thought, there ought to be a division of function between him and the military. But where should the line be drawn? And who was the general to whom he could confide the power to control? Lincoln was to go through some bitter and agonizing experiences before he got the answers to these questions. In the process, he and the army and the nation were to learn a lot about command. By 1864 the United States would have a modern command system. Lincoln did not know

---

1 Rawley 2003, 222-223.
2 Guelzo 2012, 97.

it in 1861, but he was going to make a large and permanent contribution to the organization of the American military system.[1]

Perhaps one of the more insightful vignettes of Lincoln as commander-in-chief can be gleaned from a conversation between Lincoln, Stanton, and Grant that occurred after Stanton impatiently complained that the general had reassigned artillerymen that Stanton thought were required for the defense of Washington. "I think I rank you in this matter, Mr. Secretary," was Grant's quiet answer. "We shall have to see Mr. Lincoln about that," Stanton replied. "All right," said Grant. "Mr. Lincoln ranks us both." They went to the White House. "Won't you state your case, General Grant?" said Stanton. Grant replied, "I have no case to state; I am satisfied as it is." After Stanton detailed his own case, Lincoln, sprawled in his chair, watching his infuriated Secretary reflectively, slowly answered: "You and I, Mr. Stanton, have been trying to boss this job, and we have not succeeded very well with it. We have sent across the mountains for Mr. Grant, as Mrs. Grant calls him, to relieve us, and I think we had better leave him alone to do as he pleases."[2]

Abraham Lincoln emerges as a seminal figure in American political and military history. And although he was occasionally unrealistic about the capabilities of his military commanders, he did not take the view that war was an aberration, nor did he chose to ignore his own responsibility with respect to preserving and enhancing the Union's military capability. On the contrary, Lincoln harbored an aggressive, pragmatic perception of conflict. With no knowledge of the principles of war, and no technical military training, he nonetheless became a viable tactician. One in which his pursuit of presidential leadership necessitated a very different image of the chief executive as a military leader.

In the end, Lincoln was able to steer through the morass of meddlesome congressional representatives, arrogant political generals and scheming, envious cabinet members and effectively lead the Union to victory. Therein, perhaps, reflecting back to his "House Divided Speech" of 1858 in which he identified his own era as a turning point in the long quest for human dignity. From the opening paragraph to the splendid peroration, his message is charged with an electric feeling for the drama of a crisis in which the citizens of the United States "shall nobly save, or meanly lose, the last best hope of earth."[3]

---

1 May and Braziller 1960, 89.
2 Church 1897, 249.
3 Lincoln 1946, 40.

Works Cited

Abel, Annie Heloise. *The American Indian in the Civil War, 1862-1865* (Lincoln, NE: University of Nebraska Press, 1992)

Allan, William. "Lee the Soldier." *Lee the Soldier*, ed. Gary W. Gallagher (Lincoln, NE: University of Nebraska Press, 1996)

Ambrose, Stephen E. *Americans at War* (Jackson, MS: University Press of Mississippi, 1997)

Andrews, J. Cutler. *The North Reports the Civil War* (Pittsburgh: University of Pittsburgh Press, 1955)

Angle, Paul M. and Schenck Miers. *Tragic Years, 1860-1865: A Documentary History of the American Civil War*, Volume. 1 (New York: Simon and Schuster, 1960)

Apperson, John Samuel, and John Herbert Roper. *Repairing the "March of Mars": The Civil War Diaries of John Samuel Apperson, Hospital Steward in the Stonewall Brigade, 1861-1865* (Macon, GA: Mercer University Press, 2001)

Armstrong, Marion V. *Unfurl Those Colors!: McClellan, Sumner, and the Second Army Corps in the Antietam Campaign* (Tuscaloosa, AL: University of Alabama Press, 2008)

Baggett, James Alex and Joseph G. Dawson III. "Charles Griffin." *Handbook of Texas Online* (Denton, TX: Texas State Historical Association, 2012)

Bailey, Anne J. *The Chessboard of War: Sherman and Hood in the Autumn Campaigns of 1864* (Lincoln, NE: University of Nebraska Press, 2000)

Ballard, Colin R. *The Military Genius of Abraham Lincoln: An Essay* (Cleveland, OH: World Publishing, 1952)

Barrett, Joseph Hartwell. *Abraham Lincoln and his Presidency*, Volume. 2 (Cincinnati: The Robert Clarke Company. 1904)

Bartlett, Irving H. *Brahmin Radical* (Boston: Beacon Press, 1961)

Basler, Roy P. *A Short History of the American Civil War* (New York: Basic Books, 1967)

Baylor, George. *Bull Run to Bull Run; Or, Four Years in the Army of Northern Virginia.* (Richmond: B. F. Johnson Publishing Company, 1900.)

Behn, Richard J. "Robert A. Schenck (1809-1890)." *Mr. Lincoln's White House* (The Lincoln Institute, 2012)

_____. "The Officers." *Mr. Lincoln and Friends* (The Lincoln Institute, 2013)

Belz, Herman. *A New Birth of Freedom: The Republican Party and Freedmen's Rights, 1861 to 1866* (New York: Fordham University Press, 2000)

Beymer, William Gilmore. *Scouts and Spies of the Civil War* (Lincoln, NE: University of Nebraska Press, 2003)

Binning, William C., Larry E. Esterly, and Paul A. Sracic. *Encyclopedia of American Parties, Campaigns, and Elections* (Westport, CT: Greenwood Press, 1999)

Birchfield, D.L. *The Encyclopedia of North American Indians*, Volume. 7 (New York: Marshall Cavendish, 1997)

Boman, Dennis K. *Lincoln and Citizens' Rights in Civil War Missouri Balancing Freedom and Security* (Baton Rouge: Louisiana State University Press, 2011)

Booker, Christopher B. *I Will Wear No Chain: A Social History of African-American Males* (Westport, CT: Praeger, 2000)

Boyle, John Richards. *Soldiers True: The Story of the One Hundred and Eleventh Regiment Pennsylvania Veteran Volunteers and of Its Campaigns in the War for the Union, 1861-1865.* (New York: Eaton & Mains, 1903)

Brockett, L. P. *The Life and Times of Abraham Lincoln, Sixteenth President of the United States* (Philadelphia: Bradley & Co., 1865)

Browne, Ray B. *Lincoln-Lore: Lincoln in the Popular Mind* (Bowling Green, OH: Popular Press, 1974)

Bruce, Robert V. *Lincoln and the Tools of War* (Indianapolis: Bobbs-Merrill, 1956)

Bryant, James K. *The Battle of Fredericksburg: We Cannot Escape History* (Charleston, SC: History Press, 2010)

Burton, Brian K. "Seven Days' Battles." *Encyclopedia Virginia* (Charlottesville, VA: Virginia Foundation for the Humanities, 2012)

Cannan, John, *The Antietam Campaign: August-September 1862* (Conshohocken, PA: Combined Books, 1994)

Carman, Ezra Ayers, and Joseph Pierro. *The Maryland Campaign of September 1862: Ezra A. Carman's Definitive Study of the Union and Confederate Armies at Antietam* (New York: Routledge, 2008)

Carpenter, John A. *Sword and Olive Branch: Oliver Otis Howard* (New York: Fordham University Press, 1999)

Carr, Lucien. *Missouri: A Bone of Contention* (Boston: Houghton, Mifflin, 1888)

Castel, Albert. *A Frontier State at War: Kansas, 1861-1865* (Ithaca, NY: Cornell University Press, 1958)

Catton, Bruce. *This Hallowed Ground: The Story of the Union Side of the Civil War* (Garden City, NY: Doubleday, 1956)

Chase, Salmon P. *Inside Lincoln's Cabinet: The Civil War Diaries of Salmon P. Chase*, ed. David Donald (New York: Longmans, Green, 1954)

Chesson, Michael B. "35: Prison Camps and Prisoners of War," in *The American Civil War: A Handbook of Literature and Research*, ed. Robin Higham and Steven E. Woodworth (Westport, CT: Greenwood Press, 1996)

Church, William Conant. *Ulysses S. Grant and the Period of National Preservation and Reconstruction* (New York: G.P. Putnam's Sons. 1897)

Colaizzi, Janet. *Homicidal Insanity, 1800-1985* (Tuscaloosa, AL: University of Alabama Press, 1989)

Collins, Donald E. "War Crime or Justice? General George Pickett and the Mass Execution of Deserters in Civil War Kinston, North Carolina," in *The Art of Command in the Civil War*, Steven E. Woodworth ed. (Lincoln, NE: University of Nebraska Press, 1998)

Conger, A. L. *The Rise of U. S. Grant* (New York: Century, 1931)

Connor, Henry G. *John Archibald Campbell: Associate Justice of the United States Supreme Court* (Boston: Houghton Mifflin Company, 1920)

Conyngham D. P. *The Irish Brigade and Its Campaigns*, ed. Lawrence Frederick Kohl (New York: Fordham University Press, 1994)

Cooling, Benjamin Franklin., *Counter-Thrust: From the Peninsula to the Antietam* (Lincoln, NE: University of Nebraska Press, 2007)

Coppée, Henry. *Grant and His Campaigns: A Military Biography* (New York: Charles B. Richardson, 1866)

Cozzens, Peter. *This Terrible Sound: The Battle of Chickamauga* (Urbana: University of Illinois Press, 1992)

Cuomo, Mario M. and Harold Holzer. *Lincoln on Democracy* (New York: Fordham University Press, 2004)

Davis, Charles E. *Three Years in the Army. The Story of the Thirteenth Massachusetts Volunteers from July 16, 1861, to August 1, 1864* (Boston: Estes and Lauriat, 1894)

Drumond, Dwight Lowell. *Antislavery: The Crusade for Freedom in America* (Ann Arbor, MI: University of Michigan Press, 1961)

Dupuy, Ernest R. Trevor N. Dupuy. *Military Heritage of America* (New York: McGraw-Hill, 1956)

Eckenrode, H. J. and Bryan Conrad. *George B. McClellan, the Man Who Saved the Union* (Chapel Hill, NC: University of North Carolina Press, 1941)

Ellinghouse, Cletis Ray. *Old Wayne: A Brit's Memoir.* (Philadelphia: Xlibris, 2010)

Engle, Stephen D. *Struggle for the Heartland: The Campaigns from Fort Henry to Corinth, Great Campaigns of the Civil War* (Lincoln, NE: University of Nebraska Press, 2001)

Fetherling, George. *The Book of Assassins: A Biographical Dictionary from Ancient Times to the Present* (New York: Wiley, 2001)

Freeman, Joanne. *Time Line of the Civil War.* (Washington D.C: Library of Congress, 2013)

French, Samuel Livingston. *The Army of the Potomac from 1861 to 1863: An Inside View of the History of the Army of the Potomac and Its Leaders* (New York: Publishing Society of New York, 1906)

Furqueron, James R. and Albert A. Nofi. "A Short Biographical Guide to Persons Mentioned in the Text," in *James Longstreet: The Man, the Soldier, the Controversy*, ed. R. L. Dinardo and Albert A. Nofi (Conshohocken, PA: Combined Publishing, 1998)

Gaines, W. Craig. *Civil War Gold and Other Lost Treasures: On the Trail of Various Grey Ghosts* (Conshohocken, PA: Combined Publishing, 1999)

Gallagher, Gary W. "The Shenandoah Valley Campaign of 1862." *The Shenandoah Valley Campaign of 1862* (Chapel Hill, NC: University of North Carolina Press, 2003)

_____. "The Shenandoah Valley in 1864," in *Struggle for the Shenandoah: Essays on the 1864 Valley Campaign*, ed. Gary W. Gallagher (Kent, OH: Kent State University Press, 1991)

Gerteis, Louis S. *The Civil War in Missouri: A Military History* (Columbia, MO: University of Missouri Press, 2012)

Gorham, George C. *Life and Public Services of Edwin M. Stanton* (Boston: Houghton Mifflin Company, 1899)

Grant Ulysses S. *Personal Memoirs*, ed. E. B. Long (Cleveland, OH: World Pub., 1952)

_____. *The Papers of Ulysses S. Grant: December 9, 1862–March 31, 1863*, ed. John Y. Simon, Volume. 7. (Carbondale, IL: Southern Illinois University Press, 1979)

_____. *The Papers of Ulysses S. Grant: December 9, 1862–March 31, 1863*, ed. John Y. Simon, Volume. 10. (Carbondale, IL: Southern Illinois University Press, 1982)

_____. *The Papers of Ulysses S. Grant: December 9, 1862–March 31, 1863*, ed. John Y. Simon, Volume. 11. (Carbondale, IL: Southern Illinois University Press, 1984)

_____. *Personal Memoirs*, ed. E. B. Long (Cleveland, OH: World Pub., 1952)

Green, Michael S. *Freedom, Union, and Power: Lincoln and His Party during the Civil War* (New York: Fordham University Press, 2004)

Guelzo, Allen C. *Abraham Lincoln: Redeemer President* (Grand Rapids, MI: William B. Eerdmans, 1999)

_____. "Lincoln and Leadership- An Afterword," in *Lincoln and Leadership: Military, Political, and Religious Decision Making*, ed. Randall M. Miller (New York: Fordham University Press, 2012)

Hahn, Steven. *A Nation under Our Feet: Black Political Struggles in the Rural South from Slavery to the Great Migration* (Cambridge, MA: Belknap Press, 2005)

Harris, William C. *With Charity for All: Lincoln and the Restoration of the Union.* (Lexington, KY: University Press of Kentucky, 1997)

Hattaway, Herman, and Archer Jones. *How the North Won: A Military History of the Civil War* (Urbana: University of Illinois Press, 1991)

Hay, John. *Lincoln's Journalist: John Hay's Anonymous Writings for the Press, 1860-1864*, ed. Michael Burlingame (Carbondale, IL: Southern Illinois University Press, 1998)

Headley, Phineas C. *The Life and Campaigns of General U. S. Grant from Boyhood to His Inauguration As President of the United States Including an Accurate Account of Sherman's Great March from Chattanooga to Washington* (New York: Leavitt, 1869)

Hebert, Walter H. *Fighting Joe Hooker* (Lincoln: University of Nebraska Press, 1999)

Heidler, David Stephen, Jeanne T. Heidler, and David J. Coles. *Encyclopedia of the American Civil War: A Political, Social, and Military History* (Santa Barbara, CA: ABC-CLIO, 2000)

Hess, Earl J. *Banners to the Breeze: The Kentucky Campaign, Corinth, and Stones River* (Lincoln, NE: University of Nebraska Press, 2000)

Holland, J. G. *Life of Abraham Lincoln* (Springfield, MA: Gurdon Bill, 1866)

Holzer, Harold, ed. *Dear Mr. Lincoln: Letters to the President* (Reading, MA: Addison-Wesley, 1993)

_____. *Lincoln on War.* (Chapel Hill NC: Algonquin Books, 2011)

Horn, John. *The Petersburg Campaign: June 1864-April 1865* (Conshohocken, PA: Combined Publishing, 1999),

Horn, Stanley F. *The Army of Tennessee: A Military History* (Indianapolis: Bobbs-Merrill, 1941)

Horner, David. "Stress on Higher Commanders in Future Warfare," in *The Human Face of Warfare: Killing, Fear and Chaos in Battle*, ed. Michael Evans and Alan Ryan (St. Leonards, NSW: Allen and Unwin, 2000)

Hubard, Jr., Robert T. *The Civil War Memoirs of a Virginia Cavalryman*, ed. Thomas P. Nanzig (Tuscaloosa, AL: University of Alabama Press, 2007)

Illinois Infantry. *Military History and Reminiscences of the Thirteenth Regiment of Illinois Volunteer Infantry in the Civil War in the United States, 1861-1865* (Chicago: Woman's Temperance Association, 1892)

Johnson, Allen, ed. *Readings in American Constitutional History, 1776-1876* (Boston: Houghton Mifflin Company, 1912)

Johnson, Cecil. "Wired Lincoln: How the President Made Technology Work for Him." Review of *Mr. Lincoln's T-Mails*, by Tom Wheeler. *Columbia Daily Tribune* (November 11, 2006)

Keller, Rudi. "150 Years Ago: Colonel Disparages Congressmen in Letter to Lincoln." (Columbia MO: *Columbia Daily Tribune*, 2012)

Kohl, Lawrence Frederick. "Introduction: The Irish Brigade," in *The Irish Brigade and Its Campaigns*, D. P. Conyngham, ed. (New York: Fordham University Press, 1994)

Krause, Michael D., and R. Cody Phillips. *Historical Perspectives of the Operational Art.* (Washington, D.C.: Center of Military History, United States Army, 2005)

Lincoln, Abraham, Earl Schenck Miers, and Paul M. Angle. *The Living Lincoln: The Man, His Mind, His Times, and the War He Fought* (New Brunswick, N.J.: Rutgers University Press., 1955)

Lincoln, Abraham, Marion Mills Miller, and Henry Clay Whitney. *Life and Works of Abraham Lincoln.* (New York: Current Literature Pub. Co, 1909)

Lincoln, Abraham. *An Autobiography of Abraham Lincoln: Consisting of the Personal Portions of His Letters, Speeches, and Conversations*, ed. Nathaniel Wright Stephenson (Indianapolis: Bobbs-Merrill, 1926)

_____. *New Letters and Papers of Lincoln*, ed. Paul M. Angle (Boston: Houghton Mifflin, 1930)

_____. *The Martyr's Monument: Being the Patriotism and Political Wisdom of Abraham Lincoln, As Exhibited in his Speeches, Messages, Orders, and Proclamations, from the Presidential Canvass of 1860 until his Assassination, April 14, 1865* (New York: American News Co, 1865)

_____. *Abraham Lincoln: His Speeches and Writings*, ed. Roy P. Basler (Cleveland, OH: World Publishing, 1946),

_____. *Collected Works of Abraham Lincoln*, Volume 4. (New Brunswick, N.J.: Rutgers University Press, 1953)

_____. *Collected Works of Abraham Lincoln*, Volume 5. (New Brunswick, N.J.: Rutgers University Press, 1953)

_____. *Collected Works of Abraham Lincoln*, Volume 6. (New Brunswick, N.J.: Rutgers University Press, 1953)

_____. *Collected Works of Abraham Lincoln*, Volume 7. (New Brunswick, N.J.: Rutgers University Press, 1953)

_____. *Collected Works of Abraham Lincoln*, Volume 8. (New Brunswick, N.J.: Rutgers University Press, 1953)

_____. *Lincoln on Democracy*, ed. Mario M. Cuomo and Harold Holzer (New York: Fordham University Press, 2004)

Logan, John A. *The Great Conspiracy: Its Origin and History* (New York: A. R. Hart and Company, 1886)

Lossing, Benson J. *A Pictorial History of the Civil War* (Hartford CT: Thomas Belknap, 1877).

Ludwig, Emil, Paul Eden and Paul Cedar. *Lincoln* (Boston: Little, Brown, 1930)

Ludwig, Emil. *Lincoln* (Boston: Little, Brown, and Company, 1930)

Marszalek, John F. "Abraham Lincoln and William T. Sherman," in *The Lincoln Forum: Rediscovering Abraham Lincoln*, ed. John Y. Simon, Harold Holzer, and D. W. Ruark (New York: Fordham University Press, 2002)

Martin, David G. *Jackson's Valley Campaign: November 1861-June 1862* (Conshohocken, PA: Combined Books, 1994)

Marvel, William. *Burnside* (Chapel Hill, NC: University of North Carolina Press, 1991)

Matloff, Maurice. *American Military History* (Washington: Office of the Chief of Military History, U.S. Army, 1969)

May, Ernest R. and George Braziller. *The Ultimate Decision: The President as Commander in Chief* (New York: G. Braziller, 1960)

McClellan, George Brinton. *The Army of the Potomac: Gen. McClellan's Report of Its Operations While Under His Command* (New York: G.P. Putnam, 1864)

McFeely, William S. *Grant: A Biography* (New York: Norton, 1981)

McMurry, Richard M. *The Fourth Battle of Winchester: Toward a New Civil War Paradigm* (Kent, OH: Kent State University Press, 2002)

McPherson, James M. *Battle Cry of Freedom: The Civil War Era* (New York: Oxford University Press, 1988)

_____. *Crossroads of Freedom: Antietam* (New York: Oxford University Press, 2004)

_____. "Lincoln as Commander in Chief," in *The Lincoln Forum: Rediscovering Abraham Lincoln*, ed. John Y. Simon, Harold Holzer, and D. W. Ruark (New York: Fordham University Press, 2002)

Meade, George Gordon. *Life and Public Services of Major-General Meade* (Philadelphia: T.B. Peterson, 1864)

Means, David Chambers and Earl Schenck Miers. *Largely Lincoln* (New York: St. Martin's Press, 1961)

Miller, Randall M. "Lincoln and Leadership," in *Lincoln and Leadership: Military, Political, and Religious Decision Making*, Randall M. Miller ed. (New York: Fordham University Press, 2012)

Milton, George Fort. *The Age of Hate: Andrew Johnson and the Radicals* (New York: Coward-McCann, 1930)

Moore, Frank. *The Portrait Gallery of the War, Civil, Military, and Naval A Biographical Record* (New York: G.P. Putnam for Derby & Miller, 1864)

Mosgrove George Dallas. *Kentucky Cavaliers in Dixie: The Reminiscences of a Confederate Cavalryman* (Lincoln, NE: University of Nebraska Press, 1999)

National Archives. *The Emancipation Proclamation* (Washington: The National Archives and Records Administration, 2012)

Neely, Mark E. *The Fate of Liberty: Abraham Lincoln and Civil Liberties* (New York: Oxford University Press, 1991)

_____. "Abraham Lincoln," in *The American Civil War: A Handbook of Literature and Research*, ed. Robin Higham and Steven E. Woodworth (Westport, CT: Greenwood Press, 1996)

Nevins, Allan. *Fremont, Pathmarker of the West* (Lincoln, NE: University of Nebraska Press, 1992)

Nicolay, John G. and John Hay. *Abraham Lincoln: A History*, Volume 8 (New York: The Century Company, 1909)

Nicolay, John George. *A Short Life of Abraham Lincoln: Condensed from Nicolay and Hay's Abraham Lincoln: A History* (Charleston, SC: BiblioLife, 2008)

Nofi, Albert A. *A Civil War Treasury: Being a Miscellany of Arms and Artillery, Facts and Figures, Legends and Lore, Muses and Minstrels, Personalities and People* (New York: Da Capo Press, 1995)

Noyalas, Jonathan A. "Harpers Ferry During the Civil War." *Encyclopedia Virginia* (Charlottesville, VA: Virginia Foundation for the Humanities, 2011)

Patchan, Scott C. *Shenandoah Summer: The 1864 Valley Campaign* (Lincoln, NE: University of Nebraska Press, 2007)

Patterson, Robert Michael. *Rufus Saxton, Major General, United States Volunteers* (Washington: Arlington National Cemetery, 2012).

Pinsker, Matthew. *Lincoln's Sanctuary: Abraham Lincoln and the Soldiers' Home* (New York: Oxford University Press, 2003)

Pollan, Carolyn. "Ft. Smith under Military Rule: September 1, 1863–Fall 1865." *Ft. Smith Historical Society Journal.* Volume 6, Number 1 (April 1982)

Pond, George E. *The Shenandoah Valley in 1864*, Volume 11 of *Campaigns of the Civil War* (New York: Charles Schribner's Sons, 1883)

Pope, John. *The Military Memoirs of General John Pope*, ed. Peter Cozzens and Robert I. Girardi (Chapel Hill, NC: University of North Carolina Press, 1998)

Porter, Horace. *Campaigning with Grant* (Lincoln, NE: University of Nebraska Press, 2000)

Porter, Horace. *Campaigning with Grant* (Lincoln, NE: University of Nebraska Press, 2000)

Randall, J. G. *Mr. Lincoln* (New York: Dodd Mead, 1957)

Randall, J. G., and Richard Nelson Current. *Lincoln the President: Last Full Measure* (Urbana: University of Illinois Press, 2000).

Rawley, James A. *Abraham Lincoln and a Nation Worth Fighting For* (Lincoln, NE: University of Nebraska Press, 2003)

Raymond, Henry J. *The Life and Public Services of Abraham Lincoln* (New York: Derby and Miller, 1865)

_____. *History of the Administration of President Lincoln: Including His Speeches, Letters, Addresses, Proclamations, and Messages* (New York: J.C. Derby & N.C. Miller, 1864)

Raymond, Henry J., and F. B. Carpenter. *The Life and Public Services of Abraham Lincoln* (New York: Derby and Miller, 1865)

Remlap, L. T. *The Life of General U. S. Grant: His Early Life, Military Achievements, and History of His Civil Administration, His Sickness, Together with His Tour Around the World* (San Francisco: A. Roman, 1885)

Rhodes, J.F. "The First Six Weeks of McClellan's Peninsular Campaign Spring." *The American Historical Review.* Volume 1, Number 3 (April 1896)

Richardson, Albert D. *The Secret Service, the Field, the Dungeon, and the Escape* (Freeport, NY: American Publishing Company, 1971)

Ritter, Charles F. and Jon L. Wakelyn. *Leaders of the American Civil War: A Biographical and Historiographical Dictionary* (Westport, CT: Greenwood Press, 1998)

Rothschild, Alonzo. *Lincoln, Master of Men* (New York: Houghton Mifflin Company, 1906)

Ruckman, P.S. and David Kincaid. "Inside Lincoln's Clemency Decision Making." *Presidential Studies Quarterly.* Volume 29, Number 1 (March, 1999)

Sanders, Charles W. *While in the Hands of the Enemy: Military Prisons of the Civil War* (Baton Rouge: Louisiana State University Press, 2005)

Schofield, John M. *Forty-Six Years in the Army* (New York: The Century Company, 1897)

Simpson, Brooks D. "Facilitating Defeat: The Union High Command and the Collapse of the Confederacy," in *The Collapse of the Confederacy*, ed. Mark Grimsley and Brooks D. Simpson (Lincoln, NE: University of Nebraska Press, 2001)

Smith, M. T. "Benjamin F. Butler (1818–1893)." *Encyclopedia Virginia* (Charlottesville, VA: Virginia Foundation for the Humanities, 2011)

Spring, Leveritt. "American Commonweals: Kansas." *The California Teacher and Home Journal.* Volume 5, Number 5 (December, 1885)

Starnes, Sam. *Widener Magazine* (Chester, PA: Widener University, 2012)

Starr, Stephen Z. *The Union Cavalry in the Civil War: From Fort Sumter to Gettysburg, 1861-1863* (Baton Rouge: Louisiana State University Press, 1979)

Stevens, Walter B. *Centennial History of Missouri (the Center State) One Hundred Years in the Union, 1820-1921* (Chicago: S.J. Clarke Publishing Company, 1921)

Stewart, Richard W. *American Military History*. Volume. 1, *The United States Army and the Forging of a Nation, 1775-1917* (Washington, DC: Center of Military History, United States Army, 2005)

Stoker, Donald Stoker. *The Grand Design: Strategy and the U.S. Civil War* (New York: Oxford University Press, 2010)

Sutherland, Daniel E. *A Savage Conflict: The Decisive Role of Guerrillas in the American Civil War* (Chapel Hill, N.C.: University of North Carolina Press, 2009)

Swint, Kerwin C. *Mudslingers: The Top 25 Negative Political Campaigns of All Time* (Westport, CT: Praeger, 2006)

Thayer, William Roscoe. *The Life and Letters of John Hay* (Boston: Houghton Mifflin Company, 1915)

Thomas, Benjamin P. *Abraham Lincoln: A Biography* (New York: Alfred A. Knopf, 1952)

U.S. Writers' Program. *Indiana, a Guide to the Hoosier State* (New York: Oxford University Press, 1941)

Upton, Emory, Joseph Prentiss Sanger, William D. Beach, and Charles Dudley Rhodes. *The Military Policy of the United State.* (Washington: Government Printing Office, 1917)

Usilton, Fred G. *History of Kent County, Maryland: 1630-1916* (Bowie, MD: Heritage Books, 1994)

Van Horne, Thomas Budd, and Edward Ruger. *History of the Army of the Cumberland.* Volume 2 (Cincinnati: R. Clarke, 1875)

Weitz, Mark A. *A Higher Duty: Desertion among Georgia Troops during the Civil War* (Lincoln, NE: University of Nebraska Press, 2000)

Welles, Gideon. *Diary of Gideon Welles.* Vol.2 (Boston: Houghton Mifflin, 1911)

Welsh, Jack D. *Medical Histories of Union Generals* (Kent, OH: Kent State University Press, 1996)

Wert, Jeffry D. *The Sword of Lincoln: The Army of the Potomac.* (New York: Simon & Schuster, 2005)

Wertenbaker, Thomas J. *Norfolk: Historic Southern Port*, ed. Marvin W. Schlegel (Durham, NC: Duke University Press, 1962)

West, Richard S. *Mr. Lincoln's Navy* (New York: Longmans Green, 1957)

Wheeler, Richard. *Witness to Gettysburg* (Mechanicsville, PA: Stackpole Books, 1987)

White, Ronald, C. *A. Lincoln: A Biography* (New York: Random House, 2009)

Williams, Frank J. *Judging Lincoln* (Carbondale, IL: Southern Illinois University Press, 2002)

Williams, T. Harry. *Lincoln and His Generals* (New York: Gramercy Books, 2000)

Winters, William. *The Musick of the Mocking Birds, the Roar of the Cannon: The Civil War Diary and Letters of William Winters*, ed. Steven E. Woodworth (Lincoln, NE: University of Nebraska Press, 1998)

Woodbury, Augustus. *Major General Ambrose E. Burnside and the Ninth Army Corps: A Narrative of Campaigns in North Carolina, Maryland, Virginia, Ohio, Kentucky, Mississippi and Tennessee, During the War for the Preservation of the Republic.* (Providence: S.S. Rider, 1867).

Woodworth, Steven E. *Six Armies in Tennessee: The Chickamauga and Chattanooga Campaigns* (Lincoln, NE: University of

_____. *This Grand Spectacle: The Battle of Chattanooga* (Abilene, TX: McWhiney Foundation, 1999)

Wright, John D. *The Language of the Civil War* (Westport, CT: Oryx Press, 2001)

Index